FOCUS ON WRITING

FOCUS on WRITING

What College Students Want to Know

Laurie McMillan

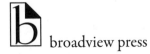

broadview press

BROADVIEW PRESS – www.broadviewpress.com
Peterborough, Ontario, Canada

Founded in 1985, Broadview Press remains a wholly independent publishing house. Broadview's focus is on academic publishing; our titles are accessible to university and college students as well as scholars and general readers. With over 600 titles in print, Broadview has become a leading international publisher in the humanities, with world-wide distribution. Broadview is committed to environmentally responsible publishing and fair business practices.

© 2019 Laurie McMillan

Library and Archives Canada Cataloguing in Publication

McMillan, Laurie, author
    Focus on writing : what college students want to know / Laurie McMillan.

Includes bibliographical references and index.
ISBN 978-1-55481-388-9 (softcover)

    1. College readers. 2. English language—Composition and exercises. 3. English language—Rhetoric. 4. Report writing. I. Title.

PE1417.M33 2018   808'.0427   C2018-904757-7

Broadview Press handles its own distribution in North America:
PO Box 1243, Peterborough, Ontario K9J 7H5, Canada
555 Riverwalk Parkway, Tonawanda, NY 14150, USA
Tel: (705) 743-8990; Fax: (705) 743-8353
email: customerservice@broadviewpress.com

Distribution is handled by Eurospan Group in the UK, Europe, Central Asia, Middle East, Africa, India, Southeast Asia, Central America, South America, and the Caribbean. Distribution is handled by Footprint Books in Australia and New Zealand.

 Broadview Press acknowledges the financial support of the Government of Canada for our publishing activities.

Edited by Michel Pharand
Book Design by Em Dash Design

PRINTED IN CANADA

For my past students:
I appreciate all the ways you have been wise and generous teachers

To future students:
I look forward to learning with you

CONTENTS

CHAPTER TWO
What Is the "Rhetorical Situation" and Why Should I Care about It? 99

CHAPTER THREE
What Do Effective Writers Do? 159

CHAPTER FOUR
What Do Effective Researchers Do? 235

CHAPTER FIVE
How Do I Translate My Academic Writing into Public Genres? 297

CONCLUSION
Now What? 365

ACKNOWLEDGMENTS

I became immersed in the world of writing studies by participating in the WPA listserv and the Conference on College Composition and Communication. Thanks to the many amazing colleagues I've worked with in person and the even greater number who have influenced me with your words, your research, and your generous insights on the pages and screens of the writing studies world. I especially appreciate the Writing about Writing work of Doug Downs, Elizabeth Wardle, Barbara Bird, Jan Rieman, Christy Wenger, Steve Smith, and the anonymous reviewers who provided feedback. Thank you to Marjorie Mather who invited me to propose a Writing about Writing textbook, to Michel Pharand for his impeccable copyediting, to managing editor Tara Lowes, and to the others at Broadview Press who have generously supported this project. I've been fortunate to have incredible colleagues—from graduate school at Duquesne University through my faculty appointments at Marywood University and now Pace University in Pleasantville, NY. Y'all know who you are. A specific thanks goes to my NYC writing partners Meaghan Brewer-Wert and Mara Lee Grayson, and I've been grateful more than I can say to be in the company of writing studies scholar-friends Rob Mundy, Michael Turner, and Olivia Worden. Thank you! I'm also lucky to have smart and kind family members: my parents, Esther and Carroll, and my siblings, Carole, Stephen, Michael, Janet, and Diane. Last but not least, my immediate family has been incredibly patient and supportive. Scot, Callie, Jace: You put the fun in discourse community. Love you!

INTRODUCTION: WHAT SHOULD I KNOW ABOUT THIS BOOK?

Welcome

Welcome! The beginning of the semester can be scary and nerve-wracking, but it can also be full of hope and possibility. To encourage the latter, I want to spend a little time setting the stage, letting you know what you can expect of this text and how it might be helpful.

First I want to acknowledge that I don't know you personally. You might be someone who enjoys school or who dreads school. You might be fifteen years old or ninety years old or somewhere in between. You might be comfortable with one or more dialects of English, or you might be most fluent in another language. You might prefer working individually or with others. A gazillion other preferences, identity markers, personality traits, and experiences may affect what you are thinking and feeling right now about your first-year writing course.

During my years of teaching, even when I thought I knew students, I would regularly find my assumptions were wrong. I am thus okay with not knowing you personally but still doing my best to support you. Usually, if I let students know my role is to help them succeed and work toward their goals, most students are willing to take some risks, put in some effort, and do what they can to produce meaningful work. They tend to learn a good bit about writing in the process.

That's what I wish for you.

Now back to telling you about this book so you know what to expect. If you're at all like me, you may associate textbooks with information presented in a dry academic style. One of my colleagues who teaches history told me that if he found a textbook that didn't bore him and his students, he would assign it in every class.

When I read boring textbooks, I feel frustrated because I've spent enough time in school to know that most learning and thinking and research experiences have fun and fascinating sides, even when work and patience are also required. I can't unequivocally promise hours of fun and fascination, but I have set up this book in ways that I hope will spark your interest.

A number of **premises** guide the content and organization of this book, some of which are about writing and research in general and some of which are specifically about students:

CONNECT

This "Connect" box and the ones that follow interrupt the text and offer places for you to pause and respond. Reading is more interesting when you "talk back" to the text, and it's more meaningful if you connect it to your experiences, your ideas, and your past learning. Your "past learning" may even include other readings completed this semester. Making connections is smart.

CONNECT

1. What kind of writing do you expect to find when you pick up a textbook?

2. Have there been textbooks that have surprised you in a good way? Explain.

- Inquiry guides learning and research. *Ask questions. Wonder. Be curious!*
- Learning happens through reading, writing, thinking, talking, and listening; these linked practices inform one another. *Have conversations on the page, in your head, and in real life.*
- Students already know a lot about writing; even those of you who may struggle with school assignments may be experts when it comes to a particular kind of writing, whether it's texting or tweeting or writing associated with a particular sport, activity, or workplace. *You have resources to draw on!*
- Explicitly identifying what is known helps us transfer our skills from one situation to another situation. *You can build up more resources to draw on!*
- As students read about writing and write about writing, you are more likely to transfer what you learn to new writing situations. *If you're taking a class, it helps to know how you might apply what you learn, yes?*

FOCUS ON WRITING: WHAT COLLEGE STUDENTS WANT TO KNOW

- Academic research and writing often involve responding to prior research. *You can add to academic conversations. I'll say more about research soon, so now you have something to look forward to!*

Reading *Focus on Writing*

WHAT TO EXPECT

You'll notice that each chapter title is a question. That's because learning tends to be more interesting if it's based on *inquiry*—questions we want to know the answers to. Inquiry also highlights the way questions tend to lead not only to answers but also to more questions.

Each chapter has three sections:

1. ***Exploring the Question*** considers why the title question matters and offers some preliminary answers to the question that have been found through research, usually in the overlapping fields of composition studies, writing studies, rhetorical studies, linguistics, and education—all fields associated with communication and learning. I use a conversational tone in these sections, as I do in this intro, in hopes of drawing you in and helping you remember there's a person behind the writing.

2. ***Extending the Conversation*** offers a sample of writing selections that respond to the chapter title question. These texts represent a range of genres, so they offer not only helpful ideas but also potential models of writing you can draw on in your own work. The selections are authored by writing studies researchers and writers at various stages in their careers—from first-year students to well-established scholars and professional writers. Before each selection, I provide contextual information and response questions for you to keep in mind as you read. I also include a selection of supplementary readings available via open access online resources.

3. ***Joining the Conversation*** provides several writing prompts meant to inspire formal writing. Some of these prompts lead to traditional academic writing while others ask for creative responses, digital work, or other multimedia engagement.

READING ACTIVELY, READING RHETORICALLY

It's easy to read without processing the ideas, but it ends up being a waste of time when you'll be using the ideas in some way. Trust me—I've had to reread texts more often than I'd like to admit.

You can make better use of your time and process what you're reading by marking up the text and otherwise responding:

- Write notes in the margins
- Use quick marks such as ? ! and :) or :(to call attention to points that elicit a reaction from you
- Answer some of the questions that interrupt the main body of text
- Connect the ideas to your own experiences, either mentally or in writing
- Take notes to help you extract key ideas you want to remember or return to
- Pay attention to terms in bold italics; I define these as I use them

CONNECT

What other active reading strategies help you pay attention and make good use of your time?

You may have spent time in school learning the active reading strategies mentioned above and being taught to recognize the use of secondary research, primary research, and other typical parts of research articles (which I'll review below). Such strategies are useful, but research in writing studies shows that the most effective and efficient readers also use *rhetorical reading strategies* to help them process texts (Downs; Haas and Flower). Reading rhetorically means asking: **Why was this text written? What kind of purpose is it filling?** To answer these questions, consider:

- Who wrote this text? What kind of role or position led to the authoring of the text?
- When and where was this text originally written or published? What was occurring that contributed to the publication?
- To what genre does this text belong?
- What is this text responding to?
- How would you characterize the text's original primary audience?
- How would you characterize the text's current primary audience?
- How does the new context of publication affect the text's purpose?
- What might you do with the text?

Sometimes these questions are tricky to answer, but you often figure out most of these answers in your everyday life without even realizing it. For example, imagine you are visiting a friend (Fred) and you see a sticky note on the refrigerator:

My favorite son—DON'T FORGET!
Haircut 3:30 Friday

Without a trace of Sherlock Holmes in you, you make a lot of assumptions to decode that message. It's likely that Fred's mom or dad wrote the note sometime recently, and it may have originally been elsewhere but was taped to the refrigerator door so it wouldn't be lost. The *genre*, or category, of writing is the personal reminder note, so you understand the purpose is to remind Fred of his appointment. Fred's parents may think his hair is too long, perhaps he has forgotten appointments before, or maybe they want him to look nice for an upcoming event. Any of these factors would contribute to the note's *exigence*—the situation that compelled the writer to write in hopes of influencing a particular state of affairs. The upcoming date would affect *kairos*, which is the suitability of timing; the note would not make sense once the appointment has passed, and if the note is posted too soon, Fred may not pay attention to it when he needs to. The combination of the phrase "my favorite son" and the caps used in "DON'T FORGET!" suggests a bit of light-heartedness, but you still know that Fred better remember this appointment. As you read the text, you now know you won't ask Fred to make plans with you on Friday afternoon, and you may be ready to either compliment or tease him about his haircut when you see him again, depending on the kind of friendship you have.

Some of the questions involved in rhetorical reading strategies are not relevant in this situation, but most of the questions are answered instinctively. The note would not be read as poetry or as part of a novel or as a homework assignment; the original writer's purpose and the audience is clear; and you can make use of the note in a limited way.

When you're reading the selections included in the various chapters, you can use my textual introductions to help you think through the rhetorical situation. You will probably appreciate the reading more if you also think about your own rhetorical situation:

CONNECT

1. Even though the note seems simple, many elements of the original rhetorical situation—the context of the writing—are not fully known. Review the list of questions that are considered when we read rhetorically. Which questions are most difficult to answer?

2. Why are we bothering to think about this made-up note and how it might be read rhetorically?

- Why are you being assigned this reading?
- How does it fit with your course and the other readings and assignments?
- How do the ideas resonate with what you already know?
- How can you make use of the reading to think about your own writing in helpful ways?

It might help to know that, as I have selected readings, I have thought both about *what* each reading says and *how* it says it. You, too, can turn to texts as sources of ideas and as writing models to help you become familiar with new genres. I kept the original citation styles in the selected readings, so even in that small detail you can begin noticing how writing choices vary from one publication to another.

READING ACADEMIC ARTICLES

Often I refer to academic writing as a ***scholarly conversation***. "Conversation" refers to people exchanging ideas and building on what others have said by adding new information. The word "scholarly" suggests that the topics being discussed are ones deemed worthy of research within a particular discipline. "Scholarly" is often aligned with a formal tone and style, and it also implies that appropriate disciplinary evidence is being used to develop an argument. Most often, this evidence includes

a) a familiarity with past scholarly research on a given topic and
b) primary research methods that can be replicated and that effectively answer the question being investigated.

Many of us who teach writing courses appreciate the metaphor of an ongoing discussion that scholar Kenneth Burke used:

Imagine that you enter a parlor. You come late. When you arrive, others have long preceded you, and they are engaged in a heated discussion, a discussion too heated for them to pause and tell you exactly what it is about. In fact, the discussion had already begun long before any of them got there, so that no one present is qualified to retrace for you all the steps that had gone before. You listen for awhile, until you decide that you have caught the tenor[1] of the argument; then you put in your oar. Someone answers; you answer him; another comes to your defense; another aligns himself against you, to either the embarrassment or gratification of your opponent, depending upon the quality of your ally's assistance. However, the discussion is interminable. The hour grows late, you must depart. And you do depart, with the discussion still vigorously in progress. (110–11)

As you read, try to think of writers as having conversations that develop gradually over time, even when the writing itself seems formal and academic. You can also join these conversations, whether by summarizing what others have said, noting connections between various writers, evaluating the various contributions to the conversation, or offering new insights to the conversation.

Do you remember I promised I would discuss research before long? Well, this is the moment you've been waiting for! Understanding the relationship between secondary and primary research will help you when you're reading and writing academic texts.

Secondary research involves consulting the research of others and using it to better understand or contextualize your own research question. Usually this research has been published and is accessible via books, periodical articles, or online venues.

Primary research is a way of investigating a research question through a study you develop and perform yourself, perhaps by conducting interviews, analyzing texts, completing lab experiments, administering surveys, or collecting and analyzing data through observation.

Often an academic research article will meet the following aims, so being aware of these likely moves will help you watch for them and recognize them:

1. *introduce* the focus of the research and its importance by briefly recapping a problem or a discussion that leads to an open question; the research article will attempt to answer this *open question*

> **CONNECT**
>
> Can you think of another metaphor for contributing to a scholarly conversation? For example, consider a food metaphor, a sports metaphor, or a metaphor of place.

> **CONNECT**
>
> 1. Describe a time you used secondary research to answer a question.
>
> 2. Describe a time you used primary research to answer a question.

---

1 Catching the *tenor* of an argument means you understand the main positions and ideas being disputed.

2. *synthesize* a number of *secondary sources* that frame the primary research project; this part of academic writing is called a ***literature review***; note that the word "literature" does not refer to creative writing in this context
3. *explain* the *methods* used to gather evidence, such as interview, survey, textual analysis, observation, and so forth
4. *identify* the results of the *primary* research
5. *discuss* the *significance* and implications of these results
6. *conclude* with a call to action or an acknowledgment of further research to be conducted

CONNECT

Teachers can be a resource for you by modeling what to do when reading is difficult. Ask your teachers about times when they needed to read difficult texts and what strategies they used to help them meet the challenge.

As you encounter difficult academic writing, reviewing the above advice about reading actively, reading rhetorically, and recognizing common moves in an academic research article will help you read more effectively. Also, at times you might want to aim for glimmers of understanding rather than thorough comprehension. It's okay if you have trouble reading an article that was written for an audience of professors.

WHY WRITING ABOUT WRITING?

First-year composition classes try to prepare students for all writing that students will ever do, whether in your other college classes, in your future workplaces, or in your personal and civic lives (***civic*** refers to your role as a citizen who participates in the democratic process and contributes to the community).

Teaching how to write in every situation is an impossible task to accomplish in only one or two semesters. It's also impossible in seven or eight semesters because *so* many writing tasks arise over the course of a lifetime that more learning is always necessary. Don't be depressed. I'm still learning, and it's actually enjoyable most of the time!

Still, a lot of people expect students to learn everything about writing by the end of their first year of college, either because these people don't realize how complicated writing is or because they don't remember that their own learning about writing took place over many years and experiences.

Despite the impossibility of full preparation for all writing situations you will ever encounter, Writing about Writing (WAW) approaches are designed to give you tools and ways of thinking about writing that you can apply in new situations. All first-year composition classes—whether they use **WAW** or not—involve a lot of writing because one of the best ways to learn how to write is to actually write.

However, classes vary in terms of what students write *about*. Some composition classes have students read about pop culture or social issues or specific themes and then respond to those readings. Students practice writing in these classes, but the content they write about does not actually help them become better writers.

In **WAW** courses, students read about writing and respond to those readings. That way, you are learning *content* (what do we already know about writing effectively?) that can help you improve your writing, and you have the chance to think through, apply, and respond to that content as you write.

Sometimes students initially envision a long and boring semester as we read and write about writing. Yes. That's what I'm aiming for.

Just kidding! The reality is that not every reading or writing assignment is likely to excite you, so I won't lie and tell you they all will. However, because reading and writing are such integral parts of our lives, it's often easier to connect to these conversations than you'd imagine.

To get a sense of the semester ahead, look at the chapter titles. Some of the information may be helpful to you even if no one is assigning you to read it. To the degree that you're open to learning, **WAW** is designed to help you learn about writing in ways that can be applied in a wide variety of situations.

CONNECT

Choose a chapter title and see if you can anticipate or predict answers that might be provided in that chapter. What kinds of smaller questions might be asked in each chapter?

1. Why write?

2. What is the "rhetorical situation" and why should I care about it?

3. What do effective writers do?

4. What do effective researchers do?

5. How do I translate my academic writing into public genres?

The Wider Conversation

I've been telling you that researchers are involved in ongoing discussions with one another and suggesting that you can be part of these discussions. Now I'd like to point out that this textbook and your writing class are also connected to texts that inform our work and that we respond to in various ways. Some of these texts I have already cited or quoted from.

Two documents, however, are so foundational to first-year composition courses that I am including them here (they are also available online): *The WPA Outcomes Statement for First-Year Composition (3.0)* and the *Framework for Success in Postsecondary Writing*. I provide a bit of background before each document to help you make sense of them. Your own college writing program may have adopted or adapted some of the principles found in these documents.

WPA OUTCOMES STATEMENT FOR FIRST-YEAR COMPOSITION (3.0)

Approved July 17, 2014 by the Council of Writing Program Administrators

Background

The "WPA" is short for "Writing Program Administrators"—that is, faculty who run college writing programs. In 1997, a group of writing faculty decided to develop outcomes to articulate learning goals common to first-year writing courses at most colleges where such courses are required (Dryer et al. 129).

The first version of the *WPA Outcomes Statement* was the result of collaborative work that involved an impressive amount of time and conversation. It was endorsed by the Council of Writing Program Administrators in 2000, and it was designed to be adaptable rather than rigid in its application (Dryer et al. 130). In 2008, a section titled "Composing in Electronic Environments" was added to the earlier version of the *Outcomes* to reflect the rise in digital writing. Finally, in 2014, version 3.0 was published to reflect changing assumptions about composing and the work of first-year writing classes. Again, an incredible amount of time and conversation was involved in this publication, including surveys of writing faculty and conference workshops to help crowdsource ideas.

In this most recent version, more attention is given to **multimodal** texts (that is, texts using

CONNECT

Why might writing faculty be interested in identifying and publicly communicating learning outcomes that are common across many first-year writing courses?

CONNECT

As you read the *Outcomes Statement*, consider

1. Which outcomes seemed most relevant in high school courses that involved writing?

2. Which outcomes surprise you or seem different from what you would expect?

3. Which outcomes fit with your own goals for becoming a more effective writer?

4. Why do you suppose I included the *Outcomes Statement* in the intro of this textbook?

image, video, sound, and/or alphabetic writing); writing skills are presented as the ability to respond to evolving technologies and changing contexts using key ideas from writing theory; and students are positioned not simply as writers but also researchers who contribute to scholarly conversations (Dryer et al. 138–40). In brief, as composing practices have taken new forms and as writing courses have responded to such changes, the *Outcomes Statement* has also been revised to better fit current writing practices.

WPA *Outcomes Statement for First-Year Composition (3.0)*

Rhetorical Knowledge

Rhetorical knowledge is the ability to analyze contexts and audiences and then to act on that analysis in comprehending and creating texts. Rhetorical knowledge is the basis of composing. Writers develop rhetorical knowledge by negotiating purpose, audience, context, and conventions as they compose a variety of texts for different situations.

By the end of first-year composition, students should

- Learn and use key rhetorical concepts through analyzing and composing a variety of texts
- Gain experience reading and composing in several genres to understand how genre conventions shape and are shaped by readers' and writers' practices and purposes
- Develop facility in responding to a variety of situations and contexts calling for purposeful shifts in voice, tone, level of formality, design, medium, and/or structure
- Understand and use a variety of technologies to address a range of audiences
- Match the capacities of different environments (e.g., print and electronic) to varying rhetorical situations

Critical Thinking, Reading, and Composing

Critical thinking is the ability to analyze, synthesize, interpret, and evaluate ideas, information, situations, and texts. When writers think critically about the materials they use—whether print texts, photographs, data sets, videos, or other materials—they separate assertion from evidence, evaluate sources and evidence, recognize and evaluate underlying assumptions, read across texts for connections and patterns, identify and evaluate chains of reasoning, and compose appropriately qualified and developed claims and generalizations. These practices are foundational for advanced academic writing.

By the end of first-year composition, students should
- Use composing and reading for inquiry, learning, critical thinking, and communicating in various rhetorical contexts
- Read a diverse range of texts, attending especially to relationships between assertion and evidence, to patterns of organization, to the interplay between verbal and nonverbal elements, and to how these features function for different audiences and situations
- Locate and evaluate (for credibility, sufficiency, accuracy, timeliness, bias, and so on) primary and secondary research materials, including journal articles and essays, books, scholarly and professionally established and maintained databases or archives, and informal electronic networks and internet sources
- Use strategies—such as interpretation, synthesis, response, critique, and design/redesign—to compose texts that integrate the writer's ideas with those from appropriate sources

Processes

Writers use multiple strategies, or ***composing processes***, to conceptualize, develop, and finalize projects. Composing processes are seldom linear: a writer may research a topic before drafting, then conduct additional research while revising or after consulting a colleague. Composing processes are also flexible: successful writers can adapt their composing processes to different contexts and occasions.

By the end of first-year composition, students should
- Develop a writing project through multiple drafts
- Develop flexible strategies for reading, drafting, reviewing, collaborating, revising, rewriting, rereading, and editing
- Use composing processes and tools as a means to discover and reconsider ideas
- Experience the collaborative and social aspects of writing processes
- Learn to give and to act on productive feedback to works in progress
- Adapt composing processes for a variety of technologies and modalities
- Reflect on the development of composing practices and how those practices influence their work

Knowledge of Conventions

Conventions are the formal rules and informal guidelines that define genres, and in so doing, shape readers' and writers' perceptions of correctness or appropriateness. Most obviously, conventions govern such things as mechanics, usage, spelling, and citation practices. But they also influence content, style, organization, graphics, and document design.

Conventions arise from a history of use and facilitate reading by invoking common expectations between writers and readers. These expectations are not universal; they vary by genre (conventions for lab notebooks and discussion-board exchanges differ), by discipline (conventional moves in literature reviews in Psychology differ from those in English), and by occasion (meeting minutes and executive summaries use different registers). A writer's grasp of conventions in one context does not mean a firm grasp in another. Successful writers understand, analyze, and negotiate conventions for purpose, audience, and genre, understanding that genres evolve in response to changes in material conditions and composing technologies and attending carefully to emergent conventions.

By the end of first-year composition, students should

- Develop knowledge of linguistic structures, including grammar, punctuation, and spelling, through practice in composing and revising
- Understand why genre conventions for structure, paragraphing, tone, and mechanics vary
- Gain experience negotiating variations in genre conventions
- Learn common formats and/or design features for different kinds of texts
- Explore the concepts of intellectual property (such as fair use and copyright) that motivate documentation conventions
- Practice applying citation conventions systematically in their own work

FRAMEWORK FOR SUCCESS IN POSTSECONDARY WRITING— EXECUTIVE SUMMARY

Developed by the Council of Writing Program Administrators, the National Council of Teachers of English, and the National Writing Project
January 2011

The second approach to framing first-year writing was written at a time of increasing emphasis on standardized tests and the spread of Common Core standards across much of the United States. College and high school writing faculty created a statement that emphasized traits (called "habits of mind" in this document) that would help first-year students be successful in their college writing classes.

In the introduction to the document, the writers make an argument about appropriate ways to teach writing:

> At its essence, the Framework suggests that writing activities and assignments should be designed with genuine purposes and audiences in mind (from teachers and other students to community groups, local or national officials, commercial interests, students' friends and relatives, and other potential readers) in order to foster flexibility and rhetorical versatility. Standardized writing curricula or assessment instruments that emphasize formulaic writing for nonauthentic audiences will not reinforce the habits of mind and the experiences necessary for success as students encounter the writing demands of postsecondary education. (Council et al. 3)

The writers also identify the audiences who they hope will find the *Framework* helpful: not only educators but also "parents, policy makers, employers, and the general public" (Council et al. 2). I am not sure why students are not mentioned as a potential audience for the document, but that omission will be interesting to keep in mind as you read the "Executive Summary" of the *Framework*.

CONNECT

As you read the *Framework for Success*, consider

1. Why were these particular traits associated with success in college writing?

2. In what ways did your high school experiences help you develop some of these traits?

3. How are these "Habits of Mind" different from and similar to the *Learning Outcomes* above?

4. Which "Habits of Mind" do you perceive as your own strengths and as challenges?

5. How might the *Learning Outcomes* and *Framework for Success* be important for teachers?

6. How might the two documents be useful for students like you?

Framework for Success in Postsecondary Writing—Executive Summary

THE CONCEPT OF "college readiness" is increasingly important in discussions about students' preparation for postsecondary education.

This Framework describes the rhetorical and twenty-first-century skills as well as habits of mind and experiences that are critical for college success. Based in current research in writing and writing pedagogy, the Framework was written and reviewed by two- and four-year college and high school writing faculty nationwide and is endorsed by the Council of Writing Program Administrators, the National Council of Teachers of English, and the National Writing Project.

Habits of mind refers to ways of approaching learning that are both intellectual and practical and that will support students' success in a variety of fields and disciplines. The Framework identifies eight habits of mind essential for success in college writing:

- Curiosity—the desire to know more about the world
- Openness—the willingness to consider new ways of being and thinking in the world
- Engagement—a sense of investment and involvement in learning
- Creativity—the ability to use novel approaches for generating, investigating, and representing ideas
- Persistence—the ability to sustain interest in and attention to short- and long-term projects
- Responsibility—the ability to take ownership of one's actions and understand the consequences of those actions for oneself and others
- Flexibility—the ability to adapt to situations, expectations, or demands
- Metacognition—the ability to reflect on one's own thinking as well as on the individual and cultural processes used to structure knowledge.

CONNECT

I began this textbook by identifying assumptions about how a writing course works best, explaining what to expect from the text, and offering you advice about how to approach the reading. You might want to think about your own assumptions, expectations, and needs as you begin the semester, and your instructor might be interested in hearing your answers.

1. What has helped you learn to write so far in your life?

2. What do you most want to learn this semester?

3. How can your professor support your learning of writing this semester?

4. What will you do to make the semester effective for yourself?

5. What might you do to support your classmates this semester?

This last question may surprise you. However, college professors continue to recognize the importance of collaboration (Bruffee; Harris). We tend to learn not as isolated individuals but as members of many small communities. This principle doesn't have to be hokey—sometimes it just means listening to others or having a good time together while doing our work. As Vanilla Ice says, "Collaborate and listen."

Bruffee, Kenneth A. "Collaborative Learning and the 'Conversation of Mankind.'" *College English*, vol. 46, no. 7, Nov. 1984, pp. 635–52.

Burke, Kenneth. *The Philosophy of Literary Form: Studies in Symbolic Action*. 3rd ed. 1941. U of California P, 1973.

Council of Writing Program Administrators. *WPA Outcomes Statement for First-Year Composition (3.0)*, July 2014, <wpacouncil.org/positions/outcomes.html>.

Council of Writing Program Administrators, National Council of Teachers of English, and National Writing Project. *Framework for Success in Postsecondary Writing*. CWPA, NCTE, and NWP, 2011, <ncil.org/files/framework-for-success-postsecondary-writing.pdf>.

Downs, Doug. "Teaching First-Year Writers to *Use* Texts: Scholarly Readings in Writing-About-Writing in First-Year Comp." *Reader: Essays in Reader-Oriented Theory, Criticism, and Pedagogy*, Fall 2010, pp. 19–50.

Dryer, Dylan B., et al. "Revising FYC Outcomes for a Multimodal, Digitally Composed World: The *WPA Outcomes Statement for First-Year Composition* (Version 3.0)." *WPA: Writing Program Administration*, vol. 38, no. 1, Fall 2014, pp. 129–43.

Haas, Christina, and Linda Flower. "Rhetorical Reading Strategies and the Construction of Meaning." *College Composition and Communication*, vol. 39, no. 2, 1988, pp. 167–83.

Harris, Joseph. "The Idea of Community in the Study of Writing." *College Composition and Communication*, vol. 40, no. 1, 1989, pp. 11–22.

Vanilla Ice. "Ice Ice Baby." *To the Extreme*, SBK, 1990.

Guide for Writing Instructors

When I was asked to write a proposal for a Writing about Writing textbook, I did so quickly, based on my own teaching over many years and my attention to the wide and wonderful world of writing studies. You will notice the presence of both in the pages ahead. I rely on what I have learned from many smart writing studies researchers, whether through conversation, conference presentations, or, most often, their published works; and my teaching experiences and writerly practices are used to explain and develop ideas.

The actual development of the textbook took much longer than the initial proposal, as I tried to write in ways that might engage students and help writing instructors—both tasks were daunting for different reasons, as you might imagine.

RATIONALES INFORMING TEXTUAL FEATURES

Exploring the Question sections

From the time I began writing the proposal, I knew I wanted to include ideas about writing and research that I talk about with students almost every time I teach a writing course. Often these discussions are crowd-sourced rather than instructor-led, so I imagine student readers will have more to say on many of the subjects raised.

My tone in these sections is sometimes light and silly, sometimes matter-of-fact and practical, and sometimes earnest. Those tones are consistent with my real-life classroom presence. I know my style is unlikely to appeal to everyone, so I'm sorry if it's not your thing, but bringing some of my personality to the page makes sense. As I challenge students to engage, I need to show my own engagement.

When I use a term that may be unfamiliar to students, it's marked in bold italics and defined in the text. The hope is that some of these key words will become part of your classroom lexicon, allowing students to communicate about writing in thoughtful ways.

I end each "Exploring the Question" section with a Works Cited list to sample some of the texts that have informed my thinking and to provide resources in case you or your students would like to do additional reading. I am certain I have failed to credit many writers and researchers who have influenced my pedagogies; such omissions are unintentional.

Connect questions

I break up the reading with "Connect" questions regularly, just as I would stop and do something interactive if I were in a classroom and found myself talking on and on. These questions show that the discussions are not closed, and informal writing in response to "Connect" questions can thus can lead into formal assignments. As students notice ambiguities, uncertainties, and open questions, they can find topics worth further investigation. Both individual answers and a classroom database of responses can provide useful material for primary research.

"Connect" questions also appear at the start of each anthologized reading. Although it's more typical for questions to appear at the close of a text, I consistently tell students to read the questions first so they can keep them in mind while

INTRODUCTION: WHAT SHOULD I KNOW ABOUT THIS BOOK?

reading. I see these questions, too, as ways for students to engage in their reading with thoughtful reflection.

Extending the Conversation sections

I chose sources that fit each chapter topic but that addressed it in a focused way in hopes that students would see how any large question is informed by many smaller questions, and research leads to more research as new questions arise.

In some cases I've included excerpts rather than full sources. My reasoning is two-fold. One, focusing closely on a shorter reading can be more productive than spending time on a longer reading and struggling to find a way in. Two, keeping the length of the book reasonable makes it more affordable.

I frame the sources reprinted here in a few ways. To help students think of sources *rhetorically*, I explain "Why I included it" in terms of a) the ideas students might learn from and b) the approaches to writing or research that students might imitate. In addition, the "Background" section provides information about the conversation and other contextual factors that gave rise to the text. Finally, "Reading hints and vocabulary" tells students what to expect, suggests strategies to help them with difficult material, and anticipates terms they might find difficult. These key terms can supplement those found in the "Exploring the Question" sections.

At the end of each chapter's "Extending the Conversation" section, I offer a list of several online sources with brief descriptions. Although I have not provided extensive introductions, these readings and videos are worth checking out, and they make this textbook a much richer resource.

Joining the Conversation

At the close of each chapter, I provide a sampling of formal assignments to help students engage and apply relevant ideas. Many of these assignments lead to traditional academic writing in genres including narrative, evidence-based research, and textual analysis. Each chapter also includes options for creative and digital projects. Personally, I compose in a wide variety of academic, creative, and digital genres and find value in each, so throughout the textbook I emphasize how helpful it can be to recognize both similarities and differences when moving from one genre to another. I hope the variety of assignments contributes to this message.

Although I do not include questions that encourage meta-cognition with each set of assignment suggestions, I do recommend having students reflect on their writing each time they submit a formal assignment (and at other times as well during drafting, workshop, and revision processes). In an article about his implementation of methods to teach for transfer (TFT) in a first-year writing class, Howard Tinberg provides a series of questions he has students answer:

- Did this assignment remind you of any writing that you've done previously? Please describe that work.
- What was new about this assignment? Please be precise.
- What kinds of knowledge/writing skills did you draw on to produce this draft? Please begin to use some of the key terms that have begun to form the basis of your theory of writing. For example, did you draw upon your understanding of audience awareness or genre? How so?
- When drafting, what choices did you make? Please explain.
- What questions do you have for readers about the piece? (Tinberg)

This ongoing self-monitoring will help students assess their learning at the end of the course as suggested in the final chapter: *Conclusion: Now What?*

Overall organization

I wanted to provide structures and coherence that could support newer teachers while offering flexible options that could be used with a variety of WAW pedagogies. The chapter titles can be used to guide a sequence of units and assignments, or you might move back and forth between the overviews of writing concepts provided in each chapter and the focused approaches of the articles, essays, and online texts.

To facilitate your thinking about course design, I align parts of the textbook to

1) The *WPA Outcomes Statement* (see Table 1)
2) The "Habits of Mind" (see Table 2)
3) Select threshold concepts from *Naming What We Know: Threshold Concepts of Writing Studies* (Adler-Kassner and Wardle) (see Table 3)

I also group the readings in several categories that may be helpful as you seek models for the kinds of writing you hope your students will produce.

ALIGNING CHAPTERS OF *FOCUS ON WRITING* WITH THREE PEDAGOGICAL FRAMEWORKS

The following tables offer brief glimpses of where various outcomes, dispositions, and writing concepts receive attention, with the upper-case X representing a primary area of attention and the lower-case x representing an implicit area of attention. To some degree, each part of the textbook fits most of the criteria. Tables full of Xs probably wouldn't be helpful, however, so I used discernment when generating these alignments.

TABLE 0.1

WPA Outcomes Statement (CWPA)	Introduction	Chapter 1	Chapter 2	Chapter 3	Chapter 4	Chapter 5	Conclusion
RHETORICAL KNOWLEDGE			X				
Learn and use key rhetorical concepts through analyzing and composing a variety of texts			X				
Gain experience reading and composing in several genres to understand how genre conventions shape and are shaped by readers' and writers' practices and purposes	x	x	x	x	x	x	x
Develop facility in responding to a variety of situations and contexts calling for purposeful shifts in voice, tone, level of formality, design, medium, and/or structure			X				
Understand and use a variety of technologies to address a range of audiences					X		
Match the capacities of different environments (e.g., print and electronic) to varying rhetorical situations		X	X		X		
CRITICAL THINKING, READING, AND COMPOSING					X		
Use composing and reading for inquiry, learning, critical thinking, and communicating in various rhetorical contexts	X			X	X		
Read a diverse range of texts, attending especially to relationships between assertion and evidence, to patterns of organization, to the interplay between verbal and nonverbal elements, and to how these features function for different audiences and situations	x	x	X	x	X	x	x
Locate and evaluate (for credibility, sufficiency, accuracy, timeliness, bias, and so on) primary and secondary research materials, including journal articles and essays, books, scholarly and professionally established and maintained databases or archives, and informal electronic networks and internet sources					X		

WPA Outcomes Statement (CWPA)	Introduction	Chapter 1	Chapter 2	Chapter 3	Chapter 4	Chapter 5	Conclusion
Use strategies—such as interpretation, synthesis, response, critique, and design/redesign—to compose texts that integrate the writer's ideas with those from appropriate sources					X		
PROCESSES				X			
Develop a writing project through multiple drafts				X			
Develop flexible strategies for reading, drafting, reviewing, collaborating, revising, rewriting, rereading, and editing				X			
Use composing processes and tools as a means to discover and reconsider ideas				X			
Experience the collaborative and social aspects of writing processes				X			
Learn to give and to act on productive feedback to works in progress				X			
Adapt composing processes for a variety of technologies and modalities				X		X	
Reflect on the development of composing practices and how those practices influence their work				X			
KNOWLEDGE OF CONVENTIONS			X	X			
Develop knowledge of linguistic structures, including grammar, punctuation, and spelling, through practice in composing and revising				X			
Understand why genre conventions for structure, paragraphing, tone, and mechanics vary			X				
Gain experience negotiating variations in genre conventions			X				
Learn common formats and/or design features for different kinds of texts	X	x	x	X	X	X	x
Explore the concepts of intellectual property (such as fair use and copyright) that motivate documentation conventions					X		
Practice applying citation conventions systematically in their own work					X		

TABLE 0.2

Framework for Success in Postsecondary Writing: "Habits of Mind" (CWPA, NCTE, and NWP)	Introduction	Chapter 1	Chapter 2	Chapter 3	Chapter 4	Chapter 5	Conclusion
Curiosity—the desire to know more about the world		X					
Openness—the willingness to consider new ways of being and thinking in the world		X					
Engagement—a sense of investment and involvement in learning		X					
Creativity—the ability to use novel approaches for generating, investigating, and representing ideas							X
Persistence—the ability to sustain interest in and attention to short- and long-term projects		X		X			
Responsibility—the ability to take ownership of one's actions and understand the consequences of those actions for oneself and others					X		
Flexibility—the ability to adapt to situations, expectations, or demands		X	X				X
Metacognition—the ability to reflect on one's own thinking as well as on the individual and cultural processes used to structure knowledge	x	x	X	x	x	x	X

TABLE 0.3

Select Threshold Concepts adapted from *Naming What We Know: Threshold Concepts of Writing Studies* (Adler-Kassner and Wardle)	Introduction	Chapter 1	Chapter 2	Chapter 3	Chapter 4	Chapter 5	Conclusion
Writing is always a social rather than isolated activity (even if we are alone when we write; even if we are alone and are writing to ourselves)		x	X	X			
Writing and reading activities always occur within specific situations, never in a vacuum or in a way that is "general" or universal		x	X				
Writing makes things happen			X		X	X	
Writing is a way we construct our social identities		x	X				
Words and texts are always in relationships with other words and texts					X		
Writing helps us learn as we think on the page				X			
Returning to our own writing helps us move from understanding our own perspective to using recognizable forms that help us communicate our ideas to others				X			
Because writing situations always change, we are always learning how to write			X				X

MODELS: APPROACHES TO WRITING AND RESEARCH

Many of the readings below may be helpful to students as sources to cite in their writing or even inspiration about how writing can matter. The focus in this section, however, is using writing to model approaches for students to adopt or adapt in their own writing. The following categories thus reflect various genres, purposes, audiences, styles, and use of evidence.

I hesitated before creating a category of student-authored texts because that designation seems to signal they are less worthy. I have found, however, that when I share texts my former students have published beyond our university, this provides more incentive for my current students to produce work worth sharing. The writing listed here is substantive and worth reading; it is impressive no matter who authored it.

All the works listed have either been reprinted in this text or are available online, as indicated.

Writing authored by students
"Domestic Sphere vs. Public Sphere"
"Writing What Matters: A Student's Struggle to Bridge the Academic/Personal Divide" (online)
"Texting and Writing" (online)
"A Response to Michaela Cullington" (online)
"Powerless Persuasion: Ineffective Argumentation Plagues the Clean Eating Community"
"Tag: Classroom Genres" (online)
"'I Realize Writing Is a Part of My Daily Life Now': A Case Study of Writing Knowledge Transfer in One Section of ESL Writing" (online)
"To 'Play That Funky Music' or Not: How Music Affects the Environmental Self-Regulation of High-Ability Academic Writers" (online)
"Excuse My Excess" (online)
"*Respondeo etsi Mutabor*: The Comment and Response Assignment, Young Scholars, and the Promise of Liberal Education" (online)
"Eavesdropping on the Conversation: Situating an Undergraduate's Role within the Scope of Academic Journals" (online)
"Typeface and Document Persona in Magazines" (online)
Teach-a-Theory Videos (online)

"Domestic Sphere vs. Public Sphere"

from *Bird by Bird: Some Instructions on Writing and Life*

"Teaching the Other Self: The Writer's First Reader"

"Why I Write" (online)

"Writing What Matters: A Student's Struggle to Bridge the Academic/Personal Divide" (online)

"Reflections on Teaching" (online)

"Story as Rhetorical: We Can't Escape Story No Matter How Hard We Try" (online)

"Excuse My Excess" (online)

Case studies

"The Pursuit of Literacy"

"Materiality and Genre in the Study of Discourse Communities"

"Understanding Composing"

"Going Public: Exploring the Possibilities for Publishing Student Interest-Driven Writing beyond the Classroom"

"Writing What Matters: A Student's Struggle to Bridge the Academic/Personal Divide" (online)

"'I Realize Writing Is a Part of My Daily Life Now': A Case Study of Writing Knowledge Transfer in One Section of ESL Writing" (online)

Focus on student texts and student reflections

"Literature, Literacy, and (New) Media"

"Understanding Composing"

"Research Is Elementary: How *Blue's Clues* Can Help Teach Communication Research Methods"

"The Low Bridge to High Benefits: Entry-Level Multimedia, Literacies, and Motivation"

"Going Public: Exploring the Possibilities for Publishing Student Interest-Driven Writing beyond the Classroom"

The Meaningful Writing Project: Learning, Teaching, and Writing in Higher Education (online)

"Texting and Writing" (online)

Writing across Borders (online)

"*Respondeo etsi Mutabor*: The Comment and Response Assignment, Young Scholars, and the Promise of Liberal Education" (online)

from *Bird by Bird: Some Instructions on Writing and Life*
"The Wrong Way to Teach Grammar" (online)
"Easy Reading Is Damn Hard Writing" (online)
"Excuse My Excess" (online)
"All about Beta Readers" (online)
"Reading, Writing, and Research in the Digital Age" (online)
"Multimodal Composing, Sketchnotes, and Idea Generation" (online)

Pedagogical advice (for a faculty audience)
"Literature, Literacy, and (New) Media"
"Materiality and Genre in the Study of Discourse Communities"
"Teaching the Other Self: The Writer's First Reader"
"What Can a Novice Contribute? Undergraduate Researchers in First-Year
    Composition"
"Research Is Elementary: How *Blue's Clues* Can Help Teach Communication
    Research Methods"
Introduction to *Situated Language and Learning: A Critique of Traditional
    Schooling*
"The Low Bridge to High Benefits: Entry-Level Multimedia, Literacies, and
    Motivation"
"Going Public: Exploring the Possibilities for Publishing Student Interest-
    Driven Writing beyond the Classroom"
*The Meaningful Writing Project: Learning, Teaching, and Writing in Higher
    Education* (online)
"Story as Rhetorical: We Can't Escape Story No Matter How Hard We Try"
    (online)
"Informal Local Research Aids Student and Faculty Learning" (online)

Protocol analysis used for research
"Understanding Composing"
"Writing Research and the Writer"

**Texts and people: Rhetorical analysis / genre analysis / discourse community /
ethnography**
"Domestic Sphere vs. Public Sphere"
"Materiality and Genre in the Study of Discourse Communities"

"Powerless Persuasion: Ineffective Argumentation Plagues the Clean Eating Community"

"Tag: Classroom Genres" (online)

"Why Do People Say 'AX' instead of 'ASK'?" (online)

"People Are Sharing Words that Only Their Family Uses, And It's Hilariously Relatable" (online)

"Eavesdropping on the Conversation: Situating an Undergraduate's Role within the Scope of Academic Journals" (online)

"Typeface and Document Persona in Magazines" (online)

"From Pencils to Pixels: The Stages of Literacy Technology" (online)

Enjoy the readings, enjoy the writing, enjoy your students!

WORKS CITED

Adler-Kassner, Linda, and Elizabeth Wardle. *Naming What We Know: Threshold Concepts of Writing Studies*, Utah State UP, 2015.

Council of Writing Program Administrators. *WPA Outcomes Statement for First-Year Composition (3.0)*, July 2014, <wpacouncil.org/positions/outcomes.html>.

Council of Writing Program Administrators, National Council of Teachers of English, and National Writing Project. *Framework for Success in Postsecondary Writing.* CWPA, NCTE, and NWP, 2011, <ncil.org/files/framework-for-success-postsecondary-writing.pdf>.

Tinberg, Howard. "Teaching for Transfer: A Passport for Writing in New Contexts." *Peer Review*, vol. 19, no. 1, 2017, <https://www.aacu.org/peerreview/2017/Winter/Tinberg>.

1 WHY WRITE?

Exploring the Question

During a class near the beginning of the semester, my students and I make lists of all the writing we've done so far that day. Sometimes students hesitate, and I remind them that texting and Instagramming and tweeting and Snapchatting are forms of writing. Students remember that they have created notes, doodles, lists, and other kinds of everyday writing.

We combine our individual lists to make a fuller class list, and then we take it even further by writing down what we *read*, that day or even that week. You can imagine how the list grows exponentially; once we start paying attention, it seems that written text is *everywhere*. We list stop signs,

CONNECT

Before you begin reading, try this exercise either individually or as a class:

1. List all the kinds of writing you have done so far today, whether you used a pen, a pencil, a computer, a tablet, or a cell phone.

2. List all the kinds of items you have read so far today. Look around you right now to notice writing that may be part of your everyday life.

3. If you can, compare lists with other people. Did anyone list writing and reading activities that involved reading images, objects, people, or situations? Sometimes "writing" and "reading" imply alphabetic texts, but often these words are used to suggest activities of constructing and interpreting meaning that may or may not involve written words.

4. What, if anything, surprises you about the above lists? Explain why.

menus, billboards, room numbers, store names, cereal boxes ... and the list goes on and on.

If we think of writing and reading as activities that involve not only alphabetic text but also images, objects, people, situations, and so forth, the list again multiplies.

In short, it doesn't take long for us to realize that writing and reading are activities that are intertwined with all aspects of our lives in a variety of ways.

Even if we think of writing in terms of alphabetic texts alone, the question arises, WHY? Why is writing such an integral activity in our lives? And how can we apply answers to the question of "why" to the very real writing we are often required to do in academic settings?

CONNECT

What is your initial response to the question "Why write"? To answer this, you might do the following:

1. Choose one of the kinds of writing you do several times a week or more and explain what motivates you to engage in that writing.

2. Now choose a writing assignment you completed in school that you felt motivated to work on. What factors contributed to your motivation?

RELATIONSHIP WITH WRITING: IT'S COMPLICATED

If you're at all like me, you write regularly without thinking twice about it, but at other times you find yourself making every excuse in the world to avoid writing. When thinking through the question "Why write?" then, it helps to consider what compels us to write in some situations and what hinders our writing in other situations.

Filling a purpose

Much writing is undertaken because it accomplishes something. Remember the note on the refrigerator I discussed in the Introduction?

My favorite son—DON'T FORGET!
Haircut 3:30 Friday

That note operated as a reminder for Fred to keep his haircut appointment. That haircut might have been important because of an upcoming sporting event or formal celebration, which would make the reminder note even more crucial. The motivation for writing the note increases if the purpose for the note is not simply a typical monthly haircut.

The note was also a reinforcement of a particular kind of relationship. It would be unusual for a child to leave such a reminder note for a parent, though it is possible. It would also be unusual for a parent to leave such a reminder note for a very young child. The note itself implies that Fred is old enough to read and to keep haircut appointments himself, but his parents do not believe he is fully independent— not only because they share the same household but also because they think he *needs* the reminder note.

CONNECT

1. Can you think of other purposes the reminder note might fill?

2. Look at the kinds of writing on your list from the start of this chapter. How many kinds of writing reinforce relationship bonds, even if they simultaneously fill another purpose?

It is also possible the child does not need the reminder note but the parents *want* to have a role in his life; the note establishes a role for them.

Motivation

Some writing we do is ***intrinsically motivated***. We write because we want to, and we find satisfaction or another kind of reward in this writing. You might experience this motivation if you text a friend because you want to share a funny thought or if you write reflections in a personal journal.

Other writing is ***extrinsically motivated***. In these situations, we write in order to gain a reward or to avoid a negative consequence. You might experience this if you fill out a form when you visit a doctor or you complete a class writing assignment because you want to earn a high grade.

Many times we might have a combination of motivations when we write. As a matter of fact, I find it difficult to invest in a writing project if I am focused solely on extrinsic factors. If I'm not initially excited about writing I need to complete, I give myself a good talking to until I either feel invested in the work or I convince myself to just get it done.

For example, part of my work as a college faculty person involves writing an annual report about my activities. I have to explain how I have fulfilled my responsibilities in order to be evaluated. Every year when it's time to complete this report, I am not excited, even though the report can result in a salary increase.

To get motivated, I remind myself it's helpful to see what I've done for my own reasons. I can feel good about what I've accomplished, I can think about my current professional status, and I can plan where I am headed next.

I *also* talk myself into just getting the report done so that I can focus on work I enjoy more. When I avoid work, I feel like I'm carrying it around wherever I go, and the best way to feel free is to get the work done.

1. Teachers can be a resource by modeling what to do when writing is difficult. Ask your teachers about times when they did not want to write and how they coped with the situation.

2. How about you? Describe a time when you were annoyed with a writing requirement but you found a way to become invested in it.

I'm not certain if I would complete an annual activity report if I weren't required to do so. I do know, however, that the reason why I complete the work with good will is not because of potential money, but for the intrinsic rewards. I also keep the report in perspective. I know it doesn't need to be a grand masterpiece but instead simply needs to be complete. I enjoy checking that task off my "to do" list.

A burden or a gift?

You might be familiar with Mark Twain's novel *The Adventures of Tom Sawyer*. Early in the book, young Tom has been caught misbehaving, and his punishment involves whitewashing a fence. Tom's friends come by and tease him because he has to work on a beautiful day, but Tom pretends he has chosen to whitewash the fence and he acts like he's having a lot of fun doing it.

Soon enough, Tom's friends want to whitewash the fence because they buy into his pretense. Tom doesn't allow anyone else to whitewash the fence immediately— he keeps that possibility just out of reach to increase desire. The friends end up offering Tom gifts in exchange for an opportunity to paint the fence.

Writing is an awful lot like painting a fence.

If you've grown up in a school system that has required you to write, you might associate writing with work and even punishment. But you might have thought about writing differently when you were a kid. You might have felt excitement when you learned how to write letters, or form words, or create a story.

For many of us, when we were kids and were first learning to write, we were like Tom Sawyer's friends who wanted to whitewash that fence. We saw older people in our lives writing, and we wanted to be able to do it, too.

Unfortunately, that feeling goes away for a lot of us during years upon years of schooling, as we are told to write on demand and much of that writing is evaluated. Grading places the focus on *extrinsic* rewards, and being compelled to write may take some of the pleasure away from the activity. We might also not always recognize the purpose of writing tasks we are assigned in school.

A required first-year composition course may also feel like the punishment form of whitewashing a fence simply because it's *required* rather than being a choice.

Am I depressing you yet?

I like to be honest. Sometimes writing feels like a burden and an obligation. It is much more difficult to write in those circumstances.

But even when we are required to take a course, when we are expected to write, when we are supposed to meet a deadline, and when we are producing writing that is going to be graded—we can still channel our inner Tom Sawyer. We can start *pretending* we want to write and that many people would be jealous if they were witnessing our writing process.

The way it works, however, is that it doesn't take long to realize that we *are* lucky to be writing, even when it's something that someone else has told us to do (like my faculty activity report or a paper you are completing for a class). The truth is, our ability to take time to write and think and process ideas is an incredible privilege that is denied to many people the world over. The truth is, people with few resources often make great sacrifices in order to learn how to write and improve their education.

CONNECT

1. Some people struggle when first learning to write and thus may not associate early writing with a kind of joy. What about you? What were your earliest associations with writing?

2. Can you think of an example of writing being used as a form of punishment?

3. Can you think of an example of writing being used as a form of reward?

What sometimes feels like a burden may actually be a gift. And Tom Sawyer probably enjoyed whitewashing that fence more than he ever expected, all because he first *pretended* that it was something he wanted to do.

Writing for ourselves, writing for others

If you look back at the list of examples of writing and reading completed by you and your classmates, you'll notice there are many ways to categorize the writing. The chapter question "Why write?" suggests that *purpose* matters a lot. In addition, audience affects how we write, and these two factors are often paired in the ways they shape writing.

For example, if you write a shopping list or a "to do" list for yourself, the purpose may be to help you remember. If you write a similar list for another person, your purpose is to communicate what needs to be done to someone who may otherwise have no idea what you're thinking. The way that you write the lists thus changes based on purpose (memory versus communication) and audience (self versus other).

In writing tasks that are more complex than shopping lists, it's easy to feel frustrated when writing to meet the expectations of others. I actually encourage students (and remind myself) to initially write with *some* general sense of readers' expectations but without worrying *too* much about being judged or evaluated.

If you are not used to writing and speaking in a particular setting, you might be confused about the expectations. That can be frustrating from the start. When I have no idea what I'm aiming for, I tend to procrastinate; it seems like a waste of time for me to begin writing without any sense of how the finished product should look. The key for me has been to find an example of the kind of writing I need to complete. Once I have a model, I am better able to begin drafting.

However, I do not get too hung up on what other people will think of my writing when I get started so worries and concerns about being criticized or misunderstood don't get in the way of drafting and thinking on the page.

At some point, it's important to focus on what readers will expect and how we can shape our ideas in order to communicate effectively. Sometimes we will want to fully meet our readers' expectations so our writing will be most likely to fill its purpose.

Sometimes we might know the expectations, but we have a reason for writing in unexpected ways. For example, sometimes when writing my faculty activity report, I'll think about my dean reading a whole stack of these reports and getting bored, so I'll insert something funny. Humor generally does not belong in a faculty activity report. But if I have a dean who appreciates a laugh, my choice to ignore expectations might be smart. I would not, however, refuse to list my activities. Such a refusal would be counterproductive because I would not be filling the purpose of the writing task.

Sometimes people who use unexpected approaches let their audience know they are going to do so and explain why. This dynamic happened at a conference talk I attended. The speaker was an African American professor named Ersula Ore who was speaking to an audience of college professors of various racial and ethnic identities. Ore was discussing black experience and cultural expectations, and she explained at the start of her talk that she would be using African American vernacular *and* the language of academics because both languages fit her identity. Even though one style is considered informal and the other formal, she was showing that the two styles can have a different effect when used together. This practice of bringing various dialects together is called ***code meshing*** (Young et al.).

The speaker helped audience members adjust their expectations. If she hadn't done so, some people might have thought she was being inauthentic when using African American vernacular, while others might have accused her of being inauthentic when using academic discourse. She might have had a more difficult time communicating effectively if people in the audience focused on her tendency to mix two different speaking styles and were thus distracted from her argument.

Here's the deal. Writer-centered prose means that you're writing for yourself. Reader-centered prose means that you're writing for your readers. Rather than there being only two extreme choices, you can pick and choose what you do and how you do it so your writing meets the purpose you'd like it to meet, or at least has a reasonable chance of doing so. On a good day, your writing may serve you as well as your readers.

When you first write, make sure you have a basic sense of what you're working on, and then just write. If you saw the first draft of this chapter, you'd be wondering, "What is she talking about?" and "Why is this lady so boring?" If you're still thinking that now that I've revised and worked to appeal to you by clarifying ideas and deleting irrelevant tangents, I'm sorry! But please let me know (in a polite way that won't make me cry) so I can revise and improve for the next edition. Thank you!

CONNECT

1. Describe a time you felt good about communicating in your own distinctive way.

2. Describe a time when you appreciated someone else's surprising or unique approach to writing.

WHY WRITE IN A COLLEGE COURSE?

Many writing teachers advocate for *authentic* writing in our classrooms. "Authentic" suggests that the writing engages a real-world audience and purpose, as opposed to writing for the teacher or writing for a grade. Some courses use service learning, civic engagement, online writing, campus publications or research forums, and other tools to position course assignments in wider frames so that students will hopefully find the work meaningful.

If your course writing assignments tend to be positioned in such a way, the answer to "Why write?" may already be apparent to you.

However, whether in your current course or in another course, chances are that sometimes you are going to be assigned writing that seems aimed at a teacher who will be evaluating your work. That can be a daunting dynamic, and it may be difficult to feel motivated.

It usually helps if you have a sense of *why* the professor has assigned the work. Is it to guide you in writing in a genre that you will be required to use again in the future? Is it to challenge you to synthesize ideas about a topic to increase your understanding of those ideas? Is it to help you practice specific disciplinary conventions? Is it a way of having you engage deeply in a text via close analysis?

If you know the purpose, you might find the work more meaningful.

In addition, composition scholar Toby Fulwiler advises students to "make the assignment your own" by putting the assignment in your own words and relating it to something you care about (9). That way, the assignment may fill a purpose for *you* as well as a purpose within the context of the course. Fulwiler also says that it helps if you "try to teach your readers something," even if your reader is a teacher (9). Teachers really can and do learn from students! It's not just a cliché.

From everyday writing to academic writing

Sometimes students tell me they hate to write. I ask if they text people or use social media.

"Yes."

"Does anybody force you to do that?"

"No."

"Well, why do you text and use social media if you hate to write?"

When students tell me they hate to write, they usually mean they hate to write for school, on demand, with constraints developed by a teacher, and with a grade at the end of the process.

I am not simply being snarky when I point out times students enjoy writing and do it by choice. I value diverse kinds of writing, and I want us to question why some practices are not perceived as "real writing" while others are, both in academic and non-academic contexts (Winsor).

In addition to valuing texting and social media writing in their own right, I also appreciate how becoming aware of our expertise in one kind of writing can help us develop expertise in other kinds of writing.

My interest in connecting everyday writing to academic writing might seem odd to you. Often people rail against the amount of time teens and young adults spend in front of a screen, and research certainly shows some drawbacks to spending too much time on social media or on a phone (Twenge). Still, the potential for negative repercussions does not mean that every facet of screen time is bad. People today write and read more than any generation that has come before, and that has to count for something.

One way to improve writing is to begin noticing similarities and differences as you move from one situation to another. When researcher Lucille McCarthy followed a

CONNECT

1. If you had to argue that smartphones are unhealthy based solely on your own experiences, what would you cite as evidence?

2. If you had to argue that smartphones are healthy based solely on your own experiences, what would you cite as evidence?

3. Have you ever changed your phone habits? If so, why? If not, what might compel you to do so?

FOCUS ON WRITING: WHAT COLLEGE STUDENTS WANT TO KNOW

student as he worked on papers for various college courses, she found he approached each class as if there was no connection to writing he had done before. The student thus struggled, while students who notice both similarities and differences can apply and adapt what they have learned in past situations to help them complete new writing tasks.

CONNECT

What similarities and differences can you think of between writing in a high school English class and a high school science class?

For example, students who adapted more quickly and effectively to new writing situations noticed that most academic settings required ideas to be developed with evidence. What counted as "evidence," however, differed from one discipline to the next.

Just as students who identify the similarities and differences from one classroom to the next have an easier time writing in new situations, noticing what you know about writing in everyday situations can help you think more about how to develop writing appropriate to academic settings.

How texting and social media writing connect to academic writing

According to both my personal experience and more reliable research studies published online by the Pew Research Center, teens spend a lot of time reading, writing, and viewing digital texts (Lenhart). After a casual conversation with digital humanities professor Amanda Licastro at an academic conference many years ago, I began thinking more about intersections between students' use of social media and their academic writing. Once I asked a class of about twenty students whether academic writing and social media had more in common or more that was different. Initially, all but one of the students pointed to differences. You can probably imagine the reasons they provided (these are from memory and are not exact quotes):

- "I quickly post on social media to my friends without thinking."
- "I use social media to make my friends laugh or to flirt with someone."
- "I don't worry about my spelling or how I say something when I text."
- "I use gifs and selfies and emojis when texting."
- "I would never use terrible language in a paper, but I do all the time when texting with my friends."
- "When I post on Twitter or Instagram, I know that a lot of people are going to see it. It matters more. Only a teacher sees my papers."
- "People will say anything online. At least when it's anonymous."
- "Social media is short and quick. That's not at all like writing a paper."

Certain themes recur in the above paraphrases from a class discussion. When describing differences between one kind of writing and another, students most often discussed purpose, audience, content (that is, what material would be appropriate), length of the writing process, and style (informal or formal, text-based or image-based, sloppy or well-edited, short or long, and so forth).

CONNECT

Before reading further, think about your own response. To what degree do you find that texting and writing on social media platforms seem disconnected from academic writing? What areas of similarity do you see?

One of the most obvious connections between texting or social media writing and academic writing is awareness that

1) *certain elements matter: purpose, audience, content, writing process, and style*
2) *writers make choices as we move from one situation to another*

A host of other connections can be drawn from social media expertise and applied to academic writing. Such connections might not be obvious at first because informal digital writing embeds information about author, recipient, date, time, and even sources (via links and sharing), so conscious attention to context and audience is often minimized (Mattingly and Harkin 15). Students who write easily via texting or social media may struggle writing appropriately in professional or academic contexts (Mattingly and Harkin 15–17), but noticing similarities and differences can help writers adjust and adapt.

For example, not all texting and social media writing is alike. If you use Snapchat and Instagram and Twitter, you may notice the way each functions differently, both in terms of possibilities and constraints. These differences between platforms parallel differences between academic **disciplines**, so it's expected that your approach to writing in a history class would be different from a psychology class.

Audiences also shift from class to class, even within a single discipline, just as they do on social media as you write to particular friend groups. Each professor (or friend group) may have slightly different priorities, so part of communicating well is noticing the shift in audience expectations.

Genres, too, make a difference. A private or direct message on social media functions differently than a public post, and we all need to learn what is appropriate in which space in order to communicate and avoid alienating others. Similarly, emailing a professor, taking notes in class, writing an in-class essay exam, and submitting a semester-long research paper are all different genres and need to be treated as such.

I also like to point out that texting and social media writing may often be dashed off without much thought, but many of us have taken our time and labored over a particular post that had higher stakes attached to it. Most students I talk to can recall a time when they revised their writing or asked for advice before making writing public. For some, it was because they were at a turning point in a relationship. For others, it was because they wanted to express a difference of opinion with someone but didn't want to cause offense. Others took their time figuring out what to say because they wanted to share something deeply sad or troubling such as the death of a loved one or their own story of surviving trauma.

In such situations, a **writing process** that involves time, reflection, feedback from others, revision, and editing is part of self-motivated social media writing. A similar process is often expected in academic writing situations, even though the finished product will probably be quite different from the social media posting. The general principle is that *high stakes writing* (writing associated with serious and consequential communication) takes more time and is a more complex process than *low stakes writing* (informal writing that may involve thinking through ideas or gradually building a relationship).

Reflecting on our writing expertise in one situation to better understand expectations in a less familiar situation is an excellent habit to develop. Building strong friendships through texting and social media writing is not exactly the same as developing your academic reputation through course writing assignments, but noticing both the differences and the similarities can help you appreciate the value of the various kinds of writing you do.

CONNECT

1. Much academic writing involves responding to reading or using sources to help develop an argument. What aspects of texting or social media writing have similar dynamics?

2. Most people craft a particular kind of public identity on social media. Think of examples from people you follow. Do people also craft a particular identity in their academic writing? If so, how would this identity be similar to or different from their social media identity?

3. Although I focused on digital writing in this section, you probably have expertise in many kinds of everyday writing. Can you think of an example of writing that might have some lessons to keep in mind as you write in school settings?

WORKS CITED

Fulwiler, Toby. *College Writing: A Personal Approach to Academic Writing*, 3rd ed. Boynton/Cook, 2002, <www.heinemann.com/shared/onlineresources/0523/0523.pdf>.

Lenhart, Amanda. "Teens, Social Media, & Technology: Overview 2015." *Pew Research Center*, 9 April 2015, <http://www.pewinternet.org/2015/04/09/teens-social-media-technology-2015/>.

Mattingly, Rebecca de Wind, and Patricia Harkin. "A Major in Flexibility." *What We Are Becoming: Developments in Undergraduate Writing Majors*, edited by Greg A. Giberson and Thomas A. Moriarty, Utah State UP, 2010, pp. 13–31, <https://digitalcommons.usu.edu/cgi/viewcontent.cgi?referer=&httpsredir=1&article=1026&context=usupress_pubs>.

McCarthy, Lucille P. "A Stranger in Strange Lands: A College Student Writing across the Curriculum." *Research in the Teaching of English*, vol. 21, no. 3, Oct. 1987, pp. 233–65.

Twain, Mark. *The Adventures of Tom Sawyer*. American Publishing, 1884. Project Gutenberg, 2016, <http://www.gutenberg.org/files/74/74-h/74-h.htm>.

Twenge, Jean M. "Have Smartphones Destroyed a Generation?" *The Atlantic*, September 2017, <https://www.theatlantic.com/magazine/archive/2017/09/has-the-smartphone-destroyed-a-generation/534198/>.

Winsor, Dorothy A. "What Counts as Writing? An Argument from Engineers' Practice." *JAC: A Journal of Rhetoric, Culture, and Politics*, vol. 12, no. 2, 1992, pp. 337–47, <http://sophclinic.pbworks.com/f/winsor-jac-engineering-writing-2.pdf>.

Young, Vershawn Ashanti, et al. *Other People's English: Code-Meshing, Code-Switching, and African-American Literacy*. Teachers College P, 2014.

Extending the Conversation

To think more about the question "Why write?" I have gathered together four selections reprinted here and six readings you can find online. Each piece overlaps with my initial approach to the question in some way, but each piece also extends the question "Why write?" in a particular direction. As we answer questions that may seem simple at first, complexities and nuances develop that call for more exploration.

For each text reprinted here, I tell you why I included it, provide some background about its initial publication, and offer hints that may guide your reading, including vocabulary terms when relevant. I also provide "connect" questions to help you engage and respond as you read.

For each online source I recommend, I offer a brief introduction—just enough to guide you as you decide what further reading might be helpful, inspiring, enjoyable, or challenging.

DEBORAH BRANDT'S "THE PURSUIT OF LITERACY" (2001)

Why I included it

I appreciate that Brandt answers the question "Why write?" by connecting literacy—the ability to read and write—to economic, historical, and social conditions during the twentieth century. Because this is an excerpt of a book introduction, it provides an overview of what the book does rather than specific details from the literacy study. Still, even this overview says a lot.

As you read about Brandt's research methods, you might be inspired to interview one or two people or reflect on your own experiences. You can review the Appendix and focus your own research according to your interests.

Background

Brandt's study looks back at the twentieth century from the vantage point of 2001. This timing allows her to think historically. Her research responds to a wider movement centered on understanding literacy as contextual; that is, reading and writing always take place in particular times and places, so they should not be understood in abstract or universal ways but instead should be connected to other cultural dynamics.

Brandt explains that literacy (the ability to read and write) is a useful resource that some people can access more easily than others and that is tied to economic and historical change. Brandt describes the process of interview that she used to reach conclusions, and she offers a framework (the "literacy sponsor") that allows her to discuss issues of access to literacy. Brandt's term "literacy sponsor" has been used regularly since this 2001 publication because scholars have continued to research questions of literacy, access, and social power.

Remember that this selection is an excerpt. Where the asterisks appear, text is omitted, and the reading experience may thus be jumpy in those places.

Three sections are included here. The first pages of the introductory chapter provide a sense of the book's focus. The section titled "Parameters of the Study" outlines Brandt's research methods. The third section, titled "The Analytical Framework: Sponsors of Literacy," explains that whenever people are supported in their efforts to read and write, the individual or institutional "sponsor" also stands to benefit in some way. This last section is probably the most difficult part.

Try thinking about each section individually in terms of its purpose, and then think about it in relation to the other sections. Brandt assumes scholarly readers who have an interest and background in studies of literacy, so her text may seem difficult to you at times. In places, however, her writing is straightforward and will likely be clear to you. Using these places of clarity to guide you, try to figure out what she hopes to accomplish with this text. Why would she ask 80 people about their experiences with literacy? What might she hope to accomplish as she tells of the patterns she's found in their stories?

The Appendix at the end of the selection will help you gain a better sense of the interviews Brandt conducted, so you may want to look at that document early in your reading.

literacy: the ability to read and write, especially within a particular situation. For example, although Brandt doesn't use the term "computer literacy," that is a particular kind of literacy. Literacy thus may look different over time as reading and writing expectations shift.

literacy sponsor: a person or institution supporting the literacy development of a person or group of people. This relationship benefits the person who

CONNECT

As you read, consider responding to the following questions to help you process the material.

1. I said that Brandt is assuming her audience is scholarly and interested in literacy studies. What clues in the first section helped me to draw that conclusion? Are there any signs that she has a wider audience in mind?

2. In what ways do Brandt's study parameters help her discover information about literacy? In what ways is the study limited? If you wanted to find out more, what kind of study would you design?

3. How did you learn to read and write? What people or institutions sponsored your literacy? Were you expected to conform or otherwise meet expectations of those who sponsored your literacy?

4. Have you ever noticed unequal access to literacy? Now that Brandt is pointing it out, can you imagine being raised in different circumstances that would provide you with either more or less access to literacy?

is gaining literacy, but it is often under conditions that also benefit the sponsor; thus, access to literacy may come at a price. Considering the role of the literacy sponsor allows Brandt to move from individual stories to recognizing changing economic and historical conditions.

Excerpt from: Brandt, Deborah. "The Pursuit of Literacy." Introduction to *Literacy in American Lives*. Cambridge UP, 2001, pp. 1–24.

LITERACY IS SO much an expectation in this country that it has become more usual to ask why and how people fail to learn to read and write than to ask why and how they succeed. In a society in which virtually every child attends school and where some kind of print penetrates every corner of existence, only the strongest sorts of countervailing forces—oppression, deprivation, dislocation—seem able to exclude a person from literacy. Asked to imagine how their lives would be different if they didn't know how to read and write, people I have spoken with are often baffled and pained. "I would be totally in the dark," they say. Or, "It would be like not having shoes."

To think of literacy as a staple of life—on the order of indoor lights or clothing—is to understand how thoroughly most Americans in these times are able to take their literacy for granted. It also is to appreciate how central reading and writing can be to people's sense of security and well-being, even to their sense of dignity. At the same time, these analogies ask us to take a deeper look. They remind us that, as with electricity or manufactured goods, individual literacy exists only as part of larger material systems, systems that on the one hand enable acts of reading or writing and on the other hand confer their value. Changes in these systems change the meaning and status of individual literacy much as the newest style of shoes—or method of producing shoes—might enhance or depreciate the worth of the old. Further, these analogies remind us that, despite a tendency to take the resource of literacy for granted, acquiring literacy—like acquiring other basic staples of life—remains an active, some-times daunting process for individuals and families. This process is exacerbated by turbulent economic changes that do not merely raise standards for literacy achievement from one generation to the next but often ruthlessly reconfigure the social and economic systems through which literacy can be pursued and through which it can find its worth.

This book is about how ordinary people have learned to read and write during the century just concluded. It is also about how they have made use of that learning at various stages of their lives. Learning to read and write has taken place amid convulsive changes in economic and social life, educational expectations, and communication technologies. This has been a time when the meaning of what it is to be literate has seemed to shift with nearly every new generation. Inevitably, pursuing literacy in the twentieth century entailed learning to respond to an unprecedented pace of change in the uses, forms, and standards of literacy. One of the major aims of this book is to look closely at the sources of the changing conditions of literacy learning and especially at the ways that Americans have faced the escalating pressure to provide for themselves and their children the kinds of literate skill demanded by life in these times.

Literacy has proven to be a difficult and contentious topic of investigation largely because its place in American culture has become so complex and even conflicted. Expanding literacy undeniably has been an instrument for more democratic access to learning, political participation, and upward mobility. At the same time, it has become one of the sharpest tools for stratification and denial of opportunity. Print in the twentieth century was the sea on which ideas and other cultural goods flowed easily among regions, occupations, and social classes. But it also was a mechanism by which the great bureaucracies of modern life tightened around us, along with their systems of testing, sorting, controlling, and coercing. The ability to read and, more recently, to write often helps to catapult individuals into higher economic brackets and social privilege. Yet the very broadening of these abilities among greater numbers of people has enabled economic and technological changes that now destabilize and devalue once serviceable levels of literate skills. Unending cycles of competition and change keep raising the stakes for literacy achievement. In fact, as literacy has gotten implicated in almost all of the ways that money is now made in America, the reading and writing skills of the population have become grounds for unprecedented encroachment and concern by those who profit from what those skills produce. In short, literacy is valuable—and volatile—property. And like other commodities with private and public value, it is a grounds for potential exploitation, injustice, and struggle as well as potential hope, satisfaction, and reward. Wherever literacy is learned and practiced, these competing interests will always be present.

[***]

Parameters of the Study

This is a study, then, about how people across the past century learned to read and write, actively, passively, willingly, resistantly, and, always, persistently, over a lifetime. It focuses on the experiences of ordinary people, some who read or write constantly and some who do so rarely, some who are able to take reading or writing with them into virtually any sphere of life where it can do some good and others who usually must trade on other means to make out. In any case, in this study, an understanding of literacy is built up from people's accounts of their lived experiences, embracing those instances in which anyone said they learned anything about reading or writing. Although encounters with literacy often blended with other activities (some people learned about writing, for instance, while drawing, calculating, reading, listening to the radio, watching television, talking), the study maintains a primary focus on the acquisition and use of alphabetic script. The interest is in reading and writing as people would mundanely and practically distinguish them from other sorts of recognizable activity (or at least as they were being recognized in the 1990s!). The study makes no attempt to measure people's literacy skills against any kind of standard (although it notices, at times, how such measurements are made). Rather, the driving concerns have to do with how people say they came to acquire or develop the resources of reading or writing—at all.

It has been commonplace, as I mentioned, to consider literacy in the plural, as sets of social practices, diverse routines that must be understood in relationship to the particular social aims and habits associated with their contexts of use. In this study, perhaps because the focus is less on how people practice literacy and more on how they have pursued it, literacy appears less settled than the term *practice* might imply. It appears more elusive, as a want, as an incursion, as an unstable currency. When literacy does appear in this study as a social practice, it is as a practice that is often jumping its tracks, propelled into new directions by new or intensifying pressures for its use.

This study is based on 80 in-depth interviews I conducted in the mid-1990s with a diverse group of Americans ranging in birth date from the late 1890s to the early 1980s. In the interviews, we traced together their memories of learning to write and, to a lesser extent, their memories of learning to read. The inquiry focused especially on the people, institutions, materials, and motivations that contributed to literacy learning, both in school and out, from birth to the present. I also explored with the people I interviewed the uses and values that literacy has had for them at various stages of life. This study follows in the tradition of life-story research, which is a loose confederation of historical, sociological, psychological, and phenomenological inquiry. This form of research serves multiple purposes and employs various methodologies, including the collection of open-ended autobiographical monologues, structured and less structured interviews, and biographical surveys. What these diverse traditions have in common is an interest in people's descriptions of their own life experiences. A significant focus for analysis is the life span. Social psychology uses life stories to explore people's subjective worlds, seeking relationships among social structure, personality, and behavior. Other sorts of inquiries examine the linguistic forms and functions of narrative accounts themselves to uncover the meaning structures that people call on to bring order to their experiences. Perhaps the best known line of life-story research is oral history, which uses interviews to gather information about the social conditions of ordinary lives, information that is otherwise unrecorded and often overlooked in conventional histories of important people and events. In other cases, oral history is used to document multiple perspectives on public events. My study is aligned in many ways with oral history perspectives as articulated by Paul Thompson (1975, 1988, 1990) and Trevor Lummis (1987) and with the biographical sociology of Daniel Bertaux (1981, 1984).[1] I treat autobiographical accounts for their historical value, for their illumination of people's relationships to the social structures of their times and places, especially those in which literacy learning is implicated. Rather than searching for uniqueness or subjective differences, this study concerns itself with similarities of experience among people who experience similarly structured positions and relations. As Trevor Lummis explained,

> … people live their lives within the material and cultural boundaries of their time span, and so life histories are exceptionally effective historical sources because through the totality of lived experience they reveal relations between individuals and social forces which are rarely apparent in other sources. Above all, the information is historical and dynamic in that it reveals changes of experience through time.[2]

---

1   Also see Bertaux and Thompson (1997). Social structure and social change are at the heart of the investigations of these three researchers. Individual cases are valued for what they can reveal about economic and social relationships. For weaknesses in this approach, see the Popular Memory Group's (1982) critique of Thompson's *The Voice of the Past* (1988), which they fault for not attending to the cultural constructions involved in life-story interviewing and life stories themselves, for disguising premises of researcher and researched in "the empirical fact." My study, in fact, is limited in the same way.

2   Lummis, 1987, page 108.

FOCUS ON WRITING: WHAT COLLEGE STUDENTS WANT TO KNOW

Direct accounts about how ordinary people have acquired reading and writing and their motivations for doing so are largely missing from the record of mass literacy development. Most studies of the past have had to rely on indirect evidence, such as signature rates, book circulation, or the growth of schooling, with only an occasional excerpt from diaries or letters or autobiographies to provide a more contextualized sense of the means and meaning of literacy in various eras. Only recently have we begun to accumulate more systematic and direct accounts of contemporary literacy as it has been experienced. Nevertheless, many current debates about literacy education and policy continue to be based largely on indirect evidence, such as standardized test scores or education levels or surveys of reading habits. It is the persistent interest of this study to characterize literacy not as it registers on various scales but as it has been lived.

The point of view of this investigation is roughly through birth cohorts, a method of analysis meant to capture literacy learning within what Lummis called "material and cultural boundaries" of a time span. Norman Ryder discussed the merits of birth cohort analysis in studying social change:

> Each new cohort makes fresh contact with the contemporary social heritage and carries the impress of the encounter through life. This confrontation has been called the intersection of the innovative and the conservative forces in history. The members of any cohort are entitled to participate in only one slice of life—their unique location in the stream of history.[3]

This approach has proven especially amenable to a treatment of the changing conditions of literacy learning, especially given the ways that literacy-based technologies have been introduced across the century, entering people's lives at different ages and so with different impacts and possibilities. At the same time, though, tracing literacy through successive generations illuminates the "conservative forces" that Ryder mentioned, as we can see how older, fading forms of literacy roll along with new and emerging ones, creating new material and ideological configurations for literacy learners at any stage of life. Literacy preserves, and one of the things that it is best at preserving is itself, so an encounter with literacy will always in some sense be an encounter with its history.

---

3   Ryder, 1965, page 844. Ryder captured the value of this perspective for the study of literacy learning when he wrote that "the principal motor of contemporary social change is technological innovation. It pervades the other substructures of society and forces them into accommodation" (p. 851).

Consequently, what is new in literacy learning comes not merely from new technologies and their implications but from the creation of new relationships to older technologies and ways of writing and reading. Cohort analysis is especially useful for apprehending this process. Finally, the comparative perspective recognizes the close connections between social structures and communication systems and how changes in both are interrelated; literacy is not merely an expression of social structure but a dynamic element in it. What people are able to do with their writing or reading in any time and place—as well as what others do to them with writing and reading—contribute to their sense of identity, normality, possibility.

Of course, as with any investigative approach, life stories have their limitations and dangers. Especially complicating is the fact that accounts of past events inevitably are rendered through the perspective of the present. People reflect on—indeed, refashion—a memory in terms of its significance for how things have turned out, whether in terms of personal circumstances or shared culture. This is a thorny matter for the interviewer as well as those interviewed. It is especially tricky in an investigation of changing meanings of literacy, as past senses of writing or reading are apprehended through more recent realities and perspectives and the blend is hard to separate. One way to mitigate this problem, as Daniel Bertaux has suggested, is to focus people's attention on the past by remembering concrete activities and material surroundings.[4] Such a tactic cannot claim to yield something more objective or true but does potentially grant a return to the material scenes of past learning, a move that especially interested me. I devised an interview script by which I tried to lead participants through a chronological account of both ordinary and extraordinary encounters with writing and reading, lingering to explore their detailed recollections of the literal settings, people, and materials that animated their memories. (See Appendix [at the end of this excerpt].) Of course, such an approach only leads to the additional complication of the role of the questions and questioner in structuring life-story accounts. In an effort to be cooperative, those being interviewed will try to render their responses according to the perceived desires of the questioner.[5] Undoubtedly, the heavy hand of

---

4 Bertaux, 1981, page 130.
5 Briggs's (1986) book is a useful reminder that oral history interviews are as systematically related to the present (especially the ongoing demands of the interview itself) as to the past. He also called for more attention to what he called the "metacommunicative repertoires" of the social groups from which interviewees come, especially so that the interviewer can learn the lessons offered in a particular exchange.

my interview script, shaped by the theoretical interests motivating my study, imposed itself on the participants, becoming at times at odds with the communication norms they preferred and knew best. Other times, of course, the script receded as conversations meandered into stories, jokes, jibes, and other tangents during which I tried to listen closely for the lessons about literacy that they offered. In any case, one of the great advantages of conducting autobiographical interviews at the end of the twentieth century was the ubiquitous models of the interview format available through television, radio, and print, making the roles of interviewer and interviewee not quite so strange for either party. Nevertheless, the methodological limitations I mention as well as the ones I fail to notice myself are indelibly present in (and absent from!) this presentation, there (and not there) for the discriminating reader to weigh against my claims.[6]

A few more deliberate limitations must be noted. First, although reading development is not ignored in this study, the central focus is on writing and learning to write. One reason is simply to help to redress the neglect of the social history of writing in comparison to reading. As Michael Halloran has observed, "Writing has been a virtually invisible topic in the material history of modern culture."[7] I have been amazed throughout the process of researching for this book at how invisible writing remains as a researched phenomenon in economics, history of education, and communication studies.[8] Although the situation is improving, much more is left to be known about the practices, meanings, and values of writing for ordinary citizens. A focus on writing is especially pertinent now because the pressure to write is perhaps the main new feature of literacy to have emerged in the second half of the twentieth century. It is a second wave, one might say, of the mass (reading) literacy achieved for many groups by the second half of the nineteenth century.

Second, I decided early on not to ask participants to show me their writing. Partly this was a practical matter, for most of the writing done by ordinary people is by nature transitory, consumed, discarded. Most of the texts people recalled no longer existed anyway. Partly this was a philosophical matter, for too much of our understanding about literacy and writing development is based on the analysis of texts, and this study is meant to emphasize other dimensions.

6 For additional psychological treatments of autobiographical memory, see the collection by Thompson, Skowronski, Larsen, and Betz (1996).

7 Halloran, 1990, page 155.

8 More attention needs to be paid to the fact that many reading assessments require students to write out their responses to reading as proof of comprehension. The intermingling of writing ability with reading ability in these settings is not usually addressed. The National Assessment of Educational Progress in Reading, for instance, judges reading comprehension on the basis of students' written answers.

Partly, too, this was a personal matter, a reluctance to force into my relationship with the participants the long shadow of the teacher ready to uncover shameful inadequacies of expression. As the interviews demonstrated, the disapproving teacher looms large enough still in many people's memories and was best, I thought, left alone. In several cases, people spontaneously offered me examples of their writing, sometimes journals, letters, poems and fiction, autobiographies, old school reports, or professional projects and publications. But they were never solicited.

Finally, I steered away in the interviews and certainly in the write-ups from probes and disclosures of most personal matters. These excisions from the presentation, even when bits of the shape of literacy learning might have been cut along with them, were motivated by a desire not to hurt or embarrass the people who helped me so much in this project. I hope I have succeeded.

A note about transcriptions: All quotations from the interviews have been edited into standard written English with hesitations, misstarts, and pauses eliminated. Such editing indeed washes out the dialectical diversity of the people I spoke with. However, not trained as a linguist, I lacked the skill to transcribe accurately the range of regional accents and dialects that I heard. Although the racism of our society often invites researchers to hear and inscribe aspects of the most stigmatized dialects (for instance, Ebonics or the "broken" English of second-language speakers), the speech of the nonstigmatized is not so closely scrutinized for its deviations from the accepted standard. It is out of a sense of evenhandedness, then, that I have converted all the speech that I quote into standard edited English. Dropping the hesitations and misstarts risks loss of nuance, but in each case I listened carefully to the contextual meaning of passages I have chosen to quote to be sure that such editing would not flagrantly distort meaning as I understood it. What is gained by these decisions, I hope, is greater clarity and efficiency for the reader.

[***]

The Analytical Framework: Sponsors of Literacy

In his sweeping history of adult learning in the United States, Joseph Kett described the intellectual atmosphere available to young apprentices who worked in the small, decentralized print shops of antebellum America. Because printers also were the solicitors and editors of what they published, their workshops served as lively incubators for literacy and political discourse. By the mid-nineteenth century, however, this opportunity faded when the invention of the steam press reorganized the economy of the print industry. Steam presses were so expensive that they required capital outlays beyond the means of many printers. As a result, print jobs were outsourced, the processes of editing and printing were split, and, in tight competition, print apprentices became low-paid mechanics with no more access to the multiskilled environment of the craft shop.[9] Although this shift in working conditions may be evidence of the deskilling of workers induced by the Industrial Revolution,[10] it also offers a site for reflecting on the dynamic sources of literacy and literacy learning. The reading and writing skills of print apprentices in this period were an achievement not simply of teachers and learners or of the discourse practices of the printer community. Rather, these skills existed vulnerably, contingently within an economic moment. The pre-steam press economy enabled some of the most basic aspects of the apprentices' literacy, especially their access to material production and the public meaning or worth of their skills. Paradoxically, even as the steam-powered penny press made print more accessible (by making publishing more profitable), it brought an end to a particular form of literacy sponsorship and a drop in literacy potential.

Kett's study, which focused on the competition among providers of education in the United States, helped me to formulate an analytical approach to literacy learning that I came to call sponsors of literacy. As I suggested earlier, literacy looms as one of the great engines of profit and competitive advantage in the twentieth century: a lubricant for consumer desire, a means for integrating corporate markets, a foundation for the deployment of weapons and other technology, a raw material in the mass production of information. As ordinary citizens have been compelled into these economies, their reading and writing skills have grown sharply more central to the everyday trade of information and goods as well as to the pursuit of education, employment, civil rights, and status. At the same time, people's literate skills have grown vulnerable to unprecedented turbulence in their economic value, as conditions, forms, and standards of literacy achievement seem to shift with almost every new generation of learners. In my analysis of the life histories, I sought ways to understand the vicissitudes of individual literacy development in relationship to the large-scale economic forces that set the routes and determine the worldly worth of that literacy.

My own field of writing studies has had much to say about individual literacy development. Especially in the last quarter of the twentieth century, we have

---

9   Kett, 1994, pages 67–70.
10 Nicholas and Nicholas (1992).

theorized, researched, critiqued, debated, and sometimes even managed to enhance the literacy potentials of ordinary citizens as they have tried to cope with life as they find it. Less easily and certainly less steadily have we been able to relate what we see, study, and do to these larger contexts of profit-making and competition. This even as we recognize that the most pressing issues we deal with—tightening associations between literacy skill and social viability, the break-neck pace of change in communications technology, persistent inequities in access and reward—all relate to structural conditions in literacy's bigger picture. When economic forces are addressed in our work, they appear primarily as generalities: contexts, determinants, motivators, barriers, touchstones. But rarely are they systematically related to the local conditions and embodied moments of literacy learning that occupy so many of us on a daily basis.[11]

This study does not presume to overcome the analytical failure completely. But it does offer a conceptual approach that begins to connect literacy as an individual development to literacy as an economic development, at least as the two have played out over the last century. The approach is through what I call sponsors of literacy. Sponsors, as I have come to think of them, are any agents, local or distant, concrete or abstract, who enable, support, teach, and model, as well as recruit, regulate, suppress, or withhold, literacy—and gain advantage by it in some way. Just as the ages of radio and television accustomed us to having programs brought to us by various commercial sponsors, it is useful to think about who or what underwrites occasions of literacy learning and use. Although the interests of the sponsor and the sponsored do not have to converge (and, in fact, may conflict), sponsors nevertheless set the terms for access to literacy and wield powerful incentives for compliance and loyalty. Sponsors are delivery systems for the economies of literacy, the means by which these forces present themselves to—and through—individual learners. They also represent the causes into which people's literacy usually gets recruited.[12] Sponsors are a tangible reminder that literacy learning throughout history has always required permission, sanction, assistance, coercion, or, at minimum, contact with existing trade routes.

Intuitively, *sponsors* seemed a fitting term for the figures who turned up most typically in people's memories of literacy learning: older relatives, teachers, religious leaders, supervisors, military officers, librarians, friends, editors, influential

---

11 Three of the keenest and most eloquent observers of economic impacts on writing and teaching and learning have been Faigley (1999), Miller (1991), and Spellmeyer (1996).

12 For a more positive treatment of sponsors, see Goldblatt (1994), who explored the power of institutions to authorize writers.

authors. Sponsors, as we ordinarily think of them, are powerful figures who bankroll events or smooth the way for initiates. Usually richer, more knowledgeable, and more entrenched than the sponsored, sponsors nevertheless enter a reciprocal relationship with those they underwrite. They lend their resources or credibility to the sponsored but also stand to gain benefits from their success, whether by direct repayment or, indirectly, by credit of association. *Sponsors* also proved an appealing term in my analysis because of all the commercial references that appeared in these twentieth-century accounts—the magazines, peddled encyclopedias, essay contests, radio and television programs, toys, fan clubs, writing tools, and so on, from which so much experience with literacy was derived. As the twentieth century turned the abilities to read and write into widely exploitable resources, commercial sponsorship abounded.

In whatever form, sponsors deliver the ideological freight that must be borne for access to what they have. Of course, the sponsored can be oblivious to or innovative with this ideological burden. Like Little Leaguers who wear the logo of a local insurance agency on their uniforms, not out of a concern for enhancing the agency's image but as a means for getting to play ball, people throughout history have acquired literacy pragmatically under the banner of others' causes. In the days before free public schooling in England, Protestant Sunday schools warily offered basic reading instruction to working-class families as part of evangelical duty. To the horror of many in the church sponsorship, these families insistently, sometimes riotously demanded of their Sunday schools more instruction, including in writing and math, because it provided means for upward mobility.[13] Through the sponsorship of Baptist and Methodist ministries, African Americans in slavery taught each other to understand the Bible in subversively liberatory ways. Under a conservative regime, they developed forms of critical literacy that sustained religious, educational, and political movements both before and after emancipation.[14] Most of the time, however, literacy takes its shape from the interests of its sponsors. And, as we will see throughout this book, obligations toward one's sponsors run deep, affecting what, when, why, and how people write and read.

---

13 Laqueur (1976, p. 124) provided a vivid account of a street demonstration in Bolton, England, in 1834 by a "pro-writing" faction of Sunday school students and their teachers. This faction demanded that writing instruction continue to be provided on Sundays, something that opponents of secular instruction on the Sabbath were trying to reverse. The legacies of this period on contemporary reading and writing are explored in Chapter 5 [of Brandt's book].

14 See Cornelius's (1991) absorbing study, which provides ample evidence of how competing interests —economic, political, and religious—set the conditions for literacy and illiteracy among African Americans in slavery.

The concept of sponsors helps to explain, then, a range of human relationships and ideological pressures that turn up at the scenes of literacy learning—from benign sharing between adults and youths to euphemistic coercions in schools and workplaces to the most notorious impositions and deprivations by church or state. It also is a concept useful for tracking literacy's materiel: the things that accompany writing and reading and the ways they are manufactured and distributed. *Sponsorship* as a sociological term is even more broadly suggestive for thinking about economies of literacy development. Studies of patronage in Europe and *compadrazgo* in the Americas show how patron-client relationships in the past grew up around the need to manage scarce resources and promote political stability.[15] Pragmatic, instrumental, ambivalent, patron-client relationships integrated otherwise antagonistic social classes into relationships of mutual, albeit unequal, dependencies. Loaning land, money, protection, and other favors allowed the politically powerful to extend their influence and justify their exploitation of clients. Clients traded their labor and deference for access to opportunities for themselves or their children and for leverage needed to improve their social standing. Especially under conquest in Latin America, *compadrazgo* reintegrated native societies badly fragmented by the diseases and other disruptions that followed foreign invasions. At the same time, this system was susceptible to its own stresses, especially when patrons became clients themselves of still more centralized or distant overlords, with all the shifts in loyalty and perspective that entailed.[16]

In raising this association with formal systems of patronage, I do not wish to overlook the very different economic, political, and education systems within which US literacy has developed. But where we find the sponsoring of literacy, it will be useful to look for its function within larger political and economic arenas. Literacy is a valued commodity in the US economy, a key resource in gaining profit and edge. This value helps to explain, of course, the length people will go to secure literacy for themselves or their children. But it also explains why the powerful work so persistently to conscript and ration the resource of literacy. The competition to harness literacy, to manage, measure, teach, and exploit it, intensified throughout the twentieth century. It is vital to pay attention to this development because it largely sets the terms for individuals' encounters with literacy. This competition shapes the incentives and barriers

---

15 Thanks to Ann Egan-Robertson for suggesting patronage as a useful model for thinking about literacy and sponsorship. See Bourne (1986), Hortsman and Kurtz (1978), and Lynch (1986).
16 Hortsman and Kurtz, 1978, pages 13–14.

FOCUS ON WRITING: WHAT COLLEGE STUDENTS WANT TO KNOW

(including uneven distributions of opportunity) that greet literacy learners in any particular time and place. It is this competition that has made access to the right kinds of literacy sponsors so crucial for political and economic well-being. And it also has spurred the rapid, complex changes that now make the pursuit of literacy feel so turbulent and precarious for so many.

Each of the following chapters [in Brandt's book] applies the analytical concept of the sponsor to life-history accounts to address fundamental questions about literacy learning in the twentieth century: How do regional economic transformations change the conditions for literacy learning for people in that place? What do sharply rising standards for literacy feel like in the lives of ordinary Americans? How is literacy passed across generations under conditions of rapid social change? What barriers and opportunities in social structures matter to literacy learning at the current time? In several chapters, I have chosen to concentrate on extended exemplar cases to provide detailed examination of the material and ideological conditions that carry potential answers to these questions. Where exemplar cases are used, they have been chosen for the clarity and robustness with which they illustrate findings from the larger body of life accounts. In other chapters, the data have been sliced more thickly, across groups and at times across the entire set of interviews. Although in the end it has been necessary to focus in depth on only a few of the many interviews that I collected, it was only by collecting and analyzing many interviews (indeed, I wish there could have been more) that I could find the recurrent patterns and themes that I here illustrate with fewer, in-depth cases.

[***]

Appendix: Interview Script

Demographic Questions
Date of birth
Place of birth
Place of rearing
Gender/race
Type of household (childhood)
Type of household (current)
Great-grandparents' schooling and occupations, if known
Grandparents' schooling and occupations, if known
Parents'/guardians' schooling and occupations, if known

Names and locations of all schools attended
Other training
Degrees, dates of graduation, size of graduating class
Past/current/future occupations

Early Childhood Memories
Earliest memories of seeing other people writing/reading
Earliest memories of self writing/reading
Earliest memories of direct or indirect instruction
Memories of places writing/reading occurred
Occasions associated with writing/reading
People associated with writing/reading
Organizations associated with writing/reading
Materials available for writing/reading
Ways materials entered households
Kinds of materials used
Role of technologies

Writing and Reading in School
Earliest memories of writing/reading in school
Memories of kinds of writing/reading done in school
Memories of direct instruction
Memories of self-instruction
Memories of peer instruction
Memories of evaluation
Uses of assignments/other school writing and reading
Audiences of school-based writing
Knowledge drawn on to complete assignments
Resources drawn on to complete assignments
Kinds of materials available for school-based writing/reading
Kinds of materials used
Role of technologies

Writing and Reading with Peers
Memories of sharing writing and reading
Memories of writing and reading to/with friends
Memories of writing and reading in play
Memories of seeing friends reading and writing

Memories of reading friends' writing

Extracurricular Writing and Reading
Organizations or activities that may have involved writing or reading
Writing contests, pen pals, and so forth

Self-Initiated Writing or Reading
Purposes for writing and reading at different stages
Genres
Audiences/uses
Teaching/learning involved

Writing on the Job
Same questions as above

Civic or Political Writing

Influential People
Memories of people who had a hand in one's learning to write or read

Influential Events
Significant events in the process of learning to write

Purposes for Writing and Reading Overall

Values
Relative importance of writing and reading
Motivations
Consequences

Current Uses of Reading and Writing
All reading and writing done in the six months prior to the interview

Sense of Literacy Learning
Interviewee's own sense of how he or she learned to read and write
Sense of how people in general learn to read and write

Bibliography

Bertaux, D. (Ed.) (1981). *Biography and society: The life history approach.* Beverly Hills: Sage.

Bertaux, D., & Thompson, P. (1997). *Pathways to social class: A qualitative approach to social mobility.* Oxford: Clarendon Press.

Bourne, J.M. (1986). *Patronage and society in nineteenth-century England.* London: Edward Arnold.

Briggs, C.C. (1986). *Learning how to ask: A sociolinguistic appraisal of the role of the interview in social science research.* New York: Cambridge University Press.

Cornelius, J. (1991). *"When I can read my title clear": Literacy, slavery, and religion in the antebellum South.* Columbia, SC: University of South Carolina Press.

Faigley, L. (1999). Veterans' stories on the porch. In B. Boehm, D. Journet, & M. Rosner (Eds.), *History, reflection, and narrative: The professionalization of composition,* 1963–1983. Norwood: Ablex.

Goldblatt, E. (1994). *'Round my way: Authority and double consciousness in three urban high-school writers.* Pittsburgh: University of Pittsburgh Press.

Halloran, M. (1990). From rhetoric to composition: The teaching of writing in America to 1900. In J.J. Murphy (Ed.), *A short history of writing instruction from ancient Greece to twentieth-century America* (pp. 121–150). Davis, CA: Hermagoras Press.

Hortsman, C., & Kurtz, D.V. (1978). *Compadrazgo in post-conquest middle America.* Milwaukee: Milwaukee-UW Center for Latin America.

Kett, J.F. (1994). *The pursuit of knowledge under difficulties: From self-improvement to adult education in America, 1750–1990.* Stanford, CA: Stanford University Press.

Laqueur, T. (1976). *Religion and respectability: Sunday schools and working class Culture, 1780–1850.* New Haven, CT: Yale University Press.

Lummis, T. (1987). *Listening to history: The authenticity of oral evidence.* London: Hutchinson.

Lynch, J.H. (1986). *Godparents and kinship in early medieval Europe.* Princeton, NJ: Princeton University Press.

Miller, S. (1991). *Textual carnivals: The politics of composition.* Carbondale, IL: Southern Illinois University Press.

Nicholas, S.J., & Nicholas, J.M. (1992). Male literacy, "deskilling," and the Industrial Revolution. *Journal of Interdisciplinary History,* 23, 1–18.

Popular Memory Group (1982). Popular memory: Theory, politics, method. In R. Johnson, G. McLennan, B. Schwarz, & D. Dutton (Eds.), *Making histories: Studies in history writing and politics* (pp. 205–252). London: Hutchinson.

FOCUS ON WRITING: WHAT COLLEGE STUDENTS WANT TO KNOW

Ryder, N.B. (1965). The cohort as a concept in the study of social change. *American Sociological Review*, 30, 843–861.

Spellmeyer, K. (1996). After theory: From textuality to attunement with the world. *College English*, 58, 893–913.

Thompson, C.P., Skowronski, J.J., Larsen, S.F., & Betz, A. (1996). *Autobiographical memory: Remembering what and remembering when.* Mahwah, NJ: Erlbaum.

ALEEZA LASKOWSKI'S "DOMESTIC SPHERE VS. PUBLIC SPHERE" (2016)

Why I included it

I appreciate the way Laskowski made a course assignment her own while still meeting the requirements. Her writing helps me think about the way families and schools have ways of approaching learning that may be in conflict with one another. Although she writes about attitudes towards learning in general, I think her ideas can be applied more specifically to learning how to write more effectively.

Background

Laskowski submitted this in response to her first essay assignment in a writing course during her first semester of college. The class read several selections offering both positive visions and critiques of education systems. In response, students were asked to write a narrative asking them to identify key words that defined what it meant, in their experience, to be a student. This narrative was to be shared with me, the instructor, and with the rest of the class. Laskowski engaged in writing workshops during class and revised her writing several times with this audience in mind.

CONNECT

As you read, consider responding to the following questions to help you process the material.

1. Laskowski's narrative casts her in a negative light at one point. How does this part of the essay contribute to the overall impact on readers?

2. Laskowski unpacks one set of contrasts between her family's values and her school's values. Are there other contrasts between family values and school values that you've encountered, whether in your own experience or in the experiences of people you know?

3. To what degree have you embodied the values of Laskowski's mother? To what degree have you embodied the values that Laskowski recognizes in her school experiences?

4. Are there any downsides to the values that Laskowski's mother encourages?

Because the assignment asked for a "narrative" rather than an analysis, Laskowski uses storytelling to develop her ideas. As you read, notice the way the title sets up a contrast and see if you can trace the two kinds of attitudes Laskowski has identified. Pay particular attention to places where Laskowski breaks from storytelling to directly state her point for her readers.

Laskowski, Aleeza. "Domestic Sphere vs. Public Sphere." ENG 120 Critical Writing, Pace University, Fall 2016.

IF MY MOTHER has taught me anything, it is the true meaning of pride and motivation. To her, these two values are key to being a successful student, and over time they have become mine. However, these teachings inside of my own household were hard to grasp easily because they ran counter to the two very different teachings I learned in the classroom.

Mariana, my mother, came from humble roots. She was one of ten children born and raised in the slums of Dominican Republic. Education was accessible but not in the way it had become when she entered the United States. Like many other immigrants my mother is a strong believer in the "American Dream." America was like Heaven; you entered the gates expecting only the best of the best. "I came here at the age of sixteen," she'd say to me, "and only knew one English word—No." She often repeated this, as a way to etch it into my mind that this came from the same woman who went on to take AP Physics and AP Calculus. My mother did not let things like language barriers get in her way. She was motivated and cared enough to express her gratification for her seat in the classroom. As a student she felt as thankful as a servant would be to his king, and this was what pride meant to her.

At the age of nineteen Mariana had received her high school diploma and also gave birth to her first child. She worked numerous jobs but a stable career was out of reach due to lack of education. To my mom a college degree would be synonymous with prosperity. In 2016, my mother graduated with her Bachelor's Degree in Nursing (with honorable mention), three kids and thirty years later. As a single mother raising four kids, she worked full time as a nurse in surgery and still managed to sit through her classes for 12 hours one day out of the week each week. My mother cared enough for the opportunity to even sit in a classroom. She was proud to be studying and mastering something that only she motivated herself to do.

Growing up as a student of hers, I wanted to completely believe and devote myself to this view. But for the forty hours a week I spent in school, those same beliefs on what it means to be a student were not being taught. I received two very different perspectives that battled with the one my mother had been trying to instill in me.

I went to public school from kindergarten all the way to eighth grade. In public school, the kids rarely care about their actions and consequences. If they fail there's always summer school; if they fail summer school then they get held back or switched to another school. If they're constantly fighting, they get removed and placed into another school. The whole system felt like a constant cycle, a repetitive routine, and this aura was upheld in the actual classroom as well. Teachers followed the guidelines for what was to be taught strictly and there was no room for creativity. This confinement that was upheld by the Board of Education caused me to lose sight of what I was actually doing this for. The pride that was upheld in public school was carelessness and complete lack of motivation.

My mother was trying to teach me how to "take an education rather than merely receive a schooling" (Gatto 115). The Prussian system in which my public education originated from (Gatto 117) worked to stifle my mother's teachings at home. I'd watch my mother sit on the porch for hours when she first attempted to get her bachelors when I was in middle school. She'd have huge textbooks laid out with notes open, ready to absorb all the information. I'd get up from bed to get a drink of water and there'd she be, still working. I couldn't help but admire how she didn't give up. I wondered though what motivated her to do this, because I myself had nothing to push me to do well in school. Not even the sight of her struggling pushed me because I had learned over the course of nine years in public school that motivation and pride had nothing to do with being a student. Conformity and routine on the other hand was the epitome of it.

My switch to Catholic school for my high school experience was a drastic change. Education now became a product I bought, and it better be the best product I ever spent my money on. I held a certain pride, "you can't do this, you can't take away my phone, you can't suspend me, and you have no right." I noticed instantly how the money we poured into the school gave us power. One day I entered into my trigonometry class still waking up and realized we had a scheduled test that I forgot to study for. Instead of freaking out and rummaging through notes to try to absorb anything, I sat in my seat nonchalantly and waited for my teacher to walk into class.

"Okay class, take out a sheet of loose-leaf and number it—"

"We won't be taking the test today, Mrs. Conklin."

I did not ask. I stated a fact: we would not be taking it. And we would not be taking it because I pay for this class so no, you are not in charge, I am. She eventually agreed without much having to convince her and I was able to avoid a potential failed grade.

Because I was paying for the education I felt entitled to do as I please. I began to treat my teachers as "cashiers at a department store, who [were] there to serve and satisfy [my] every need" (Lugo-Lugo 195). And, more often than not, the teachers would succumb to the demands and preferences the students presented. Instead of identifying a student with humility and care like my mother would, I began to identify it with arrogance and entitlement.

My mother taught me how to be humble. There was no room, no time, and no money to waste. Being a student required her to be selfless. After time away from the teachings I learned in the classroom setting, I have become committed to the teaching my mother has taught since day one. Being a true student is about pride—associated with caring about your work—and motivation.

Works Cited

Gatto, John. "Against School." *Rereading America: Cultural Contexts for Critical Thinking and Writing*. Ed. Gary Colombo, Robert Cullen, and Bonnie Lisle. 10th ed. Boston: Bedford/St. Martin's, 2016. 114–22. Print.

Lugo-Lugo, Carmen R. "A Prostitute, A Servant, and A Customer-Service Representative: A Latina in Academia." *Rereading America: Cultural Contexts for Critical Thinking and Writing*. Ed. Gary Colombo, Robert Cullen, and Bonnie Lisle. 10th ed. Boston: Bedford/St. Martin's, 2016. 188–98. Print.

MARCEA K. SEIBLE'S *THE TRANSITION FROM STUDENT TO PROFESSIONAL: A PEDAGOGY OF PROFESSIONALISM FOR FIRST-YEAR COMPOSITION* (2008)

Why I included it

This dissertation excerpt synthesizes a good bit of research about what motivates students to write. As you read what researchers have discovered, you can compare their findings to your own experiences. This reading also provides a nice counterbalance to the other selections in this book because it focuses exclusively on secondary research.

Background

Seible's doctoral dissertation argues for focusing on professional writing in the first-year classroom. Even though the excerpt below synthesizes secondary research rather than proffering an argument, Seible frames the information to eventually introduce her own research study.

Usually, a dissertation would be read in its entirety. The primary readers would be Seible's dissertation committee—a few professors in the field who guided the research project and suggested revisions and edits as she completed her work. Seible might be thinking about eventually turning her dissertation into an article or a book, so she likely considered a wider audience of composition professors.

Reading hints and vocab terms

It's important to remember that this reading is an *excerpt* rather than a complete piece. You'll notice it begins and ends abruptly because I pulled this section out of a longer text.

This excerpt is part of a ***literature review*** (often shortened to "lit review") that recaps past research on a particular topic. That way, readers can understand how the new research being conducted is responding to earlier research. You're probably familiar with "literature" referring to creative texts such as poetry and fiction, but when used with academic research writing, the term "literature" refers to secondary research that addresses a topic.

As mentioned above, this particular dissertation focuses on attention to professional writing in the first-year composition classroom. The lit review thus provides information about what has already been found about motivating students and teaching first-year composition effectively. You'll notice two sections of the lit review excerpt. You can use these divisions to trace the way the discussion shifts. Consider reviewing relevant vocab as you read each part.

The first section focuses on general principles regarding student motivation. As you read the first section, notice what improves motivation and why it's sometimes difficult to motivate students in a first-year composition course.

mastery goal learning: associated with intrinsic rewards; based on interest in the learning task and self-motivation

CONNECT

As you read, consider responding to the following questions to help you process the material.

1. Identify a part of Seible's research that resonates with your own experience. Paraphrase or summarize Seible's explanation of research findings, and then tell a relevant story about your experience.

2. Based on the excerpted lit review, how do you imagine Seible might respond to the course website of professional interview profiles, Writing When I Grow Up? <sites.google.com/a/maryu.marywood.edu/lauriem/course-websites/writing-when-i-grow-up>.

3. Review the vocabulary. Choose two terms that seem most helpful in thinking about writing and explain why.

4. Compare the benefits of this kind of informational text versus the benefits of a narrative essay such as that of Aleeza Laskowski. What does each offer readers?

performance goal learning: associated with extrinsic rewards; based on competition against others

flow: becoming absorbed in an activity so that you want to continue; happens when there is a good balance between challenge and ability to meet the challenge

service writing course: a writing course usually taken in the first semester of college that is designed to prepare students to write in other classes; the course is thus viewed as "serving" other college courses

future time perspective (FTP): thinking about what's important now based on how useful it will be at a future point

Generation NeXt: name for millennial generation with a focus on future goals

The second section focuses on approaches to first-year composition that help motivate students.

current-traditional approaches: methods of teaching writing by focusing on the end product and providing students with typical structures and rules to apply; considered outdated in contemporary composition research

process approaches: focus on complex processes of writing; writing is treated as rhetorical, social, and a means of learning

post-process approaches: continues to consider writing processes, but also recognizes writing as public, interpretive, and situated

Excerpt from: Seible, Marcea K. *The Transition from Student to Professional: A Pedagogy of Professionalism for First-Year Composition* (Order No. 3323939). ProQuest Central; ProQuest Dissertations & Theses A&I. (304606678). 2008.

Self-interest Practicality and Control: Understanding Student Motivation

FINDING WAYS TO motivate students about course content has long plagued educators. Because motivation depends on one's personality, it is difficult for educators to speak to the needs of several students, each with different motivators, at once within a single classroom. However, research on student motivation shows there are general principles, or values, that drive students' motivational impulses. Marilla Svinicki's research into student learning and motivation has helped instructors focus on increasing student motivation. Svinicki describes five different values students place on goals that contribute to their motivation for learning: value from expected outcomes (what is "the reward at the end of the line"?) (147), value from satisfying a need (achieving basic physical needs) (148), value from intrinsic qualities of the task (personal interest of the material to students) (152), value derived from utility (what is the need for learning the material?) (154), and value from choice and control (having the freedom and power to choose what is interesting) (155).

Donelson R. Forsyth and James H. McMillan, in their seminal piece "Practical Proposals for Motivating Students," also call upon such established motivating factors as students' need to achieve, expectations for success, and setting and recognizing valuable goals. Others like Wlodkowski and Ginsberg in their Motivational Framework for Culturally Responsive Teaching list such motivational elements as a feeling of inclusion (students feeling respected and connected); positive attitudes about learning (students maintaining choice and finding relevance in the material); meaningfulness (classroom experiences provide students with challenges and value students' perspectives and ideas); and competence (students believe they have the potential to be successful) (qtd. in Svinicki 168). Similarly, Michael Theall and Jennifer Franklin's motivational model lists inclusion, attitude, meaning, competence, leadership, and satisfaction as elements affecting student motivation (qtd. in Svinicki 169). More recently, educational theorists such as Ken Bain choose to highlight students' need for control, stating that students who feel more in control of their learning will exhibit greater motivation and success in a course.

Though this is only a sampling of what theorists claim is important to understanding student motivation, this list demonstrates general similarities found among researchers. Self-interest, control over learning, and setting valuable goals are commonalities that motivational models share, and given their significance, they should not be ignored when investigating how to improve students' learning experiences in higher education courses today. Forsyth and McMillan claim that all students have basic needs in the classroom and that instructors can help improve student learning and success by focusing on these basic needs they have as learners. Thus, research indicates that the key to motivating students lies heavily in tapping into these needs, including students' intrinsic motivators, by discovering what they really value and what interests them. One way that instructors can do this is by allowing students to set personal and professional goals and by giving them control and responsibility over their learning.

Teaching by tapping into students' intrinsic and extrinsic motivators has long occurred in classrooms. Carole Ames in "Classrooms: Goals, Structures, and Student Motivation" more fully examined student motivation by discussing the difference between students' mastery and performance goals. Performance goal learning, also known as extrinsic motivation, promotes one students' success over another's, fueling a desire for public recognition and competition in the classroom. While some students are more motivated by this sense of competition, it can ultimately affect their sense of self worth and ability, and as a result, negatively influence their learning (Ames 262).

Conversely, mastery goal learning involves motivating students intrinsically, which is often considered the preferable side to the age-old intrinsic/extrinsic motivational binary. Researchers consider mastery goal learning to be a more positive way of encouraging students to learn because it encourages them to do so for the sake of learning and not for an extrinsic reward such as a grade. In their seminal article, Forsyth and McMillan describe mastery goal orientation as a way of providing students with attainable goals that are within their reach, in essence showing them that their success in the class is within their control (553). Carole Ames builds on Forsyth and McMillan's ideas, stating that mastery learning is more successful because it "promotes a motivational pattern likely to promote long-term and high-quality involvement in learning" (Ames 262–63). Like Forsyth and McMillan, Ames believes that utilizing students' mastery goals in any classroom is vital to building student motivation because students need tasks that engage them personally and push them toward personal success rather than public competition.

Mihalyi Csikszentmihalyi uses the term "flow" to describe a person's behavior when motivated intrinsically about a topic or task. Essentially, "flow" describes the state of consciousness a person undergoes when taking part in an activity that causes him or her to become so absorbed by that activity that he or she becomes unaware of all surroundings. Such absorption into a topic or task leads to a state something like euphoria:

> It [flow or psychic entropy] obtains when all the contents are in harmony with each other, and with the goals that define the person's self. These are the subjective conditions we call pleasure, happiness, satisfaction, and enjoyment. (Csikszentmihalyi, "The Flow Experience" 24)

Writers, too, often experience a sense of flow when fully engaged in a writing task, so much so in fact that they become engrossed in the act of writing to the point where they lose track of time and self. Their motivation for the task is driven by an intrinsic need and desire to move forward and to continue experiencing the pleasure of the moment. For students to experience flow, they need to have a "balance between the challenges perceived in a given situation and the skills" they bring to it (Csikszentmihalyi, "The Flow Experience" 30). In other words, they must believe they can do the task (experience the ability to succeed), but they must also find the task challenging enough to pursue it; if it becomes too easy, the sense of flow, enjoyment, and motivation to continue is lost. To help students find their intrinsic motivation and attain a sense of flow about writing in the classroom, one that positively affects their motivation to write, instructors must be able to provide challenging experiences that allow students to work with what interests them and what challenges them at the same time.

When it comes to motivation, students in service writing courses such as first-year composition typically exhibit low motivation for a variety of reasons, one of which is because of a course's required general education and non-major status. Because they are required to take the course, students may experience a loss of control over their learning. This negatively affects their motivation because control, according to motivational theorists, is one of the primary features of motivation for learning. Additionally, the generality of the course content, given that many service writing courses teach general academic writing meant to be applied in any academic situation, affects students' sense of challenge because they may feel they already know how to write for academic contexts. Such generality may have a negative effect on students because they cannot see the usefulness of the course, leaving them to question its purpose and relevance. As Csikszentmihalyi would describe it, students are not motivated to find their sense of flow because they find no challenge in doing something they think they already know how to do.

In his article, "Enhancing Student Motivation in Freshman Composition," Larry Anderson supports the theory that students need a greater sense of personal motivation in order to succeed in the course. Anderson claims it is difficult to get students to become intrinsically motivated, or to become mastery learners in service courses such as first-year composition, because their interest in writing is strictly performance—they write to get a grade and to be extrinsically rewarded (30). Anderson calls for writing instructors to use student motivation as a "lens to view (your own) pedagogy"; ultimately, he calls for instructors to better understand what motivates students and to use that to alter their pedagogical practices, for he believes that an instructor's approach to teaching writing can positively or negatively affect student motivation (31). To positively affect students' motivation, Anderson claims instructors need to help students see the relevance of writing to their lives because when students see the value of what they do, they become more successful learners (31).

In his article "Enhancing Student Motivation: Make Learning Interesting and Relevant," Edward Hootstein supports Anderson's claims about relevance and motivation. Hootstein believes that learning in any classroom, including composition, can and should be made relevant to students' lives. Using expectancy-value theory, stating that "motivation is determined jointly by the learner's expectancy for success and by incentive value of the goal," Hootstein claims that teachers should place more emphasis on what students value because those who are not invested in activities (such as writing) will not be motivated to do them (475). His theory corresponds with the beliefs of scholars like Ames; Anderson; and Forsyth and McMillan: when students expect success and see the value in what they are doing, they will be more motivated and successful in the classroom (Hootstein 475).

Scholars such as these all claim that part of understanding student motivation is recognizing what students value, including practicality, usefulness, and the personal challenges associated with a task. As a result of understanding this, instructors can incorporate those student values into their course design. Hootstein claims that not enough instructors are attending to the importance of what motivates students, and, therefore, students are not given the chance to explore and discover what is meaningful about the course to them. In the end, this lack of personal and professional relevance has a significantly negative effect on student motivation, which can result in decreased learning and a negative, if not hostile, learning environment for both teachers and [students].

Students' need for practical and professional relevance is detailed in Jenefer Husman and Willy Lens's concept of Future Time Perspective (FTP), or "the degree to which and the way in which the chronological future is integrated into the present life-space of an individual through motivational goal-setting processes" (114). In other words, the term FTP describes how students perceive what they are doing now with how useful it will be to their future; this, according to Husman and Lens, directly corresponds to students' motivation for learning. Since many college students state they are in college for practical purposes—to get an education, to get a degree, to get a job—for instructors, knowing the value students place on the future (FTP) can greatly affect their learning in class. Ames believes that students who see the relevance of a task to their overall goals, what Husman and Lens describe as students' FTP, become more engaged with the task and approach learning in a different, more motivated way (263).

FTP and student motivation share a common link in the notion of professional relevancy. When students see the relevance of the course to their present, and, more particularly, to their future, they exhibit more motivation for learning. Similarly, when students understand the professional relevancy of a course, their ability to recognize what it means to be and act as a professional in their field is also affected. For them, developing the skills needed to become a professional is something seen as important to their future and something they believe they should get from their college courses. When they do not see the immediate connection between their coursework and their majors/future careers, their motivation for the course and their ability to learn the subject matter of the course suffer.

In service writing classes, instructors can attend to this understanding of students' intrinsic motivation and their FTP/need for professional relevancy by adding a dimension of professionalism studies to the course, in particular, by expanding the dimensions of writing in the classroom or in an academic context to taking writing into situated sites of practice. In essence, by showing students how writing is relevant to their personal and professional lives and by asking students to consider what it means to be and write like a professional in their field, instructors will utilize students' intrinsic motivation to teach them about writing. Doing so invites students to make the course professionally relevant to them and calls upon them to create linkages between writing, their academic majors, and their future roles/jobs as professionals. Keying into students needs for professional relevance is even more important in light of today's generation of students.

Modern scholars of student behavior and motivation have described today's students' behavior and learning styles as unlike any generation to come before them. Mark Taylor, a scholar of student behavior, has recently described today's generation of college students as "Generation NeXt," claiming that the generation formerly considered "Millenials" actually has several characteristics that make them unlike any other student group. Students of this "Generation NeXt" population reflect major shifts in how our society functions, including exhibiting a greater dependence on parents, television, and entertainment in addition to exhibiting a greater consumerist attitude in relation to education (Taylor, "Generation NeXt"). Given the major shift in how these students learn and interact with each other and instructors, Taylor claims that instructors need to (re)learn how to interact with students by shaping their pedagogies to meet their needs as learners.

Much like the students Husman and Lens discussed in their 1999 article, Taylor believes that students today need to see how the work they are doing will benefit them in the future. But today's generation of students is faced with even greater challenges than their counterparts ten years ago. They are faced with more choices and more distractions (personal, technological, and otherwise) which make it more difficult to get them to recast their view of education as something they, as consumers of education, "purchase" and get them to focus on making learning meaningful in a learning-for-the-sake-of-learning way. Thus, it becomes essential for educators to (re)examine today's students' intrinsic motivators, including their need for personal and professional relevancy, in order to find the best pedagogical methods for reaching them.

Taylor suggests that universities and educators attend to one of the time-honored suggestions of motivational theorists: "provide meaning through real-life application" ("Gen NeXt" 104). Because many of today's postmodern students fall into the student-as-consumer population, Taylor claims that students need very pragmatic, applicable content. In "Generation NeXt Goes to Work: Issues in Workplace Readiness and Performance," Taylor suggests that for students to be fully prepared for the workplace, they need academic programs that help them connect to the professional world and that help them work on their future orientation and goal setting skills. Taylor states:

> Given the high proportion of students who are working while attending college, especially at community colleges, schools must make every effort to see that these work experiences relate meaningfully to students' career exploration, career choices, and career skills and help students develop

FOCUS ON WRITING: WHAT COLLEGE STUDENTS WANT TO KNOW

realistic expectations of what will be required of them after graduation ... Cooperative education, internships, assistantships, job help and
job matching, required contact hours, and all mechanisms for getting
students into the career-oriented workplace can help students develop
both clearer expectations and meaningful workplace skills. (Taylor 39)

Taylor clearly emphasizes the importance of FTP in today's students' success as
well, noting:

Much of the extreme focus on their immediate personal development,
especially in the core and liberal arts classes where links to the workplace
are often more tangential than in major or vocational classes, encourages
students to not look ahead. As has always been true for young people, but
especially for Generation NeXt, goal setting is critical. Students' ability
to see themselves in the future helps more of today make sense, especially the less fun parts. The conflicts students face daily to study or play,
if looked at immediately, tend to favor the fun of play. Looking ahead to
tests, grades, and workplace competitiveness and success is what can make
study a better choice. ("Generation NeXt Goes to Work" 39)

To meet the needs of today's students, instructors in service writing classes can
integrate content that speaks to students' needs for professional relevancy to
enhance students' motivation for learning. Pedagogies that integrate forms of
situated learning are particularly useful in helping students find the professional
relevancy they desire because these help students visualize the connections
between the classroom and the real world. Because situated learning pedagogies situate students in realistic professional contexts, performing realistic tasks
and immersing them in the culture and discourse of the workplace, they can
offer ways for students to see their academic work in a professional context and
give them the chance to develop a sense of self as a professional in their field.
Students in situated learning experiences are often asked to engage in activities
with working professionals and observe the tasks and communication patterns
that take place in non-academic contexts. As a result, situated learning pedagogies can have a positive effect on student motivation in writing classes, for
not only do they aim to teach students about writing, but they may also help
prepare students for their roles as professionals, contributing to the goals set by
both teacher and university.

In the next section of this literature review, I discuss how current composition pedagogies already lend themselves to building student motivation by attempting to help students see the relevancy of writing to their lives. Building on process and post-process composition theories, I show how activity theory and situated learning pedagogies can contribute to building student motivation in writing classes, in particular those considered as service classes to the university.

Motivation and Situated Learning: Aligning the Writing Classroom with the "Real" World

In some ways, today's university writing classes already attempt to connect writing to the world outside of the classroom. The process approach to writing teaches students that writing is a complex activity and that in order to learn about writing, students need to understand the "process" that real writers undergo. By making the shift from the current-traditional paradigm to more rhetorically-focused process and post-process approaches to writing, composition studies is already taking writing out of a classroom-only context and bringing it more in line with the activities of "real" writers.

Since the 1960's process movement, more writing instructors have been teaching students to view writing as a process, one that is, among other things, non-linear and that involves what Gary Olson describes as a generalizable process with systemized elements (8). Process theories support instructors' attempts to help students see writing as recursive, as a social activity, as a means of learning and discovery, and as rhetorical (Olson 7). Such a view helps situate writing in a new light, one that aims to create a more complete picture of writing as both academic and professional practice. Such a shift in writing pedagogy also clearly emphasizes the importance of teaching writing as a complex and dynamic activity, requiring student writers to perceive writing as more than just knowing the modes of writing or learning writing through a set of skills and drills. Essentially, it aims to teach students that knowing the process of writing will be useful to them for the rest of their lives.

While process approaches have all but replaced current-traditional practices with newer, more comprehensive frameworks for teaching writing, such an approach does not yet fully articulate the complexities associated with "real" or "professional" writing. As a result, post-process theorists have argued that though teaching writing as a process has been a necessary component of writing education, the act of writing itself involves a larger and more complex system, one that is less easy to generalize or that can be "applied to all or most writing

FOCUS ON WRITING: WHAT COLLEGE STUDENTS WANT TO KNOW

situations" (Olson 7). As Thomas Kent describes, post-process theorists claim three assumptions about writing: "(1) writing is public; (2) writing is interpretive; and (3) writing is situated" ("Introduction" 1). Within these assumptions comes an understanding that writing is more than just a systematic process, one that is easy for student writers to emulate; instead, when viewing writing through the lens of post-process theory, writing becomes situated in a complex interplay of audiences, communities, beliefs, and values. The combination of these elements (plus others) produces complex rhetorical situations that writers also need to consider as part of their larger understanding of the "process" of writing. As Bruce McComiskey explains, post-process writing more fully develops students' abilities to extend writing beyond the classroom by placing knowledge construction within "the social world of discourse" (41).

Given that instructors know that writing involves complex interplays between language, societies, communities of practice, and ideologies, it becomes clear that teaching students about writing, and the practices of real writers, requires attending to the world outside of the classroom. In this capacity, post-process approaches to teaching writing work well with other "real world" theories and pedagogies to align students' perceptions of writing as a process with the complex processes at work in real writing situations. As a result of this view of writing, students gain better insight into how writing functions in the non-academic professional world and how it can contribute to their professional lives as well. As David Russell argues in his article, "Activity Theory and Process Approaches: Writing (Power) in School and Society," organizations have their own writing processes, and in order to become "real" writers, student writers need to analyze "the various writing processes of different networks of human activity—variously theorized as social or discursive practices, communities of practice, or discourse communities" (81). Such organizational writing processes are described by Clay Spinuzzi as "Activity Networks," or the ways in which organizations utilize various tools and subjects to reach their objectives and outcomes (340). In order for student writers to become a writer within such a network, they must understand how such an Activity Network functions with all its interrelated parts (Spinuzzi 340).

In the next section [a reference to Seible's dissertation; you can read an excerpt from her next section in Chapter Two of this text], I discuss how instructors of writing can strengthen their process and post-process approaches to teaching writing by combining these theories with other pedagogical practices and theoretical lenses in order to build on the belief that writing is indeed complex. Activity theory and situated learning practices provide useful pedagogical frameworks for post-process writing classes, and as a result of such integration, instructors can help students build their awareness of professionalism practices and engage them in writing that is both professionally relevant and, ultimately, more motivating.

References

Ames, Carole. "Classrooms: Goals, Structures, and Student Motivation." *Journal of Educational Psychology* 84.3 (1992): 261–72.

Anderson, Larry. "Enhancing Student Motivation in Freshman Composition." *Journal of College Writing* 3.1 (2000): 27–34.

Csikszentmihalyi, Mihaly. "The Flow Experience and Its Significance for Human Psychology." *Optimal Experience. Psychological Studies of Flow in Consciousness*. Eds. Mihaly Csikszentmihalyi and Isabella Selega Csikszentmihalyi. New York: Cambridge UP: 1988. 15–35.

Forsyth, Donelson R., and James H. McMillan. "Practical Proposals for Motivating Students." *Teaching and Learning in the College Classroom*. 2nd ed. Eds. Kenneth A. Feldman and Michael B. Paulsen. Boston: Pearson, 1994. 551–59.

Hootstein, Edward. "Enhancing Student Motivation: Make Learning Interesting and Relevant." *Education* 114.3 (1995): 475–79.

Husman, Jenefer, and Willy Lens. "The Role of the Future in Student Motivation." *Educational Psychologist* 34.2 (1999): 113–25.

Kent, Thomas. "Introduction." *Post-Process Theory: Beyond the Writing-Process Paradigm*. Ed. Thomas Kent. Carbondale: Southern Illinois UP, 1999. 1–6.

McComiskey, Bruce. "The Post-Process Movement in Composition Studies." *Reforming College Composition: Writing the Wrongs*. Eds. Ray Wallace, Alan Jackson, and Susan Lewis Wallace. Westport, CT: Greenwood P, 2000. 37–53.

Olson, Gary A. "Toward a Post-Process Composition: Abandoning the Rhetoric of Assertion." *Post-Process Theory: Beyond the Writing-Process Paradigm*. Ed. Thomas Kent. Carbondale: Southern Illinois UP, 1999. 7–15.

Russell, David. "Activity Theory and Process Approaches: Writing (Power) in School and Society." *Post-Process Theory: Beyond the Writing-Process Paradigm*. Ed. Thomas Kent. Carbondale: Southern Illinois UP, 1999. 80–95.

Spinuzzi, Clay. "Pseudotransactionaliy, Activity Theory, and Professional Writing Instruction." *Teaching Technical Communication: Critical Issues for the Classroom*. Ed. James M. Dubinsky. Boston: Bedford/St. Martin's: 2004. 337–47.

Svinicki, Marilla D. *Learning and Motivation in the Postsecondary Classroom*. Bolton, MA: Anker, 2004.

Taylor, Mark. "Generation NeXt: Today's Postmodern Student—Meeting, Teaching, and Serving." *Higher Learning Commission of the North Central Association of Colleges and Schools: 2005 Collection of Papers on Self-Study and Institutional Improvement.* Becoming a Learning Focused Organization: The Learning Environment. April 2005. 99–107.

—. "Generation NeXt Goes to Work: Issues in Workplace Readiness and Performance." *2007 Higher Learning Commission: A Collection of Papers on Self-Study and Institutional Improvement.* Vol. 2. Programs, Strategies, and Structures to Support Student Success. 2007. 35–42.

Theall, Michael, and Jennifer Franklin. "What Have We Learned? A Synthesis and Some Guidelines for Effective Motivation in Higher Education." *New Directions for Teaching and Learning: No. 78. Motivation from Within: Approaches for Encouraging Faculty and Students to Excel.* Ed. M. Theall. San Francisco: Jossy-Bass, 1999. 99–109 in Marilla D. Svinicki, *Learning and Motivation in the Postsecondary Classroom.* Bolton, MA: Anker, 2004.

ANDREA LUNSFORD'S "LITERATURE, LITERACY, AND (NEW) MEDIA" (2012)

Why I included it

Andrea Lunsford is one of my personal heroes. That alone is not enough reason to include her writing, of course. Lunsford is not only widely respected by her peers but she also shows a sense of appreciation and respect for students. I do not look at students through rose-colored glasses; I know you're human and have as many imperfections as the rest of us. I *do* appreciate, however, the many writing researchers who seek to help and support students while recognizing that students already have plenty to bring to the table. This approach seems important for two reasons. First, it fosters healthy teacher-student relations, and such relations make effective teaching and learning more likely. Second, recognizing what people already know helps us build on those foundations, which, again, makes effective teaching and learning more likely.

Lunsford summarizes some of the ways writing and reading practices have changed as students have participated actively in online platforms. Her method of observing practices, recording observations, and extracting patterns and lessons from the collected data is something you might be asked to do, both in academic and professional settings.

Lunsford's article appeared in the *ADE Bulletin*, a professional journal that is widely read by English department faculty and administrators. It favors short articles rather than full research pieces, and most of the articles focus on teaching, running a department, and other issues related to the work of an English department.

While many of the composition articles I've included in this textbook have been published in journals or books with an audience of writing professors, this particular journal has a large readership of professors who specialize in literature rather than writing. Literature faculty might not hold the same assumptions about students, social media, digital writing, and literacy that composition (writing) faculty might hold. Lunsford's positive characterization of "new literacies" may thus be surprising to many of her readers, a point she only briefly hints at as she ends her essay. Lunsford uses the phrase "the dumbest generation" at the end of her essay without citing it, but it alludes to a book by another English professor, Mark Bauerlein, titled *The Dumbest Generation: How the Digital Age Stupefies Young Americans and Jeopardizes Our Future (Or, Don't Trust Anyone Under 30)*. Lunsford's article challenges Bauerlein's argument, but Lunsford only acknowledges that agenda as she concludes.

Reading hints and vocabulary

Lunsford quickly presents her topic and her research methods in her first paragraph. This is an unusual move, but she is summarizing findings rather than offering the kind of full research article that would be appropriate in another kind of journal. Lunsford briefly defines terms by relying on other researchers, and then she cites a few examples to develop her argument. At about the halfway point, she begins offering her own interpretation of what students are doing in the digital age, first in terms of writing and then in terms of reading. She ends by calling for new ways of teaching and summing up a perspective that values the new literacies students are using.

old literacies: academic argument, research, adherence to copyright codes, and other writing and reading habits associated with schools prior to the rise of digital literacies

new literacies: digital reading and writing associated with new media and the ability to not only read or consume public texts but also to write and produce public texts, often using or directly responding to texts that already exist

web 2.0: in its early stages, the world wide web was a place people visited to read, access, and perhaps download content; as various platforms allowed and encouraged people to interact, participate, produce, and upload content, the term "web 2.0" was coined to mark the shift in digital activities

textual ownership or **intellectual property**: these phrases reference the idea that writing (and other creative endeavors) is authored by a particular person (or group of people), and that people ought to receive credit or compensation if their writing (or other creative work) is used by others

CONNECT

As you read, consider responding to the following questions to help you process the material.

1. Why does Lunsford wait until the end of her essay before explicitly opposing the association of digital media and stupidity? Think about her audience and how they might respond differently if she had begun her essay with such a stance.

2. How many characteristics associated with twenty-first century students fit you? To what degree do the characteristics seem inaccurate?

3. Look at the five ways of reading Lunsford identifies. Can you think of an example of each one from your own life?

4. Lunsford does not necessarily offer a utopian view of digital literacy, but she definitely focuses on the positive aspects for students. What downsides might digital literacy have on students?

5. Compare Lunsford's views with those of Michaela Cullington (whose research is available online; see the article citation below). How do their research methods seem similar? different?

Lunsford, Andrea A. "Literature, Literacy, and (New) Media." *ADE Bulletin*, vol. 152, 2012, pp. 49–53.

IT'S NO LONGER an exaggeration to say that writing has changed more dramatically in the last two decades than during any previous time in the last 2,500 years. Like many others, I have been invested in tracing such changes in the biggest literacy revolution the world has seen in a very long time, a revolution that is affecting all of us and our ways of communicating, especially our ways of writing and reading. To do so, I followed a group of Stanford University undergraduates, tracking their writing and learning and interviewing a subgroup of them at least once a year for six years. I have learned more than I could ever have imagined at the beginning of this research, and certainly more than I can easily summarize. But I can focus on some of the most significant findings about student uses of literacy today and consider the implications they hold for us as teachers of writing and reading.

To begin with, this group of students embodies what many are calling the "new literacies," as opposed to the "old literacy" that I grew up with and still value. What are these new literacies? Most researchers agree with Michele Knobel and Colin Lankshear, who argue that new literacies—those encouraged by Web 2.0 —are "more 'participatory,' 'collaborative,' and 'distributed' in nature than conventional literacies. That is, they are less 'published,' 'individuated,' and 'author-centric' than conventional literacies. They are also less 'expert-dominated' than conventional literacies" (9). One way to sum up the shift Knobel and Lankshear describe is to say that student writers today are turning from consuming texts (often those deemed most worthy by schools and other institutions) to producing texts. Thus new literacies involve a different kind of mind-set than literacies traditionally associated with print media. In their introduction to *A New Literacies Sampler*, Knobel and Lankshear contrast what they refer to as a "physical-industrial" mind-set—the mind-set that I certainly grew up inhabiting—with a "cyberspatial-postindustrial mind-set" (10).

According to Knobel and Lankshear, those whose experience grounds them primarily in a physical-industrial mind-set tend to see the individual as "the unit of production, competence, intelligence." They also identify expertise and authority as "located in individuals and institutions." Those who inhabit a cyberspatial-postindustrial mind-set, in contrast, increasingly focus on "collectives as the unit of production, competence, intelligence" and tend to view expertise, authority, and agency as "distributed and collective" (11).

Students in twenty-first-century universities exhibit the mind-set Knobel and Lankshear describe: they work in teams on everything; they work effortlessly across genre and media; they tell us that good writing is writing that makes something happen in the world, that is performative; and they no longer hold to traditional notions of copyright and textual ownership (see Lunsford and Ede). I'd like to introduce you to a few students and their work, stressing another important finding from our longitudinal study: the literate practices about which students are most passionate occur outside class. Meet "sparker2," for example, an avid contributor to *Twitter*:

Rain's over, going to Trader Joe's to buy some Healthy stuff to fight this cold ... suggestions? (13 Mar. 2010, 9:21 a.m.)

FOCUS ON WRITING: WHAT COLLEGE STUDENTS WANT TO KNOW

Watching Queen Seon Duk 선덕여왕 on @dramafever, love it so far! Your assessment? http://www.dramafever.com/drama/56/#nowplaying (10 Jan. 2011, 1:16 a.m.)

Here sparker2 tweets with a purpose, whether it's to get or to give information from those who follow her. An avid fan of Korean cinema, she tweets every day or two with what amount to 140–character film reviews. Her writing is performative and collaborative and aimed at action.

A second example comes from Stanford's required second-year course on writing and rhetoric. Not content with doing the course assignments, which were hefty enough, these students set out to use the skills they were learning to create ads of their own—ads that would, in turn, parody their course, PWR 2.

This spoof ad was created by a group of students working together on their laptops and making use of programs like *Photoshop*—and they were producing discourse rather than analyzing advertisements or reading what others have to say about them. They were doing such analyses in class, but they also insisted on creating advertisements of their own. And they certainly were practicing new literacies, that is, literacies that are participatory, collaborative, and performative. Note also that these students don't blink at using photos from the Web. Indeed, no finding was more interesting to me in our longitudinal study than the complex notions students held about textual ownership. In short, we found that deeply participatory electronic forms of communication provide new opportunities for writerly agency, even as they challenge notions of intellectual property that have held sway now for over three hundred years, leading to diverse forms of multiple authorship and to the kind of mass authorship that characterizes sites such as *Wikipedia* and *Google News*.

To make this point, let me introduce you to Mark, a student who wrote and performed a spoken-word poem during the first weeks of his first year. Titled "The Admit Letter," this poem was performed at the Writing Center's annual celebration of writers held during Parents' Weekend. It opens with a "so-called friend" saying to the writer of the poem, "Oh sure, you got into Stanford: you're Black." What follows is Mark's imagining of what his "so-called friend" thought his admission letter to Stanford might have said. The two imaginary versions of the letter are biting—and very, very funny. Together, they not only put the so-called friend in his place forever but manage to send up the university as well. On the Stanford campus, news of this poem spread like proverbial wildfire, and Mark was called on to perform it in numerous venues. During one such performance, the poem changed significantly: now it was performed by Mark and a Chicana student, who powerfully wove together versions of their "admit letters."

"The Admit Letter" went through additional permutations over Mark's college career, and during one of the interviews with him I asked, "So is this poem yours? Do you own it?" In a lengthy conversation, Mark said that he considered the poem to be his—but not exclusively his; in fact, he said, his work is usually written and performed collaboratively, and he sees it as part of a large poetic commons. He was already effectively moving into new media literacy and into new territory regarding textual ownership. Mark's poem also illustrates what students have told me over and over again: that "good writing" is performative; it makes something happen. Mark's poem certainly did that (in fact, it is still being performed on campus).

But students are using writing and rhetoric to make things happen in many other ways as well. Amrit made a poster as part of the work he and fellow students were doing to support AIDS research. Anna and her colleagues in the Stanford Labor Action Coalition designed a Web site to call attention to the plight of temporary workers on the Stanford campus and to convince campus administrators that these workers deserve a living wage. Another student resisted writing a traditional essay in favor of producing a film and using it as a way to raise issues he felt he could not address as tellingly in print. After a series of negotiations with his teacher, this student went on to make the film and then to present it along with an analysis and a set of recommendations to the campus community. In this instance, the student was able to satisfy both the demands of old literacies for analysis and academic argument while also embracing the new.

What we learned from these and many other students and their uses of literacies challenged us to rethink our curricula and, in fact, to focus the second-year writing course at Stanford on the oral and multimedia presentation of research—that is, to try to combine the best of the old literacies (academic argument and research) with opportunities for engaging in new literacies and to do new media writing in the way that the student making the film did. In this course students move from articulating a research question and doing the research necessary to answer it in a traditional academic essay to "translating" that essay into other media. Thus this course focuses on the fifth canon of rhetoric, delivery, recognizing the many choices that student writers now have available to them.

At the same time that we are looking at how writing is changing, we are also tracking changes to readers, since new literacies and new media writing are influencing reading practices as well as the texts students read. In addition, new literacies are challenging us to rethink what we mean by *literature* and to entertain broadening that term to mean *letters*, as it did in earlier times. Moreover, we might expend the kind of effort we have given to high literary texts to other texts as well, the kind of attention Michael Armstrong displays so brilliantly in his reading of stories written by children. Most of all, our findings suggest that the new literacies ask us to diversify our notion of texts. As Juan Poblete argued during the 2011 ADE Summer Seminar West, we urgently need to pluralize reading ("What Is a Reader?").

In my graduate seminar The Future of English Studies, we have been investigating these claims, and recently we have been trying to monitor and describe our different ways of reading. Our findings match in some ways what the students in the longitudinal study have told us about how they read, and on that basis we've been talking about five particular ways of reading:

- The informational reading students do every day—such as searching the Web to look for some particular fact or date. This kind of reading is similar to that which Louise Rosenblatt labeled "efferent" in her groundbreaking *The Reader, the Text, the Poem*, opposing it to "aesthetic" reading for pleasure.
- The ludic or playful reading students also do daily, from checking status updates and *Twitter* feeds to "reading" games and films.
- The rhetorical reading students do when they want to know not what something means but how it means, that is, how it creates its effects on readers. This kind of reading also often aims at action, at making something happen in the world, to make or support a case or claim.
- Hermeneutical reading, the kind of close reading students learn to do in school. While my students often say this kind of reading is "nit-picking" and "hunting for symbols and other hidden things, especially in poems," they value the ability to read between the lines.
- The creative reading students do when they use reading to make something of their own. As Richard Miller put it during the 2010 ADE Summer Seminar East, in this kind of reading, "the value of the aesthetic object is to invite readers to create on their own."

This list only gestures toward the many kinds of reading we and our students might identify, but it suggests the need to broaden our understanding of reading practices in general and to pay more careful attention to students' ways of reading in particular.

If we need more expansive ways of understanding and describing our students' reading practices, I believe we must also engage a broader range of texts students are reading. I try to follow this advice in my courses by including texts such as Lynda Barry's *What It Is*; Mark Danielewski's *House of Leaves*; Apostolos Doxiadis, Christos Papadimitriou, Alecos Papadatos, and Annie Di Donna's *Logicomix*; Jonathan Safran Foer's *Tree of Codes*; Gilbert "Beto" Hernandez's *Chance in Hell*; Shelley Jackson's *Patchwork Girl*; David Mazzucchelli's *Asterios Polyp*; Dwayne McDuffie's *Icon*; and Steve Tomasula and Stephen Ferrell's *TOC: A New Media Novel*. This selection includes comic books, hypertexts, and works that mix media or play with format in other ways, and one (*Tree of Codes*) is a "remix" of the author's favorite book, Bruno Schulz's *The Street of Crocodiles*. Reading these texts calls for all the kinds of reading I mentioned above—and then some—and for recognizing that literature is a category capacious enough to include these texts in provocative and produc-tive ways. I find that reading together with students challenges all of us to work together, to do a kind of social, group reading that opens the texts up to us in ways that individual reading does not. Thus if writing is increasingly collabora-tive, participatory, and social, so I would argue is reading.

To sum up, the research and teaching I have done over the last decade convince me that students today are reading and writing more than ever before and that they are increasingly insistent on producing as well as consuming texts. They are accustomed to and comfortable with mixing media and genre, with producing remixes and mash-ups, with transforming what they find (usually online) into still other kinds of texts. Unlike those who think that literacy is on the decline and that today's students are the dumbest generation, I am struck every day by the intelligence and creativity of the readers and writers I see at work. They have a lot to teach us about what it means to be a reader and a writer today.

Works Cited

Armstrong, Michael. *Children Writing Stories*. London: Open UP, 2006. Print.

Barry, Lynda. *What It Is*. Toronto: Drawn and Quarterly, 2006. Print.

Danielewski, Mark. *House of Leaves*. New York: Pantheon, 2000. Print.

Doxiadis, Apostolos, Christos Papadimitriou, Alecos Papadatos, and Annie Di
    Donna. *Logicomix*. London: Bloomsbury, 2009. Print.

Foer, Jonathan Safran. *Tree of Codes*. London: Visual, 2010. Print.

Hernandez, Gilbert "Beto." *Chance in Hell*. Seattle: Fantagraphics, 2002. Print.

Jackson, Shelley. *Patchwork Girl*. Watertown: Eastgate, 1995. CD-ROM.

Knobel, Michele, and Colin Lankshear. "Sampling 'the New' in New Literacies." *A New Literacies Sampler*. Ed. Knobel and Lankshear. New York: Lang, 2007. 1–24. Print.

Lunsford, Andrea A., and Lisa Ede. "'Among the Audience': On Audience in an Age of New Literacies." *Writing Together: Collaboration in Theory and Practice*. By Lunsford and Ede. New York: Bedford/St. Martin's, 2012. 236–57. Print

Mazzucchelli, David. *Asterios Polyp*. New York: Pantheon, 2009. Print.

McDuffie, Dwayne. *Icon: A Hero's Welcome*. New York: DC Comics, 1997. Print.

Miller, Richard. "Undergraduate Study in English: Where Do We Go from Here?" ADE Summer Seminar East. Univ. of Maryland, College Park. 6 June 2010. Address.

Poblete, Juan. "What Is a Reader? A Roundtable on the New Literacy and the English Curriculum." ADE Summer Seminar West. Stanford Univ., Palo Alto, CA. 24 June 2011.

Rosenblatt, Louise M. *The Reader, the Text, the Poem: The Transactional Theory of the Literary Work*. Carbondale: Southern Illinois UP, 1978. Print.

Tomasula, Steve, and Stephen Ferrell. *TOC: A New Media Novel*. N.p.: Fiction Collective 2, 2009. DVD-ROM.

RECOMMENDED ONLINE SOURCES

For direct links to these sources, please visit <sites.broadviewpress.com/focusonwriting>.

1. To enjoy personal expressive writing with a poetic style: Williams, Terry Tempest. "Why I Write." 1998. *Why I Write: A Celebration of the National Day on Writing*. National Writing Project, 2011, <rvannoy.asp.radford.edu/rvn/312/whyiwrite.pdf>.

2. To consider motivation in school writing and to appreciate accessible academic research: Strasser, Emily. "Writing What Matters: A Student's Struggle to Bridge the Academic/Personal Divide." *Young Scholars in Writing*, vol. 5, 2007, <cas.umkc.edu/english/publications/youngscholarsinwriting/documents/MATTERS.pdf?cn21>.

3. To explore accessible scholarly research about the kinds of academic assignments students find meaningful: Eodice, Michele, Anne Ellen Geller, and Neal

Lerner. *The Meaningful Writing Project: Learning, Teaching, and Writing in Higher Education*. Conference on College Composition and Communication Research Grant, 2010–11, <http://meaningfulwritingproject.net>.

4. To hear how a thoughtful writing professor connects our everyday lives to our classroom work: Cusick, Christine. "Reflections on Teaching." *Assay: A Journal of Nonfiction Studies*, 29 Jan. 2018, <https://assayjournal.wordpress.com/2018/01/29/christine-cusick-reflections-on-teaching/>.

5. To trace how a student researcher journeys from wondering whether texting has a negative effect on student writing to finding answers to her question: Cullington, Michaela. "Texting and Writing." *Young Scholars in Writing: Undergraduate Research in Writing and Rhetoric*, vol. 8, 2011, pp. 90–95, <https://arc.lib.montana.edu/ojs/index.php/Young-Scholars-In-Writing/article/view/164/116>.

6. To see how one scholar might respond to another in a public venue: Cooper, Julia. "A Response to Michaela Cullington." *Young Scholars in Writing*, vol. 11, 2014, pp. 91–93, <https://arc.lib.montana.edu/ojs/index.php/Young-Scholars-In-Writing/article/view/283/210>.

Joining the Conversation

The following formal writing prompts are ways of helping you think through the ideas you've been reading about by *using* the ideas in some way to help you create a text of your own.

LITERACY NARRATIVE

Compare a time when you were motivated to write to a time when you were not motivated to write. How might you apply what you discover to future writing situations, especially when it is difficult to find motivation?

PROFILE

Interview a professional to discover how writing, reading, and research are part of a career field. Present your findings in a genre that might reach people interested in that profession. Consider, for example, a blog post, an article for LinkedIn, or a YouTube video. You might even ask the professional for samples of writing that are appropriate to share publicly. For inspiration, visit this website: *Writing When I Grow Up*. Class Website, Marywood University, 2009, <sites.google.com/a/maryu.marywood.edu/lauriem/course-websites/writing-when-i-grow-up>.

TEXTUAL ANALYSIS

Find a common theme such as motivation, audience, purpose, or identity addressed in two reading selections (including the online readings). What can writers understand better from reading both selections rather than just one of the selections?

For a more creative version of this assignment, write an imaginary dialogue between two or more authors based on the ideas they discuss and the approaches or styles they use.

PERSONAL ESSAY

Choose a specific kind of writing you do regularly and write about your motivation in the style of Terry Tempest Williams's essay, "Why I Write." For example, you might title your essay "Why I Take Notes," "Why I Snapchat," or "Why I Write 'To-Do' Lists."

MULTIMEDIA PROJECT

Work either individually or with classmates to create a multimedia project that answers the question "Why Write?" for a specific audience. For example, you might create a Pinterest board that highlights the importance of writing for people who engage in craft projects, or you might compose and perform a song that helps remind musicians of the roles writing might play in their work. Consider what kind of genre you might use to celebrate writing used by baseball players, people who love to cook, or the staff of your high school yearbook.

2 WHAT IS THE "RHETORICAL SITUATION" AND WHY SHOULD I CARE ABOUT IT?

Exploring the Question

Each time we speak and each time we write, the situation is slightly different. The combination of factors that affect communication is labeled the **rhetorical situation** or the **rhetorical context**.

Now you know what the rhetorical situation is. Why should you care about it? For two reasons:

1. Since every communication is more or less effective in meeting a purpose based on the rhetorical situation, noticing the rhetorical situation can help you become a *more effective writer* and a *stronger reader*.

2. Recognizing the rhetorical situation will also help writing and reading be *easier* for you because you'll be prepared to notice similarities and differences as you move from one rhetorical situation to another.

As described in Chapter One, people who don't notice similarities in rhetorical situations may encounter each new writing task with extreme nervousness and confusion about how to begin (McCarthy). Likewise, people who don't notice

CONNECT

Before you begin reading, think about all the different kinds of writing you've been assigned in school.

1. What expectations for writing assignments are consistent whether completed for English, science, history, or another class?

2. How do expectations for various kinds of classes vary?

differences in rhetorical situations may treat each new writing task as if it were identical to prior writing, which would likely lead to missteps and a lot of revision.

If writing is like a dance, being aware of the rhetorical situation allows the dancer to change from ballet moves to club moves based on what fits the music, the audience, the purpose, and so forth.

Let's look at some of the factors that contribute to the rhetorical situation so you can look good on the dance floor.

CONNECT

Sometimes the word "rhetoric" is used to mean baloney, as in "That's just rhetoric." The implication is that language is being used persuasively to manipulate people, but there is little of substance beyond the language.

If you do an online search for definitions of "rhetoric," what do you find? Are the definitions connected to one another?

THE RHETORICAL TRIANGLE AND BEYOND

Often when people begin researching a particular field, they create categories, sub-categories, and criteria that help define what they're talking about and what matters. You've probably noticed this in the way science is divided into chemistry, biology, physics, and so forth. You probably also know that the animal kingdom is divided into phyla and then into six classes: math, English, social studies.... No! Not *that* kind of class. The animal kingdom is divided into phyla and then into six classes (invertebrates, birds, fish, mammals, amphibians, and reptiles), and each class is divided into orders; each order is divided into families; and so on, until the most specific division of species. All of these divisions are determined by criteria—the factors that are deemed most important.

In 1971, James Kinneavy published *A Theory of Discourse: The Aims of Discourse* with hopes of creating such a system that would help people discuss and research writing and rhetoric. Today, writing and rhetoric are not codified in ways the animal kingdom is, but Kinneavy's model helped writing studies become a more defined and focused discipline. As writing scholars have considered ways of systematizing writing and rhetoric, they have worked to articulate what matters most, just like scientists studying animals needed to decide which differences are most and least significant to advance understanding. That's why a whale is categorized as a mammal even though to non-scientists like me, the whale seems more similar to fish than to other mammals.

Since we are actually discussing writing, not animals, it's helpful to have a basic understanding of factors that writing experts commonly use to discuss the rhetorical situation. Those factors provide ways to discuss, research, and better understand writing even as writing constantly evolves with each new context. Writers able to

FOCUS ON WRITING: WHAT COLLEGE STUDENTS WANT TO KNOW

recognize how rhetorical situations shift will likely write and read more effectively and efficiently just as scientists who understand criteria used to classify animals will be better prepared to do their work.

At this point, it's a good idea to revisit the multiple kinds of written text we produce and consume in the course of a given day or week. That way we can consider criteria we might use to think productively about writing. See the start of Chapter One for a guide to brainstorming your own list. Here is a short list of alphabetic texts I write or read regularly. I've excluded image- and aural-based texts for the sake of simplicity.

cell phone texts
emails
tweets
Facebook posts
grocery lists
lists of things to do
notes to prepare for class
billboards
road signs
writing on television news
research notes
conference papers
menus

CONNECT

What other groupings can you create? How would you label each group?

I could group these texts in multiple ways. I might put emails, tweets, and Facebook posts together and label this group "online communication to connect with others." I might put emails, notes to prepare for class, research notes, and conference papers in a group and label it "writing done for work." I could place grocery lists, lists of things to do, notes to prepare for class, and research notes in a group and title it "informal writing to help myself remember and organize."

Each kind of writing could potentially belong to more than one group depending on the organizing principles. Furthermore, even when we place kinds of writing in a group, that doesn't mean those types of writing are the same; it simply means that the kinds of writing have something in common.

This "something in common" is often either *purpose* or *audience*. For example, some kinds of writing I do are driven by purposes of communication and connection (texting, Facebook posts) while other kinds have a purpose of helping me accomplish a task (lists, notes). Some writing is directed to my family and friends, some is directed to my work colleagues or students, and some is directed to myself. Because purpose and audience shape writing so much, it's no accident that these elements arose in the prior chapter that asks, "Why write?"

CONNECT

1. Can you think of other types of writing that change in style and content as the purpose and audience shift? Consider the examples of writing listed above or other kinds of writing that you're familiar with.

2. Google "How to email a professor." In what ways does the advice you find consider audience, purpose, or genre?

Purpose and audience matter even when writing within a single genre (with *genre* referring to a category of writing that has identifiable characteristics regarding content, structure, and style). For example, I write emails to students, friends, colleagues, and other people. Although these emails have many elements in common, as I write to different audiences for a variety of purposes, the content and style of my emails change. Understanding that I need to shift style and content according to whom I'm writing (my audience) and why I'm writing (purpose) is crucial. I could end up composing some very inappropriate emails otherwise.

Chapter One that asks "Why write?" also focuses on writers themselves. A writer's motivation and investment in writing often affects the text that is produced. Our backgrounds and education and homes and stories also influence the ways we write, both in terms of language or phrasing we use and in terms of processes we follow and feelings we have as we write.

These three elements—purpose, audience, and writer—strongly define the *message* that is communicated, so they are often represented as parts of a ***rhetorical triangle***—a simple graphic that represents basic criteria used to define a rhetorical situation.

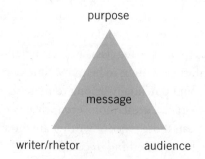

The ideas depicted in the rhetorical triangle are rooted in the work of Aristotle, a scholar in Ancient Greece who offered guidelines for persuasive oral speeches.

Aristotle was an early *rhetorician*—a person who studies how *rhetoric* (persuasion) works. Many of Aristotle's ideas about oratory have been applied to writing, images, and design, as these modes of communicating have become important sites of persuasion.

Communication tends to be persuasive to a degree even when that is not the main intent in any obvious way. The visual element of the triangle helps expose this persuasive element. The rhetor/writer and the audience member/reader are in two different positions and thus have different views of the message. The writer's job is to motivate the audience to view the message in a particular way that will fulfill the purpose of the communication.

In order to accomplish this job, the rhetor needs to understand that the audience is in a different position than the rhetor. If the rhetor assumes the audience will see things in the same way as the rhetor, there's a good chance the purpose won't be filled. And if the rhetor only repeats what the audience already knows and believes, reading will have served no purpose.

You can see how this works even when I write down a list of things I need at the grocery store. Present Me is the rhetor who writes the list, and Future Me is the audience who will be pushing a grocery cart, inevitably with one squeaky wheel, trying to figure out whether boxes of raisins are sold near the fresh fruit, the canned fruit, or the candy. Present Me is focused but knows that Future Me will be distracted, so Present Me writes a list that can be processed easily and that provides enough information so that Future Me knows what to buy. If Present Me provided only information that was easy for Future Me to recall, Present Me should not have bothered writing. And if Present Me wrote a paragraph or a story about the items needed at the grocery store, Future Me would be really annoyed while trying to find raisins.

Luckily, Present Me did a good job of serving the purpose of communication by understanding that Future Me would have a very particular perspective at the grocery store and made the message work well for Future Me. Are you wondering exactly what the purpose was? It was buying milk, eggs, and bread so Present Me and Future Me could make French toast during the big storm. French toast with extra raisins.

CONNECT

1. Can you give another example of how a rhetor/writer manages to fill a purpose by communicating in ways that are sensitive to the perspective or situation of the audience/reader?

2. Can you give an example of a rhetor communicating in a way that seemed unaware of the audience's perspective and was thus unsuccessful in filling the purpose of communication?

103

CHAPTER TWO: WHAT IS THE "RHETORICAL SITUATION" AND WHY SHOULD I CARE ABOUT IT?

This idea that writers help an audience see a message in a particular way is why all communication can be understood as persuasive to some degree. This viewpoint is reflected in a composition textbook titled *Everything's an Argument*. The authors, Andrea Lunsford and John Ruszkiewicz, offer a way of looking at the entire world as a series of communications that shape thinking. That textbook is not as good as this one, but don't tell Lunsford I said so because as I mentioned in Chapter One, she is one of my heroes.

The connection between the rhetorical triangle and persuasion can also be understood by viewing each point in terms of a persuasive element, with all three elements holding the triangle together when a text is rhetorically effective.

purpose
logos

message

writer/rhetor
ethos

audience
pathos

CONNECT

1. How might using appeals to pathos or logos increase ethos? Provide an example.

2. How might appeals to pathos or logos minimize ethos? Provide an example.

CONNECT

Do a search for images of the rhetorical triangle. What do you find? Is there a particular image you especially like? Why?

The message should establish that the rhetor/writer can be trusted by appealing to **ethos**; in other words, the text demonstrates the writer's intelligence, integrity, and good will. The audience or reader may be more or less receptive to the message depending on the appeal to **pathos**; in other words, the message can be crafted to affect the emotional state of the audience and make them more likely to see the message from the rhetor's perspective. Finally, appealing to **logos** uses arguments of reason and order to fill the purpose of the message.

When analyzing arguments or other obviously persuasive texts, appeals to ethos, pathos, and logos can be articulated as separate elements, but the three appeals tend to overlap and intersect.

I have a confession to make. I've chosen the labels in the triangles above because those labels seem helpful to me. I added "rhetor" to the "writer" label because it includes not only writers but also speakers, filmmakers, visual artists, and so forth, but I kept "writer" both because it's a more familiar word than "rhetor" and because this course focuses on *writing*. I also chose which label to put on top. That was instinct, not rational decision-making. Even foundational concepts may be framed in various ways depending on purpose.

The rhetorical triangle is often pictured inside a circle that suggests a fuller context.

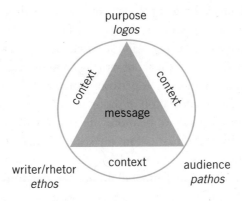

This context can be understood in an overwhelming number of ways, so fasten your seatbelt:

- all that has been written or said on the subject prior to this communication;
- elements of shared language, shared values, and shared genres;
- the immediate occasion and conditions that enable communication;
- the constraints that limit the communication that is possible or that is likely to be effective;
- and literally any other element that shapes the writer, the audience, the purpose, or the message.

Whew. It's even trickier because the context for writing and the context for reading are different—at times extremely different. Furthermore, a message might have many writers or many audiences (Grant-Davie). Even though considering context is almost like wrapping your mind around infinity, it is both possible and useful to focus on specific elements of context that can help us be more effective and efficient writers and readers.

CHAPTER TWO: WHAT IS THE "RHETORICAL SITUATION" AND WHY SHOULD I CARE ABOUT IT?

THE OCCASION: AN OVERLY BRIEF EXPLANATION

In a 1968 essay, Lloyd Bitzer focused on the way particular situations call for spoken or written language that responds to the situation and affects it in some way. The *exigence* is the reality that the discourse aims to shape or change.

For example, I write a text message to make lunch plans because I know I will be passing through the town where my good friend works. I write this textbook because Writing about Writing approaches to teaching college writing are widely used, and professors are looking for textbooks that support student learning. I write a toast because my sister is getting married and has asked me to say a few words. In each case, the rhetorical act of writing "functions ultimately to produce action or change in the world" as "it performs some task," with language used to shape "reality through the mediation of thought and action" (Bitzer 3–4). An act of speaking or writing is likely to be more effective if *kairos*—appropriate timing—is in place. If I write a toast before my sister has decided to get married or after the wedding has occurred, I have missed the kairotic moment, and my toast will probably not be appreciated and will not lead to the drinking of champagne.

Reading also occurs for a reason or is elicited by a particular situation. Maybe your phone buzzed, so you read a text message. It probably was not me trying to make lunch plans, but if it was, let me know, because that would be an amazing miracle, wouldn't it? Maybe your professor assigned this chapter, so you're getting a huge kick out of it as you do every time you are required to read something. Maybe you are going to hear (rather than read) my toast because my sister heard you are awesome and invited you to her wedding.

In each case, the exigency implies an audience of those who are able to respond to the rhetor. The audience for my text message is my friend who can consider meeting me for lunch. One audience for this textbook is professors, believe it or not, because they are the ones who decide whether to assign this book in their classes. A second audience is you, the students, because I hope to help you approach writing with thoughtful awareness (and professors will only assign the book if they believe it may have such influence). The audience for my wedding toast is my sister, her spouse, and the guests who are holding flutes of champagne waiting for my remarks to come to a close as a signal it is time to clink glasses and drink.

All that has been written or said on the subject prior to this communication
An occasion may be more complex than what is suggested with my small examples, but thinking in terms of exigence and kairos can be tremendously helpful in academic reading and writing. As a reader, pay attention to what scholars are

FOCUS ON WRITING: WHAT COLLEGE STUDENTS WANT TO KNOW

responding to. As a writer, make the exigence and kairos for your own writing clear to your readers.

Because reading and writing are cyclical activities as scholars respond to one another, you sometimes need to offer a full and complex explanation rather than a brief gesture toward exigence. When writing in academic genres, it is typical to first see what others have written and then place one's own research in the context of earlier findings.

This dynamic may make more sense if you consider a long text conversation that enacts a cycle of reading and writing. It would be odd to reply to a group text conversation without having some familiarity with the prior remarks. You might end up repeating something or going off track or even eventually getting kicked out of the group chat because you hold the conversation back instead of moving it forward. To think about it in terms of that triangle we recently bonded over, if you write in a group chat or in an academic setting without having some sense of what has already been said, you aren't really noticing the position of your audience. If you don't notice the audience's position, it is unlikely you will be able to reach them.

As you recognize how complex communication is, you can feel proud of all the writing and reading you do effectively and also begin realizing that it's okay to struggle with writing and reading on a regular basis. Although it's complicated, learning some of these behind-the-scenes secrets will hopefully help you analyze rhetorical situations in ways that can help you learn.

Some of the most common ways composition teachers help students think about contexts involve discourse communities and genres. I don't want you to miss out, so let's get into those topics next.

DISCOURSE COMMUNITIES

Although writing is often pictured as an individual practice involving a writer sitting alone with a laptop or pen and paper, writing is always social. We write using language and conventions we have learned within a culture—within a group of people who communicate with one another.

A community of people with shared communication practices can be called a *discourse community*. I will complicate this basic definition in a moment, but it can be helpful to start with a simple example before noticing the gray areas.

For several years, I worked in restaurants as a server. During this time, I learned certain words and phrases that eventually felt natural to me as I became more

107

CHAPTER TWO: WHAT IS THE "RHETORICAL SITUATION" AND WHY SHOULD I CARE ABOUT IT?

immersed in the work (these words and phrases associated with a discourse community are called a **lexis**). "Behind ya" was a phrase I used when I wanted another server or worker to be aware I was right there. We used this regularly to avoid calamity when carrying big trays of drinks and food. Other phrases were related to a particular system we had of ringing in food orders, such as PLU (Price Look Up), which referenced a number coding system for most of the foods on the menu.

"Laurie please" meant that I was needed, either because an order for one of my tables was ready or because the cook had a question. Sometimes at family parties, my brother would use this phrasing to get my attention because four members of my family worked at the same restaurant chain; my brother brought the restaurant lexis into our family discourse community, and it was a fun and funny gesture because it wasn't as natural there.

CONNECT

When thinking about discourse communities, it's often helpful to think about learning to speak in a new context, noticing when another person hasn't quite grasped how to speak within a particular context, or recognizing how noticeable it can be when habits from one communication context are used in a different communication context. In other words, it's often easiest to recognize discourse communities by noticing when the boundaries are transgressed in some way.

Can you think of instances that fit any of these situations?

To some degree, the phrase "discourse community" is inaccurate when describing the workplace because "discourse" focuses on language, but using the language effectively was simply one part of the community. I also needed to learn how things were to be done in a particular restaurant—trays were used to serve drinks, appetizers were served before salads, ramekins were used for tartar sauce, ketchup was kept on all the tables, and so forth. To learn the customs, I trained with experienced servers, attended "pre-meal" meetings at the start of each shift, completed additional trainings for all restaurant workers, and took exams to test me on my knowledge. To this day, I can tell you that a plate of nachos at that particular restaurant included 64 chips (eight tortillas were each cut into eight parts and then deep fried for each plate of nachos).

Because most communities combine language practices with other kinds of practices, the phrase "discourse community" is sometimes replaced with "**community of practice**." The latter phrase takes the focus off of spoken or written discourse, though discourse is still *part* of a community of practice.

Are you with me so far? Here is a quick review:

- writing is always social!
- a discourse community is a group of people who share language practices

- a community of practice is a group of people who share language practices and other conventions

CONNECT

Think of a time when you felt like an "outsider" or when you noticed someone else seemed like an "outsider," whether online or in real life.

1. What signs showed outsider status?

2. To what degree did this outsider status change as the individual became part of the community of practice? Did the individual need to change in some way for this to happen?

Now I am going to complicate the ideas, though I am going to rely on the term "discourse community" from here on out because I am going to focus on language and communication. Scholars who seriously investigate discourse communities need a clearer definition of the terms in order to set parameters for their arguments. If I am researching a subject, even something like "dogs," I need to clearly define what I mean by "dog" in order to conduct and communicate my research in ways that others can use.

One researcher who has established criteria for defining a "discourse community" is John Swales. Swales wrote in 1990 that discourse communities have six criteria. Many teachers use these criteria to help students identify and understand the way communication operates within a particular discourse community:

1. A discourse community has a broadly agreed set of common public goals.
2. A discourse community has mechanisms of intercommunication among its members.
3. A discourse community uses its participatory mechanisms primarily to provide information and feedback.
4. A discourse community utilizes and hence possesses one or more genres in the communicative furtherance of its aims.
5. In addition to owning genres, a discourse community has acquired some specific lexis.
6. A discourse community has a threshold level of members with a suitable degree of relevant content and discoursal expertise. (Swales, *Genre*, 24–27)

Recently, John Swales revisited his thinking about discourse communities and he created a slightly new list. I paraphrase his revisions in italics just below. Part of the reason I share the versions published in 1990 as well as 2017 is to show that even ideas published, read, cited, and used by a lot of people can undergo revision.

109

CHAPTER TWO: WHAT IS THE "RHETORICAL SITUATION" AND WHY SHOULD I CARE ABOUT IT?

1. A discourse community has a broadly agreed set of goals; *these goals may or may not be explicitly stated, and there may be sets of differing goals for different segments of a single community.*
2. A discourse community has mechanisms of intercommunication among its members; *these mechanisms may be digital; some kind of communication is necessary for a set of people to be defined as a "community."*
3. A discourse community uses its participatory mechanisms to provide information and feedback; *members communicate in order to keep the community functioning or help it grow; communication helps things to get done.*
4. A discourse community utilizes and hence possesses one or more genres in the communicative furtherance of its aims; *the word "possesses" is unnecessary, though a particular community might refine a genre in a particular way.*
5. In addition to owning genres, it has acquired some specific lexis; *the lexis of a community develops over time and often includes abbreviations.*
6. A discourse community has a threshold of members with a suitable degree of relevant content and discoursal expertise; *the newer members of a discourse community gradually advance into full membership.*
7. A discourse community develops a sense of "silential relations" (Becker 1995); *some things can go unsaid because they are assumed.*
8. A discourse community develops horizons of expectation; *the community develops a value system to evaluate work, and a history and ongoing patterns lead to expectations of when and how things will happen.* (Swales, "Concept of Discourse Community")

It is worth reading the full article (available online in *Composition Forum*) to hear more about how Swales thinks about discourse communities, but I am going to turn from defining what a discourse community is to thinking about why so many of us who teach writing find the concept useful.

If all writing is situated in a particular context, and contexts constantly change, it is difficult to discuss contexts in a useful way. Recognizing and describing discourse communities, however, allows us to make the complicated world of context more manageable. Noticing discourse communities helps us see that many contexts for communication have patterns—such as particular forms, language practices, guidelines, and so forth—that enable or encourage some behavior while restricting or discouraging other behavior.

At the very least, then, paying attention to discourse communities can help writing teachers and students notice the way expectations are likely to change from one classroom to another. Each discipline can be considered a discourse community, and that is why writing expected in a biology course, a music theory course, and a developmental psychology course is likely to differ, sometimes in drastic ways.

CONNECT

I have mentioned the importance of recognizing disciplinary similarities and differences several times. When has it been helpful to notice similarities or differences in writing you've completed for school?

Paying attention to discourse communities can also help us connect how writing is similar across many classrooms. Most academic writing involves evidence-based thinking that responds to earlier research in the field, and most professors expect writing to be clear and concise. The larger discourse community of the university is a way of recognizing such common expectations.

More broadly, an awareness of discourse communities can help us think about ways that communities may be healthy and supportive or unhealthy and oppressive. Often, a single discourse community may have both healthy and unhealthy elements, or a single element might welcome some people and make others feel unwelcome.

If we return to the restaurant where I worked in my twenties, I can describe a conduct and policy manual that all workers were responsible for studying and abiding by, a menu that servers and kitchen workers needed to understand, logos and signs that helped customers identify the restaurant and key components like restrooms and smoking/non-smoking sections. (Yes, we used to have smoking sections in restaurants, as if smoke would be contained.) I made notes for myself when I took customer orders, and I translated these notes into the restaurant computer so that bartenders and kitchen workers could prepare food. All of these elements of communication helped the restaurant run smoothly, helped me learn how to do my work when I was new, and helped the restaurant fill its mission of serving good food at reasonable prices.

If you turned a critical eye to that restaurant, however, you might notice some other patterns. Almost all of us who worked there were white. An Asian immigrant who spoke little English washed dishes, and three immigrants who spoke English as a second language did prep work in the kitchen. All of the text inside and outside the restaurant—from policy manuals to menus to signs—was in English. The restaurant was in a Massachusetts town with a largely white population, so the lack of diversity wasn't odd, but the choices to keep all restaurant texts solely in English advantaged some workers and disadvantaged others, welcomed some clientele and discouraged others from eating there.

111

CHAPTER TWO: WHAT IS THE "RHETORICAL SITUATION" AND WHY SHOULD I CARE ABOUT IT?

Most servers and hostesses were female. Most bartenders were male. The manager and the three assistant managers were male. The kitchen workers were almost all male, though there was one exception when I first started working there, and she impressed me because she was a young woman in a realm that seemed to be a male space. I cannot associate these gender patterns with particular texts of that discourse community, either because it was long ago or because the divisions of labor rested on unspoken assumptions. The patterns likely matched national trends of the time, and they make me curious. Why is it that many workplace roles seem divided along gender lines, even when such a dynamic is not an explicit goal of this restaurant or, perhaps, most work spaces? And how was the discourse community affected by the unplanned way that divisions of labor in this particular restaurant tended to fall along gender lines?

I did not analyze any of these dynamics when I was actually part of the discourse community. I also didn't analyze economic class divisions, disabilities, sexuality, age, or other common ways of categorizing cultural identities. My point is that the discourse communities that we belong to may intentionally support a wider sense of fluidity, diversity, and welcome; they may legislate particular roles for particular kinds of workers; or they may fall somewhere in between, unintentionally welcoming some members in some roles while not providing access for others—often those who are in marginal rather than mainstream positions.

If my restaurant discourse community example doesn't make sense to you, let me offer another example: The movie *Elf*. In this comedy, Buddy is a human raised by elves, so he belongs to a North Pole discourse community with very particular kinds of texts, belief systems, means of communication, and purposes. When he travels to New York City, he encounters an entirely different discourse community. Poor Buddy does not understand that he is in a new discourse community, so he continues to behave as if he is in his North Pole community, and a lot of very funny episodes ensue.

In some of these episodes, Buddy is excluded because he does not know how to fit into the New York City discourse community. He gets thrown out of a toy store, thrown out of an office building, and relegated to the mailroom of his dad's company because his communication and his behavior tend to confuse, annoy, and offend others.

The operation of discourse communities is far more complex throughout the movie, but the point remains. When we communicate in ways that fit one discourse community but not another, we run the risk of exclusion. The problem may be that we need to learn a new kind of discourse, or the problem may be that the discourse community is more exclusive and unwelcoming than it ought to be. People who learn English as a second language or who speak in a regional or ethnic dialect may be especially vulnerable to exclusion. Often an expectation of "standard English" is used to welcome some people and bar others from access.

Sometimes students tell me that their high school friends speak in a local dialect and label those who resist that style as "uppity," "snooty," or "fake." Those same students notice that the use of their regional or family dialect in their college classes may lead to assumptions that they are unintelligent, local "hicks," or uneducated. Personally, when I first entered college and my new classmates teased me about my Boston accent, I coped by gradually changing the way I spoke to minimize my accent. This change didn't seem like a loss to me at the time, but when I was working in Pennsylvania almost twenty years later and had a colleague who had kept her Boston accent, I was jealous. My new friend sounded like members of my family, and I realized I was sad that I no longer sounded like my family or the friends I grew up with.

Rigid adherence to "standard English" is thus a catch-22, compelling many of us to either conform to or resist languages considered appropriate in school, with either choice involving a loss. *Code switching* is a coping mechanism that involves changing dialects when moving from one situation to another. This approach allows people to belong to several discourse communities in ways that follow the norms of each. If I had used my Boston accent with my family and childhood friends and shed it outside of those communities, that would be considered code switching.

Another strategy is to seek opportunities for *code meshing*. This strategy involves bringing a variety of dialects together, an approach that conforms in some ways to expectations of a discourse community while challenging expectations in other ways. In the Introduction, I told of a colleague who used both academic language and African American vernacular English in a conference presentation. Making such decisions may be more difficult when new to a discourse community, when less certain of expectations, and when seeking a sense of belonging.

In a writing course that encourages attention to discourse communities, your professor may be interested in opportunities for you to bring various ways of speaking and writing together. Consider when and how discourse communities may be open to diverse dialects rather than upholding rigid expectations or using speech patterns to perpetuate stereotypes.

CONNECT

1. Can you think of a movie that depicts a discourse community? How can you tell it's a discourse community?

2. What dialects are you aware of in your own life? To what degree are these dialects stigmatized in negative ways?

3. Can you think of an example of code meshing that worked effectively?

113

CHAPTER TWO: WHAT IS THE "RHETORICAL SITUATION" AND WHY SHOULD I CARE ABOUT IT?

As you begin noticing the discourse communities in which you participate, whether in school or in other parts of your life, you will hopefully be able to learn to adjust your approaches to communication to fit new spaces. I hope you may also notice how communication practices within a discourse community might be improved. Understanding discourse communities involves not only adapting your own practices to fit but also considering how the discourse community itself might be more inclusive.

GENRES

One criterion for identifying a group as a "discourse community" is the use of shared genres of writing. A *genre* is a category of writing with identifiable characteristics of content, organization, and style. Genres might be used to communicate information, improve the community, and acclimate new members to the discourse community.

Again, because understanding a full context for communication can be overwhelming, looking at patterns allows writers to grapple with the context. Genres are part of not only a single discourse community but often span many discourse communities. Paying attention to genres, then, is another way of helping writers move from one discourse community to another, bringing some expertise along and noticing how more learning or adaptation might need to occur.

In the discussions of discourse communities above, I mentioned many genres from the restaurant setting—a policy manual, menu, signs, and so forth. If you took just one of these genres, such as a menu, you could likely list the typical content that is included, typical organizational elements, and stylistic guidelines. You may even be able to generate criteria to evaluate whether or not a menu is effective.

To the degree that commonalities among menus exist across restaurants, we can identify genre conventions. Because different restaurants are different discourse communities, however, menus are also likely to vary. Some might serve all-Italian food, or all-vegan dishes, or pub food that fits the big-screen sports decor. Some restaurants might have a menu in a single paper sheet while some might offer many pages of colorful illustrations or a leather-bound wine list separate from the food menu.

CONNECT

Choose a genre you read or write as an expert—perhaps an Instagram post or notes taken during class.

1. What criteria might you use to evaluate whether a particular instance of this genre was well done or not?

2. How might developing criteria for less familiar genres be helpful?

FOCUS ON WRITING: WHAT COLLEGE STUDENTS WANT TO KNOW

Genres thus give many hints about what to expect as we read and as we write, just as a single discourse community can be analyzed to help us better communicate. Considering both genre and discourse community provides us with an even better sense of the way context affects what we are reading or writing.

RECAPPING THE RHETORICAL SITUATION

At this point, I am going to loop back to the rhetorical triangle and bring it together with the contextual elements we have discussed.

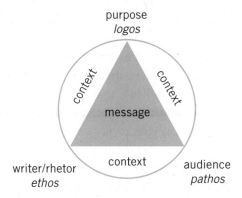

First, when **analyzing a message**, always pay attention to the original three elements to whatever degree you can:

- Who is the writer (or rhetor/speaker)?
- To what audience is the message being directed?
- What purpose or purposes is the message serving?

As far as context, any message is communicated within an **occasion**, so if you can understand the **exigence** and **kairos** that led to communication, it will help you discern the purpose. Notice how the communication is responding to and building on what has come before, whether in terms of content and information, conventions associated with a discourse community, genre conventions, or even larger cultural assumptions. Every communication is connected to earlier communications.

When possible, use your knowledge of the **discourse community** to better understand the message, and use the message to better understand the discourse

115

CHAPTER TWO: WHAT IS THE "RHETORICAL SITUATION" AND WHY SHOULD I CARE ABOUT IT?

community. While many messages are communicated within a discourse community, some messages are communicated across or between discourse communities. Most messages fall into **genres** as well, so if you are familiar with a genre, you can better understand how the message is functioning by noting how it fills some genre conventions and deviates from other genre conventions. You can also use the message to better understand how a genre operates to allow some kinds of communication and discourage other kinds of communication.

When **crafting a message** rather than analyzing one, be sure to understand that your audience needs to be motivated to see a new perspective, so make it easy for your audience to hear you and be sure to tell them something they do not already know. If the exigence isn't obvious, tell your audience—why are you communicating? what are you responding to? how are you bringing something new to the conversation?

If information needs to be recapped in order for you to add to a conversation, do so while giving credit to those who have already contributed to thinking about a topic. Such a dynamic shows your audience that you are worth listening to, both because you have done your homework and because you are building on others' ideas without claiming their work as your own.

Also be aware of discourse community conventions and genre conventions. Both allow clearer communication, and your audience is more likely to listen if you show that you can fill expectations. However, if your sense of a discourse community or genre is that it is overly restrictive, consider challenging or stretching expectations. If you feel uncertain about taking such risks because you are new to a discourse community or the stakes are high, ask for input and support from an expert.

Paying attention to rhetorical situations should help you communicate more effectively and efficiently, so if you are overwhelmed with the more complex ways of thinking about context, at the very least pay attention to why in the world someone is bothering to speak, write, or otherwise communicate. What is the purpose?

FROM "RULES" TO "GUIDELINES"

Recognizing that all writing is situated involves more sophisticated understandings of conventions.

I regularly ask students what rules they learned about writing during high school. The list is often long and interesting, including items such as "Do not use 'I'" and "Do not start a sentence with 'But' or 'And.'" I ask students where and when they violate these rules. How do they write when brainstorming? taking

FOCUS ON WRITING: WHAT COLLEGE STUDENTS WANT TO KNOW

notes? writing on social media? texting? I also wonder whether they have seen professional writers violate rules that were taught in high school classes.

If you've seen any of the *Pirates of the Caribbean* movies, you might remember that The Pirate's Code is "more of a guideline, really." That's how I like to think about writing rules. They tend to be "more of a guideline, really."

In other words, sometimes a rule applies and sometimes it does not. Yes, that's confusing, yet it's unavoidable because if the rhetorical situation changes, the writing is likely to shift right along with it.

In order to cope with this confusing situation, I often look at models of writing from a) the discourse community I'm writing within and b) the genre I'll be writing in. For example, when I needed to request travel funding for a conference or complete a self-evaluation, I looked at how other faculty from my department had written their documents. My specific information was different, but I understood the kinds of information I should include and how to organize the information based on these samples.

In classroom or work situations, it is also smart to talk with teachers or bosses about guidelines and conventions. I provide several tips about academic conventions in Chapter Three that will not be universally helpful but will at least give you some guidelines to start from. Such foundations allow you to gradually adjust approaches for specific situations. When students ask me whether they can use "I" or how many sentences should be in a paragraph, I know they are taking their past experiences with academic writing and trying to figure out what is similar and what is different in this situation. In other words, those students are transferring what they have learned about writing so that the new writing task is at least somewhat familiar, even if it might be different in

CONNECT

1. As an individual or as a class, generate a list of rules that you've been taught in various situations of school writing. What do you notice about these "rules"?

2. Have you ever noticed that most writing rules apply in some situations but not others? What increased your awareness of these shifts?

3. Have you ever laughed about a person who was texting or using social media for the first time and didn't seem to understand conventions in those spaces? What are some examples? What's similar about that situation and the kinds of conventions that teachers articulate about school writing? What's different?

CONNECT

1. When is it okay to judge another person by their dialect, spelling, use of grammar conventions, and so forth?

2. When is such judgment inappropriate?

3. In what situations is it appropriate or inappropriate to correct the way another person speaks?

117

CHAPTER TWO: WHAT IS THE "RHETORICAL SITUATION" AND WHY SHOULD I CARE ABOUT IT?

my flexible attitude toward the use of "I" and my appreciation of the occasional high-impact one-sentence paragraph.

I now suddenly feel pressure to write a high-impact one-sentence paragraph, but I'm sorry: I got nothing.

WORKS CITED

Bitzer, Lloyd. "The Rhetorical Situation." *Philosophy and Rhetoric*, vol. 1, 1968, pp. 1–14.

Grant-Davie, Keith. "Rhetorical Situations and Their Constituents." *Rhetoric Review*, vol. 15, no. 2, 1997, pp. 264–79. *JSTOR*, JSTOR, www.jstor.org/stable/465644.

Kinneavy, James L. *A Theory of Discourse: The Aims of Discourse*. Prentice-Hall, 1971.

Lunsford, Andrea A., and John J. Ruszkiewicz. *Everything's an Argument.* 7th ed. Bedford/St. Martin's, 2016.

McCarthy, Lucille P. "A Stranger in Strange Lands: A College Student Writing across the Curriculum." *Research in the Teaching of English*, vol. 21, no. 3, Oct. 1987, pp. 233–65.

Swales, John M. "The Concept of Discourse Community: Some Recent Personal History." *Composition Forum*, vol. 37, Fall 2017, < http://compositionforum.com/issue/37/swales-retrospective.php>.

—. *Genre Analysis: English in Academic and Research Settings*. Cambridge UP, 1990.

Extending the Conversation

To think more about the question "What is the 'rhetorical situation' and why should I care about it?" I have gathered together three selections reprinted here and seven readings or videos you can find online. Each piece overlaps with my initial approach to the question in some way, but each piece also extends the chapter question with a particular focus. As we answer questions that may seem simple at first, complexities and nuances develop that call for more exploration.

For each text reprinted here, I tell you why I included it, provide some background about its initial publication, and offer hints that may guide your reading, including vocabulary terms when relevant. I also provide "connect" questions to help you engage and respond as you read.

For each online source I recommend, I offer a brief introduction—just enough to guide you as you decide what further reading (or viewing) might be helpful, inspiring, enjoyable, or challenging.

MARCEA K. SEIBLE'S "ACTIVITY THEORY: SITUATED LEARNING AND STUDENT MOTIVATION" (2008)

Why I included it

You might have already encountered another excerpt from this literature review in Chapter One that focused on research about what motivates students to write. The excerpt below continues the conversation but turns the focus to "situated learning"—that is, learning in a particular rhetorical context. It thus provides a helpful bridge between Chapters One and Two. As you read what researchers have discovered, you can compare their findings to your own experiences.

Background

Seible's doctoral dissertation argues for focusing on professional writing in the first-year classroom. The following excerpt synthesizes secondary research in ways that gradually lead into her own research study (which I have not included).

Usually, a dissertation would be read in its entirety. The primary readers would be Seible's dissertation committee—a few professors in the field who guided the research project and suggested revisions and edits as she completed her work. Seible might be thinking about eventually turning her dissertation into a book, so she likely considered a wider audience of composition professors.

Reading hints and vocab terms

It's important to remember that this reading is an *excerpt* rather than a complete piece. You'll notice that it begins and ends abruptly because I pulled this section out of a longer text. This excerpt is part of a ***literature review*** (often shortened to "lit review") that recaps past research on a particular topic. That way, readers can understand how the new research being conducted is responding to earlier research.

As mentioned above, this particular dissertation focuses on attention to professional writing in the first-year composition classroom. This part of the lit review focuses on specific theories used in teaching composition that motivate students and connect to professional writing.

119

CHAPTER TWO: WHAT IS THE "RHETORICAL SITUATION" AND WHY SHOULD I CARE ABOUT IT?

activity theory: "the complex process of making knowledge by engaging oneself with a community and its already-established system and interactions" (Seible, para 1, below)

CONNECT

As you read, consider responding to the following questions to help you process the material.

1. How does this excerpt connect to ideas from this chapter about why we should care about the rhetorical context when we are reading and writing?

2. How does this excerpt help you think about the question "Why write?" in terms of a focus on rhetorical situations or situated learning?

3. Review the vocabulary. Choose two terms that seem most helpful in thinking about writing and explain why.

activity networks: communities of complex systems that use specific genres of writing

situated learning: students write in real-world settings, perhaps via internships or service-learning projects

legitimate peripheral participation: learning how to participate in an activity network (including learning to write in its genres) by starting as a beginner and gradually becoming a full-fledged member of the community

service learning: combining classroom learning with work that benefits the community

Seible, Marcea K. "Activity Theory: Situated Learning and Student Motivation." Excerpted from *The Transition from Student to Professional: A Pedagogy of Professionalism for First-Year Composition* (Order No. 3323939). ProQuest Central, ProQuest Dissertations & Theses A&I. (304606678), 2008.

ACTIVITY THEORY PROVIDES a unique lens from which to examine how students can become "real" (as in professional) writers and how they can begin a process of professionalization that will help them meet the demands of the professions they will join upon leaving the classroom. The term "activity theory" describes the complex process of making knowledge by engaging oneself with a community and its already-established system and interactions. Within this theory, "Meaning is not created through individual intentions; rather, it is mutually constituted in relations between activity systems and persons acting, and has a relational character" (Lave, "The Practice of Learning" 18). In short, knowledge is constructed through meaningful actions and "complex relations with(in) societal activity systems" (Lave, "The Practice of Learning" 18).

Activity theory has already been combined with process and post-process theories in writing classes to teach students about writing as academic and professional practice, and in the process, it has worked to situate students within professional settings and to engage them with the complexity of real writing. For example, Donna Kain and Elizabeth Wardle utilized activity theory to teach technical writing students about professional writing genres, helping them to "focus on context and the role of texts in mediating activities" (114). Others, like James Kalmbach, in his chapter "Teaching Reports as Rhetorical Practice" in *Resources in Technical Communication*, have used activity theory to teach students how to write in socially-situated contexts, showing them that technical writing, like all writing, is always rhetorically situated. Kalmbach describes technical writing in the context of activity theory: "... to write a report is to make visible the complex social practices of everyday organizational lives. Effective reports can best be understood within the context of those social practices" (26).

Lave and Wenger's concept of situated learning, described by them as a way to envision the linkages between professional practice and classroom pedagogies, is an important part of understanding activity theory and its relation to student meaning-making through organization and community engagement. A practice already in use by writing instructors through such practices as internships, client projects, and service-learning projects, situated learning activities are considered beneficial because they help students learn about "real" writing, but they are also considered beneficial for the communities and organizations students work with. At its heart, situated learning places students in active roles within an organization or particular community, allowing them to enter professional sites to learn the responsibilities, conventions, and professional discourse from those already situated within it. In addition, it allows them to gain an awareness of the complexities associated with writing, as articulated by post-process theorists.

Clay Spinuzzi's description of Activity Networks (AN) illustrates the complex systems that students must come to understand when learning through pedagogies utilizing activity theory. Spinuzzi's example of the Activity Network of a Software Development Company illustrates the vital interplay between the tools a company utilizes (computers, graphics, voices, etc.), the subjects or people involved, the objectives, and the necessary outcomes (340). In combination, these elements combine to create genres of writing that are unique to that

121

CHAPTER TWO: WHAT IS THE "RHETORICAL SITUATION" AND WHY SHOULD I CARE ABOUT IT?

organization. Though it is essential for students to understand how ANs function, it is also essential that students learn that each organization has its own
systems and genres. Activity theory provides a lens from which to introduce
students to the variety of ANs that exist by encouraging active participation in
such communities, though it is impossible for teachers to teach students how
to write in the specific manner every organization will expect of its employees.
Within activity theory, situated learning activities work on a different level to
engage students with writing in real professional contexts.

Jean Lave and Etienne Wenger's term, "legitimate peripheral participation,"
describes the defining characteristic of situated learning, in that "... learners
inevitably participate in communities of practitioners and that the mastery of
knowledge and skill requires newcomers to move toward full participation in
the sociocultural practices of a community" (29). For Lave and Wenger, situated
learning allows students to become participants in their various communities by
doing so in a peripheral manner. In other words, students act as learners in the
communities before acting as full-fledged participating members: "Legitimate
peripheral participation is proposed as a descriptor of engagement in social
practice that entails learning as an integral constituent" (Lave and Wenger 35).
Such a view describes learning as a process in which the focus is on "participation in the social world" (Lave and Wenger 43) and in which "the production,
transformation, and change in the identities of persons, knowledgeable skill
in practice, and communities of practice are realized in the lived-in world of
engagement in everyday activity" (Lave and Wenger 47).

Situated learning, or learning created through one's engagement within a
community's social practices, is also already utilized in different writing pedagogies and has been linked to an increase in student motivation in writing courses
(Adler-Kassner, Crooks, and Watters). Though questioned as a form of situated
learning, given that they do not always take place within the environment of a
workplace but rather in the classroom, client projects are one form of situated
learning that may help students begin to assimilate to professional discourse
practices. Internships, though they too do not guarantee ideal professional
workplace participation, are meant to provide a greater source of activity system
interaction for students and thus, ideally, should be considered an example of
situated learning.

Writing classes such as composition and technical communication have
found ways to integrate service learning projects as examples of situated
learning in order to help students foster a greater connection between the classroom and the "real world" (Dorman and Dorman). Such situated learning

FOCUS ON WRITING: WHAT COLLEGE STUDENTS WANT TO KNOW

environments have the potential to significantly affect students' motivation because they allow students to see themselves as real writers and as real working/writing professionals. Students begin acquiring a sense of self as a "professional" which results from their interactions with real professionals in real organizations, leading to a better understanding of how writing functions within those authentic settings as opposed to an inauthentic classroom.

Technical communication scholars also attest to the importance and value that situated learning pedagogies, such as service learning, bring to their writing classes. In particular, scholars promote its value in preparing students for their roles as ethical, responsible citizens in addition to helping students transition from the classroom to the workplace. Sapp and Crabtree claim that, like internships, service learning experiences not only offer students a chance to develop as future employees, they also give students a chance to become socially responsible citizens and gain an "education in engaged citizenship" (412). Similarly, Jeff Grabill in "Technical Writing, Service Learning, and a Rearticulation of Research, Teaching, and Service," claims that service learning provides a link between the community organizations and the university. He believes that service learning and technical communication are natural partners in the sense that they "focus on complex problems and real clients ... service learning is in many ways a natural extension of pedagogies common in technical and professional classes" (83). J. Blake Scott supports Sapp and Crabtree as well as Grabill's views of service learning as ways to engage students civically and socially in their communities. He believes that technical communication and service learning, as viewed through a cultural studies lens, emphasize the role of the student as a critical citizen and an agent of change within their communities.

Composition scholars have found that service learning brings an added dimension to the writing course, enabling students to see the applicability of writing to their lives beyond the classroom. Service-learning-in-composition scholar Thomas Huckin describes it in a positive light, claiming that service learning assignments contribute to building students academically and professionally, the latter being that its assignments "help develop project management skills and promote a socially-oriented rhetoric" (Huckin 50). Cited benefits of service learning also include a better understanding of civic issues, increased student motivation, and a greater sense of responsibility and accountability for learning and the community (Adler-Kassner, Crooks, and Watters 2–3). As a pedagogy, service learning has the potential to help bridge the gap between the classroom and the workplace and to offer a new perspective on students'

123

CHAPTER TWO: WHAT IS THE "RHETORICAL SITUATION" AND WHY SHOULD I CARE ABOUT IT?

professional development (Stone 386). Given the inauthentic, or non-realistic, settings that many writing classes provide, situated learning pedagogies face several challenges to being successful if they are not organized or implemented correctly in the writing classroom. On the downside of situated learning is that though internships, service learning, and client projects attempt to provide realistic "real-world" writing experiences, practical considerations often make them less than perfect examples of this pedagogy. Several factors affect how "situated" the situated learning environment/assignment actually is. For example, the success of students' experiences working on a client project may be affected by how invested the student is with the project, how invested the client is with both the student and the project, and how far the project goes beyond the confines of the writing classroom. When client projects remain in the classroom and do not extend into the client's Activity Network, students' writing may reflect more of what Spinuzzi describes as the pseudotransactionality problem: writing that is written more for the teacher's specifications than the client's, or "a genre adapted for meeting the object(ive)s of the particular classroom" (342).

Ann M. Blakeslee described another challenge associated with client projects as successful examples of situated learning, namely that students may not value the project or see it as an authentic representation of workplace writing. When students see the writing or the work as artificial, they may not take part in the true situatedness of the writing experience and they lessen their learning and professional development. However, based on her research into client projects, Blakeslee commented favorably overall about client projects in their role as a "bridge between school and work" (361). She believes that "classroom and workplace activity systems may overlap with the projects since students get a taste of workplace practices while still experiencing the structure, support, and familiarity of the academic learning environment (a kind of guided legitimate peripheral participation)" (Blakeslee 361). She claims that through their experiences working with clients and interacting with professionals in real settings, "Students start out at the edge of a discipline's collective life and gradually move toward its center, a conception that also resembles Jean Lave and Etienne Wenger's notion of legitimate peripheral participation" (Blakeslee 362). While client projects and internships may not always provide prime examples of professional development through situated learning, there is some acknowledgment, at least on the part of Blakeslee, that students are becoming better prepared for transitioning from the classroom to the professional world.

In some instances of poorly-planned situated learning experiences, instructors may place a greater emphasis on the classroom component of the experience than on the knowledge created within the professional environment itself. As Lizzio and Wilson note, pedagogies that attempt to combine real-world preparation practice with the classroom, as emphasized by activity theory and situated learning, face three challenges: 1) the experiences become the end rather than the means of education; in other words, they act as the culmination of learning, rather than part of the learning process; 2) these pedagogies and practices may reinforce a type of "safe superficiality" for students by not allowing them to experience wholly realistic workplace challenges in their greater focus on the classroom rather than on the workplace; and 3) practical considerations in terms of available clients and project sites make it difficult for students to experience a range of real-world challenges (472). Even though such challenges do in fact exist, the overall benefits of utilizing activity theory and situated learning pedagogies that integrate real-world learning experiences make them particularly effective for trying to motivate students. By getting them involved with their communities, getting them to do real writing, and teaching them how professionals interact in activity systems and how they write and create in the workplace, students begin to connect academic writing contexts with professional contexts and expectations.

As writers engaged in peripheral, yet real, working contexts, students can gain a more complete picture of the complexity of the (post) process of writing while taking part in experiences that prove to be professionally relevant to their future goals, an element directly tied to their intrinsic motivation. Through their observations of and direct participation in these situated communities, they can learn that writing is more than a series of steps; it is a contribution to and a product of discursive practices within professional communities. Importantly, they can learn that the process of being a writer in situated learning environments requires them to know more than just writing as a generalizable process (draft, revise, edit, revise, proofread, etc.). By relying on students' self-described needs as learners in the classroom, i.e., their need for professional relevancy, instructors can better utilize situated learning practices in process and post-process writing classes, helping students make connections between writing in professional communities and their future identities and responsibilities as professionals. Situated learning pedagogies combined with studying issues of professionalism, therefore, offer a starting point for instructors to begin constructing a pedagogy that can continue bridging the classroom-to-workplace transition gap.

125

CHAPTER TWO: WHAT IS THE "RHETORICAL SITUATION" AND WHY SHOULD I CARE ABOUT IT?

References

Adler-Kassner, Linda, Robert Crooks, and Ann Watters, eds. *Writing the Community: Concepts and Models for Service-Learning in Composition.* Washington: American Association for Higher Education and NCTE, 1997.

Blakeslee, Ann M. "Bridging the Workplace and the Academy: Teaching Professional Genres through Classroom-Workplace Collaborations." *Teaching Technical Communication: Critical Issues for the Classroom.* Ed. James M. Dubinsky. Boston: Bedford/St. Martin's, 2004. 348–71.

Grabill, Jeff. "Technical Writing, Service Learning, and a Rearticulation of Research, Teaching, and Service." *Innovative Approaches to Teaching Technical Communication.* Eds. Tracey Bridgeford, Karla Saarti Kitalong, and Dickie Selfe. Logan, UT: Utah State UP, 2004. 81–92.

Kain, Donna, and Elizabeth Wardel. "Building Context: Using Activity Theory to Teach about Genre in Multi-Major Professional Communication Courses." *Technical Communication Quarterly* 14.2 (2005): 113–39.

Kalmbach, James. "Teaching Reports as Situated Practice." *Resources in Technical Communication. Outcomes and Approaches.* Ed. Cynthia Selfe. Amityville, NY: Baywood, 2007.

Lave, Jean. "The Practice of Learning." *Situated Learning: Legitimate Peripheral Participation.* Eds. Jean Lave and Etienne Wenger. New York: Cambridge UP, 1991. 3–32.

Lave, Jean, and Etienne Wenger. *Situated Learning. Legitimate Peripheral Participation.* New York: Cambridge UP, 1991.

Lizzio, Alf, and Keitha Wilson. "Action Learning in Higher Education: An Investigation of Its Potential to Develop Professional Capability." *Studies in Higher Education* 29.4 (Aug. 2004): 469–88.

Sapp, David Alan, and Robbin D. Crabtree. "A Laboratory in Citizenship: Service Learning in the Technical Communication Classroom." *Technical Communication Quarterly* 11.4 (2002): 411–31.

Scott, J. Blake. "Rearticulating Civic Engagement through Cultural Studies and Service-Learning." *Technical Communication Quarterly* 13.3 (2004): 289–306.

Spinuzzi, Clay. "Pseudotransactionaliy, Activity Theory, and Professional Writing Instruction." *Teaching Technical Communication: Critical Issues for the Classroom.* Ed. James M. Dubinsky. Boston: Bedford/St. Martin's: 2004. 337–47.

Stone, Elisa. "Service Learning in the Introductory Technical Writing Class: A Perfect Match?" *Journal of Technical Writing and Communication* 30.4 (2000): 385–98.

AMY J. DEVITT, ANIS BAWARSHI, AND MARY JO REIFF'S "MATERIALITY AND GENRE IN THE STUDY OF DISCOURSE COMMUNITIES" (2003)

Why I included it

The authors describe an analytical method and then they model how it works. While some of the theoretical ideas discussed may be difficult to grasp, the authors look at specific scenes that clarify the value of their methods. Their analytical approach to genre in specific situations might inspire you to do similar work in a setting that interests you.

Background

This article responds to a trend in composition classes to study discourse communities and use ethnographic research. The authors note that such approaches have shortcomings, and they offer a different model for teaching that will still help students connect writing to social groups and cultural norms. Devitt, Bawarshi, and Reiff studied genre theories and their applications both before and after this article was released, suggesting their commitment to genre study as a key part of teaching writing. In this article, they propose genre analysis as a practical tool for understanding how language works in a social setting.

CONNECT

As you read, consider responding to the following questions to help you process the material.

1. Devitt analyzes jury instructions. Why do they tend to be so difficult to understand? Can you connect this difficulty to what you've learned about the role of audience or purpose in the rhetorical situation?

2. Devitt focuses on writing that may lead to a person dying. Can you think of other situations in which written clarity is a matter of life and death or otherwise extremely important?

3. Bawarshi describes the way medical settings often reflect and affirm western beliefs that physical health and mental health are separate from one another. How does Bawarshi use ethnomethodological genre analysis to develop and support that point?

4. Why does Reiff think analyzing genres within a particular context is helpful for students?

5. What parts of this article sparked your interest the most? Why?

6. What parts of this article were difficult to read? Why do you suppose the writers included these parts?

127

CHAPTER TWO: WHAT IS THE "RHETORICAL SITUATION" AND WHY SHOULD I CARE ABOUT IT?

As you read, pay attention to the purpose the authors associate with genre analysis. They offer a general defense of their approach in the first section, and then each author performs a genre analysis to show how useful such work can be: Devitt focuses on jury instructions, Bawarshi analyzes patient history forms used in medical settings, and Reiff considers how ethnography is a useful genre for students in writing classrooms.

discourse community: a group of people with a shared purpose and shared communication practices

genre analysis: recognizing rhetorical patterns used in a genre as practiced within a particular community

ethnography: the study of a community and its cultural practices

ethnomethodological: characterized by attention to community practices (rather than studying the object of interest without attention to how it operates within a community)

ethnography in composition studies: the study of the way a community's written texts are connected with a community's purposes, belief systems, and practices

Devitt, Amy J., Anis Bawarshi, and Mary Jo Reiff. "Materiality and Genre in the Study of Discourse Communities." *College English*, vol. 65, no. 5, 2003, pp. 541–58. *JSTOR*, JSTOR, www.jstor.org/stable/3594252.

OVER THE PAST two decades the concept of discourse community has been one of the most hotly contested notions in the field, subject to the range of by-now well-known critiques that claim it is too utopian, hegemonic, stable, and abstract.[1] Abstracted from real social situations, discourse communities may appear stable to advocates and critics assuming an imaginary consensus and a shared purpose that do not reflect real experience within communities.

---

1   See, for example, John Trimbur's call for a rhetoric of dissensus—a view of community based in "collective explanations of how people differ, where their differences come from, and whether they can live and work together with these differences" (610). See also Bizzell, Harris, Kent, and Leverenz.

The concept of discourse community as stable and utopian has been, to some, so seductive that it both conceals the language and the social practices that take place within it and distracts researchers from examining how its internal workings may be recognized and studied. As a result, the concept of discourse community remains of limited pedagogical value.

To make communities tangible and their discourse actions palpable to students, writing teachers have begun to use ethnographic research, which, while valuable in locating the study of discourse within the behaviors of real communities, can be difficult to implement in the classroom. According to Beverly Moss, "When ethnographers study a community as outsiders, they must spend a significant amount of time gaining access to the community and learning the rules of the community well enough to gather and eventually analyze the data" (161). The process of sifting through the massive quantities of information gathered and attempting to stake out some analytical claims can present a major hurdle, particularly for student ethnographers. How do ethnographers connect what community members know and do with what they say and how they say it—their language practices? Genre analysis has been responsive to such questions and links patterns of language use to patterns of social behavior, reflecting the composition researcher's "narrower concern with communicative behavior or the interactions of language and culture" (Moss 156). Genre study allows students and researchers to recognize how "lived textuality" plays a role in the lived experience of a group. Teaching students how to analyze genres can provide discipline and focus to the study of discourse communities.

During the last half-century, genre theory has been reconceived by literary and rhetorical theorists as, among other things, "sites of social and ideological action" (Schryer 208)—as parts of all social environments. Language genres in these contexts become less transparent and more constitutive, less the means of classifying texts and more the sites at which language's social character can be understood. In this sense language and its genres are as material as the people using them. As sites of social action, genres identify the linguistic ecology of discourse communities, making the notion of community more tangible for teachers and students.

In the three connected essays that follow, we use the idea of genre to study discourse communities.[2] We examine several contexts of language exchange in

2   We thank the many participants in a lively exchange at the 2001 Conference on College Composition and Communication, whose comments on our initial presentation have helped us clarify and elaborate our arguments.

129

CHAPTER TWO: WHAT IS THE "RHETORICAL SITUATION" AND WHY SHOULD I CARE ABOUT IT?

which the use of genre theory may yield insight into teaching, research, and social interaction: legal practice, medical practice, and classrooms. Illustrating how genres can sometimes restrict access to communities, Amy Devitt examines jury instructions as a genre, considering how the genre affects the interactions of jurors in ways that inhibit the successful execution of their duties. Anis Bawarshi suggests how a specific textual genre, the patient medical-history form, works in and provides critical access into doctors' offices. Mary Jo Reiff discusses how the combination of ethnography and genre analysis can give teachers, researchers, and students clearer ways to understand their classrooms.

Together, the essays suggest how genre analysis contributes to the use of ethnomethodology as a research technique that focuses on language and society and that is especially eligible to contribute to the pedagogy of text-dependent subject matters. Whether we are studying academic, professional, or public communities, genres, considered as material entities, enable us to enrich the idea of a discourse community by giving discipline and focus to the study of the unities of language and society.

Where communities collide: Exploring a legal genre
Amy J. Devitt

Contemporary genre analysis focuses on the actual uses of texts, in all their messiness and with all their potential consequences. Genre analysis also ties that use to actual language, to the smaller bits of language that alert analysts to underlying ideas, values, and beliefs. Such analysis often reveals the conflicts between communities that use a genre, conflicts often invisible to analysis that looks at discourse in terms of its communities alone. This essay analyzes some genres, particularly jury instructions, that are created within one professional community to be used by nonmembers of that community. While their purposes seem to be inclusive, to give nonmembers access to the community's knowledge, genre analysis strongly suggests that the specialist and nonspecialist users have different beliefs, interests, and purposes as well as levels of knowledge. The consequences for both the professional communities and the larger society are significant, potentially drawing the boundaries around professional communities even more tightly. In order to keep from substituting one abstracted concept for another, to keep from idealizing and homogenizing the realities of genres, students should also see the messiness and especially the exclusiveness of genres.

Because genres represent their communities, they effect and make consequential the communities' interests. But it is when genres encompass participants beyond a narrow community that the effects of those interests become most troublesome. Surprisingly, many genres are designed within one specialist community for functions to be filled by nonmembers of that community. Tax forms are designed by the IRS, but they are supposedly meant to be used by people who may know little of tax regulations. The fact that so many people hire specialists to complete their tax forms merely confirms the difficulty of the task of translating specialists' knowledge into laypersons' actions. An especially significant recent example is the ballot, both the propositions on it and the physical construction of it. Ballots are created by politicians but are completed by citizens. Ballots contain propositions that voters vote on, but the propositions are written by lawyers and knowledgeable proponents of an issue. To have our votes count, as we learned in the United States so vividly so recently, we must not only feel informed enough to be willing to walk into the voting booth (not always an easy task as the issues become ever more complicated and our politicians' explanations ever more simplified into sound bites); we must also be able to understand the ballot once we are in the booth. The genre of the ballot question makes it difficult to understand what is at issue. Typical ballot questions combine explanatory statements with legislative amendments, but the explanatory statements can rarely explain enough to enable the voter to understand the amendment. Even the physical layout of the ballot, we have learned, entails specialized but unstated knowledge, and good citizens must decipher where to punch, mark, and pull, and with what definiteness and strength. To mark a ballot seems a simple thing, but the community of election commissioners actually brings specialist knowledge to the interpretation of those ballots—knowledge not explained in the ballot genre. The specialists know what a chad is, for one thing, and understand what the machines will and will not count, how much must be punched for a vote to register. The specialists know that drawing a line through one candidate's name will render that ballot invalid, while the good citizen might know only that drawing such a line is a known way to register displeasure. Even without getting into the language of provisions, often unintelligible to even the most educated voters, the ballot as a genre includes complications and presumptions that serve the interests of the specialist creators but not of the nonspecialist users.

In fact, much of our civic lives involves genres that come out of a community of specialists, whether lawyers, legislators, or government employees. Doing our civic duty depends as much on our ability to understand and use genres accurately as it does on our willingness to be good citizens. Yet the difficulty remains of community-embedded genres producing action by nonmembers

131

CHAPTER TWO: WHAT IS THE "RHETORICAL SITUATION" AND WHY SHOULD I CARE ABOUT IT?

of that community. Although the borders of communities are more permeable and fluid than the community metaphor suggests, clashes of knowledge and perspective still result when specialists and nonspecialists meet, clashes that have consequences in terms of how participants interact, perform their actions, and produce certain effects in the world.

The inclusion of nonspecialists is vital to the US judicial system, with the usually final decisions made not by all-knowing judges but by everyday citizens. Instructions to juries are designed to explain enough of the law so that a jury of peers can render an appropriate verdict. But jury instructions are written by lawyers, with their details hammered out by lawyers and the judge arguing privately, away from the ears of the jurors who must use them. By the time the judge gives a jury instructions, those instructions contain presumptions, implications, specifications known well by the law community but unknown to the unsuspecting jury members. The genre thus has a significance for the legal community that it does not have for the jurors. As a result, juries do not and cannot interpret the genre the way its creators intended, as lawyers would, and cannot render verdicts that follow those instructions fully and accurately, thus resulting in significant consequences, particularly for defendants.

One recent example turned on a single word (see Mathis). Michael Sharp was convicted of child endangerment in 1999 after he held on to his three-week-old daughter while police were trying to arrest him on an outstanding warrant. His girlfriend and a police officer testified that he seemed to be holding the baby carefully. Before long, Sharp handed the child to officers. At his trial, the judge in the case instructed the jury to find Sharp guilty if they found he had put the girl in a situation where her "body or health might be injured or endangered." The jury rendered a verdict of guilty. The problem, according to Sharp's lawyer and an appeals court, is that the word "might" has a different meaning in law than in common usage. The word has a different weight to each party; it is material in different ways. Courts define "might" as saying an action was probable, not merely possible. Since the jury instructions did not explain the court's meaning of "might," the appeals court overturned the verdict and ordered a new trial. As the appeals court judge wrote in his decision, "There is a very real possibility, especially under the facts of this case, that the jury would have returned a different verdict had the term 'might' been properly defined" (qtd. in Mathis). With the community of lawyers defining "might" differently than do nonmembers, can instructions to a jury ever specify the law sufficiently to let the jury do its job according to that law? The genre of jury instructions has a perhaps insurmountable task in needing to tell citizens unaware of legal technicalities how to follow the relevant law in making their decision, a task of making community members out of nonmembers, of getting nonmembers to enact and reproduce the agendas of a specialist community.

This difficulty is especially troubling in the particular jury instructions I have examined in detail, the instructions to a jury in the sentencing phase of a capital case—instructions to a jury deciding whether to sentence a defendant to death. Originally called in to examine potential bias in the pattern of instructions (a set of approved jury instructions that judges commonly use), I eventually worked to rewrite those instructions in order to make them clearer to an ordinary jury. What I discovered is that no matter how much I elaborated, no matter how many assumptions I made explicit, I could not capture in those instructions all the information that the lawyers considered relevant to the jury's task. Clarifying for the jury's purposes clashed with adhering to legal purposes. What seemed a reasonably straightforward genre when I began proved to be a genre mired in its specialized community's expectations and potentially misleading to its nonspecialized users. What was material to me and to juries was not material to lawyers and judges, and vice versa.

Part of the difficulty when specialized communities write to nonspecialist users lies in technical language, a difficulty commonly recognized and often addressed through defining key terms, but most of the difficulty comes from differences of interest and value that definitions cannot control. In capital cases, two key terms are "aggravating" and "mitigating," for juries must weigh aggravating and mitigating circumstances. These terms are so central to the law as well as to the task at hand that no definition or rewording could capture the full technical meaning of these terms to the courts. In addition, each potential juror may have a private sense of the value of these terms. But even greater difficulties arise from the use of common terms to serve specialist interests. The list of aggravating circumstances from the *Pattern Instructions* for the state of Kansas (a set of instructions modeled on existing instructions from other states) itemizes eight possible aggravating circumstances. Some of those circumstances appear to be matters of fact, though surely still contestable: that the defendant authorized someone else to commit the crime, that the defendant was imprisoned for a felony at the time, or that the defendant committed the crime for money, to avoid arrest, or to silence a witness. Other possible aggravating circumstances, though, require jurors to assess not only whether facts were proven but also the degree of seriousness of the crime: that the defendant previously "inflicted great bodily harm, disfigurement, dismemberment, or death on another," that the defendant knowingly "created a great risk of death to more than one person," or that the defendant "committed the crime in an especially heinous, atrocious or cruel manner." "The term 'heinous,'" the instructions continue, "means extremely wicked or shockingly evil; 'atrocious' means outrageously wicked and vile; and 'cruel' means pitiless or designed to inflict a high degree of pain, utter indifference to, or enjoyment of the sufferings of others." The list of aggravating circumstances is full of gradable words with no standard of comparison: "great" bodily harm and risk of death, "serious" mental anguish or physical abuse. Mitigating circumstances similarly depend on judgments of "significant" histories, "extreme" disturbances or distress, "relatively minor" participation, or "substantial" domination and impairment. When I asked about providing some standard or clarifying what is legally defensible, I was told that there is no legally tested standard and so none could be provided.

In fact, the greatness or seriousness of the crime is precisely what the jury is being asked to evaluate. Yet nowhere do the instructions say that. Rather, the jury instructions follow the legal community's need for events to be based in fact rather than value, so circumstances are treated as either existing or not existing. That perspective appears explicitly in the next instruction about burden of proof: the State must prove "that there are one or more aggravating circumstances and that they are not outweighed by any mitigating circumstances." In fact, however, to decide whether an aggravating circumstance exists requires deciding whether the action was great, serious, or, in perhaps the most notorious language, "heinous." For a jury to decide that a crime was "especially heinous" and thus that an aggravating circumstance exists, the jury is told to define "heinous" as "extremely wicked or shockingly evil." Here in the courtroom, in the setting of this specialized community based in logic and reasoning, a jury of peers is told to "determine" and "consider" "evidence" that will allow them to decide "beyond a reasonable doubt" that a crime was "extremely wicked or shockingly evil." The clash of specialized standards with common values produces a very confused genre, not to mention jury. The material language of the genre produces material consequences, for the defendant as well as for the jury's actions and the legal community's use of those actions.

One final example from these jury instructions reveals the subtle form this clash between members and nonmembers of specialist communities can take and how it materializes in actual practices, languages exchanges, and relations. In the instruction just examined, the jury is to decide that "there are one or more aggravating circumstances and that they are not outweighed by any mitigating circumstances." The jury is not told how to weigh these circumstances but rather how not to weigh them:

FOCUS ON WRITING: WHAT COLLEGE STUDENTS WANT TO KNOW

In making the determination whether aggravating circumstances exist that are not outweighed by any mitigating circumstances, you should keep in mind that your decision should not be determined by the number of aggravating or mitigating circumstances that are shown to exist. (*Pattern* 56.00-F)

The negatives in these several instructions and the ones that follow compound, to a point that I believe most jurors would have difficulty interpreting: their decision rests on doubting (but not by counting) that some circumstances are not outweighed by others so that the defendant will not be sentenced to death. When I tried to rewrite these instructions to clarify and simplify them, though, I found that those negatives contained vital specialist presumptions. At one point, I suggested the wording, "In determining whether mitigating circumstances outweigh aggravating circumstances, you should not decide by counting the number of mitigating or aggravating circumstances that you believe exist." That revision failed to capture several legal details. Of course, it is not a matter of the jurors believing circumstances exist; they have to be shown to exist, though elsewhere jurors can be persuaded that they exist. (Note again the insistence on circumstances simply existing or not, without acknowledging that the jury must evaluate the severity of the act.) Most seriously of all, the lawyers told me, I had changed the burden of proof. The prosecutors must show that aggravating circumstances exist, first of all, and second that they are not outweighed by mitigating circumstances. The defense does not have to prove that mitigating circumstances outweigh aggravating circumstances. To serve their own purposes, jurors might well begin deliberations by weighing mitigating against aggravating (being careful now not to count), without realizing that they were shifting the burden of proof. Because the materiality of any language depends on how different communities are invested in it, language is considered to be transparent both by jurors and by judges and lawyers. Written by lawyers, the language of jury instructions assumes that the jurors will, like the lawyers, know what is important and know what to do, that the genre will enable nonmembers to behave as members would.

No amount of explication, definition, or simplification can capture the specialized legal knowledge required for a just and fair decision, as defined by the court system. The legal community—and our society—needs these distinctions, established by law and precedent, to be maintained. The genre of jury instructions is meant to guide jurors in following that law. Yet the complexity of the law, the technical nature of its precedents, and, in short, the embeddedness

135

CHAPTER TWO: WHAT IS THE "RHETORICAL SITUATION" AND WHY SHOULD I CARE ABOUT IT?

of the genre in its community make it impossible for nonspecialists to understand fully as a specialist would, no matter how well-written, detailed, or rhetorically sophisticated the jury instructions.

Leading to the linguistic and technical complexity of jury instructions is the rhetorical complexity of the situation. Lawyers and judges are in the position of maintaining the law while needing to achieve their goals through the actions of others, the relatively ignorant jurors. Jurors are in the position of deciding another human being's fate based on society's values, while being told to disregard their instincts unless they conform to the law, a law they do not fully understand. The genre of jury instructions attempts to enact those behaviors, but, like all genres, its effects depend on the actions of politically and morally interested people. Jurors must somehow address or respond to the jury instructions, giving those instructions material consequence, but jurors can respond by acting against those instructions. This reality is revealed most explicitly in the concept of jury nullification, in which individual jurors vote not according to the evidence and the law but according to their beliefs about the rightness of the law, the oppression of the defendant's group, or other beliefs and values not represented in the jury instructions or the facts of the case. Even without such explicit political motivation or deliberateness, jurors often decide in ways that may or may not match even the jurors' understanding of the instructions they received. The most immediately significant genre in a capital case is the verdict, a genre with real consequences. Jury instructions try to influence that verdict, but their effectiveness depends not just on the legal community's ability to convey important specialist information but also on the jury's ability and willingness to conform to their expected role. Jury instructions also try to influence future legal actions, whether appeals of this particular case or future similar cases. The material effects of the genre for the legal community cannot be captured in the jury's actions or the verdict alone. Although designed to transcend the narrow interests of the legal community, jury instructions also return to that community, becoming another potential precedent and more specialist knowledge.

Tax forms, ballot questions, jury instructions—all genres designed precisely to bring specialist and nonspecialist communities together—all function in complex linguistic, informational, and rhetorical situations. All genres exist through and depend on human action, so these community-spanning genres, too, depend on the cooperation of participants from multiple communities, on people accepting the roles the genres assign to them and on being able to carry out the tasks expected of them. Since people in fact often have conflicting interests and motivations, the effects of such genres may be unpredictable. Lawyers and judges, for example, surely want a fair and just verdict, but their community's values also emphasize winning, not being overturned on appeal, and building reputations as well as bank accounts. The general populace from which jurors come also wants a fair and just verdict, but that desire interacts with popular notions of fairness and rightness and with individual moral differences, ideas about social injustices, and experiences with the legal system, as well as with concerns for a speedy return to jurors' regular lives and paychecks.

The communal agendas of those who create genres may conflict with the interests of those who use them—users who would ideally reproduce the ideologies and agendas of the legal community, but who do not. To say that the genre of jury instructions—and other similar genres—simply cross community borders is to simplify the complex interaction of individuals and groups, motives and agendas, and to ignore the conflicting consequences of one genre serving different groups. To understand more fully these genres is to understand more fully how the generic materialities are their uses-in-contexts, with serious effects on people's lives.

Using genre to access community: The personal medical history genre as "form of life"

Anis Bawarshi

As Bruce Herzberg describes it, the concept of discourse community is based on the assumption that "language use in a group is a form of social behavior, that discourse is a means of maintaining and extending the group's knowledge and of initiating new members into the group, and that discourse is epistemic or constitutive of the group's knowledge" (qtd. in Swales 21). Hence the idea of discourse community is built on the premise that what we know and do is connected to the language we use. Such an understanding acknowledges the materiality of language, but does not necessarily give us access and insight into the complex motives, relations, commitments, and consequences that accompany the use of language to get things done in specific situations, as Devitt's examination of jury instructions describes.

Analyzing genres within their lived contexts reveals to students, teachers, and researchers the material strength of those communities and their power over members and nonmembers alike. Whether examining legal, medical, or pedagogical genres, genre study gives us specific access to the sites of language use that make up communities, in all their complexity. When we use genre analysis as ethnomethodological technique, we not only gain access into communities, but also begin to recognize how "lived textualities" interact with and transform "lived experiences." Such recognition becomes especially significant when we are teaching students how to use language to participate more knowledgeably and critically in various sites of language use. Using the genre of the Patient Medical History Form as an example, I demonstrate how genre analysis gives access to the workings of discourse communities in a way that renders the idea of a discourse community a more tangible, helpful concept for teachers, students, and researchers.

Attention to the Patient Medical History Form (PMHF), a commonly used medical genre, suggests how focusing on a specific textual genre helps us to identify a discourse community by relating it to a specific site of interpersonal activity that most of us have experienced. The PMHF is a good way to understand something about how doctors function and how they treat us as patients. At the same time, it also serves to show that the community is not just a backdrop to language behavior, but a growing, moving environment that includes texts and speech as its constituents, just as people are its members. We compose our discourse communities as we write and speak within them. And genre is a key part of this process.

The idea of genre, despite the work of scholars in literary and rhetorical studies over the last few decades, is still more often than not understood as a transparent lens or conduit for classifying texts. The word *genre,* borrowed from French, means "sort" or "kind," and to study sorts or kinds of things is not thought to be as substantial as to study the things themselves. Genres appear to be transparent when they are understood as ways of classifying texts. But recent scholarship in genre theory has tried to dispel this view by stipulating genres to be language forms that have identifiable and changing roles in interpersonal relations and in larger collective contexts. One of the roots of the word genre is the Latin cognate *gener,* meaning to generate. This etymology suggests that genres *sort* and *generate.* Genres organize and generate the exchanges of language that characterize what we are referring to in this essay as discourse communities.

Carolyn R. Miller has defined genres as typified rhetorical ways of acting in recurring situations (159). Following Miller, Charles Bazerman defines genres as social actions. He writes:

> Genres are not just forms. Genres are forms of life, ways of being. They are frames for social action[, ...] locations within which meaning is constructed. Genres shape the thoughts we form and the communications by which we interact. Genres are the familiar places we go to create

intelligible communicative action with each other and the guideposts we use to explore the unfamiliar. (19)

To claim that genres are environments within which familiar social actions are rhetorically enacted is to understand them as language practices. David Russell calls them "*operationalized* social action[s]" (512) within which communicants come to know specific situations as they enact them in language practices. The extent to which genres organize and generate discourse communities appears vividly in the example of the physician's office. A physician's office might be considered a local discourse community and part of a wider one insofar as its members share language practices and have comparable purposes. These purposes are enacted in social relations that are partly marked by the PMHF, a genre that within the medical profession is one of its Wittgensteinian "forms of life." As patients we recognize this form on our first visit to a physician as one that solicits information regarding our physical data (sex, age, height, weight, and so on) as well as medical history, including prior and recurring physical conditions, past treatments, and a description of current physical symptoms. Included in the genre is also a request for insurance carrier information and then a consent-to-treat statement and a legal release statement, which patients must sign. The form is at once a patient record, a legal document, and an element in a bureaucracy, helping the doctor treat the patient and presumably protecting the doctor from potential lawsuits.

But these are not the genre's only functions. The PMHF also helps organize and generate the social and rhetorical environments within which patients and doctors speak to one another. For example, the fact that the genre is mainly concerned with a patient's physical symptoms suggests that one can isolate physical symptoms and treat them with little to no reference to the patient's state of mind and the effect that state of mind might have on these symptoms. This genre assumes that body and mind are separate and also helps to perpetuate this belief. In so doing, the PMHF reflects Western notions of medicine, notions that are rhetorically naturalized and reproduced by the genre and that are in turn embodied in the way the doctor recognizes, interacts with, and treats the patient as a synecdoche of his or her physical symptoms. For example, it is not uncommon for doctors and nurses to say "I treated a knee injury today" or "The ear infection is in room 3" when referring to patients. The PMHF is at work on the individual, urging the conversion of a person into a patient (an embodied self) prior to his or her meeting with the doctor at the same time as it is at work on the doctor, preparing him or her to meet the individual as an

139

CHAPTER TWO: WHAT IS THE "RHETORICAL SITUATION" AND WHY SHOULD I CARE ABOUT IT?

embodied "patient." In this way, the genre is a site for the exchange of language within which participants influence one another and identify their discourse communities. The mental state of patients may not be considered *material* to the injury or illness; conversely, the form tends to discourage patients' reporting of mental or emotional circumstances of injury and illness, with the result that they may be incompletely or inaccurately treated.

The PMHF is one of several related genres that constitute a community one could call "the physician's office." Each of these genres—which could include greetings, oral symptom descriptions, prescriptions, referrals, physical gestures, and explanatory metaphors—is a form of life that is part of other social practices (relations between doctors and patients, nurses and doctors, doctors and other doctors, doctors and pharmacists, and so on), all of which add up to what Amy Devitt has called "genre sets." As such a set, the physician's office is a multigenre community constituted by several interconnected genres, some of which may represent conditions of social conflict. Members of this community "play" various language games: they have multiple ways of identifying themselves and relating to others within the community. In this way genres help counter the idealized view of discourse communities as discursive utopias constituted by homogeneity and consensus. As Bazerman notes, "[G]enres, as perceived and used by individuals, become part of their regularized social relations, communicative landscape, and cognitive organization" (22). These social relations, communicative landscapes, and cognitive organizations, however, are always shifting, always multiple, as they are enacted by individuals within different genres. We can think of genres as the operational sites of discourse communities.

Teachers, students, and researchers gain ethnomethodological access to discourse communities through genre analysis, which enables them to observe how and why individuals use language in specific settings to make specific practices possible. Recognizing the presence of genres helps us to recognize the palpability and complexity of our discourse communities, to reduce their abstract, symbolic status, thereby making discourse communities more visible and accessible to ethnographic inquiry.

The following example, from the research of Anthony Pare, suggests the materialization of genre and its value for ethnographic inquiry. Pare records a portion of a conversation between a social work student, Michael, and his supervisor. The supervisor is responding to Michael's draft of an assessment report, a typical social work genre:

FOCUS ON WRITING: WHAT COLLEGE STUDENTS WANT TO KNOW

That's right. So you wrote here, "I contacted." You want to see it's coming from the worker, not you as Michael, but you as the worker. So when I'm sometimes in Intake and [working] as the screener, I write in my Intake Notes "the screener inquired about." ... So it becomes less personal. You begin to put yourself in the role of the worker, not "I, Michael." [I]t's a headset; it's a beginning. And even in your evaluations ... the same thing: as opposed to "I," it's "worker," and when we do a CTMSP for placement for long-term care, "the worker." So it positions us, I think. It's not me, it's my role; and I'm in the role of professional doing this job. (67)

In this example, we notice the extent to which the genre becomes the site for the exchange of language and social interaction. The student, Michael, is learning to "play a language game," the genre of the "assessment report." This exchange between social work student and supervisor takes place within the genre, a genre that constitutes the social roles and material relations of social workers—roles as impersonal observers and "professionals"—thus constituting, in part, the community of social work.

It is in the sum of exchanges such as this one, exchanges constituted by the various and sometimes conflicting genres used in different settings, that individuals compose in and compose discourse communities.

Accessing communities through the genre of ethnography: Exploring a pedagogical genre
Mary Jo Reiff

In "The Life of Genre, the Life in the Classroom," Charles Bazerman describes genres as the "road maps" that student writers consult as they navigate "the symbolic landscape" (19). As typical responses to repeated social situations, genres are rhetorical maps that chart familiar or frequently traveled communicative paths and provide guideposts as writers adapt to unfamiliar academic terrain and study parts of society beyond the classroom. Thus understood, genre analysis is well suited for use in ethnographic approaches to writing pedagogy. Exploring the implications of genre for rhetorical instruction, Carolyn R. Miller observes, "For the student, genres serve as keys to understanding how to participate in the actions of a community" (165). Since genres embed and enact a group's purposes, values, and assumptions, they can illuminate a community's discursive behaviors; however, the question of how students gain entrance to and participate in this discursive landscape remains a source of debate.

141

CHAPTER TWO: WHAT IS THE "RHETORICAL SITUATION" AND WHY SHOULD I CARE ABOUT IT?

Taking up the issue of genre analysis in writing instruction, Aviva Freedman poses the following question: "Can the complex web of social, cultural and rhetorical features to which genres respond be explicated at all, or in such a way that can be useful to learners?" (225). Freedman objects to studying genres outside the contexts in which they are found, abstracting them from living situations. Her concern is shared by David Bleich, who argues that genres—like all language use—are not eligible for study once they are considered to be independent of their contexts of use: "[T]he process of study lies always *within* the language-using society. There is no sense in which the language one tries to understand can be thought of as located outside the living situation in which the thinker (who is all the while using the language) is working" (122). Studying genres within the actual contexts of their use—within real human groups—requires "insider" research (Freedman 234), a type of research that can be carried out through the use of ethnography. With its emphasis on participant/observation and on hands-on attention to communities, ethnography enables students to examine communicative actions within living situations and to see first-hand how communities use genres to carry out social actions and agendas.

To understand genres as situated actions, Miller has advocated an ethno-methodological approach, one that "seeks to explicate the knowledge that practice creates" (155)—knowledge rooted in the materiality of circumstances and conditions of actual use of genres. Similarly, Bazerman has argued that "[b]y forging closer links with the related [enterprise] of [...] ethnomethodology, genre analysis can play" a major role in investigating communication within social organizations (23). I consider how ethnomethodology as an academic research method and ethnography as a genre of writing that is particularly useful in writing pedagogy can provide more authentic language tasks in classrooms and can give students better access to contexts of language use beyond the classroom.

Certainly ethnography has become an increasing presence in composition as a research method and a pedagogy. However, Wendy Bishop and others distinguish between the general research method of ethnography and the more focused ethnographic writing research, which usually explores particular sites of literacy or particular literacy practices. Clarifying this distinction, Beverly Moss notes, "While ethnography in general is concerned with describing and analyzing a culture, ethnography in composition studies is [...] concerned more narrowly with communicative behavior or the interrelationship of language and culture" (156). Ethnography in composition, particularly as a pedagogical

FOCUS ON WRITING: WHAT COLLEGE STUDENTS WANT TO KNOW

approach, is concerned with the general as well as the particular: with the lived experience or behavior of a culture (as in anthropology or sociology) and with the way in which this behavior manifests itself rhetorically.

If ethnographies are understood as studies of communities and their social actions and genres taken to be rhetorical manifestations or maps of a community's actions, then genre analysis is an especially helpful path in ethnographic methodology. In order to investigate a community's social motives and actions, student ethnographers can examine the uses of language associated with these actions (the group's spoken and written genres) by gathering samples of the genre and analyzing what the rhetorical patterns reveal about the community—its purposes, its participants, and its values, beliefs, and ideologies. Ethnography is both a genre (a research narrative) and a mode of genre analysis—a research methodology used to grasp cultural beliefs and behaviors, often through the examination of genres, which are "frames for social action" (Bazerman 19). In "Observing Genres in Action: Towards a Research Methodology," Anthony Pare and Graham Smart propose how ethnographic inquiry and genre analysis work together. Understanding genre as "a rhetorical strategy enacted within a community," they say that "a full appreciation of the part that [social] roles play in the production and use of generic texts can only be gained by observing an organization's drama of interaction, the interpersonal dynamics that surround and support certain texts" (149). Ethnographic observation of a community that foregrounds genre analysis allows researchers to explore more fully the complexity of the group's social roles and actions, actions that constitute the community's repeated rhetorical strategies, or genres.

While students don't have extended periods to carry out ethnographic studies, they can carry out what Bishop has labeled "mini-ethnographies," smaller-scale studies that explore particular literacy events or local phenomena in a community. Marilyn Chapman, in an essay on the role of genre in writing instruction, lists three main teaching interests with regard to genre: "*learning genres,* or widening students' genre repertoires; *learning about genres,* or fostering awareness [...] and *learning through genres,* or using genres as tools for thinking and learning in particular situations" (473). Using ethnography in the classroom would address these goals and would have students learn one research genre (ethnography), while they simultaneously use ethnographic techniques to learn about and through other genres. As a result, incorporating ethnography into the classroom ensures that all three of the above-interrelated goals are met, giving students access to the material practices of both the classroom community and communities beyond the classroom.

143

CHAPTER TWO: WHAT IS THE "RHETORICAL SITUATION" AND WHY SHOULD I CARE ABOUT IT?

With regard to the first goal, when students are assigned ethnographies, they learn a new genre to add to their repertoire, a research genre that carries with it particular purposes, participants, and agendas. According to Moss, the main purpose of this genre is "to gain a comprehensive view of the social interactions, behaviors, and beliefs of a community or a social group" (155). This purpose casts student researchers, as users of the genre, into dual roles as both participants in the community and observers of the community's interactions. Moss compares the ethnographer to a photographer who both "takes pictures of the community" and is "in the picture at the same time" (154). The process of inquiry and first-hand participant-observation entailed by this genre requires that students engage in several rhetorical strategies: critical and reflective thinking (when deciding upon what actions and artifacts to capture through pictures); what Clifford Geertz called "thick description" (when developing the pictures so that the details are vibrant and the images come to life); an awareness of the multiple audiences who will view the pictures; and, as someone who is also "in the picture," development of an ethos as an expert or producer of knowledge. These rhetorical strategies related to purpose, audience, and persona give rise to a number of rhetorical features and conventions. In order to address an audience and create a credible ethos, writers might include a description of the data-collection methods, an explanation of the data, and a discussion of their implications. To create a representation of lived experience, students might incorporate details, dialogue, and direct quotations from community participants. Students learn a new genre as they employ patternings of language and rhetorical strategies to create an empirically grounded representation of social realities.

The second goal, learning about genres and fostering genre awareness, is also accomplished through the use of ethnography. Since the main goal of an ethnographer, according to Moss, is to gain "increased insight into the ways in which language communities work" (170), it follows that the oral and written genres of groups will play a central role in the investigation of the social context of language use. Geertz defines ethnographies as "interpretations of interpretations" (9), meaning that students must study the genres that community members use to interpret their contexts in order to fully understand and themselves interpret the community.

For example, Susan, a pre-law student in my advanced composition class, carried out a mini-ethnography on the law community. In order to find out how novice members of the community become socialized to the values, beliefs, and knowledge of the community, Susan considered genres such as opinions,

FOCUS ON WRITING: WHAT COLLEGE STUDENTS WANT TO KNOW

wills, deeds, and contracts; she focused her study on the genre of case briefs. She collected samples of constitutional law briefs, which, she recognized, "illustrated the legal community's shared value of commitment to tradition, as well as the need for a standard and convenient form of communicating important and complex legal concepts." While Susan also conducted interviews and observed lawyers in a small local firm, the genre analysis was the focus of her study, which helped to teach others about the habits and traditions of the law community. She learned about the generic features of case briefs, such as the technical terminology, rigid format, and formal style, and she became more aware of how these formal practices reflected and reinscribed the goals of the community. Recognizing that all the briefs follow the same format of presenting sections labeled "case information," "facts of the case," "procedural history," "issue," "holding," and "court reasoning," she surmised that "[e]ven the rigid structure of the format can help with our analysis by suggesting the community's emphasis on logic and order, which are two esteemed values of the profession." For students like Susan, using genre as a site for ethnographic inquiry cultivates a consciousness of the rhetorical strategies that characterize the daily work of a specific kind of professional community. By learning a community's language through its genres, students then have a more realistic sense of what it is to be a member of the community.

The third genre-related teaching interest is learning through genres, using genres to think about and understand particular situations. Ethnography gives students experience with genre analysis and with how research processes change received genres of reporting knowledge. As ethnographers seek to describe a community, they use various genres for research. Before beginning the study, students may write letters to seek permission to observe groups, or they might write proposals for their research or research plans and agendas. During the research, they use several genres such as field notes, journals or activity logs, project chronologies or summaries, progress reports, interview transcripts, even maps. When the research is completed, they may try to write in other genres that the situation warrants, like thank-you notes, self-assessments, peer assessments, or abstracts. Class time might be spent discussing the genre of the interview or the different purposes of descriptive versus analytic field notes. These genres are resources for supporting or extending thinking. Students learn a research genre that depends on genre analysis; they also learn to use, adapt, and possibly change a variety of genres during the different processes of inquiry.

When students carry out ethnographies, they become researchers who are also active social figures participating in and observing how people integrate

145

CHAPTER TWO: WHAT IS THE "RHETORICAL SITUATION" AND WHY SHOULD I CARE ABOUT IT?

their language genres with their wider collective purposes. Shifting the usual teacher/student relationship, students assume the role of investigators who are learning to speak from their own authority as researchers. As a result, classrooms become, in part, research sites at which all members are investigating, teaching, and learning. The research genre of ethnography creates a culture of inquiry, with language and genre the foci that lead to combined knowledge of rhetoric, collective values, and the broader purposes of different communities.

Students in these classrooms also help to create their own community while observing "meaningful discourse in authentic contexts," thus accomplishing what Freedman defines as the necessary criteria for learning genres: "exposure to written discourse" combined with "immersion in the relevant contexts" (247). Student ethnographers are able to study the uses of language and genre within real contexts, situations in which "speakers are alive, functioning, changing and interacting" (Bleich 120). Because ethnography is both a research genre (which functions for academic communities) and an approach to genre analysis (which explores communicative actions in groups outside the classroom), ethnographic work in class enables students to compose communities while composing in communities.

Works Cited

Bazerman, Charles. "The Life of Genre, the Life in the Classroom." *Genre and Writing: Issues, Arguments, Alternatives.* Ed. Wendy Bishop and Hans Ostrom. Portsmouth, NH: Boynton, 1997. 19–26.

Bishop, Wendy. *Ethnographic Writing Research: Writing It Down, Writing It Up, and Reading It.* Portsmouth, NH: Boynton, 1999.

Bizzell, Patricia. *Academic Discourse and Critical Consciousness.* Pittsburgh: U of Pittsburgh P, 1992.

Bleich, David. "The Materiality of Language and the Pedagogy of Exchange." *Pedagogy* I (2001): 117–41.

Chapman, Marilyn L. "Situated, Social, Active: Rewriting Genre in the Elementary Classroom." *Written Communication* 16.4 (1999): 469–90.

Devitt, Amy J. "Intertextuality in Tax Accounting: Generic, Referential, and Functional." *Textual Dynamics of the Professions: Historical and Contemporary Studies of Writing in Professional Communities.* Ed. Charles Bazerman and James Paradis. Madison: U of Wisconsin P, 1991. 335–57.

Freedman, Aviva. "Show and Tell? The Role of Explicit Teaching in the Learning of New Genres." *Research in the Teaching of English* 27 (1993): 222–51.

Geertz, Clifford. *The Interpretation of Cultures.* New York: Basic, 1973.

Harris, Joseph. A Teaching Subject: Composition since 1966. Englewood Cliffs, NJ: Prentice, 1997.

Kent, Thomas. "On the Very Idea of a Discourse Community." CCC 42 (1991): 425–45.

Leverenz, Carrie Shively. "Peer Response in the Multicultural Composition Classroom: Dissensus—A Dream (Deferred)." JAC 14 (1994): 167–86.

Mathis, Joel. "Appeal Brings Defining Moment." *Lawrence Journal-World* 4 Nov. 2000: B1.

Miller, Carolyn R. "Genre as Social Action." *Quarterly Journal of Speech* 70 (1984): 151–67. Rpt. in *Genre and the New Rhetoric*. Ed. Aviva Freedman and Peter Medway. London: Taylor, 1994. 23–42.

Moss, Beverly. "Ethnography and Composition: Studying Language at Home." *Methods and Methodologies in Composition Research*. Ed. Gesa Kirsch and Patricia Sullivan. Carbondale: Southern Illinois UP, 1992. 153–71.

Pare, Anthony. "Genre and Identity: Individuals, Institutions, Ideology." *The Rhetoric and Ideology of Genre: Strategies for Stability and Change*. Ed. Richard M. Coe, Lorelei Lingard, and Tatiana Teslenko. Cresskill, NJ: Hampton, 2002. 57–71.

Pare, Anthony, and Graham Smart. "Observing Genres in Action: Towards a Research Methodology." *Genre and the New Rhetoric*. Ed. Aviva Freedman and Peter Medway. Bristol: Taylor, 1994. 146–54.

Pattern Instructions for Kansas-Criminal 3d. Sect. 56.00-B-H. 2000.

Russell, David R. "Rethinking Genre in School and Society: An Activity Theory Analysis." *Written Communication* 14 (1997): 504–54.

Schryer, Catherine. "Records as Genre." *Written Communication* 10 (1993): 200–34.

Swales, John. *Genre Analysis: English in Academic and Research Settings.* Cambridge: Cambridge UP, 1990.

Trimbur, John. "Consensus and Difference in Collaborative Learning." *College English* 51 (1989): 602–16.

147

CHAPTER TWO: WHAT IS THE "RHETORICAL SITUATION" AND WHY SHOULD I CARE ABOUT IT?

JESSIE CANNIZZO'S "POWERLESS PERSUASION: INEFFECTIVE ARGUMENTATION PLAGUES THE CLEAN EATING COMMUNITY" (2016)

Why I included it

Cannizzo's analysis offers an excellent example of interpreting everyday language in terms of rhetorical implications that we may not typically notice; in this case, she focuses on the term "clean eating." Cannizzo also complicates notions of discourse communities while considering patterns of communication common in online settings.

This essay is a good model for what you might do in a rhetorical analysis, as Cannizzo joins a scholarly conversation, pulling together secondary research with her own textual analysis.

Background

Jessie Cannizzo wrote this paper for a first-year composition course I taught. The assignment asked students to analyze an online discourse community in terms of effective and ineffective—or productive and unproductive—approaches to conflict. Some of Cannizzo's sources were assigned to the entire class and she chose to use them because they provided a helpful context for her analysis. Other sources were ones she found to specifically address the subject of her analysis. She was writing for our class yet shaped her analysis to focus on a subject that interested her.

CONNECT

As you read, consider responding to the following questions to help you process the material.

1. Does the "clean eating community" Cannizzo describes meet the criteria of a discourse community as defined by John Swales?

2. Cannizzo offers reasons why online communication may be ineffective in times of conflict. In the situation she analyzes, the commenters do not know each other in real life. Can you think of an online conflict among people who knew each other? Were the dynamics better or not?

3. Do you participate in online conversations that are similar to the one Cannizzo describes? Why or why not?

4. What audiences might potentially be interested in Cannizzo's analysis?

Reading hints and vocab terms

As you read, notice the way Cannizzo uses the research and ideas of other scholars to provide a full context for her analysis of YouTube comments. She uses headings to help readers follow the various sections of her essay. She also follows a common structure of a scholarly research paper: An introduction, a review of secondary research, a "Methods" section, her own "Findings," a discussion of those findings, and a conclusion.

Cannizzo, Jessie. "Powerless Persuasion: Ineffective Argumentation Plagues the Clean Eating Community." ENG 120 Critical Writing, Pace University, Fall 2016.

FOOD IS MORE than just fuel. Rather, food has come to shape our culture and identity and is a dominating force on our thoughts and actions. With the prominent status of food in everyday life, proper nutrition is a major source of debate. The emergence of new diet trends sparks heated discussion within the healthy eating community. The clean eating movement is one that has generated much controversy amongst health-conscious individuals. The internet and social media have supported the rise of clean eating, as well as opposition to it. Numerous blogs and YouTube channels are dedicated to the benefits of clean eating and tips on how to achieve this healthy lifestyle. As many advocates have shared the specifics of their diet in "What I Eat in a Day" videos on YouTube, the comments section has become a battleground for followers of this movement. Analysis of these comments has shown that many commentators are encouraged to share their perspective by an ethical responsibility. Despite moral intentions, these interactions in the YouTube comments section are often ineffective in that commentators resort to personal attacks on character and make ignorant statements. These clean-eating controversies between commentators shed light on the dynamic of online conflict and the qualities of effective and ineffective argumentation in relation to ethical issues.

Clean Eating and Food Rhetoric

Though the term "clean eating" does not have a set definition, it typically emphasizes the importance of natural foods (fruits, vegetables, etc.) and advises against processed food, preservatives and additives, and added sugar (Troscianko). There are, however, some divisions within the clean eating community over the consumption of meat, dairy, and gluten products, as well as the proper caloric intake and ratio of fats, carbs, and proteins. Generally speaking, advocates of clean eating express the idea that this way of eating is not a "diet"; rather it is considered a "lifestyle." The term "clean eating" has been constructed to have a positive connotation, as it is associated with the terms "good, pure, light, simple, natural, raw, bare." The term also implies that foods that do not meet the above criteria can be categorized as "bad, contaminated, heavy, complicated, unnatural, processed, clothed" (Troscianko). This propaganda put forth by the clean eating movement contributes to a mindset in which "notions of clean and dirty are inextricably tied up with notions of right and wrong" (Anderson). Eating clean is

149

CHAPTER TWO: WHAT IS THE "RHETORICAL SITUATION" AND WHY SHOULD I CARE ABOUT IT?

elevated to a position in which adherence to this diet constitutes moral purity or superiority. Clean eating has consequently developed into a doctrine, rather than a simple guideline for nutritious eating and living.

The rhetoric used by the clean eating movement portrays eating as an identification of character and morality. Eating has become a politicized activity. In response to the influence of the food industry in shaping consumption patterns through marketing, many have come to view consumer responsibility in a new light (Grey 309; Portman 1). Opposition to the food industry manifests itself in an attempt to create an alternate food culture. Consumers take upon themselves a moral duty of dismissing the food industry's messages and seeking out "an ethical and sustainable manner" of eating (Grey 319).

The idea of a moral responsibility toward animals has been a primary factor in the debate on clean eating. Since the definition of clean eating is not explicitly stated and thus not widely agreed upon, there are several branches within the clean eating discourse community. Veganism is a major topic of debate amongst clean eaters, as there is no general consensus on whether or not consumption of animal products is considered "clean" (Anderson). Aside from the issue of the health benefits or detriments of consuming meat and dairy, vegans often take on an ethical standpoint in regard to consumption of animal products. Instead of treating veganism as a personal choice, proponents of veganism aim to "bring about positive change in the current system of food productions and consumption" (Irvine 147). This brings many to try, usually unsuccessfully, to impose their viewpoints onto others.

Online Communities

Though people tend to believe that the internet promotes connection, in reality, it promotes isolation by separating people according to common viewpoint. People associate with others who share a similar perspective when they go on the internet and social media platforms (Seife 289). It becomes common for individuals to block out views that differ from their own, and as a result, the internet becomes a harbor for extreme, unwavering positions (292).

The online environment has also brought about a different relationship between author and audience. Writers have a duty to provide quality information in order to draw an audience, and thus aim for "honesty, accuracy, fairness, and accountability." In addressing an audience, writers are tasked with examining the potential consequences of their words and thus emphasize a respectful and open attitude toward readers (Duffy). Social media and the internet, however, have promoted a culture in which the importance of an author-audience relationship is largely diminished. In an online setting, those who share information and opinions have the potential to address massive audiences. Yet the ease of introducing and spreading ideas through the internet, as well as the impersonal nature of the online world, make it so that many fail to recognize the weight of their words.

Effective and Ineffective Persuasion

The general approach to argumentation is rather ineffective in that people merely aim to persuade others and combat opposition. This approach, in which people look to convert others to their ideas and win the argument, hinders people from understanding diverse viewpoints and reevaluating their own ideas (Knoblauch 245). Persuasion is associated with "dominance, change, and control over others," as people seek to be heard, but are unwilling to listen to others. Ineffective attempts to persuade often involve "quarreling, fighting, winning, defeating opposition, and working against others." In contrast, a more effective approach to argumentation includes "mature reasoning, civil conversation, mediation, and truth seeking" (250). Invitational rhetoric, an example of productive communication, promotes a shift in argumentation technique, in which people value understanding over persuasion (252). Similarly, the Rogerian argument is another alternative approach that encourages people to open their minds to the opposing position by viewing the issue from the lens of the other party (253). However, use of these methods in written communication, particularly in the online context, is a challenge.

Productive approaches to argumentation are rather uncommon in communications relating to clean eating. Along with the faulty dynamic of online communication, the presentation of clean eating largely contributes to the ineffectiveness of discussions. The unclear definition of "clean eating," particularly in regard to meat and dairy consumption, opens the door to conflict between members who associate themselves with this online community. Clean eating is a rigid diet, as it labels specific foods and food groups as "good" and "bad"; yet the specifics of the diet are open to interpretation. Though clean eating attracts a wide audience, many members of this audience prioritize their identity as a vegan, vegetarian, etc., which hinders their openness in argument (Carmichael 1). Consequently, narrow ideas of the ideal clean eating diet have emerged and have generated conflict, thus weakening the community.

A change in the way clean eating is presented would be necessary to encourage productive conversation and a greater sense of community. Advocates of clean eating should stress the complexity of diet and urge audiences to accept and respect the fact that different people have different physical needs and

151

CHAPTER TWO: WHAT IS THE "RHETORICAL SITUATION" AND WHY SHOULD I CARE ABOUT IT?

moral standpoints. No diet is one-size-fits-all; rather, individuals should question and look critically at the information presented online.

Methods

In exploring the role of ethics in effective and ineffective argumentation, I examined the comments on popular YouTube videos regarding clean eating. I focused on Cassey Ho's video titled "What I Eat in a Day (healthy slimming recipe ideas!)." Cassey Ho (creator of blogilates) is a key face of the clean eating movement who has developed a large fan community. Cassey has faced much controversy over the dieting ideas she discusses or suggests in her videos. In this video, Cassey simply narrates one day of eating, but her video raises many concerns amongst viewers. Although Cassey does not explicitly state that audiences should follow her specific diet, impressionable viewers who look up to her and consider her to be healthy and fit may wish to do so. "What I Eat in a Day" videos may be misinterpreted by audiences, who may be suffering from eating disorders and/or poor self-image and take on diets that do not suit their body's needs. Thus YouTubers who produce such videos should make clear that the ideal diet varies from person to person.

I went about my analysis of comments section discussions (arranged by "top comments") by pinpointing the issues addressed in interactions, exploring the methods of going about discussing these issues, and evaluating the effectiveness or ineffectiveness of arguments. In doing so, I found comments that presented a critical position on the ideas shared in Cassey's video and followed the comments that sparked ongoing exchanges between viewers, focusing in on interactions that related to veganism. Though Cassey Ho does not identify as a vegan, she has incorporated vegan recipes and diet plans to help attract vegans to the clean-eating lifestyle. However, numerous members of Cassey's vegan audience have taken issue with her consumption of animal products and have expressed this view in the comments.

I expected that interactions would be largely unproductive due to the polarization that thrives on the internet. Productive arguments tend to be limited in the online setting, for commentators often offer their own ideas but fail to take those of others into account. Furthermore, eating is a sensitive topic. People will likely not respond positively when their diet preference is denounced by strangers on the internet. Veganism, as a matter of ethical principles, leads to particularly volatile exchanges.

Findings

Several argumentative strategies are attempted in the discussions on veganism that are the subject of this analysis. Examples of the five noted types of arguments—emotional, rational, religious, combative, and conciliatory—are provided in the following excerpts of comments.

Type of Argument	Example[3]
Emotional	Vegan Friend: "No no no!! Eggs may be good for your body, but they are horribly cruel to chickens."
Rational	Vegan Friend: "Sea food is very harmful to the environment. I won't be giving any facts for you at the moment. Just go look it up; 'sea food environmental damage' should come up with some good websites, videos and books you can check out."
Religious	Sarah Liana: "God put animals here for a reason. They are meant to help us. They are meant to be eaten."
Combative	Melody Arte: "No one cares. Go away, vegan."
Conciliatory	Dara (addressing another commentator): "+Pixi Terrible Why are you so concerned for animals yet so critical and condescending toward human beings with feelings? I understand that you come from a good place and are trying to do the right thing by protecting the environment, but calling people 'murderers' for doing something you don't agree with is counterproductive. Try being NICE, maybe someone will ask YOU for advice on living a vegan lifestyle. :)"

Emotional, rational, and religious arguments are used in order to support a position. Many commentators have been found to employ multiple types of arguments in doing so. For example, Vegan Friend initiates the discussion on veganism by using both emotional and rational arguments. She begins her response by using pathos as she encourages compassion for the suffering chickens, but then incorporates reason in her argument by urging others to inform themselves on the issues and look at the facts. Commentator Sarah Liana also contributes her input to the discussion by invoking religion as she takes a conflicting position. Religious commentators include a notion of what God or a religious figure intends in their statements and have thus closed their minds off to other opinions.

Combative and conciliatory arguments are also used throughout the discussion. Both aim to put an end to the conflict, but do so through radically different approaches. Through combative arguments, commentators attempt

---

3   Examples are transcribed the way each one appeared online, so please excuse any errors of grammar, usage, or punctuation.

to limit discussion, often by targeting a certain group. In response to Vegan Friend's comment, some commentators, including Melody Arte, respond in a hostile and dismissive way. It can be assumed that commentators who behave in such a way are not open to opposing viewpoints and simply disregard the statements made by others. On the other hand, some attempt to restore peace and civility in discussions by urging others to respect diverse opinions. These commentators look to shift the course of the discussion from argumentative to constructive.

Effective and Ineffective Arguments

The five arguments explored above are determined to be ineffective because they do not prompt others to expand their mindset and/or change their approach to discussion. Emotional, rational, and religious arguments tend to merely reinforce a certain viewpoint. Commentators are not open to having their views challenged by others; rather, they simply wish to prove that their belief is correct, or in some cases, convert others to their ideas. Therefore, they engage in battles, instead of debates. Although these arguments are often rooted in ethical values, they may become aggressive or revert to insults. Combative arguments are also unproductive, for they merely exacerbate the conflict. People do not respond positively when they are dismissed as unworthy of being heard by others. Conciliatory arguments, despite good intentions, also do not achieve much success in online discussions. In the discussion studied, Vegan Friend responds to Dara's constructive criticism in a civil and respectful way: "BTW, thank you for the advice, Dara. I agree, but last time I tried being gentler, someone called me an ignorant kid with autism. I believe in a greater good and am willing to harm one or two meat eaters' feelings in order to pay the animals the respect and love they deserve." Though Vegan Friend acknowledges and appears to appreciate Dara's advice, she has no intention of changing her methods of argumentation. In fact, she continues to ridicule a statement made by another commentator. Though commentators may recognize that the way they are delivering their messages is immoral, they may be so tied to the morality of their message that they do not care to change their ways. In this case, Vegan Friend is prioritizing her ethical responsibility to spread the vegan message over her ethical responsibility to address her audience with respect as a writer.

Conclusion

Consumption has transitioned from a personal matter to a topic of debate, particularly in regard to veganism. Many vegans have taken to social media to spread their moral message that animals should be treated with kindness and respect. However, in doing so, they often initiate a continuous, unproductive exchange between other commentators. These discussions have displayed the close-minded attitude that the internet and social media have given rise to. People on the internet are not looking for their opinions to be evaluated by others; rather they wish for their viewpoint to be accepted or embraced by others. This divisive nature of the internet is a major problem for current and future generations, for online life is becoming increasingly prominent. The disregard and disintegration of the duty of writers toward readers within social media is a significant problem as well, especially in the case of clean eating. Faulty information is easily spread through social media, as anyone with internet access possesses the power to reach a wide audience of people. Seeing as clean eating often appeals to young, impressionable audiences, this accessibility of information has the potential to be dangerous. Clean eating is a sensitive issue that can have unforeseen and far-reaching consequences as people rely on dieting advice from strangers on the internet. Thus, people need to write and read responsibly and reconsider the ways in which they present and interpret information and opinions.

Works Cited

Anderson, L.V. "Stop Describing Your Diet as 'Clean Eating.'" *Slate*, 8 May 2014, <http://www.slate.com/blogs/browbeat/2014/05/08/clean_eating_is_a_bad_label_with_no_real_meaning_for_your_diet_plan.html>.

Carmichael, Richard. "Becoming Vegetarian and Vegan: Rhetoric, Ambivalence and Repression in Self-narrative." *Loughborough University*, 2002, pp. 1–290, <https://dspace.lboro.ac.uk/dspace-jspui/bitstream/2134/6904/2/272914.pdf>.

Dara. Comment on "What I Eat in a Day (healthy slimming recipe ideas!)." *YouTube*, 2016, <https://www.youtube.com/watch?v=mStu6cbbchY&lc=z12oxxmaokmkw1q1522oct1zqqf0fjp1j.1455148171168292>.

Duffy, John. "Writing Involves Making Ethical Choices." *Naming What We Know: Threshold Concepts in Writing Studies*, edited by Linda Adler-Kassner and Elizabeth Wardle, Logan: Utah State, 2015. 31–32. Print.

155

CHAPTER TWO: WHAT IS THE "RHETORICAL SITUATION" AND WHY SHOULD I CARE ABOUT IT?

Grey, Stephanie H. "A Growing Appetite: The Emerging Critical Rhetoric of
Food Politics." *Rhetoric & Public Affairs*, vol. 19, no. 2, 2016, pp. 307–20.
MLA *International Bibliography*, <http://web.a.ebscohost.com/ehost/
pdfviewer/pdfviewer?sid=09c2fd3f-2fe6-47ff-b9a4-d8bb7c050035%
40sessionmgr4010&vid=1&hid=4114>.

Irvine, Rob. "Food Ethics: Issues of Consumption and Production." *Journal of
Bioethical Inquiry*, vol. 10, 2013, pp. 145–48, <https://www.researchgate.
net/publication/236654581_Food_Ethics_Issues_of_Consumption_and_
Production_Self-Restraint_and_Voluntaristic_Measures_Are_Not_Enough>.

Knoblauch, A. Abby. "A Textbook Argument: Definitions of Argument in
Leading CompositionTextbooks." *College Composition and Communication*,
vol. 63, no. 2, 2011, pp. 244–68, <http://sluenglish.pbworks.com/w/file/
fetch/49204262/A%2520Textbook%2520Argument.pdf>.

Melody Arte. Comment on "What I Eat in a Day (healthy slimming recipe ideas!)."
YouTube, 2016, <https://www.youtube.com/watch?v=mStu6cbbchY&lc=
z12oxxmaokmkw1q1522oct1zqqf0fjp1j.1455148171168292>.

Portman, Anne. "Mother Nature Has It Right: Local Food Advocacy and the
Appeal to the 'Natural.'" *Ethics and the Environment*, vol. 19, no. 1, 2014,
pp. 1–30. EBSCO*host*, <rlib.pace.edu/login?url=http://search.ebscohost.
com/login.aspx?direct=true&db=edsbl&AN=RN600312569&site=eds-
live&scope=site>.

Sarah Liana. Comment on "What I Eat in a Day (healthy slimming recipe
ideas!)." *YouTube*, 2016, <https://www.youtube.com/watch?v=mStu6cbbch
Y&lc=z12oxxmaokmkw1q1522 oct1zqqf0fjp1j.1455148171168292>.

Seife, Charles. "The Loneliness of the Interconnected." *Rereading America:
Cultural Contexts for Critical Thinking and Writing*, edited by Gay Colombo,
Robert Cullen, and Bonnie Lisle, Boston: Bedford/St. Martin's, 2016.
289–303. Print.

Troscianko, Emily T. "Dissecting the Clean-Eating Meme." *Psychology Today*, 29
Aug. 2016, <https://www.psychologytoday.com/blog/hunger-artist/201608/
dissecting-the-clean-eating-meme>.

Vegan Friend. Comment on "What I Eat in a Day (healthy slimming recipe
ideas!)." *YouTube*, 2016, <https://www.youtube.com/watch?v=m
Stu6cbbchY&lc=z12oxxmaokmkw1q1522oct1zqqf0fjp1j.1455148171168292>.

"What I Eat in a Day (healthy slimming recipe ideas!)." *YouTube*,
uploaded by Cassey Ho, 18 Sep. 2014, <https://www.youtube.com/
watch?v=mStu6cbbchY>.

RECOMMENDED ONLINE SOURCES

For direct links to these sources, please visit <sites.broadviewpress.com/focusonwriting>.

1. To consider story, narrative, and argument as persuasive and rhetorical moves in an accessible essay: Christiansen, Ron. "Story as Rhetorical: We Can't Escape Story No Matter How Hard We Try." *Rhetoric: How We Examine Writing in the World*. <https://openenglishatslcc.pressbooks.com/chapter/story-as-rhetorical-we-cant-escape-story-no-matter-how-hard-we-try/>.

2. To think about familiar genres of school writing in a series of thoughtful research articles by students: "Tag: Classroom Genres." *Grassroots Writing Research*, Illinois State University. <http://isuwriting.com/tag/classroom-genres/>.

3. To better understand how dialects can be—but shouldn't be—used to promote stereotypes: "Why Do People Say 'AX' instead of 'ASK'?" *Decoded*, MTV, 17 Jan. 2018, YouTube. <https://www.youtube.com/watch?v=l-VnitbeS6w>.

4. To engage a student research project about how learning in a first-year writing course may (or may not) transfer to other rhetorical situations: Mulcahy, Sara. "'I Realize Writing Is a Part of My Daily Life Now': A Case Study of Writing Knowledge Transfer in One Section of ESL Writing." *Young Scholars in Writing: Undergraduate Research in Writing and Rhetoric*, vol. 10, 2012. <https://arc.lib.montana.edu/ojs/index.php/Young-Scholars-In-Writing/article/view/194>.

5. To realize how writing can vary from one culture to the next in ways that go far deeper than language: *Writing across Borders*, parts 1, 2, and 3, Oregon State U, YouTube, May 2010. <https://www.youtube.com/watch?v=quI0vq9VF-c&list=PL17u1gFU9b8SgVMrsVYMrHdoeM5WQYdKH>.

6. To enjoy noticing *lexis* (a vocabulary associated with a discourse community) within family communities: Golder, Andy. "People Are Sharing Words that Only Their Family Uses, And It's Hilariously Relatable." *Buzzfeed*, 13 January 2018. <https://www.buzzfeed.com/andyneuenschwander/people-are-sharing-words-that-only-their-family-us?utm_term=.awr2KBBvlr#.bmExJjjZp3>.

7. To notice how discourse communities operate within movie plots: "Discourse Communities in Movie Clips." YouTube, 28 January 2018, <https://www.youtube.com/watch?v=pS6zJ7IsJkM&list=PL2auNWo91Io0DvgfRST-H9q50XI7WhL8s>.

Joining the Conversation

The following formal writing prompts are ways of helping you think through the ideas you've been reading about by *using* the ideas in some way to help you create a text of your own.

PLATFORM ANALYSIS

Write a blog post in which you offer guidelines for a particular group of people just beginning to use two platforms (such as Twitter and Instagram). For example, you might tailor your advice for teens, adult professionals, or senior citizens who are new to the platforms. Use specific examples of what to do and what not to do.

DISCOURSE COMMUNITY ANALYSIS

Explain the way writing, reading, and language both reflect and shape the priorities of a community to which you belong (such as a sports team, a workplace, a high school, or a fan community). You might explore this question by considering how new members become expert members, by collecting and analyzing writing samples from the community, or by using the criteria Swales associates with discourse communities (explained earlier in this chapter).

CREATIVE EXPERIMENT

Use a familiar genre to meet a new purpose. For example, transform a love note into a "to do" list or a menu, transform notes from a class into a poem or a recipe, transform clips from a horror movie into a romantic comedy, or transform clips from speeches into a song.

RATIONALE

Explain how and why your formal writing or project from any of the above prompts demonstrates or responds to some of the principles you've learned in this chapter.

3 WHAT DO EFFECTIVE WRITERS DO?

Exploring the Question

Since I began teaching writing and talking with both students and colleagues about writing habits, I've been interested in what kinds of strategies are consistently effective and what kinds of strategies are idiosyncratic. In other words, some habits work well for most people, and some habits work well for some people but not for others. And, let's be honest: Some habits may keep us from writing or keep us from making effective choices when we write.

To make thinking about writing processes even more complicated, I've also noticed that a strategy that works for me in some instances is likely to backfire and be a terrible choice in another situation.

Before you read on, then, you should be forewarned. This whole writing thing is complicated, so part of becoming a more effective writer is simply paying attention to what works and what doesn't work. When you encounter the latter, change your strategy. Also remember that an approach that seems counter-productive might work for you in another rhetorical situation.

I also want to explicitly say that I'm thinking primarily about college writing assignments in this chapter, but the research and personal experience I share is

> **CONNECT**
>
> This book is predicated on the belief that we can all learn to write in more effective ways.
>
> 1. To what degree do you believe that writing is a learned skill versus a talent that some people are born with (and some are not)?
>
> 2. What led to your beliefs?

applicable in many situations. As you think through the ideas in this chapter, you might think about the rhetorical situations you most often encounter, especially in terms of purposes, audiences, discourse communities, and genres. Notice how the ideas may or may not apply to particular rhetorical contexts.

LINEAR TO RECURSIVE MODELS

You are likely familiar with a writing process that looks like this:

1. generate ideas
2. make an outline
3. write a rough draft
4. revise the draft
5. proofread and edit the draft to produce the final essay

This model is *linear* because it follows a straightforward path from the beginning to the end of the process, and it is one way to begin thinking about writing.

However, in 1981 Linda Flower and John Hayes published their findings after studying writers who talked aloud to record their thought processes while writing. Flower and Hayes realized a linear model does not accurately reflect how most effective writers work. Writing tends to be far messier. Writers tend to generate ideas throughout the writing process; they tend to edit throughout the writing process; and they might skip steps or follow the steps in a slightly different order. This process that cycles and loops is described as a *recursive* model.

Writers might also have steps that are peculiar to them. For example, when I am working on a long paper with complex ideas, I tend to stop at some point when my draft feels confused and out-of-order. I step away from the computer and write out my ideas on notebook paper, explaining the major points in a logical way.

Why do I do this? Often when I'm drafting, I discover that the initial point I planned on developing may not be exactly what the evidence shows. As I draft and expand on my ideas, a more accurate, refined, or complex point begins to emerge. It is difficult for me to fully understand how my overall point has shifted without stepping away from my draft and using a separate space to reflect on the parts of my argument and how they fit together. Once I write out my ideas, I'm able to return to the drafting process with more direction, clarity, and confidence. I also spend time revising at this point, before finishing the first draft, so that my introduction accurately frames my argument and the early parts of my draft guide readers through the foundational ideas that the rest of my argument builds upon.

My daughter Callie has a writing process for her school papers that includes an early step of hating everything about the assignment. Sometimes I try to get her to skip this step, but I don't think she ever has. Once Callie complains about the assignment and why she doesn't like it, she gets down to the business of generating ways she might respond to the prompt. Eventually one of her ideas appeals to her, and she starts liking the assignment as she figures out how to put her own spin on it.

Callie tends to outline her ideas before drafting, and once she completes a draft she often needs to add sentences and transitions that lead her readers through her argument. She does a lot of proofreading and editing as she writes, and she also reads her paper aloud in her final round of proofreading. I always read my writing aloud, too. I cannot even tell you how much of a difference it makes.

Callie often shares her papers with me to see if I have suggestions for her to strengthen them, and she also pays attention to feedback from her teachers. I'm not usually bothered by ending sentences with prepositions or using contractions, but some teachers care about those things.

Callie also shares her writing with me at times because she is often proud of something funny or clever that she included in her paper. You probably can't tell, but I appreciate a little snark. I also appreciate how part of Callie's process is not just about meeting her teacher's expectations but also finding ways she can enjoy the writing she submits. If you have to do something, you might as well find a way to enjoy it.

As Callie writes longer and more complex papers in college, she may need to revise her process. She has some good habits such as finding something about an assignment that she cares about and reading her draft aloud for final proofreading. Other parts of her process may or may not work for more sophisticated assignments.

Part of the work of developing an effective process is noticing what works and what doesn't. When something does not work for a particular rhetorical situation, be ready to shift and experiment, visit your college writing center, and talk with your instructor. A roadblock doesn't mean that you can't do an assignment; it just means that you might need to approach the assignment in a different way than what you are used to.

CONNECT

1. How would you describe your typical writing process when given an academic assignment?

2. Ask a friend and a teacher to share their writing processes. Do they tend to feel good about their processes or do they seem frustrated about some elements of the process?

3. Draw a picture or diagram of your own writing process. Compare it to pictures others have drawn. What are common elements? How do the pictures differ?

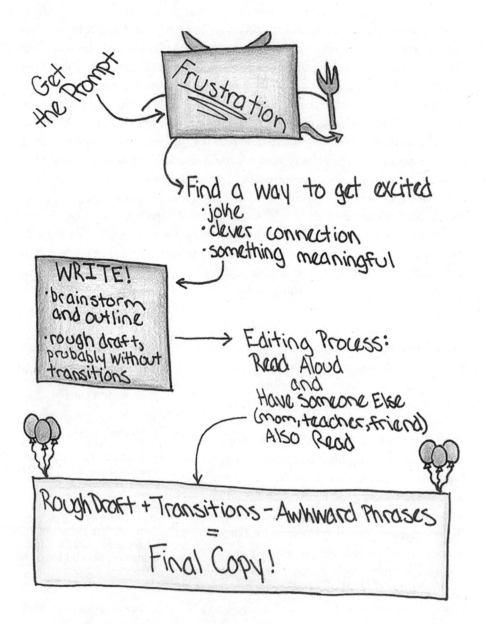

Callie's illustration of her writing process

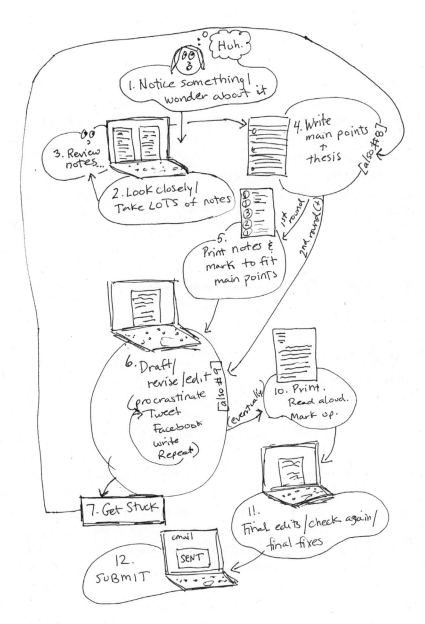

My illustration of my writing process

MATERIAL SITUATIONS

Chapter Two focused on rhetorical situations and why they matter, but I have also always loved talking with my students about *material situations*. These are the physical locations, outfits, sounds, lighting, times, and other real-world factors in which we write.

I have learned to write in multiple locations by necessity, but my favorite places are coffee shops and libraries. I like to be surrounded by other people doing work or enjoying themselves without feeling any obligation to interact with them, and I prefer to be away from my workplace and my home where responsibilities distract me from writing. I often have coffee, water, or food, but not always; I can be wearing a workout outfit or a professional outfit; I don't usually listen to music but I don't mind if it's on in the background. Some factors affect my productivity while others don't. I work best in the morning, but sometimes I begin writing at other times of day and gradually become energized.

CONNECT

1. How would you describe the ideal situation for you to write productively in terms of place, time of day, props, and so forth?

2. Compare your description to others' descriptions. What similarities and differences do you notice?

CONNECT

Do you notice the role of your body in your writing? If not, pay attention as you write or type and consider moments of movement and moments of stillness in relation to your writing.

Most often, students can similarly describe places, props, and times of day that help them mentally prepare to write. I've heard people talk about favorite writing utensils, cozy socks, hair accessories, and inspiring quotes strategically positioned on a laptop cover or above a desk.

Paying attention to the rooms where writers work can extend to thinking about writers as *embodied*—not simply minds but whole beings (Rule). In a study that involved writers watching video recordings of themselves in the act of composing, the writers discovered patterns of motion, movement, and interaction with their environments during the writing process that they had otherwise been unaware of (Rule). Thinking about the environments in which we compose thus involves also considering how writing is a physical activity. I can't tell you that a particular way of sitting or standing or moving will improve your writing. I think it's smart, however, to notice environments and strategies that help us write or that help us cope at points of struggle in the composing processes.

In terms of the chapter question, I am not certain whether particular environments or movements are common to successful writers. Still, you can pay attention to such factors to consider what works for you and what doesn't. If you have the opportunity to make writing easier for yourself in some way, you should take it.

STRATEGIES FOR STARTING

Many people use terms such as "generating ideas," "brainstorming," "invention," and "planning" to indicate the earliest stages of the writing process. Much of what follows fits these categories, but because writing processes are messy and recursive, as explained above, some strategies may not fit those terms. My own early strategies often combine a process of gathering evidence with a tendency to organize my findings, but even these steps are built on a moment—or a combination of moments—when something struck me as curious or worth investigating.

With that said, I feel compelled to confess. I often hate writing. Sometimes I find myself cleaning the bathroom sink drain in order to avoid writing. And cleaning a drain is oddly satisfying, truth be told, because you pull out disgusting goop and the water flows more freely through the pipes and on some subconscious level you try to convince yourself, "If I have time to clean this hidden part of the house, my life must be really together."

I've already mentioned that part of my daughter's writing process is to first resist writing and fuss about the writing assignment. Perhaps the apple does not fall far from the tree.

Because I struggle with the first steps, I try to make these steps as unintimidating as possible when I plan writing assignments for my students. I offer students opportunities for informal writing that doesn't feel difficult or overwhelming, and this informal writing ends up being the basis of an early draft.

That, then, is my first recommended strategy: Start drafting without realizing that's what you're doing. This may be especially important because writing is not only a means of communicating; it is also a process of discovery as we put ideas into our own words, engage in analysis, and synthesize material by combining parts in new ways to reach new conclusions (Emig).

It is difficult for many of us to engage in this discovery or thinking-on-paper phase if we are also focusing on writing a draft that will be communicating ideas to another person. The irony is that we won't have anything worth communicating if we don't allow ourselves to think through material. One way to begin working on an assignment without realizing that's what you're doing is to set other small writing goals for yourself. For example, I often have students *respond to readings* in ways that I hope will lead them to a paper topic. The most productive responses usually go beyond summary, perhaps by applying ideas from a reading, thinking through readings in relation to each other, analyzing the way a text is composed, or critiquing the limits of a writer's argument.

Verbal exchanges also tend to be helpful. Sometimes I talk with people about my ideas, and once I've said ideas aloud, I'm then able to write the ideas down. When I meet with students, I often ask them questions about their thinking and take notes on what they say. We then review the notes and talk about what is most surprising (which often ends up being the main point of the paper), and I challenge writers to consider how the ideas might be ordered to make the most sense.

For example, a student said he is interested in the rhetoric of body language and gender. That's a broad topic, so my initial questions helped the student narrow the focus:

- What kinds of body language have you noticed that seem associated with gender?
- Why does the topic interest you?
- Why do you think other people might care about this topic?

His answers led the student to focus on differences in the amount of space men and women take up in public places, a topic he had heard about in regards to "manspreading" (a term used to criticize a tendency for males in public spaces to position their legs wide apart and take up a lot of room). To help the student find an angle that would interest him and others, I asked questions that would help him explore seeming contradictions, gray areas, or puzzling points.

- When and where does this trend seem most noticeable?
- When and where do you notice exceptions to this trend?
- How does this trend seem connected to other trends?
- Why does this trend matter to people?

In this conversation, the student ended up focusing on notions of chivalry, masculinity, strength, and size. Some of the questions led to dead ends, while other questions led to thoughtful responses. As a male, the student I was talking to was interested in his own behavior and was becoming aware of contradictory messages about masculinity. He found body rhetoric interesting because it was communication without words; a person might believe he is projecting one kind of message while a completely different message is being received. The student met with me

FOCUS ON WRITING: WHAT COLLEGE STUDENTS WANT TO KNOW

with vague ideas but left my office with a plan for research and for parts of his draft, all based on a conversation we had.

These kinds of conversations take place in my writing classroom when students work with partners or small groups to think through and develop ideas.

In addition to responding to readings and talking through ideas, *heuristics* can be a helpful and low-pressure way to get started. "Heuristics" are processes for generating ideas. Here are some common ones that writers use.

Freewriting: Spend a set amount of time (such as five, ten, or fifteen minutes) writing quickly without stopping. If you have nothing to say, write about why you have nothing to say or use filler phrases, and then get right back into it. Allow yourself to go off track, and do not worry about using correct grammar, punctuation, or spelling.

Listing: Write as many facts and ideas about your topic that you can without holding anything back. Now write three to five more things. The more extensive the list, the more likely it is to include thoughtful and interesting perspectives. I use lists regularly, often in the form of taking notes about a book or movie I'm writing about. When I review a list, I notice patterns among the ideas and then mark similar ideas to create categories.

Double entry notebook: Using two columns, write your initial observations in a list in the left column. Use the right column to respond to your observations, perhaps asking more questions or explaining the significance or implications of the initial observation. This format is helpful for connecting evidence (the information in the left column) to analysis (in the right column). This approach can also be used to read actively, with quotes or paraphrases in the left column and responses, questions, or applications of the ideas in the right column.

Visual diagrams: If you place your topic in a bubble, you can create a web of sub-topics around it (a web diagram), or you can create branches below your topic bubble (a tree diagram). Many people appreciate the way visual graphics help showcase an organization in clear and immediate ways.

HDWDWW: These letters stand for the question, How Does Who Do What & Why? Rather than answer the question in a sentence, use it to generate a variety of answers, once again pushing yourself to go further than your first instincts.

Comparison matrix: Make a table with a column for each of the texts or items you'll be comparing. On the far left, make a column with labels for the major points of comparison.

Other strategies to get your draft started if you find yourself procrastinating:

- Write a letter or email to someone about what you'll be writing about.

- Break down the assignment into a series of questions and answer each of the questions in a paragraph or two.
- Write about what is confusing you or keeping you from writing clearly about the topic.

CONNECT

1. What strategies do you use most often to get started with your writing?

2. Have these strategies been effective for you? Explain.

3. Can you think of a time when you were confused because you were thinking deeply?

4. How did you work your way through your confusion?

I ask students to try these strategies, and I do the last one regularly as part of my process. Confusion when you are writing is often a good sign: It means you are thinking through a topic that is complex, and you are trying to figure out how you can explain complexities in ways that are clear to readers.

Part of becoming a more effective writer is moving toward (and through) the complexities and confusions so that you communicate something meaningful to your readers. Remember this point from the rhetorical triangle in Chapter Two: If you can't show your audience a new perspective, they probably won't be motivated to read what you have to say.

STRATEGIES FOR IMPROVING WRITING

I tend to combine drafting, revising, and editing as I write, though I eventually produce a full draft, print it out, and work from the printed version on improving it. In this section, I'm going to focus on some principles to help you "make your writing better" at this middle point, after you've begun drafting but before you're ready to do final polishing.

A writing process that often seems appealing but is rarely effective is nicknamed "one-and-done": The idea is to write one (final) draft in response to an assignment prompt. I understand this choice. Time is a precious commodity, and some writing can be completed quickly, so the one-and-done approach seems efficient.

However, as someone who appreciates effective writing and who spends a lot of time understanding how it is achieved, I usually don't support the one-and-done approach. When students rely on this strategy, they often waste my time because I take care reading and responding to work that the student didn't invest in. These students also waste their own time by writing without experiencing the benefits of deeply engaging material; without developing their own thinking and the increased likelihood that they will apply such thinking skills in other situations; and without practicing and improving clear communication.

I partly resist one-and-done writing because I haven't worked with students who write this way effectively, but I do want to point out that Muriel Harris's research suggests that many writers are able to do effective work by doing a lot of mental planning before writing. Her research is rather compelling, but I usually don't tell students much about it because I so rarely see such strategies work well. I do think that it's a problem if I expect every student to write just as I do, so I'm trying to be fair by mentioning her work here!

If you are similar to most writers I know and do need to undertake substantive revision processes in order to produce writing you're proud of, it's helpful to understand the difference between the *global* and the *local*. *Global revisions* focus on the overall ideas and organization of your writing. If your thesis doesn't make a compelling point, if you need to add examples, if you need to address counterarguments, or if you need to change the order of the ideas you address, you are working on global revisions or global issues.

CONNECT

1. Have you or someone you know benefited from the one-and-done approach?

2. If so, does that mean that it's an effective strategy?

3. In what circumstances might it be fine to use a first draft as a final draft?

Local revisions or local issues are those that focus on particular sentences and might involve rewording a sentence to improve clarity, minimizing repetition of a word, combining sentences to make writing sound better, or deleting an unnecessary detail.

I do some proofreading and editing in terms of local issues as I write, but I make sure that I'm not spending *too* long on proofreading and editing when I'm first drafting. Why? Because if I find that I need to delete parts of my work or rearrange ideas, I will end up editing all over again. Mike Rose wrote about habits of writers that worked against them, and one such habit is a tendency to spend so long worrying over word choice and phrasing that the writer gets stuck and never completes a paper. That's a case of taking a good habit and applying it in a way that leads to a big problem.

Writing is tricky because we need to move back and forth between *local decisions* (What word should I use here? How should I start this sentence? What is the next word I'm going to write?) and *global decisions* (What is the point of this paper? How might I engage the audience? How can I appropriately lead readers through the major sub-points?). Of course, the two are not separate but instead are intimately connected, and that's why I do at least a little bit of sentence-level editing as I write. I find that I clarify my big ideas that way.

As writers, we must use part of our brains to think about *what* we want to say (content), part of our brains to think about *how* we want to say it (rhetoric or style), part of our brains to process these choices in terms of our rhetorical situation (attention to audience and purpose at the very least, but most often additional attention to discourse community and genre), and part of our brains to monitor how we are approaching the writing situation. Anne Beaufort organized the kinds of expertise writers need to use into five categories:

- subject matter knowledge
- rhetorical knowledge
- discourse community knowledge
- genre knowledge
- writing process knowledge

If you ever find writing difficult, it's because it is. Feel free to fuss for a short time, and then get back to work.

Monitoring our writing habits, or, in Beaufort's schema, using "writing process knowledge," will help us recognize when a strategy has stopped working for us. If I am writing but not getting anywhere, I need to consider why and adjust what I am doing. I say more about healthy and unhealthy procrastination below, so I won't belabor the point here. I will note, however, that moving away from absolute rules that guide a writing process to flexible ideas can be challenging, but it can also help you test out what works and does not work for you in a given situation.

When thinking about global substantive revisions with students, I have two strategies that seem to work well for a lot of people.

First, we often use "glossing" or "reverse outlining" once a draft is complete or close to complete. I usually work from print copies, but this can also be done on a digital document. For each paragraph, I think about what the main point is and write it on the margins. When I am done, I look at each of these marginal notes to see how I can better organize my ideas so that similar ideas stay together, repetition is minimized, and I lead readers from ideas that are more familiar or simple to gray areas and complexities.

This process helps me think of my writing in terms of *sections* rather than *paragraphs*. Many students have experience with a five-paragraph essay that follows a

CONNECT

1. Can you give an example of a time that you moved between local and global decisions in a healthy way that helped you develop a decent draft?

2. Can you give an example of a time that you spent so much time addressing local issues that you had trouble completing a draft?

very rigid pattern. I appreciate strong organization, well-developed paragraphs, and transitions that guide readers. However, many (or even most) college writing assignments may demand a different kind of analytical thinking and may be longer than a five-paragraph essay.

The process of glossing or reverse outlining can help reveal the way certain paragraphs are working together to gradually develop a point. Together, these paragraphs comprise a section of the paper. Understanding a longer paper in terms of sections and sub-sections allows us to organize paragraphs in a logical way and to create transitions and sentences that guide readers through our main points and sub-points.

Glossing is thus an initial step: We notice what we've already said. The next step is to revisit how the parts fit together and adjust focus, organization, or key phrases so the text is more clear and coherent for readers.

The second strategy I regularly teach students is a bit easier to explain. Often the conclusion of a paper will function better as an introduction to the paper than the original introduction does. When we write an introduction, it reflects what we know before we complete a full draft. When we write a conclusion, however, it reflects our thinking on the subject after the full draft is complete. For many of us, our thinking develops in the process of writing a paper, so the conclusion says something more compelling than the original introduction; it may even offer a more specific sense of main sub-points that contribute to the overall argument.

If this is the case for you, go ahead and cut and paste the conclusion over the original introduction. Read it over to make sure it works as the introductory paragraph and revise as needed. You'll still need to write a conclusion, but you can be brief. Make sure you summarize your main point in a sentence or two, and then tell readers why it matters. What can readers do with the perspective you've just provided on the subject matter? What else needs to be understood now that you've added to the conversation? These ways of concluding will be more helpful to readers than completely spelling out all of the sub-points they have just read.

STRATEGIES FOR POLISHING WRITING

No matter how much editing I do along the way, I also spend some time near the end of my writing process devoted to polishing my writing. I usually print out my paper and read it aloud, pausing to make marks and change things as I go. You might remember from earlier in this chapter that I highly recommend this strategy. In the words of the Nike slogan, *Just Do It*.

I also spend some time double-checking my citations and my bibliography, whether it's in the form of a Works Cited page or References page or Footnotes or Endnotes.

Depending on where I'm publishing a paper, I've used a variety of style sheets. *Style sheets* are collections of rules and guidelines formed by various professional and academic organizations. You may be familiar with the MLA (Modern Language Association), the APA (American Psychological Association), and the Chicago Manual styles. No matter what style sheet I use, I need to look up some things. My advice for you? Take the time to look things up when you're unsure—at least when you're in the final stages of preparing a fully polished version of your writing.

You may have noticed the variety of style sheets used to document sources in the readings included in this textbook. I purposely kept citations in the original styles so you could notice how different publications require different bibliographic forms and how the MLA form has changed.

Often when I'm too tired to do serious thinking but know I need to work on my paper in some way or another, I spend time reviewing my entries on my Works Cited page (note that this page might be called "References" if I use an APA style sheet). That way I'm making progress and taking care of things but I'm not pushing myself in ways that are taxing my brain. Following rules is simply following rules.

You can look up most rules when you're feeling unsure. However, it's easier on you as a writer if you remember a good number of rules, and it's not too late to figure out what kinds of rules you struggle with and focus on those items. For example, I was an undergrad when I figured out how to use apostrophes correctly to indicate possession. I was in grad school when I first realized I had been spelling "occasionally" incorrectly for years. I still get mixed up with "toward" versus "towards," so that's something I look up when I'm writing formally, and I also struggle with the various forms of "lay" and "lie."

TO PROCRASTINATE OR NOT?

Usually, people will tell you that procrastinating is a bad thing. Often, they will be correct, and I'll tell you about problems with procrastination in a minute, but first I'm going to tell you that sometimes procrastination is in your best interest.

When I'm writing a formal academic argument, I often reach a point in the drafting process when my ideas seem jumbled. I find that I'm interested in what

I'm writing, but I cannot fully explain my main points to another person, and I might be more aware of how all the points seem to be connected than how I can order them and explain them clearly to someone else.

As I mentioned earlier in this chapter, sometimes I work my way through my ideas by turning away from the keyboard and picking up paper and pen. I write out the ideas and how they fit together in a systematic way that allows me to return to the draft and clarify the ideas for the reader.

Sometimes, however, I need to simply walk away from the paper altogether. I might go for a walk or clean a room or do some dishes or take a shower. While I'm doing these activities, the ideas in my draft are on the backburner of my mind, simmering away, working themselves out in my subconscious.

Eventually, I return to my writing, and the connections between the ideas have crystallized to a degree so I am able to organize the draft and spell out the argument for my readers.

That's a healthy form of procrastination. "Procrastination" may not even be the right word. I like the metaphor of ideas simmering away until they're ready to be combined with other ingredients, so maybe I can call it a "simmeration" or even a "prosimmeration." The same method works when I'm stuck on a jigsaw puzzle. If I walk away from the puzzle for a good while, when I return I can find pieces that go together easily. I have never studied this phenomenon in a scientific way, so it may be my imagination, but it seems possible that a little bit of time can provide a good bit of perspective.

We also need to discuss procrastination that is not fruitful, even though I'm tempted to continue putting it off. I regularly find myself avoiding writing in an unhealthy way that is similar to Anne Lamott in her fun book *Bird by Bird* (excerpted later in this chapter).

To be honest, I procrastinated many times when I was supposed to be working on this textbook, and it was not a healthy procrastination. Instead, I worried that my approach to writing would not be helpful to students, or that my approach would be criticized by my colleagues who teach college writing and who, in many cases, are smarter and more well-informed than I am. I also worried that I'm trying to write in a way that will actually reach students, and I thought: What if I'm too old? too serious? too boring?

I'm actually completely awesome and I'm sure it's difficult for you to imagine anyone like me having so many self-doubts. But there ya go.

I took a number of steps to cope with this unproductive procrastination. I partnered with other people who were writing so we could encourage each other and be accountable for writing. I took the big writing task—the textbook—and broke it down into all the small sections in a list so that I would be less likely to feel overwhelmed. I created a document for each chapter and put in relative notes from my original proposal.

CONNECT

1. In what ways is procrastination a healthy or unhealthy part of your writing process?

2. What are your strategies when you realize your procrastinating tendencies are becoming a problem?

I also spent time thinking about why I was procrastinating. In other situations, I've procrastinated because I wasn't sure what the end product should look like. In those cases, I found a model or a sample to guide me. But in this situation, with self-doubt holding me back, I had to face my demons and commit to producing that "shitty first draft," one piece of one section of one chapter at a time (Lamott 16–26).

As fun times and chores both competed with my writing time, I often fell into procrastination again. Whatever. I'm human. The point is that procrastination is a place many of us visit, but it doesn't mean we have to live there.

Anyone, even me, can write a really terrible draft. The key is that we can't be afraid of our own terrible writing. We just have to embrace it as part of the process.

WRITING AS SOCIAL: COLLABORATION AND FEEDBACK

As noted in both Chapters One and Two, because language develops in communities, writing is always social: Writing connects members of a community with one another and mediates identities and activities in a variety of ways.

Here, in Chapter Three, I am shifting the focus a bit. How do effective writers use the social nature of writing to inform their writing processes?

At the very minimum, effective writers spend some time imagining readers' reactions. When writing for a small audience in an informal exchange, we might simply wonder: Will the reader understand? When developing formal writing or trying to reach a large audience, we might consider not only clarity but also ask ourselves: Have I created a mutually respectful relationship with my readers? It might seem odd to think of a "relationship" with a large group of readers, but if we want to impress our readers, we should aim for clarity, work to interest readers by offering a fresh perspective, and attend to details that our readers might appreciate. At the very least, effective writers try to avoid making a poor impression on readers.

Writers can also draw on readers during the writing process. Sometimes discussing ideas verbally—whether early in the process or while figuring out how to revise a draft—helps us to refine our projects and make sense of complicated ideas. As explained earlier in this chapter, when I meet with students, I often ask them questions and I take notes on what they say. When I hand them the notes, I am literally giving them their own words to draw upon as they develop a draft. Sometimes we review all the ideas they have discussed once the ideas are written down so we can notice how the ideas are connected to one another. This process works well for a lot of people, perhaps because writers are checking to see if their thinking makes sense *as they plan*. This approach to the writing process tends to be active and enjoyable.

Writing workshops often involve these kinds of conversations, and they can happen multiple times during a writing process. The key is for writers to be willing to talk through their ideas and for readers to ask questions, take notes, and give feedback. If you doubt your ability to be helpful to other writers, remember that you have some power even if writing and reading are not your strong suits. Try some of these strategies to help your classmates:

- repeat ideas back to the writer to see if you have understood
- ask questions when you don't understand a point or when you don't understand the connections the writer is trying to articulate
- tell the writer what point, idea, or argument you find especially interesting
- notice when an example is helpful or when it doesn't fit the argument
- take notes on what the writer says

All of these ways of engaging a writer can be helpful, even if you are unsure of your ability to advise another writer.

Peer review is often part of writing workshops, and it usually occurs after some kind of draft is completed. Peer review can take many forms—in person or online, with the writer involved or not, via oral discussion or via writing, with open or focused guidelines.

Here are two forms of peer review that many of my students have found helpful. My colleague Michael Turner uses the first of these successfully and sold me on it as well.

Small peer review groups during class

1. The class reviews the most important two or three criteria for a successful paper based on the assignment.
2. The writer distributes copies of the draft to the group members and says a few words about any specific feedback they are looking for.
3. One of the readers reads the draft aloud.
4. The writer has the opportunity to reflect on the draft in terms of the two or three criteria. The writer should not insult the draft by saying phrases such as "This is so bad." The understanding is that all the drafts can be improved, and when we insult our own writing, readers are inclined to reassure the writer rather than provide meaningful feedback.
5. The readers move back and forth between the draft and the criteria, identifying places where the draft is and is not filling the criteria and offering suggestions for making the draft stronger. The writer can take notes on the feedback, ask for clarification, and so forth.
6. Each person in the group has a turn being the writer.

Analyzing the main points of another person's argument by paragraph

Each writer receives feedback from one or two readers. The readers write out full sentences that capture the arguments being made in each paragraph. If the argument of a paragraph isn't clear, the readers explain what the writer seems to be trying to say but also explains that they are not certain. If a single paragraph contains more than one argument, the readers list each of the arguments.

Writers can use this reverse outline of their essay to see if the ideas are clear, are arranged in a sensible order, are developed enough, and so forth. Writers can also use this technique to analyze their own writing, as noted above.

Writing centers and instructor feedback

Writing centers are also ways of helping check in with potential readers. It's important to provide as much rhetorical context as possible when working with a writing consultant who is not in your class—otherwise the consultant will struggle to give advice that fits the assignment, its parameters, and your teacher's expectations. When visiting the writing center, make sure you have the paper assignment with you; you may also bring feedback from your teacher on other writing assignments or notes you've taken in class. If you do not share the full rhetorical context with writing consultants, it would be easy for them to give you inappropriate feedback since appropriate writing varies from one situation to the next.

It's also smart to get in the habit of paying attention to feedback you receive to see if you notice patterns from one class to the next. If some element of writing presents a recurring challenge, taking time to work on that area will have a positive effect in multiple settings. You don't have to improve all parts of your writing at once but instead plan on gradually learning more.

PRO TIPS ON PROCESS

I have already touched on a lot of strategies that experienced writers tend to use. Here, I'm going to pull some of the highlights together and add a few more. Remember, these tips are often appropriate, but not always.

> **CONNECT**
>
> As a class, make your own list of pro tips on process.

- Find something about the assignment that interests you.
- Regularly reread the assignment sheet to keep yourself focused, especially as you start, while drafting and revising, and before you begin polishing.
- Ask for a successful sample of a writing assignment so you have a better sense of the disciplinary discourse community and genre.
- Spend some time writing on paper, especially when you need a break from writing on a screen.
- To get in the habit of writing, plan on specific times and reward yourself each time you write. Sticker charts are not just for children!
- Find a specific place where you can write productively.
- Read your writing aloud, slowly.

PRO TIPS ON PRODUCT

I hesitate to offer tips on the criteria that might make a particular piece of writing effective because, as I've mentioned about a bazillion times, writing shifts from one rhetorical situation to another. Still, here are some guidelines that *often* apply in academic writing assignments. If nothing else, you can use these guidelines to have a conversation with a teacher about expectations for a particular discipline, class, or assignment.

- Use the style sheet (often either MLA or APA) you've been assigned to set up the **format** of the paper from the start—font, title, page numbering, headings, margins, and citation style are some of the elements that show you are part of a disciplinary discourse community (or at least that you're taking enough time to fake it for now).

- **Title** your work. It should indicate the topic. Often academic titles use a colon, as in *Focus on Writing: What College Students Want to Know*. In a lot of writing I assign, students can have fun with the title and use alliteration or a pun or a metaphor. These kinds of titles are memorable and make readers motivated to read on because you've already shown that you've taken care to craft something thoughtful. In some disciplines, titles indicate the focus but tend to sound formal rather than fun.

- Know the difference between a topic and a **thesis statement**. The topic is the subject matter. The thesis statement articulates the new perspective you're bringing to the subject matter.

- If students struggle with **introductory paragraphs**, I tell them to introduce the topic in the first sentence, to identify what is already known or accepted about the topic, and then to spend several sentences previewing what they will be saying about the topic (which should offer a fresh perspective). This preview may follow the organization of the main sections of the paper—another reason the habit of glossing or doing a reverse outline is helpful. The thesis statement is at the end of the introductory paragraph and makes a specific arguable claim about the topic that the rest of the paper will systematically develop and support.

- If students struggle with **organization**, I tell them to make sure the start of each section and the start of each paragraph provides a logical progression of points that lead to the thesis. It makes sense to start with the more familiar and known information and to gradually make more specific and arguable claims. In general, moving from known to unknown helps readers follow you. Other structures follow ideas in chronological order, spatial order, or another progression.

- Notice that I used the word **section** in the point just above. Sometimes using headings for sections of your paper helps both writer and reader see a clear progression of ideas. If you use headings, most of your sections should be longer than a single paragraph. Even if you don't use headings, it's often a good idea to think about your paper in terms of two, three, or four sections, and each section might have subsections. This corresponds to the hierarchy of thinking that Hayes and Flower discuss in a reading later in this chapter: Divide ideas into a manageable number of units and sub-units so that both the writer and the reader can make sense of the material.

- In terms of individual **paragraphs**, it often works to have a structure that begins with an arguable claim (a sub-point that helps contribute to your overall thesis), that uses evidence to support and develop that claim, and that provides interpretation or analysis to connect the evidence back to the claim. Sometimes I use three questions to help students work through these elements. Claim: What is true? Evidence: When and where is it true? Analysis: How and why is it true?

- **Transitions** help guide readers as you move from one idea to the next. They can be useful within paragraphs and are crucial between paragraphs and sections of your paper.

- I'll address ways of integrating **secondary sources** into your writing in the next chapter. I know you're excited about it, but you are just going to have to wait.

- **Conclusions** can recap your argument in a sentence or two and then explain to readers what they should do now that they've learned a new perspective on the topic. They may sometimes point to further research that is needed.

- Spelling, punctuation, and grammar conventions take time and patience to learn. Start paying attention to what affects readers and what doesn't. Punctuation helps provide clarity, and some comma guidelines are easier to learn than others, so start with the easy ones. Pay attention to words that should and should not be capitalized. Notice how clearly you communicate verbally and trust that you can do so in writing, but that it might take a bit more time because verbal and written communication are not exactly the same. All the rules are actually human-made conventions, not permanent or universal rules from some divine source, so keep in mind that learning conventions is simply a way to help your audience hear what you have to say. You can gradually become better with writing conventions. Struggling with these parts of writing is more connected with experience than with anything else, so give yourself a chance to develop more experience with writing and reading.

- A few comments on usage and stylistic choices.
  - Students often ask whether they are allowed to use "I." I almost never give a straight answer but instead ask students to think through the

rhetorical implications with me. I'll summarize for you, though, since I'm not there with you in real life to have a conversation. In the end, when using "I" is necessary because the assignment asks students to draw on personal experience or when using "I" minimally helps make writing more conversational, I appreciate it. Overusing "I" can take the focus off the actual subject matter in some assignments, so I tell students that it's sometimes helpful during drafting but they might want to delete most "I" pronouns if it's adding filler that takes away from readers noticing the actual point.

– I don't mind contractions or split infinitives or ending sentences with prepositions. Some teachers do.

– Sometimes students worry about using a word repeatedly in an essay. Occasionally it's a problem because it sounds clunky. In these cases, combining sentences or finding suitable alternatives for a word can help. In other situations, a word needs to be used repeatedly because it's a key term that's being discussed. Have you been bothered by how many times I've used the words "writing," "rhetorical," or "effective"? I hope not. If I went to a thesaurus and used one synonym after another, you would likely be confused and wonder what the heck I'm talking about. Sometimes using terms consistently provides coherence for readers. Reading aloud is a useful strategy for recognizing whether the repetition of a term is likely to distract readers or help them follow the point.

– Concise writing means we omit filler words and unnecessary phrases so that the good things we want to say are not hidden in a cloud of words that distract. I have deleted "that" and "in order" many times from this manuscript because they didn't clarify or contribute to the ideas ~~that are~~ being communicated. Note: Concise writing does not mean that we don't bother to provide examples or explanations.

– Style guides often tell us to vary our sentences but also to use parallel structures. This advice seems to be contradictory, but both techniques can be used in a single essay. Stylistic choices can enhance a point or idea, so sentence variation is likely to help writers make a claim and then support it by developing and analyzing an example. Because various sentences are doing different kinds of work in this example, the sentences will likely have different structures. We can also strategically use a one-paragraph sentence or a sentence fragment to call attention to an idea. Parallelism can similarly call attention

FOCUS ON WRITING: WHAT COLLEGE STUDENTS WANT TO KNOW

to an idea. Parallel structures make sense when several sentences are performing similar work, whether offering a series of claims or a series of examples. Parallel structures can also be used to create a series of coherent phrases within a sentence; the style helps readers follow along, and often a point grows more intense as a pattern repeats.

- Gender-inclusive language is a way of inviting in readers. This awareness applies both to pronouns and to nouns that historically may have been gendered, such as "police officer" rather than "policeman." Often plural forms are used to avoid constructions such as "a writer brings his favorite pencil" or "a writer brings his or her favorite pencil." "Writers bring their favorite pencils" reads more smoothly. I have used plural pronouns with singular subjects in several places in this textbook, a practice that is slowly becoming more accepted: "A writer brings their favorite pencil."

I'll offer one more way of thinking about paragraphs because students are regularly concerned about length. I draw three pictures on the board depicting three different pages of text. You can have an idea of what I mean if you squint while looking at the three rectangles below. I ask students to think about the effect of long blocks of texts, medium-sized blocks of text, and short blocks of text. They tend to say the long block of text is overwhelming, the short blocks of text feel jumpy, and the medium blocks of text seem like they are long enough to develop a point without overwhelming or losing the reader.

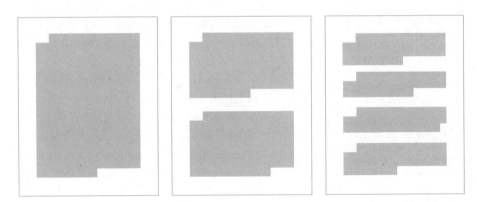

Sometimes a long block of text and a feeling of being overwhelmed might contribute to a point you're making, and short blocks of text tend to be used in newspapers and online writing. Writers will strategically use short paragraphs or long paragraphs to make a part of an argument stand out. If you are not ready to experiment with paragraph length, that's okay. If you aim for paragraphs that are between a third and three quarters of a page, you are in good shape. If a paragraph grows very long but is covering a single topic, you can break it into smaller paragraphs by sub-topic.

I'll close by offering an analogy I often use when teaching writing. Imagine that you and a friend are headed to a bookstore; she's driving but doesn't know how to get there. You start off by giving her a brief overview from the front passenger seat: "We will leave campus and go straight for three blocks, turn left onto Main Street, travel for about a mile past several car lots, and the bookstore will be on the second strip mall on the left. We will see it just to the left of the grocery store." That preview is like an introduction that explains where you're going so the driver (reader) knows what to expect, where you are ultimately headed (the bookstore/thesis), and even the kinds of things that will be encountered along the way.

As you are actually traveling, everything the driver sees in each phase of the trip is analogous to the details and examples you use to develop your argument through the sections and paragraphs of your paper.

You also need to remember to provide guidance, especially if the trip is a complicated one. In the case of this bookstore pilgrimage, it's enough to give reminders like, "This is where we go left onto Main Street" or "It's not this strip mall but the next one." In our road trip analogy, these kinds of phrases help the driver (reader) follow your argument as you move from one part of the argument to another.

Once you arrive at the bookstore, you might tell the driver why you wanted to be at the bookstore and think about what she might like to do at the bookstore. This is like a conclusion that reminds readers of what you've told them very briefly and then offers some sense of why we bothered thinking through these ideas. So what? What's next? What do we do at the bookstore?

This entire analogy seems dry and boring as I write it down, but when I tell my

CONNECT

1. How do the "pro tips on product" I offer match other advice you've been given? How do they differ? Why might differences be inevitable?

2. I will offer a different sort of organizational structure in the upcoming chapter that addresses researched writing. Do you have any sense of how a focus on secondary research might affect a paper's organization?

3. Much of this chapter has focused on the process of writing. Is attention to the end product part of the process you follow when you write? In what ways? At what stages do you spend time thinking about how the end product will work?

4. At what points in the writing process does the rhetorical situation matter most?

FOCUS ON WRITING: WHAT COLLEGE STUDENTS WANT TO KNOW

students about it, I act out the dynamics when I'm driving and someone tells me to turn left too late and I slam on the brakes and make a dangerous turn and vow never to let that person be my co-pilot again. I hope you can imagine the drama. And just wait for the next chapter when my favorite analogy for integrating research involves salad. I think you'll love it.

WORKS CITED

Beaufort, Anne. *College Writing and Beyond: A New Framework for University Writing Instruction*. Utah State UP, 2007.

Emig, Janet. "Writing as a Mode of Learning." *College Composition and Communication*, vol. 28, no. 2, 1977, pp. 122–28. *JSTOR*, JSTOR, <www.jstor.org/stable/356095>.

Flower, Linda, and John R. Hayes. "A Cognitive Process Theory of Writing." *College Composition and Communication*, vol. 32, no. 4, 1981, pp. 365–87. *JSTOR*, JSTOR, <www.jstor.org/stable/356600>.

Harris, Muriel. "Composing Processes of One- and Multi-Draft Writers." *College English*, vol. 51, no. 2, 1989, pp. 174–91, <http://www5.csudh.edu/ccauthen/575S12/harris.pdf>.

Lamott, Anne. *Bird by Bird: Some Instructions on Writing and Life*. Anchor Books, 1994.

Rose, Mike. "Rigid Rules, Inflexible Plans, and the Stifling of Language: A Cognitivist Analysis of Writer's Block." *College Composition and Communication*, vol. 31, no. 4, 1980, pp. 389–401. *JSTOR*, JSTOR, <www.jstor.org/stable/356589>.

Rule, Hannah J. "Writing's Rooms." *College Composition and Communication*, vol. 69, no. 3, 2018, pp. 402–32, <http://www.ncte.org/library/NCTEFiles/Resources/Journals/CCC/0693-feb2018/CCC0693Writing.pdf>.

Extending the Conversation

To think more about the question, "What do effective writers do?" I have gathered four selections reprinted here and seven readings or videos you can find online. Each piece overlaps with my initial approach to the question in some way, but each piece also extends the chapter question with a particular focus. As we answer questions that may seem simple at first, complexities and nuances develop that call for more exploration.

For each text reprinted here, I tell you why I included it, provide some background about its initial publication, and offer hints that may guide your reading, including vocabulary terms when relevant. I also provide "connect" questions to help you engage and respond as you read.

For each online source I recommend, I offer a brief introduction—just enough to guide you as you decide what further reading (or viewing) might be helpful, inspiring, enjoyable, or challenging.

ANNE LAMOTT'S *BIRD BY BIRD: SOME INSTRUCTIONS ON WRITING AND LIFE* (1994)

Why I included it

Anne Lamott writes fiction and essays for a general audience, so she and her work stand apart from the other writing I have included, which tends to come from academic writers and use academic styles. This particular essay shows how Lamott appeals to readers by presenting herself as a flawed human being who can laugh at herself yet still offer insights to others. My students and I enjoy saying "shitty first drafts"—the title of a section from *Bird by Bird* included here—so I hope you get a kick out of it, too.

CONNECT

As you read, consider responding to the following questions to help you process the material.

1. Which of Lamott's experiences are similar to experiences you've had?

2. What advice does she give? Are you likely to believe her advice and try to follow it? Why or why not?

3. To what degree is one writer's personal experience good evidence that a particular writing practice is effective for writers in general? Note both reasons to trust conclusions based on Lamott's experiences and reasons to doubt conclusions based on Lamott's experiences.

Background

In *Bird by Bird*, Lamott tells personal experiences and stories in hopes that readers will learn lessons along with her, with most of the lessons focused on writing, especially fiction. As a well-known popular writer, she had an audience interested in her advice and familiar with her sense of humor when her book was first published, and she continues to enjoy a wide readership. Even though the following excerpt was part of a longer work and thus might seem jumpy with the first sentence, for the most part it works well as a stand-alone text.

Reading hints

As you read, you will likely notice that this excerpt is easier to understand than much of the writing reprinted in this textbook. Pay attention to what makes the writing more accessible, and consider not only what is gained with widely accessible writing but also what is lost.

Lamott, Anne. Excerpt from *Bird by Bird: Some Instructions on Writing and Life*, Anchor Books, 1994, pp. 16–26.

THE FIRST USEFUL concept is the idea of short assignments. Often when you sit down to write, what you have in mind is an autobiographical novel about your childhood, or a play about the immigrant experience, or a history of—oh, say—say women. But this is like trying to scale a glacier. It's hard to get your footing, and your fingertips get all red and frozen and torn up. Then your mental illnesses arrive at the desk like your sickest, most secretive relatives. And they pull up chairs in a semicircle around the computer, and they try to be quiet but you know they are there with their weird coppery breath, leering at you behind your back.

What I do at this point, as the panic mounts and the jungle drums begin beating and I realize that the well has run dry and that my future is behind me and I'm going to have to get a job only I'm completely unemployable, is to stop. First I try to breathe, because I'm either sitting there panting like a lapdog or I'm unintentionally making slow asthmatic death rattles. So I just sit there for a minute, breathing slowly, quietly. I let my mind wander. After a moment I may notice that I'm trying to decide whether or not I am too old for orthodontia and whether right now would be a good time to make a few calls, and then I start to think about learning to use makeup and how maybe I could find some boyfriend who is not a total and complete fixer-upper and then my life would be totally great and I'd be happy all the time, and then I think about all the people I should have called back before I sat down to work, and how I should probably at least check in with my agent and tell him this great idea I have and see if he thinks it's a good idea, and see if he thinks I need orthodontia— if that is what he is actually thinking whenever we have lunch together. Then

I think about someone I'm really annoyed with, or some financial problem that is driving me crazy, and decide that I must resolve this before I get down to today's work. So I become a dog with a chew toy, worrying it for a while, wrestling it to the ground, flinging it over my shoulder, chasing it, licking it, chewing it, flinging it back over my shoulder. I stop just short of actually barking. But all of this only takes somewhere between one and two minutes, so I haven't actually wasted that much time. Still, it leaves me winded. I go back to trying to breathe, slowly and calmly, and I finally notice the one-inch picture frame that I put on my desk to remind me of short assignments.

It reminds me that all I have to do is to write down as much as I can see through a one-inch picture frame. This is all I have to bite off for the time being. All I am going to do right now, for example, is write that one paragraph that sets the story in my hometown, in the late fifties, when the trains were still running. I am going to paint a picture of it, in words, on my word processor. Or all I am going to do is to describe the main character the very first time we meet her, when she first walks out the front door and onto the porch. I am not even going to describe the expression on her face when she first notices the blind dog sitting behind the wheel of her car——just what I can see through the one-inch picture frame, just one paragraph describing this woman, in the town where I grew up, the first time we encounter her.

E.L. Doctorow once said that "writing a novel is like driving a car at night. You can see only as far as your headlights, but you can make the whole trip that way." You don't have to see where you're going, you don't have to see your destination or everything you will pass along the way. You just have to see two or three feet ahead of you. This is right up there with the best advice about writing, or life, I have ever heard.

So after I've completely exhausted myself thinking about the people I most resent in the world, and my more arresting financial problems, and, of course, the orthodontia, I remember to pick up the one-inch picture frame and to figure out a one-inch piece of my story to tell, one small scene, one memory, one exchange. I also remember a story that I know I've told elsewhere but that over and over helps me to get a grip: thirty years ago my older brother, who was ten years old at the time, was trying to get a report on birds written that he'd had three months to write, which was due the next day. We were out at our family cabin in Bolinas, and he was at the kitchen table close to tears, surrounded by binder paper and pencils and unopened books on birds, immobilized by the hugeness of the task ahead. Then my father sat down beside him,

FOCUS ON WRITING: WHAT COLLEGE STUDENTS WANT TO KNOW

put his arm around my brother's shoulder, and said, "Bird by bird, buddy. Just take it bird by bird."

I tell this story again because it usually makes a dent in the tremendous sense of being overwhelmed that my students experience. Sometimes it actually gives them hope, and hope, as Chesterton said, is the power of being cheerful in circumstances that we know to be desperate. Writing can be a pretty desperate endeavor, because it is about some of our deepest needs: our need to be visible, to be heard, our need to make sense of our lives, to wake up and grow and belong. It is no wonder if we sometimes tend to take ourselves perhaps a bit too seriously. So here is another story I tell often.

In the Bill Murray movie *Stripes*, in which he joins the army, there is a scene that takes place the first night of boot camp, where Murray's platoon is assembled in the barracks. They are supposed to be getting to know their sergeant, played by Warren Oates, and one another. So each man takes a few moments to say a few things about who he is and where he is from. Finally it is the turn of this incredibly intense, angry guy named Francis. "My name is Francis," he says. "No one calls me Francis—anyone here calls me Francis and I'll kill them. And another thing. I don't like to be touched. Anyone here ever tries to touch me, I'll kill them," at which point Warren Oates jumps in and says, "Hey—lighten up, Francis."

This is not a bad line to have taped to the wall of your office.

Say to yourself in the kindest possible way, Look, honey, all we're going to do for now is to write a description of the river at sunrise, or the young child swimming in the pool at the club, or the first time the man sees the woman he will marry. That is all we are going to do for now. We are just going to take this bird by bird. But we are going to finish this one short assignment.

Shitty First Drafts

Now, practically even better news than that of short assignments is the idea of shitty first drafts. All good writers write them. This is how they end up with good second drafts and terrific third drafts. People tend to look at successful writers, writers who are getting their books published and maybe even doing well financially, and think that they sit down at their desks every morning feeling like a million dollars, feeling great about who they are and how much talent they have and what a great story they have to tell; that they take in a few deep breaths, push back their sleeves, roll their necks a few times to get all the cricks out, and dive in, typing fully formed passages as fast as a court reporter. But this is just the fantasy of the uninitiated. I know some very great writers,

writers you love who write beautifully and have made a great deal of money, and not one of them sits down routinely feeling wildly enthusiastic and confident. Not one of them writes elegant first drafts. All right, one of them does, but we do not like her very much. We do not think that she has a rich inner life or that God likes her or can even stand her. (Although when I mentioned this to my priest friend Tom, he said you can safely assume you've created God in your own image when it turns out that God hates all the same people you do.)

Very few writers really know what they are doing until they've done it. Nor do they go about their business feeling dewy and thrilled. They do not type a few stiff warm-up sentences and then find themselves bounding along like huskies across the snow. One writer I know tells me that he sits down every morning and says to himself nicely, "It's not like you don't have a choice, because you do—you can either type or kill yourself." We all often feel like we are pulling teeth, even those writers whose prose ends up being the most natural and fluid. The right words and sentences just do not come pouring out like ticker tape most of the time. Now, Muriel Spark is said to have felt that she was taking dictation from God every morning—sitting there, one supposes, plugged into a Dicta-phone, typing away, humming. But this is a very hostile and aggressive position. One might hope for bad things to rain down on a person like this.

For me and most of the other writers I know, writing is not rapturous. In fact, the only way I can get anything written at all is to write really, really shitty first drafts.

The first draft is the child's draft, where you let it all pour out and then let it romp all over the place, knowing that no one is going to see it and that you can shape it later. You just let this childlike part of you channel whatever voices and visions come through and onto the page. If one of the characters wants to say, "Well, so what, Mr. Poopy Pants?," you let her. No one is going to see it. If the kid wants to get into really sentimental, weepy, emotional territory, you let him. Just get it all down on paper, because there may be something great in those six crazy pages that you would never have gotten to by more rational, grown-up means. There may be something in the very last line of the very last paragraph on page six that you just love, that is so beautiful or wild that you now know what you're supposed to be writing about, more or less, or in what direction you might go—but there was no way to get to this without first getting through the first five and a half pages.

I used to write food reviews for *California* magazine before it folded. (My writing food reviews had nothing to do with the magazine folding, although every single review did cause a couple of canceled subscriptions. Some readers took umbrage at my comparing mounds of vegetable puree with various ex-presidents' brains.) These reviews always took two days to write. First I'd go to a restaurant several times with a few opinionated, articulate friends in tow. I'd sit there writing down everything anyone said that was at all interesting or funny. Then on the following Monday I'd sit down at my desk with my notes, and try to write the review. Even after I'd been doing this for years, panic would set in. I'd try to write a lead, but instead (I'd write a couple of dreadful sentences, xx them out, try again, xx everything out, and then feel despair and worry settle on my chest like an x-ray apron. It's over, I'd think, calmly. I'm not going to be able to get the magic to work this time. I'm ruined. I'm through. I'm toast. Maybe, I'd think, I can get my old job back as a clerk-typist. But probably not. I'd get up and study my teeth in the mirror for a while. Then I'd stop, remember to breathe, make a few phone calls, hit the kitchen and chow down. Eventually I'd go back and sit down at my desk, and sigh for the next ten minutes. Finally I would pick up my one-inch picture frame, stare into it as if for the answer, and every time the answer would come: all I had to do was to write a really shitty first draft of, say, the opening paragraph. And no one was going to see it.

So I'd start writing without reining myself in. It was almost just typing, just making my fingers move. And the writing would be terrible. I'd write a lead paragraph that was a whole page, even though the entire review could only be three pages long, and then I'd start writing up descriptions of the food, one dish at a time, bird by bird, and the critics would be sitting on my shoulders, commenting like cartoon characters. They'd be pretending to snore, or rolling their eyes at my overwrought descriptions, no matter how hard I tried to tone those descriptions down, no matter how conscious I was of what a friend said to me gently in my early days of restaurant reviewing. "Annie," she said, "it is just a piece of chicken. It is just a bit of cake."

But because by then I had been writing for so long, I would eventually let myself trust the process—sort of, more or less. I'd write a first draft that was maybe twice as long as it should be, with a self-indulgent arid boring beginning, stupefying descriptions of the meal, lots of quotes from my black-humored friends that made them sound more like the Manson girls than food lovers, and no ending to speak of. The whole thing would be so long and incoherent and hideous that for the rest of the day I'd obsess about getting creamed by a car before I could write a decent second draft. I'd worry that people would read what I'd written and believe that the accident had really been a suicide, that I had panicked because my talent was waning and my mind was shot.

The next day, though, I'd sit down, go through it all with a colored pen, take out everything I possibly could, find a new lead somewhere on the second page, figure out a kicky place to end it, and then write a second draft. It always turned out fine, sometimes even funny and weird and helpful. I'd go over it one more time and mail it in.

Then, a month later, when it was time for another review, the whole process would start again, complete with the fears that people would find my first draft before I could rewrite it.

Almost all good writing begins with terrible first efforts. You need to start somewhere. Start by getting something—anything—down on paper. A friend of mine says that the first draft is the down draft—you just get it down. The second draft is the up draft—you fix it up. You try to say what you have to say more accurately. And the third draft is the dental draft, where you check every tooth, to see if it's loose or cramped or decayed, or even, God help us, healthy.

What I've learned to do when I sit down to work on a shitty first draft is to quiet the voices in my head. First there's the vinegar-lipped Reader Lady, who says primly, "Well, that's not very interesting, is it?" And there's the emaciated German male who writes these Orwellian memos detailing your thought crimes. And there are your parents, agonizing over your lack of loyalty and discretion; and there's William Burroughs, dozing off or shooting up because he finds you as bold and articulate as a houseplant; and so on. And there are also the dogs: let's not forget the dogs, the dogs in their pen who will surely hurtle and snarl their way out if you ever stop writing, because writing is, for some of us, the latch that keeps the door of the pen closed, keeps those crazy ravenous dogs contained.

Quieting these voices is at least half the battle I fight daily. But this is better than it used to be. It used to be 87 percent. Left to its own devices, my mind spends much of its time having conversations with people who aren't there. I walk along defending myself to people, or exchanging repartee with them, or rationalizing my behavior, or seducing them with gossip, or pretending I'm on their TV talk show or whatever. I speed or run an aging yellow light or don't come to a full stop, and one nanosecond later am explaining to imaginary cops exactly why I had to do what I did, or insisting that I did not in fact do it.

I happened to mention this to a hypnotist I saw many years ago, and he looked at me very nicely. At first I thought he was feeling around on the floor

FOCUS ON WRITING: WHAT COLLEGE STUDENTS WANT TO KNOW

for the silent alarm button, but then he gave me the following exercise, which I still use to this day.

Close your eyes and get quiet for a minute, until the chatter starts up. Then isolate one of the voices and imagine the person speaking as a mouse. Pick it up by the tail and drop it into a mason jar. Then isolate another voice, pick it up by the tail, drop it in the jar. And so on. Drop in any high-maintenance parental units, drop in any contractors, lawyers, colleagues, children, anyone who is whining in your head. Then put the lid on, and watch all these mouse people clawing at the glass, jabbering away, trying to make you feel like shit because you won't do what they want—won't give them more money, won't be more successful, won't see them more often. Then imagine that there is a volume-control button on the bottle. Turn it all the way up for a minute, and listen to the stream of angry, neglected, guilt-mongering voices. Then turn it all the way down and watch the frantic mice lunge at the glass, trying to get to you. Leave it down, and get back to your shitty first draft.

A writer friend of mine suggests opening the jar and shooting them all in the head. But I think he's a little angry, and I'm sure nothing like this would ever occur to you.

DONALD M. MURRAY'S "TEACHING THE OTHER SELF: THE WRITER'S FIRST READER" (1982)

Why I included it

Donald M. Murray has widely inspired both students and writing teachers. I think part of his appeal is the respect he demonstrates for students. You can see that immediately here. Murray does not ask, "What do professional writers do that students can't do?" Instead, Murray expects teachers to treat their students as if they have as much value and as much to teach us as do professional writers. I'm hoping you'll be able to test Murray's ideas against your own writing practices and your experiences with writing teachers.

Background

Research on the writing process was regularly published beginning in the 1970s, so Murray's essay contributes to that conversation. Murray himself argued in 1972 that teachers should pay more attention to writing "as a process" than "as a product," and you can see here that he continued to think about writing practices and what the role of the teacher might be. When crafting an argument about how writing should be taught, Murray often relied on a combination of his reputation as a teacher, logical reasoning, and his experience as a writer (he was a journalist as well as a professor). His writing is thus more academic than Lamott's but probably more accessible than the writing of scholars who are explaining full research studies.

Reading hints and vocab

As I mention above, this essay is more difficult than Lamott's writing but more accessible than much of the writing I've included in the volume. Probably the greatest challenge is understanding the idea of two selves. It might help if you think about the number of messages that go through your mind when writing: What word shall I type next? How is that word spelled? Is that the word I want? How will this sound when it's all put together? Will the person I'm writing to understand what I mean? and so on.

You might also use self-talk as you write, such as, "You're so stupid. You'll never make this sound right" or "Okay, that's not quite right, but get it down for now, and you can come back and make it better." I'm hoping your self-talk is more of this latter variety. At any rate, Murray chronicles two selves, but there may be a whole community of people inside our heads chatting away as we write.

affective: subjective or emotional, rooted in feelings

cognitive: objective or rational, rooted in thought and mental activity

CONNECT

As you read, consider responding to the following questions to help you process the material.

1. How are Murray's ideas about drafting and revision similar to Lamott's? How are they different?

2. Murray uses several metaphors for writers including workers, map-readers, explorers, and tennis players. Which metaphor do you like the most? Why?

3. Murray's writing is directed towards teachers. What role is he urging them to adopt? How does he suggest they help students improve their writing?

4. When you read Murray's text from the perspective of a student, do you appreciate the advice he is giving teachers? Or do you see other roles for writing teachers that Murray doesn't identify? Explain.

5. Is there a connection between the "Other Self" and ideas of motivation or audience and their role in effective writing?

Murray, Donald M. "Teaching the Other Self: The Writer's First Reader." *College Composition and Communication*, vol. 33, no. 2, 1982, pp. 140–47. *JSTOR*, JSTOR, <www.jstor.org/stable/357621>.

WE COMMAND OUR students to write for others, but writers report they write for themselves. "I write for me," says Edward Albee. "The audience of me." Teachers of composition make a serious mistake if they consider such statements a matter of artistic ego alone.

The testimony of writers that they write for themselves opens a window on an important part of the writing process. If we look through that window we increase our understanding of the process and become more effective teachers of writing.

"I am my own first reader," says Isaac Bashevis Singer. "Writers write for themselves and not for their readers," declares Rebecca West, "and that art has nothing to do with communication between person and person, only with communication between different parts of a person's mind." "I think the audience an artist imagines," states Vladimir Nabokov, "when he imagines that sort of thing, is a room filled with people wearing his own mask." Edmund Blunden adds, "I don't think I have ever written for anybody except the other in one's self."

The act of writing might be described as a conversation between two workmen muttering to each other at the workbench. The self speaks, the other self listens and responds. The self proposes, the other self considers. The self makes, the other self evaluates. The two selves collaborate: a problem is spotted, discussed, defined; solutions are proposed, rejected, suggested, attempted, tested, discarded, accepted.

This process is described in that fine German novel, *The German Lesson,* by Siegfried Lenz (Hamburg, Germany: Hoffman und Campe Verlag, 1968; New York: Hill and Wang, 1971), when the narrator in the novel watches the painter Nansen at work. "And, as always when he was at work, he was talking. He didn't talk to himself, he talked to someone by the name of Balthasar, who stood beside him, his Balthasar, who only he could see and hear, with whom he chatted and argued and whom he sometimes jabbed with his elbow, so hard that even we, who couldn't see any Balthasar, would suddenly hear the invisible bystander groan or, if not groan, at least swear. The longer we stood there behind him, the more we began to believe in the existence of that Balthasar who made himself perceptible by a sharp intake of breath or a hiss of disappointment. And still the painter went on confiding in him, only to regret it a moment later."

Study this activity at the workbench within the skull and you might say that the self writes, the other self reads. But it is not reading as we usually consider it, the decoding of a completed text. It is a sophisticated reading that monitors writing before it is made, as it is made, and after it is made.

The term "monitor" is significant, for the reading during writing involves awareness on many levels and includes the opportunity for change. And when that change is made then everything must be read again to see how the change affects the reading.

The writer, as the text evolves, reads fragments of language as well as completed units of language, what isn't on the page as well as what is on the page, what should be left out as well as what should be put in. Even patterns and designs—sketches of possible relationships between pieces of information or fragments of rhetoric or language—that we do not usually consider language are read and discussed by the self and the other self.

It is time researchers in the discipline called English bridge the gulf between the reading researcher and the writing researcher. There are now many trained writing researchers who can collaborate with the trained researchers in reading, for the act of writing is inseparable from the act of reading. You can read without writing, but you can't write without reading. The reading skills required, however, to decode someone else's finished text may be quite different from the reading skills required to chase a wisp of thinking until it grows into a completed thought.

To follow thinking that has not yet become thought, the writer's other self has to be an explorer, a map-maker. The other self scans the entire territory, forgetting, for the moment, questions of order or language. The writer/explorer looks for the draft's horizons. Once the writer has scanned the larger vision of the territory, it may be possible for him (or her) to trace a trail that will get the writer from here to there, from meaning identified to meaning clarified. Questions of order are now addressed, but questions of language still delayed. Finally, the writer/explorer studies the map in detail to spot the hazards that lie along the trail, the hidden swamps of syntax, the underbrush of verbiage, the voice found, lost, found again.

Map-making and map-reading are among man's [sic] most complex cognitive tasks. Eventually the other self learns to monitor the always-changing relationship between where the writer is and where the writer intended to go. The writer/explorer stops, looks ahead, considers and reconsiders the trail and the ways to get around the obstacles that block that trail.

There is only one way the student can learn map-reading—and that is in the field. Books and lectures may help, but only after the student writer has been out in the bush will the student understand the kind of reading essential for the exploration of thinking. The teacher has to be a guide who doesn't lead so much as stand behind the young explorer, pointing out alternatives only at the moment of panic. Only after the writer/explorer has read one map and made the trip from meaning intended to meaning realized, will the young writer begin to trust the other self and have faith that it will know how to read other trails through other territories.

The reading writer—the map-maker and map-reader—reads the word, the line, the sentence, the paragraph, the page, the entire text. This constant back-and-forth reading monitors the multiple complex relationships between all the elements in writing. Recursive scanning—or reviewing and previewing—during revision is beginning to be documented by Sondra Perl, Nancy Sommers, and others. But further and more sophisticated investigation will, I believe, show that the experienced writer is able, through the writer's other self, to read what has gone before and what may come afterward during the writing that is done before there is a written text, and during the writing that produces an embryonic text.

I think we can predict some of the functions that are performed by the other self during the writing process.

- The other self tracks the activity that is taking place. Writing, in a sense, does not exist until it is read. The other self records the evolving text.
- The other self gives the self the distance that is essential for craft. This distance, the craftperson's step backwards, is a key element in writing that is therapeutic for the writer.
- The other self provides an evolving context for the writer. As the writer adds, cuts, or reorders, the other self keeps track of how each change affects the draft.
- The other self articulates the process of writing, providing the writer with an engineering history of the developing text, a technical resource that records the problems faced and the solutions that were tried and rejected, or not yet tried, and the ones that are in place.
- The other self is the critic who is continually looking at the writing to see if, in the writer's phrase, "it works."
- The other self also is the supportive colleague to the writer, the chap who commiserates and encourages, listens sympathetically to the writer's

complaints and reminds the writer of past success. The deeper we get into the writing process the more we may discover how affective concerns govern the cognitive, for writing is an intellectual activity carried on in an emotional environment, a precisely engineered sailboat trying to hold course in a vast and stormy Atlantic. The captain has to deal with fears as well as compass readings.

We shall have to wait for perceptive and innovative research by teams of reading and writing researchers to document the complex kind of reading that is done during the writing process. But, fortunately, we do not have to wait for the results of such research to make use of the other self in the teaching of writing.

The other self can be made articulate. It has read the copy as the copy was being created and knows the decisions that were made to produce the draft. This does not mean that they were all conscious decisions in the sense that the writer articulated what was being done, but even instinctive or subconscious editorial decisions can be articulated retrospectively.

Many teachers of writing, especially those who are also teachers of literature, are deeply suspicious of the testimony of writers about their own writing. It may be that the critic feels that he or she knows more than the writer, that the testimony of writers is too simple to be of value. But I have found in my own work that what students and professional writers say about their own writing process is helpful and makes sense in relation to the text.

Writing is, after all, a rational act; the writing self was monitored by the reading self during the writing process. The affective may well control or stimulate or limit the cognitive, but writing is thinking, and a thinking act can, most of the time, be recreated in rational terms. The tennis pro may return a serve instinctively, but instinct is, in part, internalized consciousness, and if you ask the pro about that particular return the experienced player will be able to describe what was done and why. If the player thought consciously at the time of the serve, the ball would sail by. The return was a practiced, learned act made spontaneous by experience, and it can be described and explained after the fact.

This retroactive understanding of what was done makes it possible for the teacher not only to teach the other self but recruit the other self to assist in the teaching of writing. The teacher brings the other self into existence, and then works with that other self so that, after the student has graduated, the other self can take over the function of teacher.

When the student speaks and the student and the teacher listen, they are both informed about the nature of the writing process that produced the draft.

This is the point at which the teacher knows what needs to be taught or reinforced, one step at a time, and the point at which the student knows what needs to be done in the next draft.

Listening is not a normal composition teacher's skill. We tell and they listen. But to make effective use of the other self the teacher and the student must listen together.

This is done most efficiently in conference. But before the conference, at the beginning of the course, the teacher must explain to the class exactly why the student is to speak first. I tell my students that I'm going to do as little as possible to interfere with their learning. It is their job to read the text, to evaluate it, to decide how it can be improved so that they will be able to write when I am not there. I point out that the ways in which they write are different, their problems and solutions are different, and that I am a resource to help them find their own way. I will always attempt to underteach so that they can overlearn.

I may read the paper before the conference or during the conference, but the student will always speak first in the conference. I have developed a repertoire of questions—what surprised you? what's working best? what are you going to do next?—but I rarely use them. The writing conference is not a social occasion. The student comes to get my response to the work, and I give my response to the student's response. I am teaching the other self.

The more inexperienced the student and the less comprehensible the text, the more helpful the writer's comments. Again and again with remedial students I am handed a text that I simply cannot understand. I do not know what it is supposed to say. I cannot discover a pattern of organization. I cannot understand the language. But when the writer tells me what the writer was doing, when the other self is allowed to speak, I find that the text was produced rationally. The writer followed misunderstood instruction, inappropriate principles, or logical processes that did not work.

Most students, for example, feel that if you want to write for a large audience you should write in general terms, in large abstractions. They must be told that that is logical, but it simply doesn't work. The larger the audience, the more universal we want our message to be, the more specific we must become. It was E.B. White who reminded us, "Don't write about Man, write about *a* man."

When the teacher listens to the student, the conference can be short. The student speaks about the process that produced the draft or about the draft itself. The teacher listens, knowing that the effective teacher must teach where the student is, not where the teacher wishes the student was, then scans or re-scans the draft to confirm, adjust, or disagree with the student's comments.

One thing the responsive teacher, the teacher who listens to the student first, then to the text, soon learns is that the affective usually controls the cognitive, and affective responses have to be dealt with first. I grew used to this with students, but during the past two years I have also worked with professionals on some of the best newspapers in the country, and I have found that it is even more true of published writers. Writers' feelings control the environment in which the mind functions. Unless the teacher knows this environment, the teaching will be off target.

In conference, for example, the majority of men have been socialized to express a false confidence in their writing. The teacher who feels that these men are truly confident will badly misread the writer's other self. The behavior of women in conference is changing, but not fast enough. Most women still express the false modesty about their accomplishments that society has said is appropriate for women. Again the teacher must recognize and support the other self that knows how good the work really is.

I am constantly astonished when I see drafts of equal accomplishment, but with evaluations by the writers that are miles apart. One student may say, "This is terrible. I can't write. I think I'd better drop the course." And right after that on a similar paper a student says, "I never had so much fun writing before. I think this is really a good paper. Do you think I should become a writer?"

Many students, of course, have to deal first with those feelings about the draft—or about writing itself. The teacher in conference should listen to these comments, for they often provide important clues to why the student is writing—or avoiding writing—in a particular way.

The instructor who wishes to teach the other self must discuss the text with that other self in less despairing or elated tones. Too often the inexperienced conference teacher goes to the polar extreme and offers the despairing student absolute praise and the confident student harsh criticism. In practice, the effective conference teacher does not deal in praise or criticism. All texts can be improved, and the instructor discusses with the student what is working and can be made to work better, and what isn't working and how it might be made to work.

After the student learns to deal with his or her defensiveness toward criticism of a working draft, the student can move on to more cognitive matters. At first the students,.and the ineffective writing teacher, focus on the superficial, the most obvious problems of language or manuscript preparation. But the teacher, through questioning, can reorient the student to the natural hierarchy of editorial concerns.

These questions, over a series of conferences, may evolve from "What's the single most important thing you have to say?" to "What questions is the reader going to ask you and when are they going to be asked?" to "Where do you hear the voice come through strongest?"

The students will discover, as the teacher models an ideal other self, that the largest questions of content, meaning, or focus have to be dealt with first. Until there is a clear meaning the writer cannot order the information that supports that meaning or leads towards it. And until the meaning and its supporting structure are clear the writer cannot make the decisions about voice and language that clarify and communicate that meaning. The other self has to monitor many activities and make sure that the writing self reads what is being monitored in an effective sequence.

Sometimes teachers who are introduced to teaching the other self feel that listening to the student first means that they cannot intervene. That is not true. This is not a do-your-own-thing kind of teaching. It is a demanding teaching; it is nothing less than the teaching of critical thinking.

Listening is, after all, an aggressive act. When the teacher insists that the student knows the subject and the writing process that produced the draft better than the teacher, and then has faith that the student has an other self that has monitored the producing of the draft, then the teacher puts enormous pressure on the student. Intelligent comments are expected, and when they are expected they are often received.

I have been impressed by how effectively primary students, those in the first three grades in school, have a speaking other self. Fortunately this other self that monitors the writing process has been documented on tape in a longitudinal study conducted in the Atkinson, New Hampshire, schools by Donald Graves, Lucy Calkins and Susan Sowers at the University of New Hampshire. There the other self has been recorded and analyzed. The most effective learning takes place when the other self articulates the writing that went well. Too much instruction is failure-centered. It focuses on error and unintentionally reinforces error.

The successful writer does not so much correct error as discover what is working and extend that element in the writing. The writer looks for the voice, the order, the relationship of information that is working well, and concentrates on making the entire piece of writing have the effectiveness of the successful fragment. The responsive teacher is always attempting to get the student to bypass the global evaluations of failure— "I can't write about this," "It's an airball," "I don't have anything to say"—and move into an element that is working well. In the beginning of a piece of writing by a beginning student, that first concern might well be the subject or the feeling that the student has toward the subject. The teacher may well say, "Okay. This draft isn't working, but what do you know about the subject that a reader needs to know?"

Again and again the teacher listens to what the student is saying—and not saying—to help the student hear that other self that has been monitoring what isn't yet on the page or what may be beginning to appear on the page.

This dialogue between the student's other self and the teacher occurs best in conference. But the conferences should be short and frequent.

"I dunno," the student says. "In reading this over I think maybe I'm more specific."

The teacher scans the text and responds, "I agree. What are you going to work on next?"

"I guess the ending. It's sorta goes on."

"Okay. Let me see it when it doesn't."

The important thing is that only one or two issues are dealt with in a conference. The conference isn't a psychiatric session. Think of the writer as an apprentice at the workbench with a master workman, a senior colleague, stopping by once in a while for a quick chat about the work.

We can also help the other self to become articulate by having the student write, after completing a draft, a brief statement about the draft. That statement can be attached on the front of the draft so the teacher can hear what the other self says and respond, after reading that statement and the draft, in writing. But I have found this procedure far less effective than the face-to-face conference, where the act of listening is personal, and where the teacher can hear the reflection and the pause as well as the statement and where the teacher can listen with the eye, reading the student's body language as well as the student's text.

The other self develops confidence through the experience of being heard in small and large group workshops. The same dynamics take place as have been modeled in the conference. The group leader asks the writer, "How can we help you?" The other self speaks of the process or of the text. The workshop members listen and read the text with the words of the other self in their ears. Then they respond, helping the other self become a more effective reader of the evolving text.

The papers that are published in workshops should be the best papers. The workshop members need to know how good writing is made, and they need to know how good writing can be improved. I always make clear that the papers being published in workshops are the best ones. As the other self speaks of how these good papers have been made and how they can be improved, the student being published has that student's most effective writing process reinforced. You can hear the other self becoming stronger and more confident as it speaks of what worked and as it proposes what may work next. The other workshop members hear an effective other self. They hear how a good writer reads an evolving draft. And during the workshop sessions their other selves start to speak, and they hear their own other selves participate in the helpful process of the workshop.

The teacher must always remember that the student, in the beginning of the course, does not know the other self exists. Its existence is an act of faith for the teacher. Sometimes that is a stupendous act of faith. Ronald, his nose running, his prose stalled, does not appear to have a self, and certainly not a critical, constructive other self. But even Ronald will hear that intelligent other self if the teacher listens well.

The teacher asks questions for which the student does not think there are answers: Why did you use such a strong word here? How did you cut this description and make it clearer? Why did you add so many specifics on Page 3? I think this ending really works, but what did you see that made you realize that old beginning was the new ending?

The student has the answers. And the student is surprised by the fact of answers as much as by the answers themselves. The teacher addresses a self that the student didn't know existed, and the student listens with astonishment to what that other self is saying—"Hey, he's not so dumb." "That's pretty good, she knows what she's doing."

The teacher helps the student find the other self, get to know the other self, learn to work with the other self, and then the teacher walks away to deal with another Ronald in another course who does not know there is another self. The teacher's faith is built on experience. If Ronald had another self, then there is hope for Edith.

What happens in the writing conference and the workshop in which the other self is allowed to become articulate is best expressed in the play, *The Elephant Man,* by Bernard Pomerance, when Merrick, the freak, who has been listened to for the first time in his life, says, "Before I spoke with people, I did not think of all those things because there was no-one to think them for. Now things come out of my mouth which are true."

SONDRA PERL'S "UNDERSTANDING COMPOSING" (1980)

Why I included it

Perl was one of several scholars who used ***protocol analysis*** to discover what writers think about as they write. Protocol analysis involved writers "thinking aloud" while writing, and it also considered all the writing generated during the protocol. This research method is an important counterbalance to the ideas of Lamott and Murray above, which are based on writer's accounts of their experiences *outside of* instead of *during* the process of writing. Perl and other researchers also studied more than one writer to find patterns, rather than relying on a limited number of expert writers.

Perl offers an excellent example of inquiry-based research, as her work responds to clearly articulated questions. The answers are somewhat complex, which leads Perl to more questions, and more research—she is consistently motivated to learn more!

You might have noticed that Murray mentioned Perl's research in his essay above. Note that his work appeared in 1982, two years after Perl published the following piece.

Background

Perl is known for her research on composing processes. You may notice that the term "recursive" she uses is common enough today that I used it early in this chapter. Other terms she defines in this essay did not remain at the forefront of writing discussions. The patterns she articulates, however, continue to be recognized as legitimate writing practices. You may thus notice several connections to discussions in this chapter and other chapters.

This particular essay was published in the premier journal in writing studies scholarship, *College Composition and Communication*. It was thus aimed at an audience of writing professors and researchers who would be interested in knowing more about composing and who would likely be familiar with earlier conversations on this topic.

Reading hints and vocabulary

Perl summarizes her research and turns to a specific participant in her study rather than chronicle examples from many participants. Because she published several articles about composing processes, scholars in the field would likely trust her conclusions. If she was publishing her first study and told readers she was drawing on a lot of research without offering specifics, reviewers or editors probably would have asked her to revise before publishing her work so that she could provide more information (where and when did this research take place? who participated? how many participated? how exactly was the research conducted?). Perl also would likely have been asked to provide specific examples to support each of the conclusions she draws.

You can read from this position of trusting the researcher and also consider the degree to which her conclusions match your experiences and what further questions you would like answered. Familiarize yourself with the following terms to help you better understand Perl's discussion.

linear writing process: a traditional idea that writing has steps from start to end, such as "plan-write-revise"

recursive process: as writers move forward in their work, they also regularly move back, repeating earlier steps in a new way or working through an earlier part of the process to help them progress

felt sense: an internal focus on a topic that occupies the mind and body, helping a writer to conjure words, images, or ideas to get started with their writing or return to their writing after a pause

retrospective structuring: when writers use felt sense to gain a better grasp of what they have to say and what overall shape their writing should take

discovery: when writers find out what they have to say during the process of writing (instead of knowing before they write)

projective structuring: when writers pay attention to the demands of a specific situation, including audience expectations, as they craft their writing; sometimes this is done to the extreme and severs the writer's connection to the work, and sometimes audience expectations are mistakenly understood as a series of rules (which is very sad)

CONNECT

As you read, consider responding to the following questions to help you process the material.

1. Notice Perl's use of questions. What function do they serve?

2. Why does Perl focus on "Anne" in her discussion even though the patterns she describes are based on "observations of the composing processes of many types of writers"?

3. To what degree do you follow processes that Perl describes? How do your processes differ?

4. Why do you suppose some of the terms Perl uses to explain composing processes are not used regularly today when discussing writing processes?

Perl, Sondra. "Understanding Composing." *College Composition and Communication*, vol. 31, no. 4, 1980, pp. 363–69. *JSTOR*, JSTOR, <www.jstor.org/stable/356586>.

> Any psychological process, whether the development of thought or voluntary behavior, is a process undergoing changes right before one's eyes.... Under certain conditions it becomes possible to trace this development.
>   L.S. Vygotsky[1]

> It's hard to begin this case study of myself as a writer because even as I'm searching for a beginning, a pattern of organization, I'm watching myself, trying to understand my behavior. As I sit here in silence, I can see lots of things happening that never made it onto my tapes. My mind leaps from the task at hand to what I need at the vegetable stand for tonight's soup to the threatening rain outside to ideas voiced in my writing group this morning, but in between "distractions" I hear myself trying out words I might use. It's as if the extraneous thoughts are a counterpoint to the more steady attention I'm giving to composing. This is all to point out that the process is more complex than I'm aware of, but I think my tapes reveal certain basic patterns that I tend to follow.
>   Anne
>   New York City Teacher

ANNE IS A teacher of writing. In 1979, she was among a group of twenty teachers who were taking a course in research and basic writing at New York University.[2] One of the assignments in the course was for the teachers to tape their thoughts while composing aloud on the topic, "My Most Anxious Moment as a Writer." Everyone in the group was given the topic in the morning during class and told to compose later on that day in a place where they would be comfortable and relatively free from distractions. The result was a tape of composing aloud and a written product that formed the basis for class discussion over the next few days.

One of the purposes of this assignment was to provide teachers with an opportunity to see their own composing processes at work. From the start of

---

1   L.S. Vygotsky, *Mind in Society,* trans. M. Cole, V. John-Steiner, S. Scribner, and E. Souberman (Cambridge, Mass: Harvard University Press, 1978), p. 61.

2   This course was team-taught by myself and Gordon Pradl, Associate Professor of English Education at New York University.

FOCUS ON WRITING: WHAT COLLEGE STUDENTS WANT TO KNOW

the course, we recognized that we were controlling the situation by assigning a topic and that we might be altering the process by asking writers to compose aloud. Nonetheless we viewed the task as a way of capturing some of the flow of composing and, as Anne later observed in her analysis of her tape, she was able to detect certain basic patterns. This observation, made not only by Anne, then leads me to ask "What basic patterns seem to occur during composing?" and "What does this type of research have to tell us about the nature of the composing process?"

Perhaps the most challenging part of the answer is the recognition of recursiveness in writing. In recent years, many researchers including myself have questioned the traditional notion that writing is a linear process with a strict plan-write-revise sequence.[3] In its stead, we have advocated the idea that writing is a recursive process, that throughout the process of writing, writers return to substrands of the overall process, or subroutines (short successions of steps that yield results on which the writer draws in taking the next set of steps); writers use these to keep the process moving forward. In other words, recursiveness in writing implies that there is a forward-moving action that exists by virtue of a backward-moving action. The questions that then need to be answered are, "To what do writers move back?" "What exactly is being repeated?" "What recurs?"

To answer these questions, it is important to look at what writers do while writing and what an analysis of their processes reveals. The descriptions that follow are based on my own observations of the composing processes of many types of writers including college students, graduate students, and English teachers like Anne.

Writing does appear to be recursive, yet the parts that recur seem to vary from writer to writer and from topic to topic. Furthermore, some recursive elements are easy to spot while others are not.

1. The most visible recurring feature or backward movement involves rereading little bits of discourse. Few writers I have seen write for long periods of time without returning briefly to what is already down on the page.

   For some, like Anne, rereading occurs after every few phrases; for others, it occurs after every sentence; more frequently, it occurs after a

---

3   See Janet Emig, *The Composing Processes of Twelfth-Graders*, NCTE Research Report No. 13 (Urbana, Ill: National Council of Teachers of English, 1971); Linda Flower and J.R. Hayes, "The Cognition of Discovery," *CCC*, 31 (February, 1980), 21–32; Nancy Sommers, "The Need for Theory in Composition Research," *CCC*, 30 (February, 1979), 46–49.

"chunk" of information has been written. Thus, the unit that is reread is not necessarily a syntactic one, but rather a semantic one as defined by the writer.

2. The second recurring feature is some key word or item called up by the topic. Writers consistently return to their notion of the topic throughout the process of writing. Particularly when they are stuck, writers seem to use the topic or a key word in it as a way to get going again. Thus many times it is possible to see writers "going back," rereading the topic they were given, changing it to suit what they have been writing or changing what they have written to suit their notion of the topic.

3. There is also a third backward movement in writing, one that is not so easy to document. It is not easy because the move, itself, cannot immediately be identified with words. In fact, the move is not to any words on the page nor to the topic but to feelings or non-verbalized perceptions that *surround* the words, or to what the words already present *evoke* in the writer. The move draws on sense experience, and it can be observed if one pays close attention to what happens when writers pause and seem to listen or otherwise react to what is inside of them. The move occurs inside the writer, to what is physically felt. The term used to describe this focus of writers' attention is *felt sense*. The term "felt sense" has been coined and described by Eugene Gendlin, a philosopher at the University of Chicago. In his words, felt sense is the soft underbelly of thought ... a kind of bodily awareness that ... can be used as a tool ... a bodily awareness that ... encompasses everything you feel and know about a given subject at a given time.... It is felt in the body, yet it has meanings. It is body *and* mind before they are split apart.[4]

This felt sense is always there, within us. It is unifying, and yet, when we bring words to it, it can break apart, shift, unravel, and become something else. Gendlin has spent many years showing people how to work with their felt sense. Here I am making connections between what he has done and what I have seen happen as people write.

When writers are given a topic, the topic itself evokes a felt sense in them. This topic calls forth images, words, ideas, and vague fuzzy feelings that are anchored in the writer's body. What is elicited, then, is not solely the product of a mind but of a mind alive in a living, sensing body.

---

4   Eugene Gendlin, *Focusing* (New York: Everest House, 1978), pp. 35, 165.

FOCUS ON WRITING: WHAT COLLEGE STUDENTS WANT TO KNOW

When writers pause, when they go back and repeat key words, what they seem to be doing is waiting, paying attention to what is still vague and unclear. They are looking to their felt experience, and waiting for an image, a word, or a phrase to emerge that captures the sense they embody.

Usually, when they make the decision to write, it is after they have a dawning awareness that something has clicked, that they have enough of a sense that if they begin with a few words heading in a certain direction, words will continue to come which will allow them to flesh out the sense they have.

The process of using what is sensed directly about a topic is a natural one. Many writers do it without any conscious awareness that that is what they are doing. For example, Anne repeats the words "anxious moments," using these key words as a way of allowing her sense of the topic to deepen. She asks herself, "Why are exams so anxiety provoking?" and waits until she has enough of a sense within her that she can go in a certain direction. She does not yet have the words, only the sense that she is able to begin. Once she writes, she stops to see what is there. She maintains a highly recursive composing style throughout and she seems unable to go forward without first going back to see and to listen to what she has already created. In her own words, she says:

> My disjointed style of composing is very striking to me. I almost never move from the writing of one sentence directly to the next. After each sentence I pause to read what I've written, assess, sometimes edit and think about what will come next. I often have to read the several preceding sentences a few times as if to gain momentum to carry me to the next sentence. I seem to depend a lot on the sound of my words and ... while I'm hanging in the middle of this uncompleted thought, I may also start editing a previous sentence or get an inspiration for something which I want to include later in the paper.

What tells Anne that she is ready to write? What is the feeling of "momentum" like for her? What is she hearing as she listens to the "sound" of her words? When she experiences "inspiration," how does she recognize it?

In the approach I am presenting, the ability to recognize what one needs to do or where one needs to go is informed by calling on felt sense. This is the internal criterion writers seem to use to guide them when they are planning, drafting, and revising.

The recursive move, then, that is hardest to document but is probably the most important to be aware of is the move to felt sense, to what is not yet *in words* but out of which images, words, and concepts emerge.

The continuing presence of this felt sense, waiting for us to discover it and see where it leads, raises a number of questions.

Is "felt sense" another term for what professional writers call their "inner voice" or their feeling of "inspiration"?

Do skilled writers call on their capacity to sense more readily than unskilled writers?

Rather than merely reducing the complex act of writing to a neat formulation, can the term "felt sense" point us to an area of our experience from which we can evolve even richer and more accurate descriptions of composing?

Can learning how to work with felt sense teach us about creativity and release us from stultifyingly repetitive patterns?

My observations lead me to answer "yes" to all four questions. There seems to be a basic step in the process of composing that skilled writers rely on even when they are unaware of it and that less skilled writers can be taught. This process seems to rely on very careful attention to one's inner reflections and is often accompanied with bodily sensations.

When it's working, this process allows us to say or write what we've never said before, to create something new and fresh, and occasionally it provides us with the experience of "newness" or "freshness," even when "old words" or images are used.

The basic process begins with paying attention. If we are given a topic, it begins with taking the topic in and attending to what it evokes in us. There is less "figuring out" an answer and more "waiting" to see what forms. Even without a predetermined topic, the process remains the same. We can ask ourselves, "What's on my mind?" or "Of all the things I know about, what would I most like to write about now?" and wait to see what comes. What we pay attention to is the part of our bodies where we experience ourselves directly. For many people, it's the area of their stomachs; for others, there is a more generalized response and they maintain a hovering attention to what they experience throughout their bodies.

Once a felt sense forms, we match words to it. As we begin to describe it, we get to see what is there for us. We get to see what we think, what we know. If we are writing about something that truly interests us, the felt sense deepens. We know that we are writing out of a "centered" place.

FOCUS ON WRITING: WHAT COLLEGE STUDENTS WANT TO KNOW

If the process is working, we begin to move along, sometimes quickly. Other times, we need to return to the beginning, to reread, to see if we captured what we meant to say. Sometimes after rereading we move on again, picking up speed. Other times by rereading we realize we've gone off the track, that what we've written doesn't quite "say it," and we need to reassess. Sometimes the words are wrong and we need to change them. Other times we need to go back to the topic, to call up the sense it initially evoked to see where and how our words led us astray. Sometimes in rereading we discover that the topic is "wrong," that the direction we discovered in writing is where we really want to go. It is important here to clarify that the terms "right" and "wrong" are not necessarily meant to refer to grammatical structures or to correctness.

What is "right" or "wrong" corresponds to our sense of our intention. We intend to write something, words come, and now we assess if those words adequately capture our intended meaning. Thus, the first question we ask ourselves is "Are these words right for me?" "Do they capture what I'm trying to say?" "If not, what's missing?"

Once we ask "what's missing?" we need once again to wait, to let a felt sense of what is missing form, and then to write out of that sense.

I have labeled this process of attending, of calling up a felt sense, and of writing out of that place, the process of *retrospective structuring*. It is retrospective in that it begins with what is already there, inchoately, and brings whatever is there forward by using language in structured form.

It seems as though a felt sense has within it many possible structures or forms. As we shape what we intend to say, we are further structuring our sense while correspondingly shaping our piece of writing.

It is also important to note that what is there implicitly, without words, is not equivalent to what finally emerges. In the process of writing, we begin with what is inchoate and end with something that is tangible. In order to do so, we both discover and construct what we mean. Yet the term "discovery" ought not lead us to think that meaning exists fully formed inside of us and that all we need do is dig deep enough to release it. In writing, meaning cannot be discovered the way we discover an object on an archeological dig. In writing, meaning is crafted and constructed. It involves us in a process of coming-into-being. Once we have worked at shaping, through language, what is there inchoately, we can look at what we have written to see if it adequately captures what we intended. Often at this moment discovery occurs. We see something new in our writing that comes upon us as a surprise. We see in our words a further structuring of the sense we began with and we recognize that in those words we have discovered something new about ourselves and our topic. Thus when we are successful at this process, we end up with a product that teaches us something, that clarifies what we know (or what we knew at one point only implicitly), and that lifts out or explicates or enlarges our experience. In this way, writing leads to discovery.

All the writers I have observed, skilled and unskilled alike, use the process of retrospective structuring while writing. Yet the degree to which they do so varies and seems, in fact, to depend upon the model of the writing process that they have internalized. Those who realize that writing can be a recursive process have an easier time with waiting, looking, and discovering. Those who subscribe to the linear model find themselves easily frustrated when what they write does not immediately correspond to what they planned or when what they produce leaves them with little sense of accomplishment. Since they have relied on a formulaic approach, they often produce writing that is formulaic as well, thereby cutting themselves off from the possibility of discovering something new.

Such a result seems linked to another feature of the composing process, to what I call *projective structuring*, or the ability to craft what one intends to say so that it is intelligible to others.

A number of concerns arise in regard to projective structuring; I will mention only a few that have been raised for me as I have watched different writers at work.

1. Although projective structuring is only one important part of the composing process, many writers act as if it is the whole process. These writers focus on what they think others want them to write rather than looking to see what it is they want to write. As a result, they often ignore their felt sense and they do not establish a living connection between themselves and their topic.

2. Many writers reduce projective structuring to a series of rules or criteria for evaluating finished discourse. These writers ask, "Is what I'm writing correct?" and "Does it conform to the rules I've been taught?" While these concerns are important, they often overshadow all others and lock the writer in the position of writing solely or primarily for the approval of readers.

Projective structuring, as I see it, involves much more than imagining a strict audience and maintaining a strict focus on correctness. It is true that to handle this part of the process well, writers need to know certain grammatical rules and evaluative criteria, but they also need to know how to call up a sense of their reader's needs and expectations.

For projective structuring to function fully, writers need to draw on their capacity to move away from their own words, to decenter from the page, and to project themselves into the role of the reader. In other words, projective structuring asks writers to attempt to become readers and to imagine what someone other than themselves will need before the writer's particular piece of writing can become intelligible and compelling. To do so, writers must have the experience of being readers. They cannot call up a felt sense of a reader unless they themselves have experienced what it means to be lost in a piece of writing or to be excited by it. When writers do not have such experiences, it is easy for them to accept that readers merely require correctness.

In closing, I would like to suggest that retrospective and projective structuring are two parts of the same basic process. Together they form the alternating mental postures writers assume as they move through the act of composing. The former relies on the ability to go inside, to attend to what is there, from that attending to place words upon a page, and then to assess if those words adequately capture one's meaning. The latter relies on the ability to assess how the words on that page will affect someone other than the writer, the reader. We rarely do one without the other entering in; in fact, again in these postures we can see the shuttling back-and-forth movements of the composing process, the move from sense to words and from words to sense, from inner experience to outer judgment and from judgment back to experience. As we move through this cycle, we are continually composing and recomposing our meanings and what we mean. And in doing so, we display some of the basic recursive patterns that writers who observe themselves closely seem to see in their own work. After observing the process for a long time we may, like Anne, conclude that at any given moment the process is more complex than anything we are aware of; yet such insights, I believe, are important. They show us the fallacy of reducing the composing process to a simple linear scheme and they leave us with the potential for creating even more powerful ways of understanding composing.

JOHN R. HAYES AND LINDA S. FLOWER'S "WRITING RESEARCH AND THE WRITER" (1986)

Why I included it

Like Murray and Perl, John R. Hayes and Linda S. Flower are well-known and respected in the field of composition studies. This article shows both breadth and depth in their understanding of writing practices. The article is also helpful in its organization. When trying to communicate a lot of information and material, sections and sub-sections help the writer (according to the research Hayes and Flower cite), and they also help readers more easily trace the categories and sub-categories being described. If you are ever tasked with synthesizing research that spans a large subject area, this article provides an excellent model.

CONNECT

As you read, consider responding to the following questions to help you process the material.

1. What ideas from Hayes and Flower do you recognize from other parts of this text?

2. In what ways does the writing process described by Hayes and Flower match your own process? In what ways do you diverge from the processes they describe?

3. Hayes and Flower do not discuss many of the topics discussed in Chapter Two on the rhetorical situation. Where do you think attention to the rhetorical situation fits into the structure of the writing process they describe?

4. Compare the content and style of this piece to one of the other essays from this chapter. How do the ideas overlap? How are they different? How are the styles similar? How are they different?

Background

Hayes and Flower summarize their research—and the research of others—for an audience of academic psychologists who would probably be unfamiliar with this topic. The emphasis on writing cognition (how the mind is engaged in the writing process) suggests a connection between this kind of writing research and research in psychology. However, Hayes and Flower do not spend much time explaining why academic psychologists might be interested in the topic but instead begin and end the article by pointing to big changes in writing instruction. This lack of attention to exigence confused me for a moment. I then wondered if perhaps the issue of *American Psychologist* where this was published was devoted to writing or teaching. I went back to the database where I had found the article and looked at the issue. Sure enough, it was a special issue on the topic of "Psychological Science and Education." The article about teaching writing based on research findings made sense in this context.

Hayes and Flower use a very specific kind of organization, and it may help if you see it in a different form. I have thus made a reverse outline, similar to what often helps me when I am working on revisions. In this case, the reverse outline is not for revision purposes but rather because it helps me map out the parts of the article so I can see how the parts connect. I hope this outline helps you follow the ideas more easily. You might even want to create a different way of mapping this article or another article to visually represent the parts.

I. Intro
   A. There's been a move to teaching writing as a process
   B. Research has been conducted to discover the "cognitive processes that underlie writing"
   C. This article focuses on writing process research at the postsecondary (college) level

II. The Structure of the Writing Process (discovered through protocol analysis)
   A. Writing Is Goal-Directed
   B. Writing Goals Are Hierarchically Organized
   C. Writers Use Three Major Processes: Planning, Sentence Generation, Revising
      1. Planning
         a. Representation of Knowledge
         b. Source of the Writing Plan
            i. writer's topic knowledge
            ii. writer's knowledge of effective writing formats
            iii. writer's knowledge of strategies that support planning and problem-solving when known writing formats are inadequate
               a) writer forms initial task representation and body of goals
               b) the body of goals is a hierarchy with top goals and sub-goals, and the goals are linked in multiple ways
               c) the body of goals is restructured or modified as the writer's ideas or priorities shift
               d) expert writers tend to form a richer network of goals with more connections between goals
      2. Sentence Generation Process—mostly similar between expert and average writers
      3. Revision Process
         a. Experts attend more to global problems than do novices
         b. Writers have difficulty detecting faults in their own text

c. A variety of cues initiate revision, including dissonance between inten-
　　　　tion and text

　　　d. Experts detect more text problems than novices

　　　e. Some rewrite text without diagnosing a problem, and some revise (diag-
　　　　nose a problem and then address it)

III. Conclusions

　　A. Some results can be translated directly into teaching practices

　　B. Other results need to be researched more to see how they can affect teach-
　　　ing practices

　　C. A strong model of teaching writing is on the horizon

Hayes, John R., and Linda S. Flower. "Writing Research and the
Writer." *American Psychologist*, vol. 41, no. 10, Oct 1986, pp. 1106–13,
DOI: 10.1037/0003-066X.41.10.1106.

WRITING INSTRUCTION USED to be simpler. When we (the authors)
learned to write in school, we were given good models to imitate, the opportunity to practice, and redpenciled corrections from the teacher. This kind of
instruction is described as product-oriented because it focuses on the written
product the students produce rather than on the processes by which they
produce them. One of the radical departures of current instruction is to reverse
this orientation and to focus instead on writing processes. In process-oriented
instruction, the teacher attempts to intervene in the writing process itself—
to teach students what to do when they write. They do this by engaging the
students in activities designed to improve specific writing skills. For example,
students are trained in brainstorming to help them generate ideas for writing,
and they are encouraged to get peer responses to their work to develop a better
sense of audience.

　　Support for this "process movement" in composition has come in part from
research in the cognitive processes that underlie writing and from a new awareness of the connections between writing, thinking, and learning. Young, Becker,
and Pike (1970) drew on the art of invention in classical rhetoric to describe
the heuristic processes that underlie invention and persuasion and to argue for
the value of teaching writing as rhetorical problem-solving. Emig's (1971) land-
mark study of the writing of 12th graders anatomized the process in terms of
time spent on planning, reading, outlining, revising, and so on. In our studies

FOCUS ON WRITING: WHAT COLLEGE STUDENTS WANT TO KNOW

(Flower & Hayes, 1981; Hayes, Flower, Schriver, Stratman, & Carey, 1985), we have begun to model the organization of cognitive processes with particular emphasis on both planning and revision and to translate research into teachable problem-solving strategies (Flower, 1985).

Ideally, we would like instruction in writing to be informed by an accurate model of the cognitive processes that underlie writing. However, there is ample evidence that this has not always been the case. Rohman (1965) proposed a three-stage description of writing that was widely used in teaching. His stages were prewriting (e.g., idea generation and planning), writing (e.g., composing a draft), and rewriting (e.g., revising the draft). This stage model came under fire in the 1970s as an oversimplified version of the writing process that failed to recognize its recursive nature. That is, when people compose, the activities of prewriting, writing, and rewriting do not typically occur in fixed sequence but rather are interwoven with each other in a complex way. Visions of the writing process that focus on "activities" rather than on cognition continue to cause difficulty. Applebee (in press)[5] has recently charged that much of the current process-based instruction is seriously limited by its preoccupation with a set of so-called "natural process" activities (e.g., the teacher regularly requires students to spend time on pre-writing, journal-keeping, free-writing, getting peer response, revising, etc.). Such procedures, he argued, fail to recognize the role of purpose in the writing process, which dictates whether a given process is even useful. For example, free writing, a procedure in which students are asked to write down whatever they think of and to keep writing without worry about quality of ideas, may seem pointless to students who already have a clear idea of what they want to say.

Process-oriented instruction is a new frontier we have only begun to enter. The exemplary experimental research of Bereiter and Scardamalia (1982) and Scardamalia and Bereiter (1983) illustrate the difficulty and the care that must go into constructing successful interventions. However, a recent meta-analysis of writing instruction research (Hillocks, 1984) suggests that process-oriented instruction (even in these early days) is already more successful than previous product-oriented instruction. Research may have played an important role in this success. As Applebee (in press) has noted, writing instruction is one area in which research has actually had a large and visible impact on teaching.

---

5   This book chapter was published in 1989. Full original citation appears at the end of this article.

In this article, we attempt to characterize the present state of the field of adult (postsecondary) writing and to outline what we believe are the emerging trends and directions for future research. In particular, we will discuss the overall structure of the writing process and describe research on the major writing processes. (For a review of the developmental literature with a somewhat different focus, see Scardamalia & Bereiter, in press[6]).

The Structure of the Writing Process

A number of important features of the writing process have been identified through research. We will discuss evidence that writing is goal-directed, that writing goals are hierarchically organized, and that writers employ three major processes—planning, sentence generation, and revision—to accomplish these goals. Before doing this, though, it will be useful to describe the research methods used to reveal this information.

In our own attempts to characterize the writing process, we have employed a technique called protocol analysis (see Hayes & Flower, 1980). Protocol analysis has been widely used by psychologists to analyze complex task performance (see Ericcson & Simon, 1984). Protocol analysis starts with the collection of a "thinking aloud" protocol, that is, a person is asked to perform a task and to "think aloud" while performing it. In thinking-aloud studies of writing, the subject is asked not only to think aloud, but to read and write aloud as well. The writing tasks that have been studied by protocol analysis include short (hour-long) assignments completed under controlled laboratory conditions (Hayes & Flower, 1980) as well as extended (months-long) writing projects of a professional writer (Berkenkotter, 1983).

The data of thinking-aloud studies are contained in the verbatim transcript of the tape recording (with all the "um"s, pauses, and expletives) together with the essay and all the notes the writer has generated along the way. The transcript is called a protocol. These materials are then examined in considerable detail for evidence that may reveal something of the processes by which the writer has created the essay. In general, the data are very rich in such evidence. Subjects typically give many indications of their plans and goals, e.g., "I'll just jot down ideas as they come to me"; about strategies for dealing with the audience, e.g., "I'll write this as if I were one of them"; or about criteria for evaluation, e.g., "We better keep this simple." The analysis of this data is called *protocol analysis*.

---

6   This book chapter was published in 1986. Full original citation appears at the end of this article.

FOCUS ON WRITING: WHAT COLLEGE STUDENTS WANT TO KNOW

Writing Is Goal-Directed

Evidence that writing is goal-directed is easy to find in protocols. Typically, writers comment on their major goals early in the writing session. For example, one writer who was asked to write about the role of women for a hostile audience, said, "If an audience were hostile, the worst thing to do would be to defend yourself—so I would try to humor them—to make them—uh—more sympathetic maybe." A second writer assigned this same topic said, "I'm trying to decide whether ... I want to convince my audience of something specific about—uh—for instance, the Equal Rights Amendment or whether [I want to use] something general about [whether] women should have the same rights as men ... and I also need to decide if I want to actively convince my audience or simply state my point of view." A few moments later she decided "I'll try to convince them of what it is like not to have certain rights." A third writer said "I'm not really trying to persuade these people of anything. I'm simply being descriptive ... I'm saying, 'This is the way the world is.'" Because writing is goal-directed, it may well be hazardous, as Applebee suggested, to try to teach writing subskills without giving students a context of reasonable writing goals.

Writing Goals Are Hierarchically Organized

When writers have identified their major goals, for example, the particular aspect of the topic they want to discuss and their general approach to the audience, they frequently identify subgoals on the route to these major goals. Indeed, the subgoals may in turn have their own subgoals. A writer whose main goal was to write about "worries" of a particular group set up subgoals to write about the subtopics "the political issue" and "the philosophical issue." Under each of these subtopics, the writer specified a list of three or four sub-subtopics. Thus, the major goal was expanded into a hierarchical structure of subgoals.

In the same way, a writer who said that he was "simply being descriptive" elaborated his goal as follows: "I think what I really want is to present maybe one [point] with a lot of illustrations." He then went on to state the point and to develop a list of eight illustrations. In many cases, then, writers tell us in their "thinking aloud" protocols that their goals are hierarchically structured. Even if the writers didn't tell us explicitly though, there would still be plenty of evidence that writing processes are hierarchically organized. For example, many writers start writing sessions with a period of planning in which they try to develop an outline to write from. To do this they may first try to generate ideas freely. When they feel they have enough ideas, they try to organize them into an outline. Generating ideas and organizing them are parts of planning, and planning in turn is part of writing. Clearly these processes are hierarchically organized.

Writers Use Three Major Processes: Planning, Sentence Generation, and Revising
Research indicates that writers use three processes in achieving their goals: planning, sentence generation, and revising. In planning, the writer generates ideas and organizes them into a writing plan. In sentence generation, the writer produces formal sentences intended to be part of a draft. In revising, the writer attempts to improve a draft. Typically, these three processes are heavily interwoven. The interweaving has two causes: First, the writing task may be performed in parts, so that the writer plans, generates, and revises a first paragraph, then plans, generates, and revises a second paragraph, and so on. Second, the writing process may be applied recursively. For example, while revising, the writer may discover the need for a transitional paragraph. To write the paragraph, the writer invokes the whole writing process, that is, planning, generating, and revising, which are then nested within the revising process. In the remainder of this article, we will discuss research findings concerning these three major processes.

The Planning Process
If we were to build a model of planning in writing, we would want to consider, at least, the following three topics: the way people represent their knowledge, the sources of writing plans, and knowledge of writing strategies.

The Representation of Knowledge
The knowledge that a writer wants to express in a text may be stored in a wide variety of forms. Some knowledge is stored as language, perhaps in auditory form (e.g., a remembered proverb); some is stored as meanings that may be expressed in a variety of linguistic forms (e.g., "The dog is lively," or "Fido is bouncing off the walls"); some is stored as images or as skills that are harder to translate into language (e.g., the appearance of a particular facial expression or the skill of unbuttoning a coat button).

Because knowledge representations are diverse, the writing plans that writers construct to convey this knowledge must also be complex. Writing plans do not consist of knowledge representations of a single uniform type (Flower & Hayes, 1984); rather, writing plans appear to include information of at least three types: (a) pointers (in the form of cues or code words) to information that may be stored in many different forms such as schemas, episodes, images, and so on;

(b) word images, perhaps in auditory form, of particular words or phrases that could be included in the text; and (c) goals that include such things as plans for affecting the audience, for creating connections, or content-free directions to the writer, such as "add an introduction" or "go back to the drawing board."

The Source of the Writing Plan

One obvious source of expert writing plans is a well-organized body of topic knowledge. Such knowledge can provide organizing concepts that aid the writer in selecting relevant information, for example, knowing what to notice in a baseball game (Spilich, Vesonder, Chiesi, & Voss, 1979).

One of the time-honored ways of improving student writing is to allow students to choose their own topics, in the hope of increasing both knowledge and motivation (Applebee, 1982; Britton, Burgess, Martin, McLeod, & Rosen, 1975; Shaughnessy, 1977). Yet it is commonplace that knowledge of a topic will not necessarily enable an individual to produce clear, much less effective writing. For instance, subject-matter experts, for example, programmers or computer scientists, have been notoriously ineffective in writing computer documentation. At least two factors appear to contribute to the problem. First, as we will discuss later, subject-matter experts' knowledge may itself make experts insensitive to the needs of readers less informed than themselves. Second, subject-matter experts may have inadequate rhetorical knowledge. That is, they may write poorly because they do not have command of effective writing formats at the sentence, paragraph, or whole text levels. Expert writers draw on textual conventions and genre patterns and other discourse schemas to give shape to their planning (Bracewell, Frederickson, & Frederickson, 1982; Olson, Mack, & Duffy, 1981; Schumacher, Klare, Cronin, & Moses, 1984). In the writing of children and in the construction of simple stories or highly conventionalized text (e.g., the thank you note) such schemas appear to do a great deal of the work, offering a prefabricated plan for writing.

However, such rhetorical knowledge does not fully account for planning performance. The writing that older students and adults do typically calls for more complex, nonconventionalized plans unique to the immediate writing problem. As the writing task grows harder, then, less of the work can be done through the use of known formats, and the contribution of *problem-solving strategies* increases. As in Voss, Greene, Post, and Penner (1983) studies of problem-solvers in the social sciences, merely increasing the students' topic knowledge was insufficient to produce better analysts, because expert performance also depended on a repertory of strategies that included searching for

219

constraints, consolidating the search, and testing hypotheses. It appears then that the writing plan has at least three sources: the writer's topic knowledge, the writer's knowledge of effective writing formats, and the writer's knowledge of strategies that support planning and problem-solving when known writing formats are inadequate.

Strategic Knowledge

Because *strategic knowledge* plays such an important role in the more difficult or complex writing tasks, a model of writing would be quite incomplete if we did not consider it in detail. By strategic knowledge we mean a combination of three things: knowing how to define the writing task for oneself with appropriately demanding yet manageable goals; having a large body of high-level procedural knowledge on which to draw; and finally, being able to monitor and direct one's own writing process.

We can best illustrate the role strategic knowledge plays by comparing the goal-directed planning process we have observed in adults with the knowledge-telling strategy Scardamalia and Bereiter (in press[7]) have described in children.

Knowledge telling is a limited, but easily learned and efficient procedure that gets the job done for a wide variety of school writing tasks. In it, the writer's goal is simply to say what he or she knows about the topic, generating any information that is relevant to the topic rather than selecting and organizing that knowledge into a package designed for the reader. With writers who use this strategy, requests for an argument or an evaluative essay simply tend to elicit whatever the writer knows on the subject.

How does the expert planning process differ from knowledge telling? In children, the visible output (e.g., notes, etc.) and the mental "output" of planning appear to be nearly identical—the child generates a list of topics, content information, and actual language for use in the text. As students grow older, this written output can become more complex—the notes may include gists and goals that are then reordered before they appear in the text (Burtis, Bereiter, Scardamalia, & Tetroe, 1983). However, the more interesting and significant change occurs in the inner mental process of planning, that is, in the output we typically do not see and until recently have ignored in our description of good writing. Adult planning can be distinguished by four features (which themselves vary with the skill of the writer).

---

7 This book chapter was published in 1986. Full original citation appears at the end of this article.

1. During planning writers construct an initial task representation and a body of goals that in turn guide and constrain their efforts to write.
2. The body of goals is no mere temporal list of instructions, but appears to work as a hierarchical structure. That is, writers set up top-level goals that they develop with plans and subgoals. At the same time, these goals are also connected in a network in which one action can carry out multiple goals and in which individual plans or goals can be linked by a web of associations to other parts of this network. In other words, the writer's goals themselves form a complex structure.
3. The network of goals is also a dynamic structure. It is built and developed and sometimes radically restructured at even the top levels, as the writer composes and responds to new ideas or to his or her own text. The relative salience of various parts of this structure will also change as the writer works. Priorities change; attention wanders; writers forget. However, writers often return to goals that they established earlier but had seemingly abandoned. Thus, writing goals may persist even if they are currently inactive. Modifying writing goals may be essential for good writing. Writers stymied by writer's block appear to have more difficulty changing goals and plans than do other writers (Rose, 1980).
4. The differences between the goal networks constructed by experts and those constructed by novices help explain why student writers regularly have such difficulty organizing their knowledge around a problem or question or developing a focus adapted to the reader and why planning itself can be a demanding cognitive process for all writers.

In a preliminary study of expert and novice adults, we found that experts tended to generate far more elaborated networks. The goals, subgoals, plans, and evaluative comments they gave themselves provided a richer problem, more alive to the constraints of the task and their own goals. Although the sheer elaboration of working goals can be a good indication of expert planning, it is an inadequate description of that expertise. What distinguished the experts from the novices most clearly was the difference in the integration of their plans. The experts created far more connections among their goals than did the novices.

The Sentence Generation Process
Because the writing plan consists largely of pointers to information and of instructions to the writer, a great deal of work must be done to translate the writing plan into formal prose. That work involves explaining briefly sketched

ideas (e.g., "the philosophical issue"), interpreting nonverbal material in verbal form (e.g., "Just how did he look?"), and carrying out instructions (e.g., "Write a conclusion"). In a study of sentence generation, Kaufer, Hayes, and Flower (1986) found evidence that the work involved in translating plans into text is substantial. They compared the lengths of writers' outlines with the lengths of their essays. Even for the most extensive outliners, the ideas noted in the outline were expanded on the average by a factor of eight in the final essay.

Kaufer et al. (1986) found that writers compose sentences in parts. Sentence parts were defined by pauses in the thinking-aloud protocols and averaged between 7 and 12 words in length. The following is a typical sentence-generating episode observed by Kaufer et al. The dashes indicate pauses of two seconds or more in the composing process. The writer is trying to describe her job.

The best thing about it is (1)—what? (2) Something about using my mind (3)—it allows me the opportunity to (4)—uh—I want to write something about my ideas (5)—to put ideas into action (6)—or—to develop my ideas into (7)—what? (8)—into a meaningful form? (9) Oh, bleh!—say it allows me (10)—to use (11)—Na—allows me—scratch that. The best thing about it is that it allows me to use (12)—my mind and ideas in a productive way (13).

The proposed sentence parts in this episode were fragments 1, 4, 6, 7, 9, 11, and 13. Fragments 12 and 13 comprised the finished sentence that the writer included in her essay.

In general, experts and average writers constructed sentences in the same way. Both groups assembled sentence parts in a predominantly left to right fashion. That is, when writers proposed sentence parts, they were intended either to be added to the right of the last proposed sentence part, or they were intended to replace the last proposed sentence part. While producing a new draft, writers rarely revised sentence parts earlier than the one previously proposed. Further, both experts and average writers accepted about 75% of the sentence parts they proposed. That is, about 75% of the sentence parts mentioned in the thinking-aloud protocols were included in the written draft. The major differences between the two groups were (a) experts wrote significantly longer essays (786 words per essay) than average writers (464 words per essay) and (b) experts proposed significantly longer sentence parts (11.2 words per part) than average adult writers (7.3 words per part). This ability to work in larger units may be part of what it means to be a fluent writer.

The Revision Process

When Murray (1978) said, "Writing is rewriting," he was dramatizing the important role that revision can play in writing. Unfortunately, many writers lack the skill to make effective use of revision in their own writing. Bracewell, Scardamalia, and Bereiter (1978) found that 4th graders hardly revise at all, that 8th graders' revisions hurt more than they help, and that for 12th graders, helpful revisions narrowly outnumbered harmful ones. Bridwell's (1980) results suggest greater effectiveness for 12th graders' revisions than those of Bracewell et al. (1978). She found that 12th graders' second drafts were considerably better in "general merit" and mechanics than their first drafts. Pianko (1979) reported that college freshmen devote less than 9% of their composing time to reading and revising. Clearly, writers differ widely in the amount they revise. Holland, Rose, Dean, and Dory (1985) reported that the difference between good and poor adult writers in the amount of time spent on revision depends on the particular writing task. In general, though, it appears that the more expert the writer, the greater the proportion of writing time the writer will spend in revision. We will outline some observations about the nature of revision and about differences between expert and novice revisers.

Experts Attend More to Global Problems Than Do Novices

The literature suggests that experts and novices view revising in very different ways. Broadly, revision may be defined as the writer's attempt to improve the text. Within this definition, experts appear to attend systematically to different aspects of the text than do novices. There is considerable evidence that less experienced revisers focus their attention far more locally than do more experienced revisers. Stallard (1974) found that only 2.5% of 12th graders' revisions were focused above the word and sentence level. Bridwell (1980), who also studied 12th graders, found about 11% of revisions above the sentence level. Beach (1976), studying college juniors and seniors, found that students who revised extensively "tended to conceive of the paper in holistic terms" and to infer "general patterns of development" (p. 162). Students who did not revise extensively "evaluated only separate bits" (p. 162) of their papers.

Sommers (1980) found that college freshmen understand the revision process as a rewording activity, that is, they concentrate on particular words apart from their role in the text. In contrast, experienced writers, such as journalists, editors, and academics, describe their primary objectives when revising as finding the form or shape of their argument. Further, Sommers found that the experienced writers have a secondary objective; a concern for their readership. Faigley and Witte (1983), who studied writers at various skill levels, found that experts were more likely to change meaning through revision than were novices. They observed that the revisions of inexperienced college writers resulted in changed meaning in 12% of cases; the revisions of experienced college writers, in 25% of cases; and the revisions of experienced adult writers, in 34% of cases. Hayes et al. (1985) found that experts and novices differed systematically in their implicit definitions of the revision task. Experts defined revision as a whole-text task. They tended to read the whole text through before beginning revision and created global goals to guide the revision process. Novices, in contrast, saw revision largely as a sentence-level task in which the goal was to improve individual words and phrases without modifying the text structure.

Writers Have Difficulty Detecting Faults in Their Own Text

Bartlett (1981) compared revision processes in fifth grade students who were revising both their own and other writers' texts. She found that when the children were revising their own texts, they were able to find 56% of missing subjects or predicates, but only 10% of faulty referring expressions. In contrast, when the children were revising the texts of other writers, they detected about half of each type of problem. Hull (1984) has found similar results for adult writers.

One possible explanation for these results is that writers' knowledge of their own texts makes it difficult for them to detect faults in those texts. If this explanation is correct, then we would expect that prior knowledge of the content of any text would make it more difficult for the reviser to detect faults in that text. To test this hypothesis, Hayes, Schriver, Spilka, and Blaustein (1986) asked revisers to underline parts of unclear texts that they judged would cause comprehension problems for readers who did not know the subject matter. In some conditions, the revisers had read and evaluated a clear version of the text before they evaluated the unclear version. Thus, they evaluated the unclear version with prior knowledge of its content. In other conditions, the revisers had no prior experience with the content of the text. On the average, revisers who had no prior knowledge of text content discovered 50% more problems in the unclear text than did revisers with prior knowledge.

The Cues That Initiate Revision

Several researchers have suggested that the cue or initiating condition for revision is a dissonance or incongruity between intention and execution. For example, Bridwell (1980) suggested that when rereading the text, "the writer may either verify what is on the page or perceive some dissonance" (p. 220). Perception of dissonance is the cue that may lead to a decision to change the text. According to Sommers (1980), "the anticipation of a reader's judgment causes a feeling of dissonance when the writer recognizes incongruities between intention and execution" (p. 385). It is this recognition, according to Sommers, that leads the writer to make revisions. According to Scardamalia and Bereiter (1983), who proposed the Compare, Diagnose, and Operate (CDO) model of revision,

> During the course of composition, two kinds of mental representation are built up and stored in long-term memory. These are a representation of the text as written up to the time, and a representation of the text as intended. The C.D.O. process is initiated by a perceived mismatch between these two representations. (p. 4)

Although the idea that revision is initiated by the discovery of a dissonance between intention and text is attractive, there are enough clear counterexamples to warn us that this explanation can only be a partial one. For example, there are many instances in which writers appear to have written what they intended to write, but decide to revise anyway because the act of writing has led them to discover something better to say. Writing stimulates discovery, and discovery can initiate revision in the absence of dissonance. More telling is the observation (Hayes et al., 1985) that revision may be applied not only to texts but also to plans for producing texts as well. Revision of a plan cannot be triggered by comparison of intention and text because, at this point, there is no text to compare to the plan. Rather, revision is triggered by the negative evaluation of a plan, for example, "Maybe I'll give them a list of principles. No, that would bore them to flinders!" A third sort of example may be observed when writers are revising other peoples' texts. In such cases, the reviser may be cued to revise by the difficulties he or she experiences in comprehending the writer's intention, the text, or both. Failure to comprehend either the writer's intention or the text would be a reason to revise whether text matched intention or not.

Revision, then, can be triggered not only by dissonance between intention and text but also by the discovery of better things to say, by the negative evaluation of a plan, and by failure to comprehend the text. Hayes et al. (1985) have attempted to incorporate these various revision triggers in a comprehensive model of the revision process.

Detection and Diagnosis of Text Problems

Hayes et al. (1985) found that experts detected about 1.6 times as many problems in a faulty text than did novices. Further, of the problems they detected, experts were able to diagnose 74% whereas novices were able to diagnose only 42%—a ratio of 1.7 to 1. Experts, then, showed a clear advantage over novices both in the detection and in the diagnosis of text problems. Superiority in these two skills gives experts much greater strategic flexibility in revision than novices have. To appreciate this point, one needs to recognize two important facts about revision.

Diagnosis is not an obligatory step in revision

Although diagnosis is heavily emphasized in composition classes, writers often revise without diagnosing. In many instances in Hayes et al. (1985), both expert and novice revisers detected problems in the text and rewrote the problematic sections apparently without bothering to diagnose the problems. We will call this approach to revision without diagnosis the "rewrite" strategy. The most common alternative strategy is to diagnose the text problems and to fix them. We will call this the "revise" strategy.

Whether the rewrite or revise strategy is preferable depends on the text

The rewrite strategy is generally preferable when (a) it is not important to save the original text, (b) there are many problems in the original text so that diagnosis involves much effort, or (c) the purpose of the text is clear and not problematic so that extracting the gist and inventing an alternative text is easy. The revise strategy is preferable when (a) it is important to save as much of the original text as possible, (b) there are few problems in the text so that diagnosis is easy, or (c) the purpose of the text is unclear or problematic so that identification of the gist and inventing an alternative text is not easy. In such cases, diagnosis may provide the only effective means for identifying the gist or resolving problems and therefore for inventing an improved alternative text.

Because experts have strong skills in both detection and diagnosis, they can typically exercise either the rewrite or the revise strategy and therefore can choose the strategy they feel will be most effective. Novices, on the other hand, often find that their lack of skills limits their strategic choices. Experts, then, have more strategic options than do novices.

To revise a text for an audience is a very complex task. It requires the reviser to comprehend the goals of the text, to predict how well the text will accomplish those goals for the intended audience, and to propose better ways to

FOCUS ON WRITING: WHAT COLLEGE STUDENTS WANT TO KNOW

accomplish those goals when the reviser perceives the text to be faulty. It is not obvious that expert revisers operating on their intuitions can accomplish this task optimally. Duffy, Curran, and Sass (1983) found that when professional writing firms revised documents for clarity, the results were frequently disappointing when the original and revised documents were compared in tests of comprehension. Swaney, Janik, Bond, and Hayes (1981) asked a group of four document designers to revise four public documents so that they could be understood by a general audience. The designers invested about 100 hours in the project. Comprehension tests on the original and the revised documents showed that the designers' efforts had improved the comprehensibility of three of the documents but made the last one worse. Swaney et al. then revised this last document using protocol-aided revision. That is, they collected thinking-aloud protocols of readers attempting to comprehend the document and used these protocols to identify features of the text that required improvement. The document was then revised in the light of the protocols. After three revision cycles, the protocols revealed no further problems in the text. Comprehension tests showed that the text was now significantly clearer than the original (16% errors vs. 46% errors). This result is both a sensible one and a very practical one. It makes good common sense to go directly to the audience for information about readers' comprehension needs rather than relying on the writer's intuition. It is a very practical result because it can be applied quite directly to the improvement of documents. In fact, the above authors applied the technique to produce a prize-winning computer manual (Bond, Hayes, Janik, & Swaney, 1982).

Recently, Schriver (1984) constructed a set of lessons designed to increase the writer's sensitivity to readers' needs. In each lesson, students are asked to read a flawed text and to predict the sorts of troubles the reader would have in comprehending the text. Next, the students read a thinking-aloud protocol of a reader who is trying to comprehend the text. The students then revise their predictions of reader difficulties. The effect of instruction, that is, increased ability to predict reader problems, is evident after about six lessons and appears to transfer well to new texts.

Conclusions

Some of the results we have discussed can be translated directly into educational practice, but other results cannot be applied without further research. For example, it appears that protocol-aided revision could be applied not only to the revision of computer manuals but also to textbooks and instructional materials on a variety of topics, for example, statistics or history. On the other hand, although we have observed that experts define revision more globally than do novices, this fact cannot be translated directly into educational practice. It is exciting to speculate that we could improve students' revision performance by telling them, through words and examples, how experts revise and asking them to do the same. Such an improvement, achieved through changing the student's definition of the revision task, would be bought at a very small instructional cost. We have to recognize, however, that further research is required before we can recommend this sort of instruction for all students. Exposure to expert strategies might work for students who have the ability to recognize global problems and to fix them once they had been recognized. On the other hand, for students who lack these skills, the procedure might be ineffective or even harmful. Pushing students to use expert strategies too early may be like encouraging acrobats to start with the high wire. Good process instruction must be built on a sound understanding of the writing process and good diagnoses of developing writer's problems and needs.

Translating research into practice prematurely, then, can be counterproductive if research results are applied without sufficient caution. If research results are applied carefully, though, we feel that the new discoveries about the writing process will have a major impact on the effectiveness with which writing is taught. It has in fact already created a minor revolution. Teachers are extending their notion of how to teach writing from merely assigning and correcting to leading students through the full range of writing processes. This new perspective enables them to aid students in planning, exploring their own knowledge, identifying their audience, drafting, responding to peer critique, and revising.

Research in writing is beginning to show us the outlines of a theory of writing. It is giving us a much deeper understanding of the nature of writing processes and of how the writer uses them to produce text. In the near future, we can look forward to a very strong pedagogy based on a well-developed theory of writing.

References

Applebee, A. (1982). Writing and learning in school settings. In M. Nystrand (Ed.), *What writers know* (pp. 360–381). New York: Academic Press.

Applebee, A. (in press). Toward a post-process paradigm: Notes on the failure of process approaches to writing instruction. In D. Bartholomae & A.Petrosky (Eds.), *The teaching of writing*. Chicago, IL: National Society for the Study of Education.

Bartlett, E.J. (1981). *Learning to write: Some cognitive and linguistic components.* Washington, DC: Center for Applied Linguistics.

Beach, R. (1976). Self-evaluation strategies of extensive revisers and nonrevisers. *College Composition and Communication, 27,* 160–164.

Bereiter, C., & Scardamalia, M. (1982). From conversion to composition: The role of instruction in a developmental process. In R. Glaser (Ed.), *Advances in instructional psychology* (pp. 1–64). Hillsdale, NJ: Erlbaum.

Berkenkotter, C. (1983). Decisions and revisions: The planning strategies of a published writer. *College Composition and Communication, 34,* 156–169.

Bond, S., Hayes, J.R., Janik, C., & Swaney, J. (1982, August). *Introduction to CMU TOPS-20.* Pittsburgh, PA: Carnegie Mellon University.

Bracewell, R., Frederickson, C., & Frederickson, J.D. (1982). Cognitive processes in composing and comprehending discourse. *Educational Psychologist, 17,* 146–164.

Bracewell, R., Scardamalia, M., & Bereiter, C. (1978, October). The development of audience awareness in writing. *Resources in Education.* pp. 154–433.

Bridwell, L.S. (1980). Revising strategies in twelfth grade students' transactional writing. *Research in the Teaching of English, 14*(3), 107–122.

Britton, J., Burgess, T., Martin, N., McLeod, A., & Rosen, H. (1975). *The development of writing abilities.* (pp. 11–18). London: Macmillan.

Burtis, P.C., Bereiter, C., Scardamalia, M., & Tetroe, J. (1983). The development of planning in writing. In C.G. Wells & B. Kroll (Eds.), *Exploration of children's development in writing* (pp. 153–174). Chichester, England: Wiley.

Duffy, T., Curran, T., & Sass, D. (1983). Document design for technical job tasks: An evaluation. *Human Factors, 25,* 143–160.

Emig, J. (1971). *The composing process of twelfth graders.* Urbana, IL: National Council of Teachers of English.

Ericcson, K.A., & Simon, H.A. (1984). *Protocol analysis: Verbal reports as data.* Cambridge, MA: MIT Press.

Faigley, L., & Witte, S. (1983). Analyzing revision. *College Composition and Communication, 32,* 400–414.

Flower, L.S. (1985). *Problem-solving strategies for writing.* New York: Harcourt Brace Jovanovich.

Flower, L.S., & Hayes, J.R. (1981). A cognitive process theory of writing. *College Composition and Communication, 32,* 365–387.

Flower, L.S., & Hayes, J.R. (1984). Images, plans, and prose: The representation of meaning in writing. *Written Communication, 1,* 120–160.

Hayes, J.R., & Flower, L.S. (1980). Identifying the organization of writing processes. In L. Gregg & E. Steinberg (Eds.), *Cognitive processes in writing: An interdisciplinary approach*. Hillsdale, NJ: Erlbaum.

Hayes, J.R., Flower, L.S., Schriver, K., Stratman, J., & Carey, L. (1985). *Cognitive processes in revision*. (Tech. Rep. No. 12). Pittsburgh, PA: Carnegie Mellon University, Communication Design Center.

Hayes, J.R., Schriver, K.A., Spilka, R., & Blaustein, A. (1986, March). *If it's clear to me it must be clear to them*. Paper presented at the Conference on College Composition and Communication, New Orleans, LA.

Hillocks, G. (1984). What works in teaching composition: A meta-analysis of experimental treatment studies. *American Journal of Education, 93*, 133–170.

Holland, M., Rose, A., Dean, R., & Dory, S. (1985). *Processes involved in writing effective procedural instructions*. (Tech. Rep. No. 1-ONR). Washington, DC: American Institutes for Research.

Hull, G. (1984). *The editing process in writing: A performance study of experts and novices*. Unpublished doctoral dissertation, University of Pittsburgh, PA.

Kaufer, D., Hayes, J.R., & Flower, L.S. (1986). Composing written sentences. *Research in the Teaching of English, 20*, 121–140.

Murray, D.M. (1978). Internal revision: A process of discovery. In C.R. Cooper & L. Odell (Eds.), *Research on composing: Points of departure*. Urbana, IL: National Council of Teachers of English.

Olson, G., Mack, R., & Duffy, S. (1981). Cognitive aspects of genre. *Poetics, 10*, 283–315.

Pianko, S. (1979). Description of the composing process of college freshman writers. *Research in the Teaching of English, 13*, 5–22.

Rohman, G. (1965). Pre-writing: The stage of discovery in the writing process. *College Composition and Communication, 16*, 106–112.

Rose, M. (1980). Rigid rules, inflexible plans, and the stifling of language; a cognitivist analysis of writer's block. *College Composition and Communication, 31*, 389–401.

Scardamalia, M., & Bereiter, C. (1983). The development of evaluative, diagnostic, and remedial capabilities in children's composing. In M. Martlew (Ed.), *The psychology of written language: A developmental approach*. London: Wiley.

Scardamalia, M., & Bereiter, C. (in press). Written composition. In M. Wittrock (Ed.), *Third handbook of research on teaching*. New York: Macmillan.

FOCUS ON WRITING: WHAT COLLEGE STUDENTS WANT TO KNOW

Schriver, K. (1984). *Revising computer documentation for comprehension: Ten lessons in protocol-aided revision*. (Tech. Rep. No. 14). Pittsburgh, PA: Carnegie Mellon University, Communication Design Center.

Schumacher, G.M., Klare, G.R., Cronin, F.C., & Moses, J.D. (1984). Cognitive activities of beginning and advanced college writers: A pausal analysis. *Research in the Teaching of English, 18*, 169–187.

Shaughnessy, M. (1977). *Errors and Expectations: A guide for the teacher of basic writing*. New York: Oxford University Press.

Sommers, N. (1980). Revision strategies of student writers and experienced writers. *College Composition and Communication, 31*, 378–387.

Spilich, G.J., Vesonder, G.T., Chiesi, H.L., & Voss, J.F. (1979). Text processing of domain-related information for individuals with high- and low-domain knowledge. *Journal of Verbal Learning and Verbal Behavior, 18*, 275–290.

Stallard, C. (1974). An analysis of the writing behavior of good student writers. *Research in the Teaching of English, 8*, 206–218.

Swaney, J.H., Janik, C.J., Bond, S.J., & Hayes, J.R. (1981). *Editing for comprehension: Improving the process through reading protocols*. (Tech. Rep. No. 14). Pittsburgh, PA: Carnegie Mellon University, Document Design Project.

Voss, J.F., Greene, T.R., Post, T.A., & Penner, B.C. (1983). Problem-solving skills in the social sciences. In G.H. Bower (Ed.), *The psychology of learning and motivation: Advances in research and theory* (*Vol. 17*, pp. 165–213). NY: Academic Press.

Young, R.E., Becker, A., & Pike, K. (1970). *Rhetoric: Discovery and change*. New York: Harcourt, Brace & World.

RECOMMENDED ONLINE SOURCES

For direct links to these sources, please visit <sites.broadviewpress.com/focusonwriting>.

1. To consider the role of music in the writing process and appreciate the work of a student researcher: Calicchia, Sara. "To 'Play That Funky Music' or Not: How Music Affects the Environmental Self-Regulation of High-Ability Academic Writers." *Young Scholars in Writing*, vol. 11, 2014, <https://arc.lib.montana.edu/ojs/index.php/Young-Scholars-In-Writing/article/view/278>.

2. For an argument about how grammar should be taught that relies on academic research but is written for a non-academic public audience: Cleary, Michelle Navarre. "The

Wrong Way to Teach Grammar." *The Atlantic* 25 Feb. 2014, <http://www.theatlantic.com/education/archive/2014/02/the-wrong-way-to-teach-grammar/284014/>.

3. To see an example of how students can research actual writing processes in their own university: McMillan, Laurie. "Informal Local Research Aids Student and Faculty Learning." *Council on Undergraduate Research On the Web*, vol. 33, no. 1, 2012, <http://www.cur.org/assets/1/7/331Fall12McMillanWeb.pdf>.

4. For a brief and vivid blog post that provides a lesson on sentence style (I know it sounds boring, but it's really cool!): Ciotti, Gregory. "Easy Reading Is Damn Hard Writing." *Help Scout*, 3 Sept 2015, <https://www.helpscout.net/blog/damn-hard-writing/>.

5. To have a lot of fun thinking about rules and voice via a student's creative honor's thesis: Tyrrell, Lauren E. "Excuse My Excess." *Xchanges*, vol. 6, no. 1, 2010, <http://www.xchanges.org/xchanges_archive/xchanges/6.1/tyrrell/tyrrell.html>.

6. To hear video advice about acting as **beta readers** (general rather than expert readers) for one another: Moreci, Jenna. "All about Beta Readers." *Jenna Moreci*, YouTube, 9 Aug 2017, <https://www.youtube.com/watch?v=Ziykw0SmKoE&index=9&list=PLZKiZgsbgCyl1zeAGHk_U2enfc1suFsdG>.

7. For a video of students reflecting on their writing processes in college: Sommers, Nancy. *Shaped by Writing*, 2003, Harvard College, YouTube, 2014, <https://www.youtube.com/watch?v=rTOZqa__hVA>.

Joining the Conversation

The following formal writing prompts are ways of helping you think through the ideas you've been reading about by *using* the ideas in some way to help you create a text of your own.

MEDIA ANALYSIS

Choose a movie or television show that depicts writing. Explain how the depiction offers a helpful role model or not based on what you've learned about habits of effective writers. This assignment may be especially interesting if you think about ideas from the other chapters as well.

CLASS WRITING INVENTORY

As a class, develop a short survey about writing habits for all members of the class to respond to anonymously. Choose one topic from the survey to explore, comparing the habits of students in your class to what you've learned about habits of effective writers from this chapter or other chapters.

COMMUNITY ETHNOGRAPHY

Find a place where people are writing, whether on campus, at home, at work, or in the community. What do you observe? In what ways do your observations fit what you've been learning about habits of effective writers? In what ways do your observations challenge or extend what other researchers have found about writing? Create a collage, blog post, or video essay analyzing material situations and tools common to writers.

INNER DIALOGUE

Write a dramatic scene in which two or more of your inner voices have a conversation as you work on a writing assignment. These inner voices should reference class readings during the conversation. To add a twist, create a comic strip, podcast, or video that brings the scene to life.

4 WHAT DO EFFECTIVE RESEARCHERS DO?

Exploring the Question

Like the word "writing," "research" might have some negative associations for you. Maybe you've been required to read a certain number of sources or find certain types of sources to complete an assignment. When working to meet requirements, you may not have experienced interest, excitement, or wonder about the ideas.

Unfortunately, if we practice a skill that isn't attached to something we care about, the activity can feel like a chore. If this is true of you, you may feel differently when finding answers to questions that interest you.

CONNECT

1. When you hear the word "researcher," what image comes to mind? How does this image inspire you or hinder you as you perform your own research?

2. What would you like to know that could make your own experience with research more enjoyable and more effective?

You might also associate research with reading alphabetic texts and may not realize how many forms research can take. Even though I am addressing research in a chapter separate from other ways of thinking about writing, most writing is informed by research in one way or another. If I write a list of items I need at the grocery store, I may check cupboards and ask people in my household if they can think of any needed foods. If I write a personal narrative, I turn to my own experiences as texts to inform my work. If I reflect on a class discussion, that discussion is the text I use to frame my remarks. In each of these situations, my research is limited rather than extensive, but it is still research.

As far as *effective* research is concerned, what is effective is likely to vary based on the goals of the research. Still, certain approaches and strategies tend to work for many people in many situations, though some research habits are idiosyncratic—they simply depend on personal preference. In addition to trying out advice to become a more effective researcher, you can also pay attention to what strategies tend to work well.

USEFUL PRINCIPLES FROM EVERYDAY RESEARCH

The kinds of research most of us do in our everyday lives is likely driven by a desire to

- make a decision (what restaurant should I eat at? which computer should I buy? what hairstyles are popular?)
- accomplish a task (how do I back up my computer hard drive? how do I add page numbers to a Word document? what should be included in a résumé?)
- find answers to fact-based questions (what flowers grow in full sun? what happens during a government shut down?)
- find out more about a person (is that person single? do we have interests in common?)

Research papers may seem to have no connection to the research that we do willingly on our own time. However, while many differences exist that I'll discuss in a minute, our everyday research is similar to school research in some ways that can help us appreciate the latter.

Both everyday informal research and formal academic research tend to be:

1. *Inquiry-based*: A question or a desire to understand a subject matter motivates and drives the research
2. Guided by either a *focused* or *exploratory* question: Sometimes you can pinpoint exactly what you want to know (focused research), while other times preliminary (exploratory) research is used to narrow your direction
3. *Purpose-driven*: Decisions about how to conduct the research are informed by the purpose—what is the researcher trying to accomplish?

4. Guided by *primary research*, *secondary research*, or both: Depending on the question and the resources available, the researcher may combine primary and secondary sources or may decide that only one of these is appropriate

5. *Evaluative*: Potential sources of information are evaluated for relevance and credibility

You probably engage in everyday research that meets these five criteria on a regular basis. Perhaps you want to choose a restaurant. If you're in a new setting, you might look online, and you would likely filter your search according to your needs and desires at the time. You might prioritize based on factors such as cost, quality of food, type of food, dietary options, or location. You might begin with a Google search and then read Yelp reviews to make sure the place will suit your needs. This research is inquiry-based ("What restaurant should I choose?"), focused ("I want an inexpensive vegetarian meal within ten miles"), purpose-driven ("I'm hungry!"), evaluative ("These Yelp reviews seem trustworthy because there are several that consistently give positive reviews"), and relies on secondary sources (the reviews of other people who have dined at the restaurant).

If you're a savvy researcher but you're not sure what you want at first, you might look at several online menus or restaurant reviews, weigh your options, and then choose the restaurant that appeals to you. Such research is exploratory rather than focused. The specific approach to finding a restaurant varies according to the situation.

If you're in a familiar place where you've eaten out often, your research might be based on your first-hand experience rather than online searching. You might have eaten at enough restaurants to know which one might be appropriate in a given situation.

When you find the answers to research questions through direct experience, observation, or other methods other than reading the research of others, it still counts as research. This is called *primary research*; it refers to investigations performed

CONNECT

I just described two ways of choosing a place to eat. You might have criteria in mind and search for a restaurant that meets those criteria, or you might scan several restaurant options before you've developed a preference and then decide which restaurant appeals to you.

1. Can you think of times when doing online or library-based research for school that you've looked for specific information?

2. Can you think of times when doing online or library-based research for school that you've started reading sources with a general topic in mind but have focused your topic after looking at several sources?

3. Is one of these approaches better than the other?

directly by the researcher (versus reading about the research others have under-taken and ideas they have investigated). Visiting restaurants and reviewing them according to specific criteria would be considered primary research.

Secondary research refers to online or library research in which you seek the results of others' research. In the example of researching restaurants, reading a list of restaurants compiled by other people or reading Yelp reviews written by others would be considered secondary research.

ACADEMIC RESEARCH: OVERVIEW

Even though everyday research and research assigned in school are similar in some ways, the differences are also important. One of the key models that helped me better understand academic research is "the Burkean parlor," a metaphor Kenneth Burke offered back in 1941. I quoted this passage in the Introduction, and I repeat it here because I like it so much:

> Imagine that you enter a parlor. You come late. When you arrive, others have long preceded you, and they are engaged in a heated discussion, a discussion too heated for them to pause and tell you exactly what it is about. In fact, the discussion had already begun long before any of them got there, so that no one present is qualified to retrace for you all the steps that had gone before. You listen for a while, until you decide that you have caught the tenor of the argument; then you put in your oar. Someone answers; you answer him; another comes to your defense; another aligns himself against you, to either the embarrassment or gratification of your opponent, depending upon the quality of your ally's assistance. However, the discussion is interminable. The hour grows late, you must depart. And you do depart, with the discussion still vigorously in progress. (Burke 110–11)

This characterization of research as conversation has an everyday sensibility to it. However, everyday research situations like choosing a restaurant or finding out how to back up a computer hard drive tend to require a short time commitment and informal methods. In these everyday situations, the research results usually address an immediate need and only occasionally provoke a written response.

Burke's parlor, on the other hand, suggests that an academic conversation worth engaging in likely has deep roots. The researcher does not need to trace all of these roots but rather read ("listen") enough to grasp the key points and enter into the debate. The debate continues as various people publish on the same topic, responding to one another by sometimes disagreeing and sometimes adding to one another's arguments.

This parlor scene does not reference the effect these conversations have on the world beyond the room, which is a serious drawback to the analogy. While I enjoy a good parlor conversation as much as the next person (especially if the "parlor" happens to be an ice cream parlor and we can eat while we chat), I would not be motivated to spend time writing and thinking through ideas if my writing had no hope of shaping attitudes, behaviors, and actions—at the very least my own, but hopefully others' as well.

Burke does note that the researcher "must depart" when "the hour grows late," but this phrasing does not seem to imply that the researcher is going forth to take more action now that she's been inspired by the parlor conversation. (Note: I say "*more* action" rather than "action" because writing itself is an action. I use feminine pronouns for the researcher to counterbalance Burke's use of masculine pronouns.) Instead, Burke seems to suggest that the researcher retires or dies while others continue to discuss the topic. It's great that research continues beyond one person's contribution, but I hope the researcher doesn't die. That's just depressing. Let's settle on the researcher retiring and getting more involved in activism based on her research. Or maybe the researcher retires and refuses to visit the parlor anymore because the researcher is now busy using Yelp reviews to find a good restaurant. Maybe the researcher even dips her oar in and composes her own Yelp reviews because she misses the parlor and the debate a little bit. Yes. Let's imagine a combination of such activities happens when the hour grows late.

CONNECT

1. Have you heard research described as conversation before? In what ways does that analogy help you understand research assignments better? In what ways does the comparison fall short or seem misleading?

2. Why do you suppose teachers often assign research?

3. When have you felt motivated to work on a school research assignment? Why?

In any case, the key is understanding academic research as an ongoing conversation that happens in writing, thoughtfully, over time—and this conversation is one you can participate in.

As you research and write, purpose should always inform decisions. At times, researchers focus primarily on either secondary or primary research strategies, but most academic research involves both secondary and primary research methods. When being assigned academic research, notice whether you are being asked to

- Summarize secondary research: What have others said? Retrace the conversation one source at a time.
- Synthesize secondary research: What have others said? Retrace the conversation not by source but by idea, following a clear and logical structure of your own.
- Conduct primary research without secondary research: What can I discover directly? Do your own research without noticing any prior conversation.
- Conduct primary research and secondary research: What have others said, and what does my direct research add to that conversation? Do your own research and contextualize it as a response to or application of the prior conversation.

In the next sections, we will look at strategies for secondary research and primary research separately because the two activities are connected in terms of overall purpose (to answer a question, find out information) but they are very different in terms of process. First, however, I want to say a little bit about process, forming research questions, and the recursive nature of research.

Processes and research questions

As you begin research, be sure to have goals in mind and make choices accordingly.

I often shuttle between secondary and primary research in a recursive mode that mirrors the discussion of writing processes in Chapter Three.

Most often, my research questions develop when I notice that some kind of dynamic *seems* to be true, and I want to test out whether it is actually true or not. For example, when I received sexist comments on YouTube videos I had posted and simultaneously noticed that very few of the most-subscribed YouTube channels featured women, I wondered whether YouTube was an environment that tended to encourage male participation and provide an unwelcome space for females. I began collaborating with my colleague Lindsey Wotanis, and the two of us did preliminary secondary research to discover whether others had sufficiently answered the question, "Is YouTube a hostile space for women?" When we found most reports were anecdotal rather than based on researched evidence, we moved forward by

a) doing a lot of reading on relevant topics
b) conducting primary research
c) taking notes and writing findings as our research progressed.

I provide more details about our processes below, but I offer this overview to show how research often works as an ongoing process of discovery rather than a simple series of steps.

Your processes and methods may be more prescribed. A course assignment may offer parameters for your research question, so start there. It is all right to begin with a general research question and gradually narrow your focus. My students often believe a more general question will make writing easier because there will be so much to say, but a focused question gives us a better opportunity to discover and articulate a thoughtful answer that contributes to a scholarly conversation. As you develop a research direction, have a clear sense of the roles of secondary and primary research (both of which are discussed more below). Be sure to develop a genuine question—something that you and other people would like to know the answer to.

If you have a general topic but need to narrow, spend time searching terms in a library database to find subtopics; read a few articles on a single subtopic to develop a question that can be answered through your own research. Research questions may arise if articles are in conflict with one another, or if the articles provide answers to one question, but those answers lead to more questions (as in the article by Sondra Perl in Chapter Three).

Your instinct may be to use Google first to begin detecting subtopics. You can take that step, especially if you're having trouble finding keywords that work in the library databases. Still, if you are doing academic work that will likely require scholarly articles, it is smart to have some sense of what's available in library databases.

Once you have a somewhat focused research question, you can prepare to do secondary and primary research by answering:

1. What sub-questions will help answer the research question?
2. What key words from the research question and sub-questions can be used as search terms?
3. For each key word, what synonyms or alternate terms might be used for searches? What specific examples or general categories might be searchable? In other words, make sure you have plenty of terms to

CONNECT

1. Do you prefer to choose your own topic when completing a paper for a course or do you prefer to have it assigned by your professor? Explain why.

2. Do you always develop a research question when working on a research paper? If not, what other strategies can help you define and focus your research?

try out in case the first words you use for your search do not generate helpful results.

4. What kinds of databases or secondary sources are likely to provide answers to the research question and sub-questions?
5. What kind of primary research would help answer the research question?
6. Does the primary research answer a more specific question?

You should have a sense of what you will find out directly (via primary research) and what you are hoping you can learn from others (through secondary research) early in your project, though this understanding may change during the research process.

I also want to reiterate that some of your class assignments may require you to focus on either secondary or primary research rather than integrate both.

SECONDARY RESEARCH: FINDING AND EVALUATING SOURCES

The first four questions just above can guide your search for secondary sources. For example, when Wotanis and I asked, "Is YouTube a hostile environment for women?" we developed sub-questions such as:

- What is the history of YouTube and its guidelines regulating speech and behavior?
- How many women and how many men have met with YouTube success?
- How have other researchers studied online sexism?
- Have other researchers found evidence of online sexism? of sexism on YouTube in particular?
- When people have detected online sexism, what forms has it taken?
- Is online sexism connected to online racism? If so, how?

Sometimes my students have trouble with keywords when searching library databases. I have no fail-proof plan for keywords, but I recommend experimenting to see which terms yield results. I also recommend visiting a reference desk in your college library because reference librarians often have incredibly helpful advice about keywords and secondary research. I love the process of finding material and reading, but it's easy to get frustrated if you expect to find exactly what you want at the start of the search process.

In terms of sub-questions we sought to answer, the key words were clearly "YouTube," "online," and "sexism." You might notice that "online" is a wider category than "YouTube," and we used it because we had the sense that YouTube dynamics would reflect dynamics that had been recognized in other online environments. We also used many other search terms that were closely related to our initial terms, including "social media," "social network," "vlog," "feminism," "misogyny," "reception," and "civility," sometimes combining terms to narrow a search ("online civility" in quotes) or using "or" to widen a search ("social media" or "social network"). At times, we made our search more specific by entering the names of specific YouTubers.

We relied on scholarly sources for most of our research, using the online Google Scholar database as well as library databases via EBSCOhost. Most university libraries have a large selection of research available or the means to request scholarly articles through an interlibrary loan service.

We also knew that some information would not likely be available in scholarly sources. For information about the background, history, and speech policies of YouTube, we looked to the site itself. For information on the most successful YouTubers, we found online statistics of the most subscribed channels and the most views. We also found online articles about popular YouTubers and their earnings.

CONNECT

1. Can you think of a time that a teacher imposed "rules" on the research process that helped you find appropriate sources for a particular assignment?

2. Can you think of a time when guidelines about the sources you needed to find hindered your research process? Why do you suppose such moments happen sometimes during the educational process?

I'm describing an actual research process because it shows how "rules" about sources are not helpful when conducting genuine inquiry-based research. Instead, effective researchers know that different search terms yield different results, so experimentation is often necessary. Different databases or genres are useful or not depending on the question being researched.

When finding sources, researchers need to evaluate them and decide which ones are worth using. While sources can be evaluated in a variety of ways, it's helpful to think in foundational terms and gradually consider details and complexities.

When researching, the most crucial questions to ask about each source are:

1. Is it relevant?
2. Is it trustworthy?

That first question seems like it ought to be obvious, but it isn't. Relevance can be broken down into three questions:

1. Is the research from the source connected to my research?
2. Is the source appropriately current?
3. Does the source offer enough depth to be useful?

Is the research from the source connected to my research?

Often, my students are discouraged and confused and even change their research question when they cannot find any article that directly answers their specific question. I try to prevent this anxiety, but it occurs regularly, so it bears a little attention.

Just above, I told you that my colleague and I were working with this somewhat general research question:

Is YouTube a hostile environment for women?

That was a lie. We needed to narrow that broad question so that we could develop a feasible answer based on evidence. Our actual specific research question was

Is YouTube a more hostile environment for Jenna Marbles, a popular female YouTuber, than for her male counterpart, Ryan Higa? (Wotanis and McMillan)

We did not find any research, scholarly or popular, that answered our specific research question. However, our specific research question was a means of answering the general research question, or at least offering a partial answer in the larger conversation. We therefore focused our primary research on the specific question, and we focused our secondary research on the general question. If any article had answered the specific question directly, we would have had little if any reason to answer the question ourselves. Think about your ability to add to a conversation rather than simply mimic another researcher's point of view.

Can I give you another example? Great! Thanks.

One of my students wondered: "Does sharing dog photos on Instagram improve the social health of Instagram users?" She did not find any secondary research that addressed this specific question. However, she found information about two topics that together offered important frameworks for her own research: "Do dogs improve the social health of their owners?" and "Does sharing photos on Instagram (or social media in general) improve the social health of users?"

The student was able to use information she found from sources in psychology and sociology databases that answered the two slightly general questions. That secondary research led her to hypothesize that sharing dog photos on Instagram would improve social health. She then used primary research to see if her hypothesis was correct: She counted positive responses on several pet and non-pet photos, and she interviewed people she knew who regularly shared dog photos on Instagram. You, too, can frame your primary research with related (rather than identical) secondary research.

CONNECT

1. At this point in the chapter, which ideas about research seem obvious to you?

2. Which ideas are helping you see research or research processes in a new way? Explain.

Sometimes only a part of a source is relevant to your research. As long as you are not misrepresenting the source, you are allowed to use the part that overlaps with your research area and ignore the parts that do not.

Use titles, the table of contents, the index, headings and subheadings, abstracts, introductions, and discussion sections to decide whether a source seems relevant or not. If you are working with time constraints (such as a deadline and other commitments), you need to make such decisions efficiently rather than fully read every source that has the potential to be relevant.

Is the source appropriately current?

Students often hear they should use current sources and then ask, "Is a publication from 2010 too dated for me to use?" or "Is it all right if I use a newspaper article that was published in the nineties if it's about an event that happened in the nineties?"

I love these questions because the students are trying to make sense of advice directing them to use current sources. As we discuss answers to questions like these, we always end up discussing the rhetorical situation. For what purpose are they using the source? To what extent can a particular source help them meet their purpose or not based on when it was published?

When Wotanis and I were studying YouTube, older research provided information about the beginnings of the video-sharing site, but older research did not provide helpful statistics about the demographics associated with who currently posts videos, who watches videos, and what videos are most popular. On the other hand, if I wanted to focus on the beginnings of YouTube in my research, I could probably use older articles from the time period during which YouTube was first getting attention, and I could also use current research that looks back at the rise of YouTube.

One way to discern how important currency is, then, is by focusing on the subject matter and whether or not it has shifted dramatically.

CONNECT

In literary studies, both scholarly books and journals are published regularly. In comparison, in the sciences and psychology, scholarly books are rare and journal publications are common. Can you explain why in terms of the adjacent discussion about research in various disciplines?

Understanding disciplinary research can help you to make smart rhetorical decisions about your sources, too. Attention to how timely a source is can be more important in disciplines like science and psychology, where new information is not only added to old information but also old information is regularly corrected via new research. In disciplines like literary studies and history, the shift from older to newer ways of thinking about a subject matter is usually more gradual, so it is more acceptable to have slightly older sources.

Does the source offer enough depth to be useful?

Often the first place to research a question is Wikipedia. Before I tell you about the limits of Wikipedia, I will first point out that it's a fantastic place to find an overview of a topic when you're at an exploratory stage in your research, and it also includes citations and web links that can help you find sources for your research project.

Often, however, Wikipedia is not specific enough to be useful once you are working on a focused research question. Wikipedia is an encyclopedia, which is a reference work. Other reference works include dictionaries and bibliographies. Reference works tend to offer overviews rather than in-depth information, and the preferred kind of source for most academic writing is in-depth research.

Why in-depth research? I'm going to address that a bit more in the next part about how trustworthy a source is, but my short temporary answer is that when generalizations are made, a lot of information is left out. Relying on a reference article (whether from Wikipedia or another encyclopedia) is like relying on a map that shows only major highways; you will have some sense of where you're going, but you won't be able to actually

CONNECT

1. Find a newspaper article that relies on primary research (such as interviews and direct observations). How is the newspaper article similar to academic research? How is it different?

2. Find a newspaper or web-based article that presents scholarly research for a public audience. Now look at the original scholarly research article being summarized. How is the newspaper or web-based article similar to academic research? How is it different?

3. The above questions suggest that choosing sources can be complicated. Thinking about purpose can help. Based on this principle, give an example of a research question that might be answered by consulting newspaper articles.

reach your destination unless your map also shows the state routes and small roads in a more detailed and helpful view.

If you want to know more about Wikipedia in the role of undergraduate research, James P. Purdy does a nice job of writing about smart ways to approach the site.

Full disclosure: Textbooks tend to be overly general reference works. Many of the sources that I include in this volume are considered in-depth, and I have certainly read a lot of in-depth research to learn about how writing works. As I write to you, however, I am providing a great big overview—a roadmap of important highways. If you're going to cite the parts of the textbook that I've written, it would probably be more appropriate to do so in your informal writing or on social media rather than in your academic papers. You can ask your instructor about this advice, however, because it's a guideline, not a rule. Also, I find it flattering when people cite me and it allows me to imagine that we are hanging out in Burke's (ice cream) parlor together, so I won't discourage you too much.

Is it trustworthy?

So far, we have considered the **relevance** of sources by asking:

1. Is the research from the source connected to my research?
2. Is the source appropriately current?
3. Does the source offer enough depth to be useful?

Evaluating how **trustworthy** or credible a source is sounds simple, but it isn't. Don't worry: You can do it because you understand rhetorical situations and why they matter, and that helps you think through complexities.

First, let's be clear. If you care about the research you're doing, you want trustworthy sources because you're genuinely interested in the answer to your research question. If you are completing a school assignment and you don't care very much about the research question, you should still use trustworthy sources. Why? Because if you want to make a good impression on your readers, you need to use good sources. If you use unreliable sources, your lack of care becomes obvious, and then you waste your time and your reader's time.

In short: Even if you don't fully care, I recommend that you pretend you care because you'll do better work and it's possible that faking it will lead to you actually caring, at least a little bit.

Deciding whether a source is trustworthy involves distinguishing between scholarly and popular sources and, if the sources tend to be popular, recognizing bias.

Is the source scholarly, popular, or somewhere in between?

The words "*scholarly*," "*peer-reviewed*," and "*refereed*" are often used interchangeably. These kinds of sources tend to be written by experts or scholars and published in periodicals (such as print journals or online journals) or books that are intended for an audience of other faculty in that particular discipline or area of specialization. Before being published, these manuscripts are read by other faculty with expertise in the field. Only the manuscripts that are recognized as being worthy by others working in the field end up being published. Scholarly journals and books do not usually make a profit. Instead, they are subsidized by colleges and universities because these institutions not only educate people but also support the advancement of knowledge (specifically knowledge based on careful research, evidence, and analysis).

Most often, recognizing whether a book is scholarly involves looking at the publisher. If the publisher is a university press, the book is scholarly. There are several scholarly presses not affiliated with a university, however, including Routledge, Ashgrave, Rowan and Littlefield, and Palgrave Macmillan (the last of which has positive associations for me because it is almost McMillan, which is a very fine name).

Other signs that a book is scholarly are that it is written by a professor or other credentialed person in the field, it includes references, and it includes an index. However, some popular books might be authored by a professor and include references and an index, so the publisher is the clearest way to discern what is and is not a scholarly book.

Secondary Research

more scholarly	more popular
peer-reviewed periodical articles	commercial magazine articles
books published by scholarly presses	books published by commercial presses
online scholarly journal or online scholarly book	website or blog sponsored by an organization or government agency

Popular books are published by companies such as Scholastic, Random House, HarperCollins, and Simon & Schuster. These are sold at bookstores, they are sold for profit, and they are aimed at a general rather than academic audience. Books with presses such as these would be considered popular rather than scholarly.

To evaluate whether a periodical article is scholarly or popular, look at the title of the periodical. Academic journals tend to have academic-sounding names, like *Journal of Accounting Research*, *Feminist Media Studies*, and *Social Psychology Quarterly*. Academic journals may even state on their first pages that they are

FOCUS ON WRITING: WHAT COLLEGE STUDENTS WANT TO KNOW

peer-reviewed, and the editors of an academic journal are credentialed just as the article authors would be.

Popular periodicals include newspapers (such as the *Boston Globe* or the *Chicago Tribune*) and the kinds of magazines you might find in a drugstore or bookstore (whether *Sports Illustrated*, *Reader's Digest*, *Vogue*, or *People*).

Even though I've created just two categories, scholarly and popular, it's smarter to think in terms of a continuum. If a professor who is an expert in the field writes a newspaper or magazine article intended for a general audience, it's a popular source. However, that popular source is probably very trustworthy—more trustworthy than an article written by a journalist who is not an expert in the field.

In addition to thinking about the continuum of scholarly to popular (with "scholarly" generally being more trustworthy than "popular"), it's also important to remember that different sources are going to answer different questions. When I was researching YouTube, I trusted that the statistics for most subscribed channels and most popular videos were accurate because they were on a public site and the information could potentially be verified. Some specialized information will be available in popular venues but not in academic venues; so it is appropriate that you turn to the popular venues.

Currency may also be a factor that will lead you to consult a popular rather than scholarly source. Some topics require newspaper articles to provide current information; scholarly publications go through a longer process and cannot give up-to-date information. In other words, evaluating how trustworthy a source is without understanding how relevant it is does not make sense.

What about online sources?

We have access to more information than any other generation, yet it can sometimes feel like a curse rather than a blessing because we may not always be able to find the *best* information. By "best," I mean the most relevant and most trustworthy.

Let's start by better understanding what we mean when we say "online sources." An increasing amount of online material is in multimedia form (images, audio, video) rather than in alphabetic text (Manjoo). Scholarly research still more often appears in textual prose rather than in multimedia forms, but to the degree that images, audio, and video can help answer research questions, these forms are included in the remarks that follow.

An unbelievable amount of both alphabetic and multimedia texts appears in digitized form. When we are on the open web, we can access a large percentage of those digitized texts. However, a lot of material is not accessible without purchase or a subscription. If the world wide web was a physical space we could walk through, it's as if part of the space is open to everyone but part of the space is in a closed-off area, behind locked doors that require payment in exchange for access.

Much of this "closed-off area" can be accessed through a library database. A public town library probably has digitized books that are available to people with a library card, and these books have been paid for through taxes and other funding. A college or university library has digitized books and subscriptions to entire databases, with each database offering access to particular scholarly and popular publications. Universities pay for this access through a variety of sources, including student tuition and alumni donations.

One way of sifting through available information to increase the likelihood of finding relevant and trustworthy sources is to rely on college databases. They allow searching by specific disciplines, and they often have advanced search options to limit a search to "peer-reviewed" or "refereed" sources. If you typically use Google to search for information, library databases might feel unnecessary or confusing. I do not advocate using library databases all the time; for everyday questions, Google is fine. If you know you want to find scholarly sources, on the other hand, library databases can be your best friend because they do the work of evaluating whether sources are scholarly so you don't have to.

To do a more general online search rather than work through library databases, use Google Scholar to limit the findings to peer-reviewed texts. Some of the sources will be available to the public online for free (known as *open access* sources). Other sources may not be available online, but you may find those sources through your university library database.

Sometimes you will do online searches without necessarily wanting scholarly publications. Different search engines (such as Google, Bing, or YahooSearch) work in different ways, so whichever engine you use, it's worth researching how the results are listed. Google tends to list sponsored sites first, and after that the most popular sites tend to be listed at the top (though I am generalizing, and the actual metrics Google uses consider more than popularity). Wikipedia entries tend to be listed as a top result in a Google search, and then more people visit Wikipedia, and then it's more likely to be listed at the top ... you can see where this is going.

CONNECT

1. Use the same search terms in one of your library databases and then in Google Scholar. How are the results similar or different?

2. Choose two library databases to compare. Notice "Advanced Search" options and ways of refining your search by choosing year of publication, subject headings, and so forth. Do the databases you're comparing offer the same options to refine your results? What are the common elements? What are the differences?

FOCUS ON WRITING: WHAT COLLEGE STUDENTS WANT TO KNOW

In order to refine an online search, use Advanced Google search. You can choose language, a string of words, synonyms, words you do not want included in the results, and so forth. Sometimes the domain is important. For example, if you are looking specifically for government websites, you can limit the results to <.gov>.

When evaluating online sources, you can continue to notice the kinds of elements that matter in book publications and periodical publications:

- What kind of web publication is this? Consider, for example, whether it's a personal blog, a newspaper, social media, an organization's website, and so forth.
- Who is the author? Is the author credentialed in the subject matter in any way?
- How in-depth is the material? If it's a reference source, textbook, or journalistic summary of research, the original research is likely a stronger source.
- What organization sponsors the site? What is the function of this organization?
- How current is the entry or page?
- Does the page cite its sources or use hyperlinks as citations?
- Does the writing seem fair and balanced or is a particular viewpoint argued that seems questionable or one-sided?

It is more difficult to evaluate material online than in books and periodicals because sites rarely announce themselves as "untrustworthy" or "popular." If you've ever been discouraged from using online sources, that may be why. However, online sources can be incredibly useful. If you think carefully about the information you're looking for and what various venues can offer, there may be specific needs that web sources fill better than traditional resources.

Rather than eliminate online research, my advice is to be picky. Choose sources that make sense for the questions you're asking.

CONNECT

1. How comfortable are you with judging the relevance and credibility of online sources? What are your key strategies? What do you find difficult?

2. Have you used multimedia sources in the past? Can you think of circumstances when an image, audio file, or video might be appropriate for academic research?

SECONDARY RESEARCH: READING, TAKING NOTES, ORGANIZING, OH MY!

Reading rhetorically, reading critically

In the Introduction, I reviewed rhetorical reading strategies and what you can often expect from scholarly writing. If that is all hazy to you, it's worth reviewing as you think about research.

You might also notice that in each chapter I help you approach readings rhetorically by

a) showing how they might be useful to you in terms of content and as a model for writing or research (in the "Why I included it" comments)
b) providing information about the context of publication (in the "Background" comments)
c) offering questions to guide you in thinking rhetorically about purpose, audience, intertextuality, and so forth

You might thus already be fully aware that, as you read material, you become part of the rhetorical situation. You are a very particular audience, and you should read a source while keeping in mind how you might make use of it.

A secondary source might be used to

- provide background factual information or context
- define a term or concept
- reinforce a claim you're making
- provide an example to support your argument
- offer a research method that you replicate
- address a counter-argument
- find additional sources addressing the topic

As you consult multiple sources addressing a single topic or a group of related topics, you can think about them in conversation with one another. Rather than simply accept every point, pay attention to the questions you still have in regards to the conversation. Notice similarities and differences among the researchers' approaches and findings. Identify the ideas or principles that seem to be in conflict with one another; if every researcher is saying the same thing, there is no point in them taking the time to write, so you can assume that each one has at least a slightly different message.

If you struggle when working with sources because you either read them overly critically or you have trouble challenging the ideas, begin developing habits to approach sources with the ability to read both generously and critically. Honestly, this ability is important for most of us to practice because most of us tend to question material that does not fit our current worldviews while uncritically embracing material that reinforces our belief systems (Darley and Gross).

To read both generously and critically, practice slowing down. First, think about the source and agree with it in whatever way you can, even if your initial tendency is to be completely opposed to it. In what circumstances does the position make sense or seem accurate?

Then, take the opposite point of view. What are the limits of the argument? In what ways and in what circumstances is it inaccurate?

Peter Elbow, a well-known compositionist, calls this the "Believing and Doubting Game." As we slow down and see how any single source can be understood and applied in valuable ways while it also falls short or leaves questions unanswered, we learn to read sources more openly and critically. If nothing else, it is a good exercise for our minds to stretch in this way.

Strategies for recording and organizing findings

When conducting library research, be sure to keep track of sources as you go. Otherwise, you may end up with useful material but you'll have trouble citing it if you've misplaced the source.

Some people use index cards, with some cards as bibliography cards that are cross-referenced with note cards. I was forced to do this when I was young, and it never stuck.

My daughter Callie said she keeps tabs with multiple sources open on her computer and just goes back to the original sources over and over. She tends to do her writing assignments very intensively over several days, and she doesn't need to use a large number of complex sources, so her strategy works for her. For now.

If you have a strategy that continues to work for you, keep it up. If you don't, I'll tell you three strategies I've used when working on longer papers over a longer period of time while relying on a lot of sources.

First, when working on a paper over the course of a month, I would print out most of my sources and highlight the most important parts. I would put all bibliographic information on the front page of the source, and I would make brief notes about the most relevant parts that could be found within. Sometimes I dog-eared specific pages so I could flip to them easily.

As I would write a paper, I'd have my printed sources nearby and I would use them to flesh out parts of my paper as necessary. This process of moving between my own writing and my sources would happen again at various stages of drafting. My colleague Lindsey Wotanis likes to work from printed material, so we often did so when working together, though we also needed to take notes from books that were unwieldy to carry around and that needed to be returned to the library.

For most of my research activities now, I have abandoned that approach and have adopted a second strategy, partly because I write more slowly over a longer period. As I read sources for a project or part of a project, I take notes on a single long document. I enter the bibliographic information first, and then I use bullets as I read, writing down quotations for the most part but also using paraphrase, summary, or my own commentary on occasion. This way, once I've read a source, I don't ever have to go back to it. I sometimes print out the document of notes and mark it up so that when I'm working on a particular part of a project, I can quickly find all the relevant information.

CONNECT

What systems do you use for keeping track of sources and taking notes?

The third strategy is ideal when collaborating with others: Use an app meant for keeping track of sources. I have used Zotero to keep track of my sources and to share sources with others. You may be familiar with EasyBib, EndNote, Mendeley, or another tool that helps with organizing and citing sources. If you find a tool that works for you early in your college career, it will make future research projects easier. If you can find ways to keep track of sources and useful information from the time you begin a research project, later steps will be easier and you will be using your time and energy more efficiently.

SECONDARY RESEARCH: INTEGRATING SOURCES INTO YOUR WRITING ETHICALLY

You can use secondary sources in a number of ways, so I'll first review a few of the most common uses.

- You might use a secondary source briefly at the start of your paper to define a problem that your paper will address, to offer an opinion that your paper will correct, or to offer a statement that you will apply to a particular situation.
- You might use sources as needed in an analysis, drawing on sources that help support or develop your claim.

- You might use secondary sources to develop a literature review, recapping conversations and creating frameworks that inform your primary research.

No matter how you're using sources, it's important that you don't let them take over your paper. The paper should be authored by you, and the sources should simply be *used* to help you form your argument. I tell students to think about a salad. Your words and your work should make up the bulk of the salad, and sources should be used like dressing: helping your salad to be richer, but never taking over the salad. If your paper is so full of other voices that your work is minimized, it's like the end of a salad: just a few leaves of lettuce floating in a pool of dressing.

In order to prioritize your own words and work while using sources, you can begin and end most of your paragraphs with your own sentences that guide readers through your ideas. You can also use summary and paraphrase more than direct quotes. As you summarize or paraphrase sources and put ideas into your own words, you have to process them more fully. Again, that helps strengthen your voice in your paper so that sources don't take over.

CONNECT

1. Why do you suppose some writers let their sources dominate their papers?

2. Are there other ways sources might be used in academic writing that I didn't mention above?

As soon as you use sources in your writing, even at the draft stage, you should cite them. We cite sources to give credit to others' ideas, and we make it possible for someone to redo our research, making it more credible. We could put all the bibliographic material right in our papers as we use sources, but it would be messy and distracting. Instead, we use cross-reference systems. We either use a numbered system of notes or an alphabetized Works Cited or References page at the end of an essay. It's easier to document sources according to a system if you think about the purpose. Once students understand that a Works Cited or References page is a cross-reference system, they are more likely to alphabetize entries and to use in-text citations that help readers find the appropriate entry. Students are also amazed when they realize that entries on a Works Cited or References page reverse the indentations used for paragraphs—a formatting rule that helps readers distinguish a list of cited works from the rest of the essay.

Academic integrity

Often using and citing sources is discussed in terms of plagiarism and academic integrity. I want to think about these issues carefully rather than offer a simplistic stance.

First, we have discussed the ways in which writing is social no matter what because it relies on shared language, discourse communities, genres, and so forth. **Intertextuality** refers more specifically to the way any writing responds to prior writing and is located within a web of texts that influence one another.

In the United States, values of independence and individuality mean that we often emphasize individual authors, the labor they put into constructing their texts, and the resultant ownership of texts. People who represent another person's work as their own are thus guilty of intellectual theft. To avoid this situation, we give attribution when using the ideas or the language of another writer.

Understand, however, that guidelines regarding ownership of texts is cultural, not universal, so writers in other countries may have very different ideas about textual ownership and ways to treat other writers respectfully. Even in the United States gray areas exist. Literature, journalism, visual arts, music, and other forms of expression often draw on the work of others in ways that challenge simple definitions of plagiarism, intellectual property, and copyright.

In classrooms, recognizing intertextuality runs the risk of overwhelming students rather than inspiring them. Charles Bazerman notes how some research papers present information pasted together from various sources, almost as if the student writer is powerless in the face of what has already been written about a topic. Some students, however, understand there is "a lot more to writing good research papers than locating some sources and following correct bibliographic form," and these students embark on "a journey of learning, of problem formation and reformulation, of careful and thoughtful reading, of being able to interpret and restate what sources had to say, of evaluation and comment, of synthesis, of fresh argument" (Bazerman 57). This latter approach is difficult, but the appeal is that research and learning are meaningful and students have "authority" and "agency" as they use the writing of others (Bazerman 59–60).

Part of the conversation about plagiarism and academic integrity, then, is bound with the rhetorical purpose of student writing. If research is assigned as a mindless exercise in finding and citing sources or if writers do not feel comfortable speaking with authority to a particular audience, they may be more likely to rely on **patchwriting**—a practice that is "between quotation and paraphrase," as it reproduces source material with minimal changes (Jamieson and Howard 130–31).

The question of motivation and authentic writing has been engaged with regularly from the start of this textbook. However, in addition to researching questions you genuinely want to know the answers to, it also helps if you are positioned to write with authority. To some degree, this authority may come from primary research (described below) because you will be explicitly adding to existent studies. You can also think about the way you organize and present secondary research as bringing something new or unique to the table.

Reconsidering your audience may also help you develop a stronger sense of yourself as a writer. If you usually write with your teacher in mind, try to think more about directing your engagement with secondary sources to your classmates. You and your peers can learn from each other and can assert yourselves as writers and researchers in the process. Note: Your professor can also learn from you, but I know this point may be difficult to remember when writing for someone who will be grading your work, which can be daunting.

CONNECT

1. What factors help you engage in secondary sources?

2. What factors help you write with authority rather than relying too much on source material?

3. If you or someone you know has intentionally plagiarized, what negative consequences resulted?

4. Are negative consequences likely to stop people from plagiarizing? Why or why not?

Although I try to set up writing and research projects in ways that empower my students and allow them to work thoughtfully with secondary texts, I know that people often take shortcuts because time runs short and due dates are looming and grades are part of college assignments. Here, my best advice is to work steadily, in small increments that are not overwhelming. If you are behind, touch base with your professor and see how you might regain your footing.

Often when I've talked with students who have plagiarized, they tell me they panicked. They may have procrastinated on their work and then ran out of time. They usually believed the assignment was difficult and they simply weren't good enough or smart enough to do the work.

If you find yourself in a situation like this, stop and take a deep breath. You can choose to email the professor and explain the situation and see what steps you might take. You can also reach out to an advisor, a professor in another class, a reference librarian, or a Writing Center consultant who can help you see options other than plagiarizing. If your answer to panicking is to take someone else's work and represent it as your own, you are likely to make a bad situation worse. Resist taking what seems like an easy way out because it often ends up being anything but easy.

If you do make a bad choice, own up to it and see what your next options are to make the situation better. Some students impress me when I see them work hard and use their talents to produce excellent work. Other students impress me when their response to their mistakes is to take responsibility for their decisions and find ways to make the situation better. We are human; we make mistakes. Often the measure of our character is how we respond when someone calls us out. Do we deny our wrongdoing and thus continue to lie and waste everyone's time? Or do

CONNECT

Review the policies on academic integrity at your school.

1. To what degree do they support and encourage you as a researcher and writer?

2. To what degree do the policies hinder or discourage you as a researcher and writer?

we explain the circumstances, notice other possible decisions we could've made, and figure out how to move forward? Personally, I find people who fill this latter category inspiring.

In the next sections, we will explore primary research. Remember that much academic writing brings secondary and primary research together in a single paper, and many researchers move fluidly between secondary and primary research that inform one another. Don't let the linear organization of this chapter fool you!

PRIMARY RESEARCH METHODS

Imagine that no one else has yet researched "what effective researchers do," and we are the first. How could we find out the answer to the chapter question?

I'm going to give you some answers you would probably come up with on your own if I gave you a minute:

- Interview researchers who have successfully published their studies to find out their habits.
- Survey researchers who have successfully published their studies, asking them to answer a series of questions about their approaches and habits.
- Observe the behaviors of researchers who have been successful in the past as they work on a current project.
- Analyze the writing of researchers who have been successful in the past as they work on a current project.
- Perform any of the four tasks above, but also use either the interview, survey, observational, or analytic approach with unsuccessful researchers in order to notice the differences.

All of the above approaches to primary research are regularly used in writing studies to draw conclusions, and sometimes more than one approach is used in a single study. Each approach also has many permutations. An interview might focus on one or two people, or interviews could be conducted with a large number of people (as in Deborah Brandt's study of literacy from Chapter One). The results of interviews could be interpreted qualitatively by focusing on recurring themes in a nuanced way, or the results could be quantified in particular ways—such as counting how many times the interviewee changes the subject or counting the number of times the interviewee uses explicit language.

Side note: These particular examples of quantifying answers have nothing to do with "what effective researchers do," unless we have a hypothesis that effective researchers curse a lot. That would be a fun hypothesis to investigate. Imagine if such research had been conducted and it informed the advice I gave you: "Research shows that effective researchers use approximately seven swear words an hour, so if you have not yet tried this strategy, you should test it out and see if your research abilities improve."

Back to the point. I used the terms "qualitative" and "quantitative." **Qualitative research** designs focus on an open approach that involves interpretation and nuance when considering data collection. Examples include observing community behavior, interpreting online interactions, or interviewing people about their memories of research.

Quantitative research designs favor a closed approach that involves counting and measuring data to draw conclusions. Examples include multiple choice surveys, lab experiments with results that can be measured, or tracking how long subjects take to complete an activity. Qualitative and quantitative methods and results are useful, though one type of design may be more appropriate than another depending on the particular research question.

Furthermore, no matter what primary research method is used, it will have limitations. When working with sophisticated questions and complex situations, researchers are able to discover patterns and likelihoods and draw conclusions. However, there is always more to understand, and often initial findings are proven to be partial or incomplete as follow-up studies are done.

I also want to give a heads-up about correlation versus causation. Even if I were to find that effective researchers tend to swear a lot during their research process, I cannot conclude that the swearing contributes to effective research practices. It might be that unedited self-talk contributes to both swearing a lot and effective research, or it might be that effective practices lead to more swearing rather than vice versa. There may be other complex connections, or it may be coincidence, like the commonly cited example of increases in killings coinciding with

CONNECT

1. How might you use primary research to find out whether effective researchers tend to use index cards or not when engaging in secondary research?

2. What are some other questions about the habits of effective researchers you might answer by using primary research methods?

increases in ice cream sales (which may not be true, but if it is true, it's unlikely that one causes the other).

I am now thinking about ice cream again, but I feel okay about that because ice cream also makes me think of Burke's parlor. The parlor is relevant because primary research allows us to contribute to an ongoing conversation by providing new evidence. I thus have not strayed from the point at all and have no reason to use explicit language.

In academic settings, research is often guided by instructors so that students can engage in topics and questions associated with the course, exploring an idea in depth to make a course experience richer and more meaningful. Expected research varies by discipline. In biology and chemistry, lab experiments are used to test hypotheses. Social sciences tend to use a variety of methods that include field observations, surveys, interviews, and experimental designs. Historians tend to investigate textual documents, as do many rhetoricians and literary scholars, though the specific approach to a text may differ based on discipline.

Do you remember the research question I worked on with my colleague Lindsey Wotanis? It's okay, I understand that your brain is busy working and cannot possibly remember all the important things I'm telling you, so I'll remind you. In our secondary research, we found answers for a slightly general research question: "Is YouTube a hostile environment for women?" The secondary research was not conclusive, and much of the research was anecdotal, so we were interested in finding out more through primary research.

We thus made a plan. We developed a specific research question that would contribute to answering the general question about YouTube gender hostility: "Is YouTube a more hostile environment for Jenna Marbles, a popular female YouTuber, than for her male counterpart, Ryan Higa?" (Wotanis and McMillan).

We chose these particular YouTubers because they were similar to one another in popularity and video style. We were measuring a gender-based difference, so we wanted as many similarities as possible to help us control variables. Obviously, because we were working with actual YouTube channels and not strict lab conditions, our variables could not be completely controlled. We simply did what we could so that our findings would tell us something that would be at least somewhat meaningful.

Wotanis and I further controlled variables by looking at the top ten videos of each YouTuber and the hundred most recent comments for each of those videos. In everyday language, you could say that we were trying to compare apples with apples. If we had compared two vastly different YouTube personalities or if we had cherry-picked comments to analyze to support our hypothesis that YouTube is more hostile towards women, our findings would have been less convincing.

Once we chose the writing that we would analyze, we read enough comments to create categories. Some researchers begin with categories before collecting data, and after the publication of our study, other researchers used our methods and categories to conduct their own research. Either approach may work. Like the other elements of a research process, each situation calls for an approach that fills the intended purpose.

After we had categories established, we coded each comment so that we could count how many of each kind appeared in the thousand comments we had collected from each YouTuber's most popular videos. We had to decide what to do when a single comment fit more than one category and what to do when we didn't fully understand a comment. These kinds of experiences tend to occur regularly in primary research. It is a messy process. Even with the tricky gray areas, however, it is exciting when patterns emerge from the evidence you've collected.

As you make choices about primary research methods, consider not only the best way to answer your research question but also the ethical treatment of human beings who might be involved in your study. Federal policies have been developed to guide research ethics, and your university likely has an Institutional Review Board (IRB) that assesses research proposals.

CONNECT

Have you conducted science lab experiments or analyzed a poem or story? Those are both examples of primary research.

Choose one of these methods and compare it to the primary research process I followed to discover elements of gender hostility on YouTube. What is similar and what is different?

CONNECT

1. Imagine you are trying to answer the question about whether or not the YouTube platform is a hostile environment for women. What methods might you use to answer this question?

2. Do any of these methods have the potential to negatively affect the wellbeing of study participants? Explain.

3. How might you limit such possible negative effects?

The kinds of research you conduct during your first-year composition class will likely not need to go through this process, but if you're unsure, check in with your teacher. Even if you do not go through the IRB process, if you believe you'll be dealing with sensitive material, privacy issues, or have other ethical concerns, discuss these with your professor. Primary research should contribute to an ongoing conversation, but it should do so without compromising the wellbeing of study participants.

Also remember to use professional manners when inviting people to participate in a study, and be sure to thank participants afterwards, especially if they devoted more than a few minutes to helping you. Decide whether to maintain anonymity, use pseudonyms, or use participants' names when writing about your methods and findings; communicate that information to subjects when you invite them to participate. Any use of audio recordings, photographs, or video recordings should similarly be vetted with participants. Your instructor may have you use a consent form or provide guidelines specific to your institution.

All the writing we do can affect people, so we should always be considering the impact of our words. This point becomes more salient when conducting primary research and writing it up for public consumption. Ethical concerns should not keep you from researching but rather should help you make appropriate choices as you design, implement, and write about your research study and findings.

ORGANIZING COMMON RESEARCH GENRES

The arrangement of research writing changes based on the genre, discipline, purpose, and subject matter. I will offer some default arrangements, but always remember that I'm offering guidelines rather than rules.

Annotated bibliography

An annotated bibliography is a list of sources on a particular topic with descriptions of each source. Sometimes the source is also evaluated. Annotated bibliographies are published by scholars and are used as a tool by other researchers in the field. For example, Doug Downs published an annotated bibliography of sources about teaching with a Writing about Writing (WAW) focus.

I often require students to create annotated bibliographies so they have a way of slowing down the research process, noticing what each source does, and seeing how the sources work in conversation with one another. One form I ask for includes:

- The full citation in MLA format
- A paragraph that explains whether the source is scholarly or not and whether it is current or not; if the source does not fit these criteria, students explain why it is still a useful source
- A paragraph summarizing the purpose and main points of the source
- A paragraph explaining how the source might be eventually used in the full paper

Notice that the requirements help students focus on evaluating sources for relevance and credibility while also reviewing the source's argument.

Summary, synthesis, and literature review

A summary usually focuses on a single source. Sometimes a source is summarized in one sentence, sometimes in a paragraph, and sometimes at greater length. The idea is to communicate the main argument and purpose of the source, or to break the argument into sub-points if the summary is longer.

A synthesis and a literature review both put sources in conversation with one another. A synthesis is a stand-alone form while a literature review is a section of a paper; it is arranged to frame and contextualize primary research. In both cases, the key is to figure out the best way to organize the material you have found so you can create a clear overview and recap of the research for your readers. As mentioned in Chapter Three, information often moves from the old or familiar to the new and unknown, and you can also organize according to topics and subtopics.

When using a literature review to frame your primary research, you may start with general or foundational research and eventually discuss specific research that is closest to the question your primary research addresses. For example, in the research on YouTube I've discussed above, the literature review was divided into a few sections: An introduction that provided an overview of stances; YouTube as hostile environment; YouTube possibilities; and short sections about Jenna Marbles and Ryan Higa. Notice that the first sections are more general and the last two sections are specific to the primary research.

At times in that literature review, a single source was used in more than one section, and at times several sources were cited in a single paragraph because they all contributed to a particular point. A synthesis or a literature review does not necessarily discuss one source at a time but rather discusses ideas in a logical order, drawing on relevant points as necessary.

An entire research paper

Different disciplines tend to follow specific kinds of organization when presenting research. Even within a single discipline, the organization of information might change according to a writer's purpose.

Personally, I usually integrate the results of my primary research and the discussion or interpretation of those results into a single section. I did not do so in the analysis of YouTube comments I wrote with Lindsey Wotanis, but much of my published research centers on qualitative textual analyses that tend to be clearer and less repetitive when I interpret the results as I present them. For an example, you can see my analysis of slut-shaming in *Mean Girls* and *Easy A* (McMillan).

Still, it helps to have a sense of a typical structure for research, even if you know that this structure might not always work for you.

1. **introduce** the focus of the research and its importance by briefly recapping a problem or a discussion that leads to a question that remains open; the research article will attempt to answer this **open question**
2. **synthesize** a number of **secondary sources** that frame the primary research project; this part of academic writing is called a *literature review*; note that the word "literature" does not refer to creative writing in this context
3. **explain** the **methods** used to gather evidence (such as interview, survey, textual analysis, observation, and so forth)
4. **identify** the **results** of the **primary research**
5. **discuss** the **significance** and implications of these results
6. **conclude** with a call to action or an acknowledgment of further research to be conducted

Did you notice that I provided the exact same structure in the Introduction? In that context, I offered the organization as a way to guide you through the reading of academic research (even though many samples in this book do not follow that model). In this context, I offer the same model as a possible way for you to think about your own research.

CONNECT

1. Go back and look at the writing of Seible included in Chapter One and Chapter Two. What patterns of organization do you notice? What other criteria for a literature review do those samples provide?

2. Do you find it helpful or frustrating to know that a particular organization will sometimes but not always be appropriate? Explain your response.

3. Can you identify papers you completed in the past that relied solely on primary research? What about papers that relied solely on secondary research? Have you written papers that relied on both secondary and primary research? (I find this approach is often new to many college students.)

FOCUS ON WRITING: WHAT COLLEGE STUDENTS WANT TO KNOW

WORKS CITED

Bazerman, Charles. "Intertextualities: Volosinov, Bakhtin, Literary Theory and Literacy Studies." *Bakhtinian Perspectives on Language, Literacy, and Learning*, edited by Arnetha J. Ball and Sarah Warshauer Freedman, Cambridge UP, 2004, pp. 53–65.

Burke, Kenneth. *The Philosophy of Literary Form*. Berkeley: University of California Press, 1941.

Darley, John M., and Paget H. Gross. "A Hypothesis-Confirming Bias in Labeling Effects." *Journal of Personality and Social Psychology*, vol. 44, no. 1, 1983, pp. 20–33, doi: 10.1037/0022-3514.44.1.20.

Downs, Doug. "Writing-About-Writing Curricula: Origins, Theories, and Initial Field-Tests." *WPA-CompPile Research Bibliographies*, No. 12, Sept. 2010, <http://comppile.org/wpa/bibliographies/Bib12/Downs.pdf>.

Elbow, Peter. "The Believing Game—Methodological Believing." *English Department Faculty Publication Series*, vol. 5, 2008, <https://scholarworks.umass.edu/cgi/viewcontent.cgi?referer=https://www.google.com/&httpsredir=1&article=1004&context=eng_faculty_pubs>.

Jamieson, Sandra, and Rebecca Moore Howard. "Sentence-Mining: Uncovering the Amount of Reading and Reading Comprehension in College Writers' Researched Writing." *The New Digital Scholar: Exploring and Enriching the Research and Writing Practices of NextGen Students*, edited by Randall McClure and James P. Purdy, American Society for Information Science and Technology, 2013, pp. 111–33, <https://sandrajamieson.files.wordpress.com/2013/02/jamieson-sandra-rebecca-moore-howard-newdigitalscholar-ch5.pdf>.

Manjoo, Farhad. "State of the Internet." *New York Times*, 9 Feb. 2018, <https://www.nytimes.com/interactive/2018/02/09/technology/the-rise-of-a-visual-internet.html>.

McMillan, Laurie. "Mixed Messages: Slut Shaming in *Mean Girls* and *Easy A*." *Peitho*, vol. 20, no. 1, Fall/Winter 2017, pp. 85–99, <http://peitho.cwshrc.org/files/2017/12/McMillan_Mixed-Messages_20.1_corrected.pdf>.

Purdy, James P. "Wikipedia Is Good for You?" *Writing Spaces*, vol. 1, Parlor P, 2010, <http://writingspaces.org/sites/default/files/purdy--wikipedia-is-good-for-you.pdf>.

Wotanis, Lindsey, and Laurie McMillan. "Performing Gender on YouTube: How Jenna Marbles Negotiates a Hostile Online Environment." *Feminist Media Studies*, vol. 14, no. 6, 2014, pp. 912–28, <https://doi.org/10.1080/14680777.2014.882373>.

Extending the Conversation

To think more about the question, "What do effective researchers do?" I have gathered together three selections reprinted here and eight readings you can find online. Each piece overlaps with my initial approach to the question in some way, but each piece also extends the chapter question with a particular focus. As we answer questions that may seem simple at first, complexities and nuances develop that call for more exploration.

For each text reprinted here, I tell you why I included it, provide some background about its initial publication, and offer hints that may guide your reading, including vocabulary terms when relevant. I also provide "connect" questions to help you engage and respond as you read.

For each online source I recommend, I offer a brief introduction—just enough to guide you as you decide what further reading (or viewing) might be helpful, inspiring, enjoyable, or challenging.

JOSEPH HARRIS'S INTRODUCTION TO *REWRITING: HOW TO DO THINGS WITH TEXTS* (2006)

Why I included it

Harris shows how complex thinking can be presented with clarity and in a conversational tone. His approaches to thinking about texts and sources we use in our own writing are helpful and practical.

Background

Harris is another respected scholar in the field of writing studies who is known for prioritizing students and their learning. This sample of writing is from a textbook, so it is aimed at a student audience, but it also appeals to writing faculty who would make the choice to assign this book in their classes. Harris's other scholarly projects focus on collaborative writing and conflict, the use of student texts in writing classrooms, and ways of bringing the work of students and teachers together. His focus here on helping students use others' writing as they produce their own writing fits with this trajectory of publications.

Reading hints

I omitted sections of the introduction in which Harris previews what each chapter will focus on and explains how the text should be used, so the text might seem slightly jumpy in places. For the most part, however, you should be able to follow Harris's ideas because he's writing for an audience of students, and he uses tools such as section headings and definitions to help you follow along. Harris uses "intertextual" moments that operate as sidenotes to his main text. These highlight his own use of texts so that we can both read about how to use texts and see examples of someone putting the theory into practice.

CONNECT

As you read, consider responding to the following questions to help you process the material.

1. How can you tell that Harris is writing for students? How might his writing also appeal to professors choosing a text for a first-year writing course?

2. Look at the two epigraphs (the quotes at the start of the selection). Why do you suppose Harris chose to begin with those quotations?

3. I've identified Harris's audience. Can you identify his purpose?

4. Notice Harris's definitions of "text" and "interest." Choose one of these definitions and connect it to concepts you've been learning about so far this semester, such as discourse communities, the rhetorical situation, motivation, or the writing process.

Harris, Joseph. Introduction. *Rewriting: How to Do Things with Texts*. Utah State UP, 2006, pp. 1–12.

All rights reserved. Printed in the United States of America. No part of this book may be reproduced in any manner whatsoever without permission except in the case of brief quotations embodied in critical articles and reviews.
—US copyright notice

A text is made up of multiple writings, drawn from many cultures and entering into mutual relations of dialogue, parody, contestation.
—Roland Barthes, "The Death of the Author"

MY AIM IN this book is to help you make interesting use of the texts you read in the essays you write. How do you respond to the work of others in a way that is both generous and assertive? How do you make their words and thoughts part of what *you* want to say? In the academy you will often be asked to situate your thoughts about a text or an issue in relation to what others have written about it. Indeed, I'd argue that this interplay of ideas defines academic writing—that whatever else they may do, intellectuals almost always write *in response* to the work of others. (Literary theorists call this aspect of writing *intertextuality*.) But to respond is to do more than to recite or ventriloquize; we expect a respondent to add something to what is being talked about. The question for an academic writer, then, is how to come up with this something else, to add to what has already been said.

> As Jonathan Culler writes: "Literary works are not to be considered autonomous entities, 'organic wholes,' but as intertextual constructs: sequences which have meaning in relation to other texts which they take up, cite, parody, refute, or generally transform." *The Pursuit of Signs* (Ithaca, NY: Cornell University Press, 1981), 38.

My advice here is to imagine yourself as *rewriting*—as drawing from, commenting on, adding to—the work of others. Almost all academic essays and books contain within them the visible traces of other texts—in the form of notes, quotations, citations, charts, figures, illustrations, and the like. This book is about the writing that needs to go on around these traces, about what you need to do to make the work of others an integral part of your own thinking and writing. This kind of work often gets talked about in ways—avoiding plagiarism, documenting sources, citing authorities, acknowledging influences—that make it seem a dreary and legalistic concern. But for me this misses the real excitement of intellectual writing—which is the chance to engage with and rewrite the work of other thinkers. The job of an intellectual is to push at and question what has been said before, to rethink and reinterpret the texts he or she is dealing with. More than anything else, then, I hope in this book to encourage you to take a stance toward the work of others that, while generous and fair, is also playful, questioning, and assertive.

This has led some readers to ask why I've chosen a term like *rewriting* to describe this sort of active and critical stance. And, certainly, I hope it's clear that the kind of rewriting I value has nothing to do with simply copying or reciting the work of others. Quite the contrary. My goal is to show you some ways of *using* their texts for your purposes. The reason I call this *rewriting* is to point to a generative paradox of academic work: Like all writers, intellectuals need to say something new and say it well. But unlike many other writers, what intellectuals have to say is bound up inextricably with the books we are reading, the movies we are watching, the music we are listening to, and the ideas of the people we are talking with. Our creativity thus has its roots in the work of others—in response, reuse, and rewriting.

Rewriting is also a usefully specific and concrete word; it refers not to a feeling or idea but to an action. In this book I approach rewriting as what the ethnographer Sylvia Scribner has called a *social practice*: the use of certain tools (paper, pen, computer) in a well-defined context (the academy) to achieve a certain end or make a particular product (a critical essay). There are practices in all walks of life—ways of farming and gardening, of working with leather or wood, of interviewing clients and counseling patients, of teaching and coaching, of designing and engineering, of setting up labs and conducting experiments. A practice describes how the members of a particular craft or trade get their work done. A problem with many books on writing, it seems to me, is that they fail to imagine their subject in meaningful terms as such a practice. Instead, they tend to alternate between offering advice that is specific but trivial—about proofreading or copyediting, for instance—and exhortations that are as earnest as they are vague. Or at least I have never felt sure that I knew what I was actually being asked to do when called upon to "think critically" or to "take risks" or to "approach revision as re-vision." But by looking here at academic writing as a social practice, as a set of strategies that intellectuals put to use in working with texts, I hope to describe some of its key moves with a useful specificity.

> Sylvia Scribner, "The Practice of Literacy," in *Mind and Social Practice* (New York: Cambridge University Press, 1997), 190–205.

Much of my thinking about writing hinges on this idea of a *move*. My subtitle alludes to one of the quirkiest and most intriguing books I have ever read, the philosopher J.L. Austin's *How to Do Things with Words*. In this book, actually the notes from a series of lectures, Austin argues that in thinking about language his fellow philosophers have long been overconcerned with decoding the precise meaning or truth value of various statements—a fixation that has blinded them from considering the routine yet complex ways in which people use words *to get things done*: to marry, to promise, to bet, to apologize, to persuade, to contract, and the like. Austin calls such uses of language *performatives* and suggests that it is often more useful to ask what a speaker is trying *to do* in saying something than what he or she means by it.

While I don't try to apply Austin's thinking here in any exact way, I do think of myself as working in his mode—as trying to show how to do things with texts, to shift our talk about writing away from the fixed and static language of thesis and structure and toward a more dynamic vocabulary of action, gesture, and response. You *move* in tandem with or in response to others, as part of a game or dance or performance or conversation—sometimes toward a goal and sometimes just to keep the ball in play or the talk going, sometimes to win and sometimes to contribute to the work of a group. I hope in this book to describe intellectual writing as such a fluid and social activity and to offer you some strategies, some moves as a writer, for participating in it.

> J.L. Austin, *How to Do Things with Words*, 2nd ed. (Cambridge, MA: Harvard University Press, 1962).
>
> What I find of particular interest to my work here is a moment, near the very end of his lectures, when Austin offers a short list of what he calls "expositive" verbs—those that are used in "the expounding of views, the conducting of arguments, and the clarifying of usages and references"—in effect, beginning to outline his own set of "moves" for academic writing (see pp. 161–63).

To do so, I draw on my experiences over the last twenty years as a writer and teacher of academic writing. And so, while this book is filled with examples of intellectuals at work with texts, they are examples that perhaps, in the end, tell as much about my own tastes, training, and values as anything else. That is to say, in this book I use my own ways of responding to and working with texts, my own habits of reading and writing, as representative of what other academics and intellectuals do. The drawback of such an approach, I suspect, is not that it is likely to be idiosyncratic but the reverse—that I may end up simply rehashing the common sense, the accepted practices, of a particular group of writers. But that is also, in a way, my goal: to show you some of the moves that academics routinely make with texts, to articulate part of "what goes without saying" about such work.

The Structure of this book

[***]

Let me be as clear as I can about some other things that this book is *not*. It is not a guide to research; there are many such books already, and some very good ones, too. My concerns here begin at more or less the point when research ends: when you are faced with the question of what to say about a text that you have located or that you have been assigned to read.

[***]

Finally, I need to say something about two other terms that are central to this book—one a specialized term and the other a word so familiar that some of its meanings have been dulled by use. The specialized term is *text*, by which I simply mean an artifact that holds meaning for some readers, viewers, or listeners. A book (or other piece of writing) is a text, but so are movies, plays, songs, paintings, sculptures, photographs, cartoons, videos, billboards, advertisements, web pages, and the like—as well as objects like buildings, cars, clothes, furniture, toys, games, and other gadgets when they have somehow acquired meaning for their users. But not everything is a text. Unlike actions, memories, or events, texts are objects that have been made and designed—*artifacts* that can in some way be shelved, filed, or stored and then retrieved and reexamined. That is what makes them so central to academic work. We may not agree on what a certain text means, but we can return to it and try to point to those specific aspects—lines, images, phrases, scenes—that lead us to interpret it differently. Someone else should always be able to check on how you have quoted a text.

The more commonplace but equally troublesome term is *interest*. I have often heard teachers remark that describing a piece of writing as "interesting" is to say very little about it, but I don't think that this needs to be the case. The critic Raymond Williams has shown how over time the word *interest* has acquired several layers of meaning: Its first recorded uses, in the sixteenth century, appear in the realms of law and finance, as in the sense of "holding an interest" in a company or "earning interest" from an investment. But early on the word also gained a more political or partisan sense, as in the "interests of state," "self-interest," or "an interested party." (The opposite of this meaning is "disinterested," like a judge.) But *interest* did not gain its most current meaning, of attracting curiosity or attention, until the nineteenth century. (The opposite here is "uninteresting" or dull.) I find all three of these meanings useful in thinking about a piece of writing. That is, you can ask of an essay: (1) How does this writer add interest or value to what has been said before? (2) What is her interest in this issue, what perspective is she speaking for? and (3) How is her style in writing of interest or note? And so when I say that my aim in this book is to help you make *interesting* use of the work of others, I use the term in all three senses. I hope, that is, to help you write with perspicacity and wit about texts and issues that matter to you.

See Raymond Williams, *Keywords: A Vocabulary of Culture and Society*, rev. ed. (New York: Oxford University Press, 1983), 171–73, as well as the usage notes for *interest* in the online *Oxford English Dictionary*.

DOUGLAS DOWNS AND ELIZABETH WARDLE'S "WHAT CAN A NOVICE CONTRIBUTE? UNDERGRADUATE RESEARCHERS IN FIRST-YEAR COMPOSITION" (2010)

Why I included it

Downs and Wardle inspired a lot of Writing about Writing (WAW) approaches used in this textbook and in the teaching practices of many college writing professors, including me. This particular article argues for authentic research in first-year courses, so you can think about your own stance toward college writing expectations. You can also use the organizational model in your own writing, with section headings and subheadings guiding readers through the argument.

Background

Downs and Wardle are known for their work on Writing about Writing (WAW) approaches in first-year composition, and this book chapter is one of many publications explaining, theorizing, and justifying such pedagogies. It appeared in an anthology titled *Undergraduate Research in English Studies*, so the audience would likely be English professors with some interest in the topic, most likely because they are wondering how to increase or improve student research in their department. Many of the other chapters in the anthology focus on upper-level research, so it was probably smart of Downs and Wardle to begin the chapter by assuming that many professors would hesitate to engage first-year students in meaningful research projects. Stanley Fish, who is quoted at the start of the essay, is a literary scholar whose name is widely known among academics.

Reading hints and vocabulary

I included the entire chapter, so you will not need to worry about choppy transitions. You'll notice that the writers begin by representing the point of view that they oppose. This move allows them to position their thinking as somewhat controversial. As a reader, you can note the opposition that is set up to help you understand the authors' purpose.

Downs and Wardle explain what research in a first-year composition class might look like. They then have two sections that are each divided into sub-sections. The first of these offers the benefits of research in first-year composition, and the second section presents obstacles (and ways to overcome each obstacle). Use the sections and sub-sections to help you follow the specific arguments. Even though the article is directed toward teachers, you can think about your own experiences as a student.

recitative research: research that repeats the arguments and information of others rather than offering a new position, new evidence, or other meaningful contributions

contributive research: purpose-driven research that adds to a conversation or otherwise offers something to a community

IRB: acronym for Institutional Review Board, an organization on campuses that reviews research studies to make sure subjects are treated ethically and comply with government- and university-established standards

CONNECT

As you read, consider responding to the following questions to help you process the material.

1. Paraphrase the contrasting positions Downs and Wardle present at the start. Have other readings from the semester begun this way?

2. Choose one of the benefits of undergraduate research that Downs and Wardle discuss and explain whether or not you have gained that benefit from past research you've engaged in. If so, how? If not, how might you have if the research project had been designed differently?

3. To what degree do these ideas intersect with ideas from Chapters Two or Three about the rhetorical situation or writing processes? In what way? Explain.

Downs, Douglas, and Elizabeth Wardle. "What Can a Novice Contribute? Undergraduate Researchers in First-Year Composition." *Undergraduate Research in English Studies*, edited by Laurie Grobman and Joyce Kinkead, Utah State UP, 2010, pp. 173–90.

WRITING TEACHERS ARE familiar with the many complaints about and characterizations of first-year students' research papers: they are shallow, regurgitative, "grave robbing" (Russell 2002). If we listen to Stanley Fish (2002), this is perhaps all that first-years are capable of producing:

> [Students] have been allowed to believe that their opinions—formed by nothing, supported by even less—are interesting. [...] The instructor who hears them coming from the mouths of his or her students should immediately tell them, "Check your opinions, your ideas, your views at the door; they are not fungible currency here." [...] Every dean should

forthwith insist that all composition courses teach grammar and rhetoric and nothing else. (par. 13, 14, 16)

But the 1998 Boyer Commission report, *Reinventing Undergraduate Education*, rejects such passive absorption for undergraduates in general: "The ideal embodied in this report would turn the prevailing undergraduate into a culture of inquirers, a culture in which faculty, graduate students, and undergraduates share an adventure of discovery" (16). The Council for Undergraduate Research (CUR) has long argued that undergraduates can do much more than regurgitate if they are given the opportunity and appropriate guidance.

The Boyer Commission's recommendation that "undergraduates should have the opportunity to work in primary materials, perhaps linked to their professors' research projects" (1998, 17), implies that such research will take place in the major, at an upper level. Generally, only upper-level undergraduates in a major have had the opportunity to form relationships with professors and read enough in the field to be able to contribute in a meaningful way to a research project. Therefore, we wonder, along with the contributors to the fall 2008 *CUR Quarterly*, which focuses on "Undergraduate Research: An Early Start," whether there is a place for genuine, contributive research in first-year general education courses, particularly in first-year composition. This course is often charged with teaching "the research paper," but such papers are usually written in only a few weeks, outside any disciplinary knowledge, for a nonspecialist reader. Still, as Joyce Kinkead (2007) has demonstrated, composition courses already contain teaching and assignments that offer groundwork for students to become undergraduate researchers later. Is it possible to have students from many majors, with a writing studies or English studies instructor, apply that groundwork directly in the composition course? We believe it is. In this chapter we outline what we believe genuine, contributive research might look like in first-year composition and how that experience can benefit students.

A Picture of Contributive Research in First-Year Composition

While first-year composition courses can be focused in many ways, we will argue specifically for courses whose content is writing itself, including discourse, literacy, rhetoric, composition processes, new media, and the like; we believe that writing as course content increases the likelihood that the research students conduct will be genuinely contributive. We'll cover some reasons for this focus briefly, referring readers to our 2007 *College Composition and Communication*

FOCUS ON WRITING: WHAT COLLEGE STUDENTS WANT TO KNOW

(CCC) article "Teaching about Writing, Righting Misconceptions" for fuller explanation.

First, a writing course must primarily teach *writing*. Writing courses with some content other than writing—say, environmental issues—must teach *two* fields of knowledge if students are to write contributively. The likelihood of students gaining sufficient background in a content field while the course remains focused on writing is greatest when the course content is writing *about* writing. Second, undergraduate research demands mentoring by faculty in the field to which students are contributing. Although it is true that many writing instructors are *not* experts in rhetoric and composition, it seems reasonable to believe that the average writing instructor is by far the greater authority on writing and literacy than on (continuing our example) environmental issues. A third argument for writing-about-writing research is the relative accessibility of scholarly conversations on writing-related subjects. Composition studies has not only had less time to specialize than have most other academic fields (its major professional organization forming only in 1949), but it has also been a field with an ethic of inclusion and a focus on pedagogy; all of these factors yield accessibility in both the field's questions and its language. Unlike fields such as environmental biology or hydrology, then, composition allows first-year students to garner a reasonably good understanding of much of the work in the field. Another source of that accessibility is our fourth and most important reason for advocating writing about writing: students have firsthand, daily experience with language, discourse, literacy, writing, and rhetoric. If contributive research emerges from genuine questions that puzzle the researcher, all students should be able to identify a research project on writing that emerges from their own experiences.

We also find writing-about-writing courses effective because excellent opportunities for dissemination of students' research on writing and rhetoric already exist. Unlike many other fields, composition studies has an international, peer-reviewed undergraduate journal, *Young Scholars in Writing*, with a feature on first-year composition students' research on writing and rhetoric (coedited by Douglas Downs). The field has also long fostered undergraduate conference presentations, particularly through its work on writing centers. First-year composition programs have pioneered more local dissemination in the form of "celebrations of student writing" at several institutions nationwide. Finally, the past year has seen the emergence of a new venue for first-year students' work on writing and literacy: the National Conversation on Writing, a project of the Council of Writing Program Administrators' Network for Media Action, which offers a Web 2.0 clearinghouse for writers researching and talking with others about writing nationwide. When students research on writing and literacy, they can upload their work to the site for review and posting.

In our own writing-about-writing research classes, we ask that students begin by reading articles that might relate to or contrast with their own experiences with writing. As they review Sondra Perl's (1979) research on "Tony" or Nancy Sommers's (1980) research on students' understanding of revision, we ask them to explore their own experiences with writing or their own understandings of revision. Out of such reading and reflection come questions that serve as the basis for research projects, questions that are meaningful to the student and have generally not been answered in published literature. For example, our students have looked at how sports impact boys' reading habits and attitudes, how various kinds of music affect reading and writing, how students at a particular university understand plagiarism, and so on. These projects tend to take up most of a fifteen-week semester, in close imitation of the way professional scholars conduct research, with at least some opportunity to collect data, 'reflect, analyze, write, revise, and consult' with others. We also have students conduct shorter research projects that, again, begin with their own experiences and questions: students keep logs of the kinds of writing they do over several weeks, or the technologies that mediate their writing, and then compare their processes and purposes for the various texts and technologies. They keep logs of the writing they do in different classrooms, and then compare conventions and purposes across disciplines. They also conduct mini-discourse community ethnographies of groups with which they are familiar (say, church or sorority or workplace); later they conduct mini-discourse community ethnographies of language use in their desired majors. All of this work emerges from genuine questions and requires some grounding in published research and in fieldwork.

Published examples of student papers about writing and rhetoric are available to offer concrete examples of genuine inquiry at the first-year level. The inaugural first-year feature in *Young Scholars in Writing* included a commentary on the content of first-year composition (Strasser 2008), a survey-based study on perceptions of "classic" literature (Augino 2008), an ethnography of the punk scene in mid-1980s Waco (Pleasant 2008), and an interview-based study of the effects of past praise of writing on future literacy experiences (Jackson 2008). The 2009 volume included rhetorical analyses of presidential campaign speeches by first-year students. In the 2010 volume being edited as this chapter goes to press, first-year writers are revising studies on the positive and negative effects of blogging in recovery from eating disorders, on a "rhetoric of magic" in environmental discourse, on the effects of direct grammar instruction in second-language instruction, and on other equally intriguing subjects. In every case, these papers say something that hasn't been said before. They were researched and drafted during a semester in a first-year composition course. They use professional methods. They were never conceived as library research papers, regurgitation of sources to "take a stand." Rather, they respond to assignments that required primary research on an open question of import to the writer and a field, and a written account of that research and its implications. The important point, neither subtle nor intuitive, to understand about this difference in purpose is that a library research paper, for all its hope of having the writer reach a new insight, is not learning based on discovery new to *other* inquirers. Such discovery is simply not expected. In stark contrast, the teachers who made the assignments that resulted in these *Young Scholars in Writing* submissions explicitly *did* expect to read something in their students' papers that they did not already know.

What Undergraduate Research in First-Year Composition Can Offer
Clearly, first-year students cannot conduct the same sort of research that upper-division or graduate students can. They are not yet immersed in the work of a field, have not yet read broadly on any one subject, and do not have relationships with faculty in their chosen fields to serve as apprentice researchers. Yet we believe that teaching contributive research in the first year can have important benefits even if the student does not actually end up making a contribution: it can teach habits of mind and an understanding of scholarship; it can teach students how to read and use difficult scholarly texts; it can teach writing as transactional and genres as content- and purpose-driven; and it should result in better transfer (generalization) of writing-related knowledge to other courses. While we can anticipate concerns that first-year research could lower the standard for what counts as "research," we see these other benefits as lessening that pressure: success might be viewed as a contribution to the immediate class's knowledge rather than to a discipline in the pursuit of these other benefits. These students, engaged in small-scale but meaningful research in the first year, gain an understanding of what research is and how it is done that can be built on in the following years.

Teach Habits of Mind
Conducting primary research in writing courses teaches writerly and scholarly habits of mind. Sarah Wyatt (2005), in an argument for the efficacy of original

experimentation in inquiry-based learning, offers examples of what students can learn from contributive research that they *must* learn in college but are unlikely to learn in many other ways:

> Students, and teachers, have been groomed to believe there is a single correct answer and that education is about finding that answer. With original research there is no "right" answer to find; there is only data to be collected. Students must learn to think and to evaluate that data, and trust the process of so doing. They also must be willing to be wrong. (84)

In other words, training in contributive research does teach ways of thinking that benefit not only future graduate students but also the vast majority of college students, those who won't have research careers. Students' research in college is worth their time and ours, even as they pursue other directions afterward.

Therefore, even when students try but don't succeed at conducting contributive research in their first year, there is great value in the *attempt*. Failure to contribute is not synonymous with failure to learn; even failure in contribution does not diminish the value of framing undergraduate education as learning through discovery. It makes more sense to have students try to contribute and not succeed than it does to simply assume first-year students to be incapable of contribution, locking them out of the discovery culture as a whole. In arguing thus, we concur with Alan Jenkins and Mick Healey (2007) that the value of undergraduate research has to be considered more broadly than just in terms of students' actual contributions: "To say that the student learns as a researcher, is to state that the university, particularly through its curricula, supports students in gaining new insights and opportunities to learn about research and the way knowledge is constructed" (210). Institutions that would claim a culture of undergraduate research consequently seem obligated to include first-year students on principle alone.

Teach How to Read and Use Scholarship

As most teachers can attest, undergraduate students do not come to us knowing how to read scholarly research; much less do they know what to do with it, or even that they could do something with it. Students who can successfully integrate a *Time* magazine commentary into their marijuana paper do not necessarily know how to use scholarly articles and books. Reading is no mere act of text recognition (words on a page); it's an act of constructing representations of the writer's meaning by integrating text *and context* with prior knowledge. As Christina Haas and Linda Flower (1988) have demonstrated, younger students tend not to read rhetorically, understanding that the meaning of the text is contingent on the writer's motivation and the circumstances of its writing. Explicit reading instruction that demonstrates how scholars read and has students practice reading is essential to students' abilities to conduct their own research. Teaching students the "moves" (Swales 1990) in research introductions or the types of citation practices used in different disciplines (Hyland 2002), as well as the conventions of various scholarly texts, can help them focus on content and research questions in a way that supports their own research interests. No matter what their intended major, students who can read and use scholarly sources after completing first-year composition are better prepared to conduct research than those who cannot. And the fact that they are receiving this reading instruction in the composition classroom itself increases the likelihood that they can do unexpected contributive work.

Teach Writing as Transactional, Genres as Emerging from Purpose
It is by now axiomatic in rhetoric and composition that writing instruction must be situated—we cannot teach "writing" generally. Condemnation of "general writing skills instruction" is most focused in Joseph Petraglia's (1995) volume *Reconceiving Writing, Rethinking Writing Instruction,* where, for example, David Russell (1995) argues that imagining general writing skills is equivalent to imagining "general ball handling skills" for all sports involving a ball, from table tennis to American football (57–60). Petraglia labels unsituated writing assignments as "pseudotransactional" (92), asserting that first-year composition has specialized in such assignments rather than writing that genuinely participates in specific rhetorical situations. Gerald Graff and Andrew Hoberek (1999) echo this sentiment in their *College English* commentary "Hiding It from the Kids," pointing out that students "who submit writing samples that are studiously pointless would never think to speak that way in real life. It took them years of education to learn to speak with no context to no one" (252).

In marked contrast, scholarly inquiry is some of the most situated writing that teachers can assign, as contributive research grounds writing firmly in tangible audiences and purposes. As Graff and Hoberek assert, students who attempt to answer the questions most basic to scholarly inquiry—"so what?" and "who cares?"—will be situating their writing realistically (1999). The field has concrete evidence that students learn tremendously from seeing actual readers attempt to *use* their writing. Literacy researcher Gert Rijlaarsdam (2008) asked elementary students to write process instructions, watch readers try to use them (but not get direct feedback from those users), and then revise. Another group of writers did not get to watch readers but instead got additional practice writing. The group that ultimately produced the best writing was the group that wrote the least but saw readers attempting to use their document. Writers travel miles farther in the presence of genuine attempts to use their writing than in endless loops of "process" that lack any actual transaction with readers.

The connection between that finding and undergraduate research in first-year composition will be clear to teachers who have tried to publish: the attempt to create contributive writing is so genuinely recursive and interactional that writers truly get a sense of how their writing is *used* by readers, and thus where its shortcomings are. Research conducted by Downs, Heidi Estrem, and Susan Thomas (2009) on submissions to *Young Scholars in Writing* shows exactly this: the most striking aspect of students' publishing process was the interaction between readers and writers making sense of feedback by some of their intended but heretofore imagined readers.

We also want to stress that first-year students need instructors to *show* options for dissemination in order to fully imagine them. Bringing copies of *Young Scholars in Writing* into class, asking others who have presented at conferences to present to the class on those experiences, demo-ing websites that accept student work, showing videos of previous local conferences—all are strategies instructors can use to offer their students tangible goals for dissemination of their work.

Facilitate Transfer

A major consideration for first-year composition is (or should be) transfer, or generalization, from first-year composition to other classes. Much research has demonstrated the lack of transfer from school activities generally; the minimal research on writing-related transfer from first-year composition seems even bleaker. There is little evidence on whether and how students later deploy knowledge gained in first-year composition, in part because transfer seems to depend as much on context and situation at the far end as it does on first-year composition (Wardle 2007, 82). But there are ways to better encourage and facilitate transfer, and some of those methods are natural to research-based writing. For example, teaching researched writing as transactional, and genres as emerging from context and purpose, can encourage the meta-awareness about writing needed for transfer. Teaching ways of reading scholarship, and ways of understanding the conventions employed in that scholarship, teaches flexible principles rather than rigid rules, again encouraging transfer to other contexts. Elizabeth Wardle's (2007) longitudinal study of students post-first-year composition does show that the writing-about-writing version of first-year composition can "help students think about writing in the university, the varied conventions of different disciplines, and their own writing strategies in light of various assignments and expectations" (82). Although undergraduate research in first-year composition is too new for clear data on transfer to have emerged, there is at least complementarity, then, between what would be required to teach for generalization beyond first-year composition and what first-year composition as undergraduate research does.

We imagine an undergraduate research experience that sees first-year composition as the entry point and researched theses in the major as final exit points. In first-year composition, students learn how to read and use scholarly texts, how to ask meaningful questions, how to seek out answers to those questions, and how to share their findings with others. These are practices and habits of mind that can set the stage for deeper research in their chosen fields. The exact methods used in first-year composition are less important than an understanding of what methods are; that the research projects are perfectly designed and carried out is less important than an understanding that research projects should have an intentional design (along with at least a plausible possibility of dissemination, though most projects may not ultimately reach that stage). Universities that want a rich undergraduate experience should look carefully at the possibilities of first-year composition as the place where expectations are set and appropriate habits of mind are taught. English departments (which usually house first-year composition programs) should thus consider how the first-year general-education courses they host and staff fit with other undergraduate research efforts in English studies and across the university.

Impediments to Contributive First-Year Research

If teaching research as genuine contribution in first-year composition were easy, it would already be common. Teachers' own attitudes (for example, as embodied by Fish) can be a clear impediment to large-scale implementation, particularly in a course like first-year composition that is taught by such a wide variety of instructors with various levels of knowledge and preparation. Other impediments include views on how writing should be assessed (that is, whether researched writing can be as "error free" as shorter, more polished papers), problems gaining human subjects' approval, views of writing that might see collaboration as plagiarism, and the limited time available for large-scale research projects.

Teacher Attitudes and Training

Solving many, if not most, teaching problems is often a matter of attitudes, expectations, and ways of thinking. We find this to be true of building undergraduate research into first-year composition courses. Perhaps the most important attitude is respect for and belief in students themselves—what they know and what they're capable of achieving. One way of demonstrating this respect is by believing that students can exceed our expectations. Very often, they will. Such respect must also be demonstrated in our willingness to mentor (not just teach). Faculty must be *present* to students who seek their guidance and perspective, just as in higher-level subject area courses. Undergraduate researcher Amber Watson's (2008) work on how undergraduates create contributive research suggests that mentors help students understand not just subject matter, but institutional and professional structures and opportunities that are otherwise invisible to undergraduates. Mentors show students aspects of conducting research that don't appear in the published results: how to get funding, how to find calls for papers, how to submit to conferences and prepare manuscripts for submission.

Writing teachers may also need to check their own conceptions of writing. They should be aware of the distinction between recitative and contributive research, as well as the difference between writing to learn and writing to contribute. They should also be aware of the many double standards entrenched in traditional research instruction that no longer work in contributive research. For example, in traditional research instruction, students often are not allowed to include opinion unsupported by sources; in contrast, researchers use research specifically in order to think and say things that others have not. Many writing teachers have simply never compared what they themselves were taught about research writing, and thus continue to teach, to what researchers actually do. Further, the nature of contingent labor in first-year composition instruction means that many writing teachers aren't themselves actively researching. Because most do have at least MA degrees (and some others are graduate students working toward them), they would need to rely on their own graduate experiences in order to guide students' processes. They might, however, want to research along with their students, and take research classes and institutional review board (IRB) training to supplement their previous training.

Standards for Evaluating Writing

One other necessary shift in instructor attitudes pertains to evaluation of writing. Since its inception, first-year composition has been understood by most stakeholders—university administrators and faculty, writing instructors, and students—as devoted to and measured by the creation of perfect *products-shiny*, flawless documents. Just as with today's SAT writing exam, *what a writer says* is of far less concern than the fluency and correctness with which it is said. This attitude is what made David Bartholomae's (1985) essay "Inventing the University" groundbreaking: he made writing instructors ask themselves which deserves the higher grade, a perfectly written piece of fluff, or a complex piece that takes risks and stretches the writer but winds up imperfect? This was a radical idea in 1985, and is unfortunately almost as radical now—but it's an idea that teachers of contributive research in first-year composition must embrace; to ask first-years to try their hand at contributive research entails big risks and reduces time available for proofing and polishing. Teachers need to look for the merit in students' work somewhere under the surface perfection, because even the best first-year research paper may feel rough and unfinished. Downs's experience editing submissions for the first-year feature in *Young Scholars in Writing* suggests that, more than upper-division students' submissions, first-year submissions require significant additional work. However, the published articles demonstrate what the results of that additional effort can be.

This approach to first-year composition demands that teachers carefully consider evaluation, collaboration, and research ethics. How does one evaluate "unfinished" work, or assignments that emphasize accomplishing particular thinking or research work rather than refining a perfect prose style? If evaluating refinement is important, can that evaluation be delayed—as through portfolio grading—while other evaluation, of engagement or progress, happens earlier in the semester? Ultimately, what needs deciding is, as always, (1) what is important to evaluate, and (2) how to evaluate it. The same analytical challenge applies to building community: finding points where students working on related but separate projects can contribute to one another's work; or using large-scale curricular moves, such as whole-class collaboration on a research problem by having small teams investigate particular aspects of it. The curricular question is, what assignments and uses of class time will allow students to assist and learn from each other and build on each other's work as research communities do? Expect such efforts to be met by lack of student understanding—after reading scholarship, collaboration is perhaps the biggest gap in students' grasp of how research works. Writing teachers must fight years of misconception in teaching students that professionals don't write alone.

Collaboration

Students aren't the only ones who falsely understand writing as a solitary activity; their teachers often set up course assignments that perpetuate this myth, even as those teachers do their own work with the help of others. Even in the humanities, which value "lone-genius" research, researchers form communities that share and develop their members' work. Such research communities directly refute the myth that brilliance happens in the absence of interaction. Yet first-year composition research instruction traditionally turns students into islands working on choose-your-own-adventure problems (usually personal positions on social issues) without reference to each other. This arrangement ignores the possibilities, both for teaching how research actually works and for getting it accomplished, created when a class works on related problems, as is easily arranged in writing-about-writing courses. Building first-year composition research communities has long been advocated—see Michael Kleine's (1987) work on inviting students to research as faculty do, and James Reither's (1985) critique of the isolationist "process" instruction. However, the field has largely ignored such calls.

Time

If assigning students to work alone is one way teachers expect their students to adhere to requirements that they themselves do not face, then requiring students to complete "research" in a very short time is another such double standard. Many semester-length first-year composition courses feature a five-to-eight-week library research paper as a culminating project—a window within which most academics would not be able to produce much. Wardle has piloted linking first- and second-semester first-year composition courses so that students conduct preliminary research on their question in the first semester and primary research in the second. This pilot enabled some exceptionally underprepared students to produce thoughtful, contributive research projects. Such a system may not be an option at many schools, but the principle holds: expect that students can conduct quality research in direct relation to the amount of time they have to do it.

We should make the most of whatever time is available by ensuring that most or all assignments contribute to the project. The assignments, while teaching important functions and skills, should also scaffold the project: exploratory writing leading to research questions, research proposals, source summaries, annotated bibliographies, reviews of literature, separate paper sections (such as Methods), abstracts and presentations—all build to a "main" written project. It is important to ensure that assignments are recognizable and teachable genres, and equally important that students can learn without perfecting such scaffolding projects. Teachers can worry less about what students can perfect than about which assignments will help them learn about writing and accomplish research.

IRB

Contributive research in first-year composition—particularly writing-about-writing classes—may present ethical challenges involving human subjects. At the least, classes need significant instruction about guidelines for ethical research. Beyond that, teachers at some institutions will need to consider arrangements for IRB approval of undergraduate, course-based human-subjects research. If a given IRB reserves to itself oversight of individual student research projects and lacks a system for turning review over to the course instructor, large-scale undergraduate research may not be feasible. But the undergraduate research movement is giving more and more IRBs cause to create systems that do let instructors oversee their students' research rather than requiring IRB review of projects. (It helps that most writing-about-writing research is relatively low-risk.) In any event, teachers do need to consider how students' primary research is conducted safely and ethically.

Conclusion

Ultimately, we are arguing for undergraduate research as a vertical, comprehensive experience beginning in the first year. Our notion of first-year composition as a site of truly contributive undergraduate research makes such verticality feasible. What is required is a first-year composition class that seeks to instill scholarly habits of mind by encouraging students to ask and answer, via primary research, genuine questions that stem from their own experiences and their reading of published scholarship. Such a course, while unable to teach the methods and body of knowledge of all disciplines, can, by engaging students in its own scholarly field and research, teach them about the concept of methods, about the necessity of research design, and about the rewards of sharing genuine research with others—from classmates all the way to a national professional audience. Students who have completed such first-year composition courses will move on to their other classes viewing research as the norm. The burden is then on those other courses to provide further research and mentoring opportunities.

References

Augino, Lauren. 2008. Classic Is as Classic Does. *Young Scholars in Writing: Undergraduate Research in Writing and Rhetoric* 5: 123–30.

Bartholomae, David. 1985. Inventing the University. In *When a Writer Can't Write: Studies in Writer's Block and Other Composing-Process Problems*, ed. Mike Rose, 134–65. New York: Guilford Press.

Boyer Commission on Educating Undergraduates in the Research University, Shirley Strum Kenny (chair). 1998. *Reinventing Undergraduate Education: A Blueprint for America's Research Universities.* Stony Brook: State University of New York.

Downs, Douglas, Heidi Estrem, and Susan Thomas, with Ruth Johnson, Claire O'Leary, Emily Strasser, and Anita Varma. n.d. Learning with Students: Young Scholars Making Writing Visible in the Writing Classroom. In *Teaching with Student Texts*, ed. Charles Paine, Joseph Harris, and John Miles. Unpublished manuscript.

Downs, Douglas, and Elizabeth Wardle. 2007. Teaching about Writing, Righting Misconceptions: (Re)Envisioning "First-Year Composition" as "Introduction to Writing Studies." *College Composition and Communication* 58 (4): 552–84.

Fish, Stanley. 2002. Say It Ain't So. *Chronicle of Higher Education*, June 21. http://chronicle.com/article/Say-It-Aint-So/46137.

Graff, Gerald, and Andrew Hoberek. 1999. Opinion: Hiding It from the Kids (with Apologies to Simon and Garfunkel). *College English* 62 (2): 242–54.

Haas, Christina, and Linda Flower. 1988. Rhetorical Reading Strategies and the Construction of Meaning. *College Composition and Communication* 39 (2): 167–83.

Hyland, Ken. 2002. *Disciplinary Discourses: Social Interactions in Academic Writing.* Ann Arbor: University of Michigan Press.

Jackson, Erika. 2008. Past Experiences and Future Attitudes in Literacy. *Young Scholars in Writing: Undergraduate Research in Writing and Rhetoric* 5: 131–36.

Jenkins, Alan A., and Mick Healey. 2007. Critiquing Excellence: Undergraduate Research for All Students. In *International Perspectives on Teaching Excellence in Higher Education: Improving Knowledge and Practice*, ed. Alan Skelton, 117–32. London: Routledge.

Karukstis, Kerry K., and Timothy E. Elgren, eds. 2007. *Developing and Sustaining a Research-Supportive Curriculum: A Compendium of Successful Practices.* Washington, DC: Council on Undergraduate Research.

Kinkead, Joyce. 2007. How Writing Programs Support Undergraduate Research. In Karukstis and Elgren 2007, 195–208.

Kleine, Michael. 1987. What Is It We Do When We Write Articles Like This One—and How Can We Get Students to Join Us? *Writing Instructor* 6 (Spring-Summer): 151–61.

Perl, Sondra. 1979. The Composing Processes of Unskilled College Writers. *Research in the Teaching of English* 13 (4): 317–36.

Petraglia, Joseph, ed. 1995. *Reconceiving Writing, Rethinking Writing Instruction.* Mahwah, NJ: Lawrence Erlbaum.

Pleasant, Eric. 2008. Literacy Sponsors and Learning: An Ethnography of Punk Literacy in Mid-1980s Waco. *Young Scholars in Writing: Undergraduate Research in Writing and Rhetoric* 5: 137–45.

Reither, James A. 1985. Writing and Knowing: Toward Redefining the Writing Process. *College English* 47 (6): 620–28.

Rijlaarsdam, Gert. 2008. The Yummy Yummy Case: Learning to Write—Observing Readers and Writers. Presentation, Writing Research across Borders: 3rd International Santa Barbara Conference on Writing Research. Santa Barbara, CA.

Russell, David R. 1995. Activity Theory and Its Implications for Writing Instruction. In Petraglia 1995, 51–77.

—. 2002. *Writing in the Academic Disciplines: A Curricular History.* 2nd ed. Carbondale, IL: Southern Illinois University Press.

Sommers, Nancy. 1980. Revision Strategies of Student Writers and Experienced Adult Writers. *College Composition and Communication* 31 (4): 378–88.

Strasser, Emily. 2008. Writing What Matters: A Student's Struggle to Bridge the Academic/Personal Divide. *Young Scholars in Writing: Undergraduate Research in Writing and Rhetoric* 5: 146–50.

Swales, John M. 1990. *Genre Analysis: English in Academic and Research Settings.* Cambridge: Cambridge University Press.

Wardle, Elizabeth. 2007. "Understanding 'Transfer' from FYC: Preliminary Results of a Longitudinal Study." *WPA: Writing Program Administration* 31 (1/2): 65–85.

Watson, Amber. 2008. Motivation through Mentorship: Making Publishable Research Available for Novices. Paper presented at the annual meeting of the Council of Writing Program Administrators, Denver.

Wyatt, Sarah. 2005. Extending Inquiry-Based Learning to Include Original Experimentation. *Journal of General Education* 54 (2): 83–89.

DAVID GESLER'S "RESEARCH IS ELEMENTARY: HOW *BLUE'S CLUES* CAN HELP TEACH COMMUNICATION RESEARCH METHODS" (2007)

Why I included it

The article summarizes and gives examples of common characteristics of academic research processes in an accessible way. Gesler starts by defining a problem, and this problem provides the exigence for the rest of the article: He thus proceeds to offer a solution, explain it fully, and identify the benefits. This problem-solution structure is fairly typical in academic writing, so it's helpful to recognize it when you're reading, and you will likely have opportunities to use this arrangement in your own writing.

Background

As indicated in the article title, Gesler teaches communication research, and his article was first published in *Communication Teacher*. It thus makes sense that the advice is directed specifically to professors who teach communication studies, and readers of the journal would expect teaching advice. The article was published in 2007, a time when many college students would have watched the TV show *Blue's Clues* as children. *Blue's Clues* aired from 1996 to 2004 and is currently available on nickjr.com. If you aren't familiar with the format of the show, the article may be more difficult to follow.

CONNECT

As you read, consider responding to the following questions to help you process the material.

1. The text summarizes the results of a sample lesson in a table. Why might this table appeal to readers, both in terms of content (what it shows) and form (how it shows it)?

2. Gesler notes students' dislike and fear of research. Do you characterize research in such negative ways? If so, why? If not, how do you think of research? Why?

3. Do you agree that research methods can be taught by showing how a children's television show embodies each step? Why or why not?

4. Do the six characteristics of research seem common beyond communications courses? Where or when do they seem inappropriate?

5. To what degree does this article overlap with the Downs and Wardle article, whether in terms of content or in terms of organization?

Reading hints and vocabulary

As you read, notice the way Gesler identifies a problem, previews the solution he will offer, presents and explains how his solution works, and then describes benefits of this solution. Gesler's table is also worth looking at closely.

Gesler assumes that his audience will be familiar with the "six characteristics of research," but you may not be, so I provide a brief explanation here so you'll feel more prepared.

1. *Research starts with questions.* Research is motivated by inquiry, questions that we don't yet know the answers to, or questions we *may* know the answers to, but we need to test our hypotheses.
2. *Research is systematic.* A carefully crafted plan is followed, step-by-step, with clear connections between the questions guiding the research and the research methods.
3. *Research is replicable.* Others could perform the same research by following the same step-by-step methods.
4. *Research is self-critical.* Careful judgments are used when interpreting data and limitations or when complexities are recognized.
5. *Research is cumulative.* Over time, more is known as current research builds upon past research.
6. *Research is cyclical.* As questions are answered, new questions arise.

Gesler, David. "Research Is Elementary: How *Blue's Clues* Can Help Teach Communication Research Methods." *Communication Teacher*, vol. 21, no. 4, 2007, pp. 118–22.

BLUE'S CLUES IS a children's preschool TV show, which targets the 2–5-year-old age group and can be found on Nick Jr. (a 5-hour block on the Nickelodeon channel catering to preschoolers every weekday morning, available on basic cable), and Noggin (a commercial-free educational channel dedicated to preschoolers 12 hours a day, 7 days a week, currently available on digital cable and satellite), as well as on VHS and DVD. Each episode invites viewers to help "Joe" (or "Steve" in earlier episodes) figure out what Blue (Joe/Steve's puppy) wants to do that day. Blue leaves the viewers clues to what she wants to do in the form of paw prints (the paw print indicates that whatever the paw print was found on is a clue). Once a paw print is found, "Joe" will write the clue in his "handy-dandy" notebook. Once three of *Blue's Clues* are found, Joe retreats to his "thinking chair" to review the three clues and to guess what Blue is telling him she wants to do for that day.

Rodrick and Dickmeyer (2002) point out, "There are many students who need to be 'sold' on research, and a teacher who can engage students, while alleviating their fears and resistance, will be more successful in helping students find value in the class" (p. 43). Using the preschool show "*Blue's Clues*" to illustrate and exemplify the characteristics of research not only helps students to view the research process visually, but also helps to ease students' fears and anxiety about taking the research methods class. The thought is if "*Blue's Clues*," a children's "preschool" show, is an example of research, then they should not only be able to understand research, but also be able to have a little fun and reduce their collective "research methods anxiety." *Blue's Clues* shows students that the research process should not be viewed as "threatening," but rather should be viewed as "fun, creative, and within their capabilities of doing."

Activity

Before showing your chosen episode to the class, it is a good idea to preview the episode and take notes indicating examples for each characteristic from the show. Previewing the show before using it in class also ensures that the episode will be a good illustrator of the characteristics of research. With the exception of a few hour-long specials, each episode follows the same basic format, and should be able to be used for this activity.

This activity depends upon the students' initial familiarity with the characteristics of research (see Table 1); therefore, review the six characteristics of research before showing *Blue's Clues*. The six characteristics of research are: research starts with questions, research is systematic, research is replicable, research is self-critical, research is cumulative, and research is cyclical (Frey, Botan, & Kreps, 2000). Once the characteristics of research have been talked about and explained, and once you are satisfied that the students know the material, tell the students to make six columns on a sheet of paper (it helps if they turn their papers to "landscape" orientation), labeling each column one of the characteristics of research. As the students watch the episode of *Blue's Clues*, they should identify and record at least two examples of each research characteristic in their respective columns. A *Blue's Clues* episode runs about 22 minutes, so there should be ample time to watch the program and follow it with an in-depth discussion.

TABLE 1 Using *Blue's Clues* to Illustrate Characteristics of Research

Characteristic	Examples from *Blue's Clues* Episode 30: What Does Blue Want to Do with Her Picture?
Research is based upon asking questions: Research starts with a person's desire to find an answer to a question posed. At the heart of all research are questions and answers.	▪ This episode is based upon the question, "What does Blue want to do with her picture?"
Research is a systematic process: Research is planned, orderly, and proceeds in a careful, step-by-step process.	▪ Each clue is written in the "handy-dandy" notebook. ▪ After all three clues are found, Steve goes to his "thinking chair" to answer the question. ▪ Song at the beginning of the show explains the systematic process of playing *Blue's Clues*.
Research is potentially replicable: Research should be able to be reproduced by others, stemming from the systematic, step-by-step process.	▪ Each clue is written in the "handy-dandy" notebook. ▪ Spatula and Bowl rearranging recipe cards to make banana bread.
Research is reflexive and self-critical: The research process is examined and flaws or threats to validity are reported.	▪ Steve reviews the three clues with the viewers and then Steve asks the viewers if they think his answer is correct. Steve also asks Blue if his answer is correct. ▪ Felt Friend "feels funny" in his clothes. Steve helps him to review his process of putting on his clothes, and corrects the process.
Research is cumulative and self-correcting: Research allows for the accumulation of information which creates a shared history.	▪ Steve helps Spatula and Bowl rearrange a muffin recipe to bake muffins, based upon Steve's past knowledge of baking. ▪ Steve has viewers help Felt Friend put his clothes on correctly by asking, "which goes on first, socks or shoes?" based upon the viewer's previous knowledge.
Research is cyclical: Research ends up back where it started. New questions emerge based upon answers to previous questions.	▪ Steve asks Blue who she wants to send her picture to after affirming that she wants to send her picture to someone. ▪ Another episode comes on the next day with a new question about what Blue wants to do.

Note. Definitions of the characteristics are adapted from Frey, Botan, and Kreps (2000).

CHAPTER FOUR: WHAT DO EFFECTIVE RESEARCHERS DO?

Debrief

Discussion of the episode should start after *Blue's Clues* is over and students have had a chance to finish writing down their observed examples of the characteristics of research. Asking a few general questions about the show and the research process helps students see an overall connection of these two topics. Some general questions to consider are (the first two questions could be used to set up the program, before watching as well):

1. Explain your idea of the research process prior to taking this course.
2. Is/can research be fun, creative, logical, and all about discovering new things?
3. Are you more relaxed about learning the research process?
4. Had you seen the characteristics of research in everyday life before watching *Blue's Clues*?
5. Was *Blue's Clues* an effective illustration of the research process?
6. Were some research characteristics illustrated in *Blue's Clues* better than others? Which ones? Why?
7. Is the research process really this simplistic? Is there more to it? Why or why not?

Once these general questions have been addressed, students should define each characteristic of research and offer their examples of each as seen in *Blue's Clues*. Discussion should focus on if these examples are good illustrators of each characteristic, and also for the poor examples, how they could be made better.

Appraisal

The *Blue's Clues* activity has been a successful addition to the communication research class. However, there are some limitations in using this activity. This activity requires a fair amount of preparation time. The instructor must record or find an episode to use, preview the episode to ensure it will be a strong illustrator of the six characteristics of research, and lastly write down examples of each characteristic. Also, the instructor will need to devote a full class period to this activity to not only show the episode but also create the desired learning and understanding.

Despite these limitations, the *Blue's Clues* activity has many strong points. First, this activity shows students that social science research is non-threatening and is really about play, discovery, creative thinking, being logical, and being methodical in finding answers to questions. This seems to put students at ease

FOCUS ON WRITING: WHAT COLLEGE STUDENTS WANT TO KNOW

with learning about research, reduces their anxiety, and often puts their negative preconceived notions about research to rest. This activity shows students that research inherently is non-threatening, and that the perceived "threat" of the research class being hard, difficult, and unbearable is unfounded. As one particular student in the past has said after engaging in the *Blue's Clues* activity, "Wow, I was scared about this [research methods] class, but after watching *Blue's Clues*, I think I can do this!" Second, *Blue's Clues* is a good illustrator (albeit a simplistic one) of the six characteristics of research. The activity forces the students to go beyond typical rote learning and apply their learning to a seemingly incongruous situation. The use of a children's show to illustrate the research process is something students do not think about or understand at the beginning of the activity. Students' thoughts tend to center around "research is complex," "research is difficult," and "research is not fun or creative," compared to views of *Blue's Clues* which students tend to see as "simplistic," "fun," and "creative." Matching these two very different entities with one another gives the activity power, and makes the learning stronger. One cynical student remarked after the activity, "I really didn't see how a kid's show was going to teach me about academic research, but it did." Through this process, students' understanding deepens and because of the nature of the show, the students tend not to forget the lesson (students from many semesters past still come up to me and ask me if I am still teaching with *Blue's Clues*). Third, students realize that the research process consists of more than statistics and mathematics. Although statistics can be a part of the research process, they do not define the research process, again, as evidenced by *Blue's Clues*.

References

Denham, B. (1997). "Teaching research methods to undergraduates." *Journalism and Mass Communication Educator*, 51, 54–62.

Frey, L.R., Botan, C.H., & Kreps, G.L. (2000). *Investigating communication: An introduction to research methods* (2nd ed.). Boston: Allyn & Bacon.

Rodrick, R., & Dickmeyer, L. (2002). "Providing undergraduate research opportunities for communication students: A curricular approach." *Communication Education*, 51(1), 40–50.

RECOMMENDED ONLINE SOURCES

For direct links to these sources, please visit <sites.broadviewpress.com/focusonwriting>.

1. To consider the ethics and processes of primary research in a friendly form: Driscoll, Dana Lynn. "Introduction to Primary Research: Observations, Surveys, and Interviews." *Writing Spaces: Readings on Writing, Vol. 2.* Parlor P, 2011, <http:// writingspaces.org/sites/default/files/driscoll--introduction-to-primary-research.pdf>.

2. For an accessible and practical explanation of secondary research: Haller, Cynthia R. "Walk, Talk, Cook, Eat: A Guide to Using Sources." *Writing Spaces: Readings on Writing, Vol. 2.* Parlor P, 2011, <http://writingspaces.org/sites/default/files/haller- -walk-talk-cook-eat.pdf>.

3. To think about research and writing as conversational in terms of honest student experiences: O'Rourke, Sean Patrick, Stephen Howard, and Andrianna Lee Lawrence. "*Respondeo etsi Mutabor*: The Comment and Response Assignment, Young Scholars, and the Promise of Liberal Education." *Young Scholars in Writing: Undergraduate Research in Writing and Rhetoric* 10 (2012), <https://arc.lib.montana. edu/ojs/index.php/Young-Scholars-In-Writing/article/view/192/129>.

4. For a student perspective on reading academic journals intended for professors rather than students: Wojciechowski, Kylie. "Eavesdropping on the Conversation: Situating an Undergraduate's Role within the Scope of Academic Journals." *Grassroots Writing Research Journal*, vol. 5, no. 1, 2014, pp. 67–77, <http://isuwriting.com/ wp-content/uploads/2015/03/Eavesdropping-on-the-Conversation.pdf>.

5. To hear a teacher reflect on the difficulties of teaching students to navigate library databases in a brief accessible article written for other teachers: Fister, Barbara. "Burke's Parlor Tricks: Introducing Research as Conversation." *Inside Higher Ed*, 11 Nov. 2011, <https://www.insidehighered.com/blogs/library-babel-fish/ burkes-parlor-tricks-introducing-research-conversation>.

6. For an array of resources based on research of students' use and citation of sources: Jamieson, Sandra, Rebecca Moore Howard, and Tricia Serviss. *The Citation Project: Preventing Plagiarism, Teaching Writing*, <http://citationproject.net>.

7. For case studies of how internet searches are used for academic projects in a creative online publication: Purdy, James P., and Joyce R. Walker. "Digital Breadcrumbs:

Case Studies of Online Research." *Kairos*, vol. 11, no. 2, spring 2007, <http://kairos.technorhetoric.net/11.2/topoi/purdy-walker/index.htm>.

8. To view information from a plenary talk on how people are using libraries, books, and online research: Zickhur, Kathryn. "Reading, Writing, and Research in the Digital Age." *Pew Research Center*, 4 Nov. 2013, <http://www.pewinternet.org/2013/11/04/reading-writing-and-research-in-the-digital-age/>.

Joining the Conversation

The following formal writing prompts are ways of helping you think through the ideas you've been reading about by *using* the ideas in some way to help you create a text of your own.

DISCIPLINARY INVESTIGATION

Choose an academic discipline and identify the kinds of secondary and primary research practices commonly used. You might examine syllabi, paper assignments, academic journal articles, or conference presentations. You might also interview a faculty person or student immersed in the discipline. If several students (or a whole class) work on such a project, the results could cover multiple disciplines and could be shared on a collaborative blog or website as a guide for both students and teachers.

CREATIVE / ANALYTIC PROJECT

Compare perfunctory or unmotivated approaches to research with approaches motivated by genuine inquiry and a desire for answers. What would the steps look like if broken down into parts? Consider using side-by-side videos, a split video screen, or another visual way of contrasting the two approaches.

GENRE ANALYSIS

Analyze a genre associated with research. You might focus on popular culture and informal research via Yelp, Amazon reviews, movie reviews, how-to videos, instructional websites, and so forth. You might consider explanations of research processes many fiction writers include at the end of their books. You might consider notes, marginalia, and other ephemera—the writing that is generated during the research process. Whatever your focus, look for patterns of significance and focus on what is surprising, complicated, or nuanced when trying to understand the genre.

ANALOGY

Often researchers are compared to detectives. What other extended metaphor can you develop for your activity as you conduct research you care about? Another way to develop an analogy would be to compare your past views of research with your developing sense of yourself as a researcher who can investigate meaningful questions.

DIGITAL ARCHIVE

Create a website to collect "sites of research." These may take the form of photos of places where secondary research work is being done, links or screenshots to online resources for secondary research, and photos of places associated with primary research—campus labs, archaeological digs, digital sites, library archives, and so forth. Organizing material using tags and categories can show multiple patterns and relationships across a wide array of research sites.

5 HOW DO I TRANSLATE MY ACADEMIC WRITING INTO PUBLIC GENRES?

Exploring the Question

In part of Chapter One, I discussed connections between everyday writing—specifically social media writing—and formal academic writing. This chapter brings us full circle as we consider how we can take what we have learned through academic writing and research that we can bring back into wider public realms.

Online writing certainly makes it easier to share learning with public audiences rather than communicating only with a professor or a class. We will also discuss other non-digital ways of engaging public audiences, including oral presentations.

Before proceeding, I want to point out that I tend to rely on a false divide between "digital" and "non-digital." All the writing in this textbook has been digital in one way or another. I used a Mac, wrote and edited using Microsoft Word, researched using online tools and library databases and physical copies of books and journals that were typeset and manufactured; I printed out pages, used a variety of pens to annotate and edit, visited coffee shops using my Waze app to find the easiest routes ... The list could go on. A variety of digital technologies mediates my everyday activities directly and indirectly, and these digital technologies allowed me to write this text.

Digital technologies contribute to the process of writing for all of us. They also contribute to the product. As attention is given to the increasing presence of image-, audio-, and video-based writing in online spaces (Manjoo), it is easy to forget that even traditional alphabetic forms rely on visual and aural elements. Font choices, headings, paragraph indentations, and lists all provide visual cues to facilitate communication between writers and readers. Letters and words themselves are a complex system of signs, small pictures that are imbued with meaning depending on how they are arranged. I read my writing aloud when editing because even written text ought to sound right in the mind's ear.

Thus, although it seems like I'm separating out "public" and "digital" writing as confined to this chapter and thus absent from the rest of the text, my view is the opposite. You might remember I made the same point about "research" in Chapter Four and suggested that research is ubiquitous, implicitly informing writing even when we are not invoking formal research processes. Similarly, the writing I have shared throughout this textbook exists across a continuum with "traditional academic prose" on one end and "popular multimedia text" on the other, with the latter characterized as *more* public and *more* digital than the former.

Awareness of false divisions is helpful when remembering that technologies are not good or evil but rather grant us certain affordances and certain constraints. We can be mindful about the technologies that mediate our everyday lives so we can exert agency and make choices rather than mindlessly embrace or reject new forms of communication and digital tools.

While I have no patience for demonizing digital technologies, I try to recognize complexities as I move between various sites of writing. I am finding that time away from screens is important for my own physical, emotional, and mental health, and I appreciate the way **maker spaces**—campus centers designed to stimulate multimodal composing processes and experimentation with a variety of tools—can serve not only digital composing but also manipulation of materials and creative work that happens with minimal (or no) screen time. In short, I strive to make time for various modes of writing, and I hope you are able to experiment with a variety of forms as well.

In this time of rapid technological change, the ability to adapt and transform our writing so that it can speak in a variety of places to a variety of audiences seems more important than ever. Taking time in this chapter to focus specifically

CONNECT

1. Have you shared writing you have done for school assignments with a public audience in the past? If yes, describe the assignment and why your writing appealed to a non-academic audience. If not, describe an assignment you completed that may have been interesting to a non-academic audience.

2. I mentioned a number of connections between texts considered "digital" and "non-digital." What other connections can you think of?

FOCUS ON WRITING: WHAT COLLEGE STUDENTS WANT TO KNOW

on some common forms of public communication is a way of acknowledging the challenges of moving from academic writing to other genres.

COLLEGE WRITING AND "THE REAL WORLD"

Often people talk about "the real world" as a place that is completely distinct from academic classrooms or college campuses. As a person who spends a lot of time on college campuses, I take issue with such a distinction. As far as I can tell, I'm not living in a dream state or a fantasy land every time I'm at work. Even though I try to make the classroom an engaging place, I don't think it fits into any kind of fantasy ideal for my students, either.

However, I understand the distinction people are trying to convey. Classrooms seem like places where students complete assignments and write for teachers in order to prove they have learned some things. The students get their diplomas to show they have passed the tests and are now ready for "the real world."

This narrative suggests that the work done in schools is different from work done in other places. In schools, it is for show or for practice, but in "the real world" work is the means to accomplishing something. In this scenario, we meet requirements as a necessary step before getting hired or engaging fully as citizens, not because the requirements are themselves worthwhile.

Let's change that narrative.

We can characterize much of the work done in classrooms in four ways. Some of the work is busy work, without rhyme or reason. This kind of work has no place on college campuses.

The second category is work that is distinctly different from work done in professional or civic settings. This work is meaningful, as it allows room for growth, aesthetic appreciation, thinking about big questions of existence and meaning, developing empathy. This kind of work allows college to be more than preparation for what is next.

The third category is work done in classrooms that can be viewed as practice, as exercise, as training—as the kind of work that people who play sports or who play an instrument do in order to hone their skills. It might be practice with communication, or with thinking through ideas, or with considering the ethics and implications of a decision. If this kind of practice is believed to be irrelevant to "the real world," we are all in trouble.

The final category is classroom work that is akin to work in professional or civic settings. University campuses are the sites of research that is immediately applicable

299

CHAPTER FIVE: HOW DO I TRANSLATE MY ACADEMIC WRITING INTO PUBLIC GENRES?

CONNECT

How would you categorize the kinds of work and learning you do as a college student? Are there important categories I have missed?

to the rest of the real world. Sometimes this happens in classes, especially upper-level classes in your major, when you investigate a question and provide an answer through a well-designed study. Even in first-year courses, student research in the classroom can be helpful to people outside of that classroom.

Here are a few of the topics my students have written about over the last several years that can have immediate relevance beyond the classroom:

- Does texting negatively affect student writing?
- How is reading used to help people with severe intellectual disabilities?
- How are family bonds reinforced through tattoos?
- Does graffiti have a positive effect on community activism?
- What does the trend of promposals suggest about the priorities of current high school students?
- How does a Facebook group support the siblings of opioid addicts?

Although university research is indeed part of "the real world," it is often treated as distant, removed, and irrelevant.

Why is there an academic/public divide?

To address this question, I am going to review what you probably already know about academic discourse communities.

Within academic disciplines, research tends to appear in somewhat standardized forms. If you look at three articles in an academic science journal, three articles in a psychology journal, and three articles in a history journal (or another discipline that interests you), you will likely see commonalities within each discipline but differences from one subject area to the next. Each discipline values slightly different forms of research, so the expectations for articles vary to fit those values.

Even with the differences between disciplines, academic research tends to a) respond to prior research, b) identify the methods used to draw conclusions, c) share what was found, and d) interpret what was found. The research is judged by other academics in the field, and only research that meets the standards of the field is published in a peer-reviewed journal.

Because academic researchers are writing to an audience of other academic researchers in genres that highlight the criteria for appropriate research, such writing can seem like it's not part of "the real world." Often, students are asked to mimic such styles of writing during coursework to learn the values and priorities of a discipline. Because students may not be likely to use these academic styles in other places, the assignments may seem useless. However, doing serious disciplinary research and communicating in an academic style requires writers to think through each step and decision.

The process of contributing to a disciplinary conversation thus seems worthwhile to faculty like me, both because we see such research as valuable and relevant and because we regularly see students become more thoughtful communicators as they engage in academic writing. People who are not regularly engaged in disciplinary conversations, on the other hand, may assume that material aimed at a narrow audience is frivolous.

Mending the divide

Even though I believe academic research has value in and of itself, such work does not have to stop with the academic research paper. We can share with the larger public, especially with any audiences who might be especially interested in our findings.

Such sharing is done regularly by journalists, often by those covering specialty areas such as science, law, or education. Typically, journalistic articles give minimal attention to literature reviews and methods and tend to focus on findings. Such reporting is a mixed blessing. On the one hand, academic research is communicated to a wider audience. On the other hand, such reporting may be skewed, as it provides a less nuanced picture than the original research paper or, in some cases, misleads the public by relying on a single article rather than accounting for inconsistent findings over a series of studies (Dumas-Mallet et al.).

Academics also sometimes share their work in public forums. I have a friend who teaches psychology and who has a parenting advice blog. His professional work and his public writing overlap. Teachers often take research findings and translate those findings for students, whether using a lecture with PowerPoint slides, a TED talk video, or a hands-on demonstration. *Public intellectuals*—academics who share their expertise in a variety of public forums (Looser)—provide benefits as scholarship is disseminated and as university classroom work becomes viewed as part of—rather than separate from—"the real world."

Rather than view a traditional research article and public genres of writing as being in competition with one another, it helps to understand the value of each and the complementary roles they can fill.

301

CHAPTER FIVE: HOW DO I TRANSLATE MY ACADEMIC WRITING INTO PUBLIC GENRES?

DIGITAL POSSIBILITIES

Digital tools are increasingly accessible and are so often integrated into both academic and professional expectations that it is smart to experiment and play to see what kinds of tools are suited for a particular purpose. Depending on the research you want to share and the audience you hope to reach, some digital tools will be more helpful than others.

Before thinking more about the rhetorical situation and processes of developing and sharing digital content, I want to say a word about anxiety. Even though sophisticated visual, audio, and video production is easier and more widely accessible than ever before, students regularly experience the same anxieties about learning new technologies that older adults face. If this is true of you, I have some pointers.

1. Remind yourself that learning takes time. It is okay to sometimes feel lost or flustered.
2. Use Google or another search engine to find advice. A lot of helpful folks have answered questions and made videos to guide learners and troubleshoot unusual problems.
3. If your stress level is high, consider walking away from the digital tool you're learning. Work on another part of the project and try the digital tool again when you are better able to cope.

I regularly put myself in situations that require learning outside my areas of expertise to help me remember how difficult learning can be. Struggling and failing is embarrassing, but it is much better than not learning and growing at all, so give yourself credit when challenging yourself.

In many ways, writing as a public intellectual in a digital space is similar to the academic writing that was the focus of much of this textbook; attention to the rhetorical situation is key, as is a process that includes collaboration and revision. Still, it's worth noting some prominent differences when adjusting for an online platform. Often college students are labeled "digital natives" with the assumption that you know everything about technology, but many students have used online spaces primarily to socialize and access entertainment (Hargittai 108). Crafting an academic, professional, or otherwise public identity may be something new to many of you.

Think about the persona you share with your closest friends, the persona you present to a wider circle of acquaintances, and the persona you'd like to develop to have people listen to and respect your ideas. Chances are these ***personas***—a term for performed identities or roles—will have some common elements that reflect your personality and interests, but they can also be somewhat different in terms of what you share (the content), where you share (the platform), and how you share (the style).

In addition to considering the persona you want to develop as you share your academic work in online spaces, you can answer other questions to clarify and shape the rhetorical situation.

CONNECT

1. What elements from the online identity you share with close friends might also characterize your "public intellectual" persona?

2. How will your public intellectual persona be different from the online identity you share with close friends in terms of content, platform, style, or other elements?

3. To what degree do you consider yourself a "digital native" who easily adapts to new digital tools?

1. The message: What elements of my work are likely to interest others?
2. The primary audience: Who, exactly, would be most likely to appreciate these ideas or findings?
3. The purpose: How might the ideas or findings I'm going to share change the attitudes, behavior, or actions of the primary audience identified in Question 2?
4. The immediate context: Is there a particular platform (such as a social media site), a particular medium (such as text, image, audio, or video), or a particular genre that is well-suited to the message, audience, purpose, and writer?
5. How can I best use the platform, medium, or genre to reach my audience and meet my purpose?

Often you may think through all of these questions at once rather than one at a time, and you might not even realize how necessary such thinking is until you try to compose without a clear purpose and a sense of your primary audience.

For example, one of my students, Caroline Migliaro, recently decided to translate her literacy narrative to a Storify platform where she could easily bring text, image, and video onto a single page. Initially, she put her entire narrative onto the page and began to add images. She suddenly stopped and said to me, "I don't know what to do next."

At that point, we reviewed her literacy narrative and talked about who else might appreciate hearing her story and why. Caroline developed a short list of potential audiences: children who were struggling to read and write the way she had, parents who might be stressed about their children's struggles, or teachers who might be able to support struggling students. Depending on the audience, the narrative

303

CHAPTER FIVE: HOW DO I TRANSLATE MY ACADEMIC WRITING INTO PUBLIC GENRES?

would shift in terms of what was included and how it was presented. Caroline eventually decided to aim her narrative toward teachers—specifically middle school and high school teachers with the opportunity of helping students enjoy reading and writing despite past difficulties.

Caroline and I then talked about the *affordances* of the Storify platform—that is, the rhetorical moves and possible ways of communicating that are enabled or even encouraged by the format of the site. The title, subtitle, and image heading together had the power to invite readers to scroll down the page, so Caroline edited to make sure her purpose was clear and the color combination made the text easy to read. Storify allows for different-sized fonts, so Caroline made her narrative smaller and the important pieces of advice for teachers more prominent. She organized the narrative into three chronological sections that presented a problem and followed with solutions. She used images to create visual interest, and she provided links to pages with more information for teachers to draw upon. At the end of the semester, Caroline presented her Storify page to the class and explained exactly why she made each decision.

You may not be working with a Storify project, but as you think through digital communication, you might find that your first instinct is to dive in and do the project rather than slow down and plan. After all, much of the writing done in online spaces requires little or no drafting process. However, if you find you have no rationale for decisions, I recommend explicitly defining the audience, purpose, and platform or genre possibilities to guide your decisions.

Blogging and more

In 2010, I was at a conference and heard Jennifer Whetham speak about using digital tools to motivate students and encourage attention to the power of their words. In the same session, Bump Halbritter told the professors in the room that if we want our students to write using new media, we need to do so ourselves. Soon after, I began vlogging recreationally to gain experience in basic video production and blogging, and I have continued to produce videos and write blog posts ever since, though I do so sporadically now.

At about the same time and in the years since, students and alumni have shared the importance of professional social media skills in their internships and career fields. I thus try to integrate blogs into much of my teaching, hoping students gain experiences that make our classroom work meaningful while also setting them up for future success.

As Jennifer Whetham pointed out during her talk all those years ago, blogging is (or can be) a public form of journaling. It allows us to think on the page (or the screen) while sharing the journey with others. A blog can be a place to respond to readings, collect research, and ponder ideas. This kind of blogging may help you engage with reading and writing assignments over the course of a semester.

Other blog posts are finished products, presenting an argument, a profile, or reflection that has been drafted, revised, and polished for public consumption. I tend to assign this kind of post for the departmental blog or a shared class website. The latter is similar to a blog except it is static rather than being updated regularly, and the organization of a website tends to be spatial, with a homepage that allows access to pages and subpages. Typical blogs, on the other hand, are organized in reverse chronology, with most recent posts first.

If you are ready to start blogging in a style of public journaling, here are some tips to keep in mind:

- Look at other blogs, similar to what you are aiming for, to figure out what works and what doesn't.
- Use free online blog servers and choose a color scheme that is easy to read and is visually appealing.
- Think about the URL, title, and your persona carefully.
- Complete "about this site" or "about me" information in ways that will help readers understand your purpose, take you seriously, and also get to know your personality.
- Proofread and edit at least a little bit so readers can follow you more easily.
- Use short paragraphs, headings and subheadings, bulleted lists, and so forth. They make online reading easier.
- Open each post with some sense of exigence: What has led you to write about this topic at this moment?
- Invite readers to comment at the end. What kinds of thoughts or experiences do you hope readers might share with you?
- Use images to engage readers; be sure to credit the work of others; use public domain images to avoid copyright infringement.
- Use videos with closed captioning to engage readers and make your site more welcoming for those with hearing impairment.
- Describe images and videos with ALT tags to make your site more welcoming for those with visual disabilities.
- Use hyperlinks to connect your writing to other relevant texts, especially if you are directly responding to a text or using information that you found online.

- Use blog post titles, tags, categories, and so forth to indicate topics and sub-topics; such information will attract readers to your post by helping it appear in searches, and blog visitors will have an easier time finding more of your writing on a topic of interest.
- Share your blog on social media.
- If you really enjoy blogging, interact with other bloggers who address similar topics, liking and commenting on their posts. They may return the favor and create a more interactive site for you to enjoy.

Blogs are well suited to ongoing engagement with a variety of topics, but they may be less collaborative than other social media platforms. Using a hashtag for the class can allow all students as well as the professor to post on Twitter, Instagram, and other sites in ways that increase interaction. Other process-based work may focus on collecting and archiving material for course projects, either individually or collaboratively. A blog can be used in this way, or sites such as Pinterest, Tumblr, or Zotero offer formats suited for collections of images, online material, and links.

Video can be used to chronicle a research process or share a finished product, with the latter use more common. A video essay might feature a *talking head* (a commentator) and include images, clips, and text to illustrate and develop a point. Video may also be used to tell a story, educate viewers, or present an argument. So many options and approaches are available that it is especially important to spend time planning, thinking through all the visual and aural elements, making a storyboard, and gathering the material needed.

These examples are ways of helping you think about **purpose** as you make choices. As public intellectuals, we can choose to share our thinking processes and our research materials; we may also decide our research findings or writing reflections ought to be shared with particular audiences as polished projects. We may be working individually, or we may be developing a class project. These contextual factors will strongly shape the platforms we use and how we use them.

POSSIBILITIES BEYOND THE SCREEN

Don't underestimate the value of old-fashioned paper and print for disseminating information to a wider public. Newspapers accept letters to the editor on current issues, and you may have opportunities to write other material for campus publications.

Most campuses also have educational information or event marketing displayed via bulletin boards, table tents in the cafeteria, and flyers on the back doors of bathroom stalls. These genres are similar to campus news publications in terms of audience, but journalism tends to be text-based while these latter forms of writing often make greater use of graphic design and visual elements to communicate with campus audiences.

The arts may also be a way to educate or persuade people. Music, painting, storytelling, comic strips, and fashion are examples of art forms that can be used to share ideas, information, or belief systems. If you have training in graphic design, music, the visual arts, marketing, or a similar field, you may find it satisfying to use such media to create a public argument or informational text.

If creative work is new to you, it's smart to start with a model text and use it as a template. You can mimic some design elements while making adjustments so it works with your content. If you take this direction, find a way to give credit to the model text, and make sure you rely on your own writing, visuals, and aural elements.

Some professors ask students to engage course content in ways that are even further outside the realm of typical academic projects. Food, sculptures, skits, playlists, collage, games, flower arrangements, jewelry, and other items can be ways of sharing information or offering a persuasive argument. My colleagues Erin Sadlack and Helen Bittel regularly include such creative assignments in their classrooms, and one of the online sources shared below showcases projects from Jody Shipka's students.

CONNECT

Look around your campus.

1. Where do you see information publicly shared?

2. What methods seem to be most effective at reaching the intended audiences? What is it about these methods that makes them effective?

3. What music or other creative works are you familiar with that aim to educate, inform, or persuade?

Oral presentations

Another common way to share research beyond alphabetic text is through an oral presentation. Many of us feel nervous about oral presentations, so each semester I ask students what our anxiety stems from and we talk about how to present effectively despite these anxieties.

Typically, fears drive anxieties. Many of us worry that we will forget what we want to say, stumble over our words, look ridiculous, and otherwise embarrass ourselves. One of the ways I personally have dealt with such fears is by challenging myself to stop thinking so much about how I feel and instead focus on how I want my audience to feel.

I also tend to be more effective when I see myself playing a role. I can act like an effective presenter even when I don't feel like an effective presenter. This strategy is commonly called "Fake it 'til you make it," and it works wonders.

Others recommend using power poses (Cuddy) to boost confidence, and any practice you have with yoga, meditation, and breathing exercises can help with managing stress.

Once a student told me that if you feel anxious when standing to present, curl your toes tightly because all your anxiety will gather in your toes and won't be visible through shaking hands or restless movements. Every time I tell a class about that advice, I ask who else in the room is curling their toes as I'm talking about it, and it turns out most of us curl our toes as soon as I suggest the strategy. Even me! I'm not curling my toes as I write this, however, so I don't know if the effect is different in writing than when shared aloud with a group. Anyhow, it always cracks me up to think of a whole bunch of us curling our toes in the middle of class.

I hope right now you're thinking that my advice is odd because I have not said the most obvious way to give an effective presentation. I'll stop playing games now and say it, even though it is obvious.

Prepare.

That means reviewing the assignment and knowing how long the presentation should be, how you should focus your remarks, and whether you should use visuals. I recommend writing your remarks fully or creating extensive notes. Then, practice, practice, practice. I usually practice in front of a mirror, and I revise and edit my original plan during the first few rounds of practicing. That means you also need to give yourself plenty of time so that revision is possible.

When possible and appropriate, involve the audience in your presentation. Be aware of diverse abilities, so if you use a video, you should show a captioned version, and if you have handouts, you should have larger text for anyone who might be visually impaired. These kinds of inclusive gestures can make a big difference to your audience members, and they show that you are invested in your listeners.

Most of the time, presentations are more effective if you speak rather than read. In some situations, however, reading is more appropriate, so this is a guideline rather than a rule.

Make eye contact with your audience. Allow yourself to pause on occasion. Use the pace,

CONNECT

1. Do you have any worries about presenting orally? Why or why not?

2. When you enjoy a professional presentation, what qualities make it work effectively? Are these qualities that can be achieved by students?

3. What advice about oral presentations have I missed?

FOCUS ON WRITING: WHAT COLLEGE STUDENTS WANT TO KNOW

volume, and pitch of your voice to emphasize key points and keep the audience engaged.

When discussing presentations, I believe it's also important to consider how to behave like a good audience member. I ask students to visibly show me that they are interested in what I'm saying while I say the most boring thing in the world, like, "On Monday, I watched the grass grow. On Tuesday, I continued to watch the grass grow. On Wednesday, I watched the grass grow...."

No matter how boring I am, students are able to appear interested. Many lean forward, some tilt their heads a bit, some nod as I speak, a few seem to jot down notes, some look down as if they are thinking and then look up to hear the next thing I say. Cell phones and laptops are away.

One of the skills I've developed is being a good listener when people are presenting. At a few academic conferences I've attended, I have had speakers introduce themselves to me at some point during the conference when I have run into them. They have told me that I was "their person." While they were speaking, they could look at me and feel like I was with them, listening and learning. (Sidenote: One of these presenters was Jennifer Whetham; I mentioned her earlier because she spoke about having students blog instead of journaling.) I tend to take notes while I listen to speakers because it helps me pay attention, but I also look up regularly and nod as I listen. Sometimes my body language of engaged listening helps me actually listen better. And I know from being a teacher that any kind of engaged reception from students helps me be a better teacher.

CONNECT

1. How is the relationship between presenter and audience similar to the relationship between writer and reader? How are these kinds of relationships different?

2. Have you been in a situation in which having someone be "that person" who is fully supportive has made a positive difference to what you could accomplish? Explain.

What I'm saying to you is: Help other presenters succeed by being "that person" for them—the person who is on their side, listening and learning. And when you are presenting, if you can see "that person" listening to you, believe that you are having a positive effect, and keep up the good work.

309

CHAPTER FIVE: HOW DO I TRANSLATE MY ACADEMIC WRITING INTO PUBLIC GENRES?

WORKS CITED

Cuddy, Amy. "Your Body Language May Shape Who You Are." *TED: Ideas Worth Spreading*, June 2012, <https://www.ted.com/talks/amy_cuddy_your_body_language_shapes_who_you_are>.

Dumas-Mallet, Estelle, Andy Smith, Thomas Boraud, and Francois Gonon. "Poor Replication Validity of Biomedical Association Studies Reported by Newspapers." *PLoS ONE*, vol. 12, no. 2, 21 Feb. 2017, <https://doi.org/10.1371/journal.pone.0176250>.

Hargittai, Eszter. (2010). "Digital Na(t)ives? Variation in Internet Skills and Uses among Members of the 'Net Generation.'" *Sociological Inquiry*, vol. 80, no. 1, 2010, pp. 92–113, doi: 10.1111/j.1475-682X.2009.00317.x.

Looser, Devoney. "The Making of a Public Intellectual." *The Chronicle of Higher Education*, 1 Oct. 2017, <https://www.chronicle.com/article/The-Making-of-a-Public/241332>.

Manjoo, Farhad. "State of the Internet." *New York Times*, 14 Feb. 2018, <https://www.nytimes.com/interactive/2018/02/09/technology/the-rise-of-a-visual-internet.html>.

Migliaro, Caroline. "The Impact an Exceptional Teacher Can Have on Their Students." *Storify*, Dec. 2017, <https://storify.com/carolinemig/literacy-narrative#publicize>.

Shipka, Jody. *Toward a Composition Made Whole*. U of Pittsburgh P, 2011.

Extending the Conversation

To think more about the question, "How do I translate an academic argument into a public argument," I have gathered together three selections reprinted here and seven readings or videos you can find online. Each piece overlaps with my initial approach to the question in some way, but each piece also extends the chapter question with a particular focus. As we answer questions that may seem simple at first, complexities and nuances develop that call for more exploration.

For each text reprinted here, I tell you why I included it, provide some background about its initial publication, and offer hints that may guide your reading, including vocabulary terms when relevant. I also provide "connect" questions to help you engage and respond as you read.

For each online source I recommend, I offer a brief introduction—just enough to guide you as you decide what further reading (or viewing) might be helpful, inspiring, enjoyable, or challenging.

JAMES PAUL GEE'S INTRODUCTION TO *SITUATED LANGUAGE AND LEARNING: A CRITIQUE OF TRADITIONAL SCHOOLING* (2004)

Why I included it

I like the way this book's introduction quickly demonstrates how various languages and discourse communities either invite or alienate people, and the author's point about the importance of communication within a contemporary culture dominated by technology is smart, to say the least. I hope it motivates you to think about the academic languages you speak in relation to other languages, including online communication.

Gee's list of points reads like a reverse outline. I appreciate his ability to be succinct and sum up his argument. His book both says and does much more than these bare-bones points, but they are a helpful starting place for tracing the ideas the rest of his book elaborates on.

Background

Gee is known for his attention to discourse communities, situated learning, and the power of video games to motivate active learning. His background in linguistics and his interest in making education more widely accessible intersect with research in writing studies, especially as more and more composition scholars have researched technologies that enable and also constrain writing in various ways. However, as indicated by the title, Gee is speaking more broadly to educators (not just writing professors). His intentional bridging of academic and non-academic language, and his awareness that he will be criticized no matter what language he uses, is part of his work as he tries to practice what he is preaching.

Reading hints

Gee's prose tends to be accessible after the first paragraph. Take your time processing the list of main points that the rest of his book will elaborate on by thinking about how each idea might play out in an actual situation you can imagine. That kind of work helps the ideas move from an abstraction that's difficult to follow or remember to an actual argument that you could explain to another person.

311

CHAPTER FIVE: HOW DO I TRANSLATE MY ACADEMIC WRITING INTO PUBLIC GENRES?

As you read, consider responding to the following questions to help you process the material.

1. What were you thinking as you read the first paragraph? How did your thinking change as you read the following paragraph?

2. Gee repeatedly uses the term "black hole" to discuss the way people might react to a particular way of speaking or writing. What does "black hole" suggest? What kinds of speaking or writing have you encountered that feel like a "black hole" to you? Why?

3. Gee says that some people have more access to the languages used in schools than others. In your experience, does this observation seem accurate? If Gee wanted to convince readers this were true in other parts of his book, what kind of evidence might he rely on?

4. Do you play video games that require you to learn, to apply skills in new ways, or to practice and improve in order to succeed or move up a level? Can you imagine school learning occurring in video game styles? Explain.

5. What connections do you notice between Gee's observations and what you know about rhetorical situations from Chapter Two?

6. How important do you believe it is to be comfortable communicating in online environments? Explain.

7. Gee does not cite past work from his own research or the research of others, an approach that contrasts in extreme ways with the other texts included in this chapter. What are the pros and cons of citing past research?

Gee, James Paul. Introduction to *Situated Language and Learning: A Critique of Traditional Schooling*, Routledge, 2004.

I AM A linguist whose interests have changed over the years. Today I am interested in the role language plays in learning. However, earlier in my career I spent my time studying things like "naked infinitives." This is, of course, a topic that sounds a lot sexier than it is. Naked infinitives are grammatical constructions like the verb "leave" in "I saw Mary leave." In this sentence, "leave" is an "infinitive" (a verb not marked for "tense," that is not marked as "present" or "past"). In English, infinitives are usually preceded by a "to," as in "I wanted Mary to leave." Since the "to" is missing in "I saw Mary leave," "leave" is said to be "naked." I also studied "headless relatives," another topic that sounds more exciting than it is. Headless relatives are grammatical constructions like "who I want to marry" in "I will marry who I want to marry." "Who I want to marry" is a relative clause. Such clauses are normally preceded by a noun phrase called their "head," as in "I will marry the person I want to marry," where "the person" is the head of the relative clause. Thus, since there is no head in front of "who I want to marry" in "I will marry who I want to marry," it is called a "headless relative clause."

This book has nothing to do with naked infinitives or headless relatives. It does, however, have something to do with why the last paragraph, my first in the book, will not be very inviting to many readers. You don't really want to hear a lot more technical information about naked infinitives and headless relatives, do you? You lost a lot of your interest when you found out naked infinitives had nothing to do with naked bodies and headless relatives had nothing to do with decapitating people. If you didn't like school, the first paragraph reminded you a lot of school, except that school didn't even try to titillate you with nakedness and decapitation.

For some people the first paragraph was alienating, for others it wasn't. Some feared I would continue, perhaps to do something like tell them what parasitic gaps are. Some few might have hoped I would continue—too few to sell enough copies of this book to keep me alive. People who found the first paragraph alienating feared they were about to fall into the black hole of "jargon" and "academic language"—language they don't particularly like or care about. It's a black hole they experienced too often in school. On the other hand, people who can't wait for the parasitic gap discussion have, for one reason or another, made a larger peace with academic ways with words.

In the not too distant past people who had made peace with school-based academic jargon and ways with words could be pretty much assured, all things being equal, of success in modern developed countries. But the times they are achanging and things are more problematic now. Today, to hedge your bets, you probably want to make some sort of peace with academic learning—with school-based learning. But there are new ways with words, and new ways of learning, afoot in the world—ways not necessarily connected to academics or schools. These ways are, in their own fashion, just as special, technical, and complex as academic and school ways. But they are motivating for many people for whom school wasn't. At the same time, they may be alienating for many people for whom school ways were motivating. These new ways, though, are just as important—maybe more important—for success in the modern world as school ways. These new ways are the ways with words (and their concomitant ways of thinking) connected to contemporary digital technologies and the myriad of popular culture and specialist practices to which they have given rise.

We face, then, a new challenge: how to get all children—rich and poor—to be successful in school, but to ensure also that all children—rich and poor—are able to learn, think, and act in new ways fit for our new high-tech global world. We have barely begun on the first task only to have the second become more pressing by the day.

Most of you will be glad to know that I don't do theoretical linguistics any more. I have for the last number of years been an educational linguist, interested in how language and learning work at school and in society at large. But, alas, some of you will find that I still write in "jargon" and academic language. Others will find my writing a bit too "folksy"—not academic enough for rigorous reputability. It all depends on the sorts of peace you have or have not made with certain ways with words. I have tried to be as clear as I can while still using the language tools I need to get my job done—and that is part of the point of this book: that there are different ways with words because we need different tools to get different sorts of jobs done. More generally, this book is about the tension that we readers, former students all, feel about academic and school-based forms of language and thinking, that some people find alienating and others find liberating. It is about facing that tension at a time when these academic and school-based ways are challenged by new ways with words and new ways of thinking and learning.

This book [Gee's book] will constantly move back and forth between ways with words, deeds, and thoughts in school and out of school. Predominant among the out-of-school things I talk about will be computer and video games (I will in this book just use the term "video games" to mean both computer and video games). Some of my most academic readers will now themselves fear a black hole, in this case a place where they haven't been and don't want to be. I hope I can convince such readers that this is a mistake. For many people in our modern world—not all of them particularly young—video games are not a black hole, but a liberating entrée to new worlds—worlds more compelling than either the worlds they see or have seen at school or read about in academic books. But, then, the core argument of this book will be that people learn new ways with words, in or out of school, only when they find the worlds to which these words apply compelling.

This book is actually one argument, broken into pieces, that can be summarized fairly concisely. So here is a quick overview of what is to come:

1. What's hard about school is not learning to read, which has received the lion's share of attention from educators and policy-makers, but learning to read and

FOCUS ON WRITING: WHAT COLLEGE STUDENTS WANT TO KNOW

learn in academic content areas like mathematics, social studies, and science (students can't get out of a good high school, let alone get out of any decent college, if they can't handle their content-area textbooks in biology or algebra). Unfortunately, a good many students, at all levels of schooling, hate the types of language associated with academic content areas. Indeed, many people in the public don't very much like us academics and our "ways with words."

2. What's hard about learning in academic content areas is that each area is tied to academic specialist varieties of language (and other special symbol systems) that are complex, technical, and initially alienating to many learners (just open a high-school biology or algebra textbook). These varieties of language are significantly different from people's "everyday" varieties of language, sometimes called their "vernacular" varieties.

3. Such academic varieties of language are integrally connected (actually "married") to complex and technical ways of thinking. They are the tools through which certain types of content (e.g. biology or social studies) are thought about and acted on.

4. Privileged children (children from well-off, educated homes) often get an important head start before school at home on the acquisition of such academic varieties of language; less privileged children (poor children or children from some minority groups) often do not. The privileged children continue to receive support outside of school on their academic language acquisition process throughout their school years, support that less privileged children do not receive.

5. Schools do a very poor job at teaching children academic varieties of language. Indeed, many schools are barely aware they exist, that they have to be learned, and that the acquisition process must start early. At best they believe you can teach children to think (e.g. about science or mathematics) without worrying too much about the tools children do or do not have with which to do that thinking. Indeed, schools create more alienation over academic varieties of language and thinking than they do understanding.

6. All children, privileged and not, can readily learn specialist varieties of language and their concomitant ways of thinking as part and parcel of their "popular culture." These specialist language varieties are, in their own ways,

as complex as academic varieties of language. The examples I use in the book involve Pokémon and video games. (If you don't think things like Pokémon involve specialist language and ways of thinking connected to it, go get some Pokémon or Digimon cards.) There are many more such examples. While confronting specialist academic languages and thinking in school is alienating, confronting non-academic specialist languages and thinking outside school often is not.

7. The human mind works best when it can build and run simulations of experiences its owner has had (much like playing a video game in the mind) in order to understand new things and get ready for action in the world. Think about an employee role-playing a coming confrontation with a boss, a young person role-playing an imminent encounter with someone he or she wants to invite out on a date, or a soldier role-playing his or her part in a looming battle. Such role-playing in our minds helps us to think about what we are about to do and usually helps us to do it better. Think about how poorly such things go when you have had no prior experiences with which to build such role-playing simulations and you have to go in completely "cold." Furthermore, a lecture on employee-employer relations, dating, or war won't help anywhere near as much as some rich experiences with which you can build and run different simulations to get ready for different eventualities.

8. People learn (academic or non-academic) specialist languages and their concomitant ways of thinking best when they can tie the words and structures of those languages to experiences they have had—experiences with which they can build simulations to prepare themselves for action in the domains in which the specialist language is used (e.g. biology or video games).

9. Because video games (which are often long, complex, and difficult) are simulations of experience and new worlds, and thus not unlike a favored form of human thinking, and because their makers would go broke if no one could learn to play them, they constitute an area where we have lots to learn about learning. Better yet, they are a domain where young people of all races and classes readily learn specialist varieties of language and ways of thinking without alienation. Thus it is useful to think about what they can teach us about how to make the learning of specialist varieties of language and thinking in school more equitable, less alienating, and more motivating.

10. In the midst of our new high-tech global economy, people are learning in new ways for new purposes. One important way is via specially designed spaces (physical and virtual) constructed to resource people tied together, not primarily via shared culture, gender, race, or class, but by a shared interest or endeavor. Schools are way behind in the construction of such spaces. Once again, popular culture is ahead here.

11. More and more in the modern world, if people are to be successful, they must become "shape-shifting portfolio people": that is, people who gain many diverse experiences that they can then use to transform and adapt themselves for fast-changing circumstances throughout their lives.

12. Learning academic varieties of language and thinking in school is now "old." It is (for most people) important, but not sufficient for success in modern society. People must be ready to learn new specialist varieties of language and thinking outside of school, not necessarily connected to academic disciplines, throughout their lives. Children are having more and more learning experiences outside of school that are more important for their futures than is much of the learning they do at school.

Well, let's jump in. I hope it's not a black hole for any of you.

DANIEL ANDERSON'S "THE LOW BRIDGE TO HIGH BENEFITS: ENTRY-LEVEL MULTIMEDIA, LITERACIES, AND MOTIVATION" (2008)

Why I included it

Dan Anderson focuses on student learning and how it can best be served, with digital literacies being a tool to a greater end rather than a goal in itself. His use of student work and student reflection on their processes offers inspiration for potential ways to transform your own approach to assignments while offering evidence that creative production can invigorate educational practices.

Background

Anderson's essay appeared in 2008 in *Computers and Composition*, a journal begun in 1983 and aimed toward an audience of professors teaching writing who are interested in digital possibilities. Although he does not explicitly say so, Anderson may be providing other professors with ideas for multimodal classroom projects while

317

CHAPTER FIVE: HOW DO I TRANSLATE MY ACADEMIC WRITING INTO PUBLIC GENRES?

simultaneously giving them language and a rationale for explaining to colleagues why they are assigning non-traditional writing in their courses. First-year composition courses are regularly expected to provide students with writing skills that can be used in other academic situations, so Anderson may be implicitly defending creative assignments at a time when they were even less widely accepted in colleges than they are now. Note also that some of the online composing tools available now were not possibilities when Anderson was chronicling student projects that used readily available technologies.

CONNECT

As you read, consider responding to the following questions to help you process the material.

1. Anderson begins by saying computer literacies are not exciting because they are on the computer but rather because students can feel empowered as they contribute to social change. How might this initial point affect professors who are nervous about or fearful of online writing and design experiences? How might people who are excited about technological possibilities respond?

2. How does Anderson envision the relationship between human beings and digital technologies?

3. Anderson draws on the metaphor of a "construction site" for student learning. What does this metaphor suggest is important? Do you agree that this metaphor works well?

4. How does Anderson's experience of student learning fit with questions of motivation explored in Chapter One?

5. Anderson writes, "My experience is that much of education delivers cold information and boredom." How does he answer this complaint? Is his answer connected to other answers you've encountered in this text for making learning a more engaged process?

6. If Anderson were to write a follow-up today, what kinds of student projects might he include?

Reading hints and vocabulary

I cut several parts from this essay, but you can still see that it begins with an introduction, and Sections 1 and 2 provide a literature review of secondary sources. Sections 3, 4, and 5 showcase three different kinds of student projects that involve multiliteracies rather than alphabetic text. Throughout each section, Anderson works to bring together ideas about composing processes, student motivation, and public engagement, with the suggestion that all three elements are more likely to work well if teachers make time for students to thoughtfully play and construct projects using available technologies.

low-bridge technologies: free digital tools that are created for the general user (rather than experts)

flow: the state of full engagement that is more likely to occur when a task is rewarding and challenging—but it is not overwhelming

personal agency: the ability to exert power, make change, have control

FOCUS ON WRITING: WHAT COLLEGE STUDENTS WANT TO KNOW

electracy: literacies or communication capabilities connected with electronic media or digital platforms

multimodal: using more than one type of communication in a single place, such as a combination of textual, visual, and audio elements

Anderson, Daniel. "The Low Bridge to High Benefits: Entry-Level Multimedia, Literacies, and Motivation." *Computers and Composition*, vol. 25, no. 1, 2008, pp. 40–60, <https://doi.org/10.1016/j.compcom.2007.09.006>.

ABSTRACT: Low-bridge approaches to multimedia in the writing classroom rely on familiar literacies, free consumer-level software, and remix uses of materials to facilitate student production of new media compositions. The projects shed light on reconfigurations of teaching environments that foreground the classroom as a construction site or studio space. The model features an emphasis on the interplay between technical things and human goals and concerns. This emphasis requires hands-on experiences working with technologies as part of classroom activities. Skill challenges yield high levels of motivation, and student composers experience flow-like states of creativity. The writing class as new media studio becomes a site of heightened personal engagement with learning that moves from the practical to the personal to the public. These practical approaches yield significant opportunities for students to develop new media literacies through the process of making projects. Examining these projects reveals the need to focus on a sense of personal agency and the possibilities for delivering social change when we talk about new media literacy.

Keywords: Media; Flow; Creativity; Motivation; Literacy; Playlist; Collage; Video

> *There is ample evidence that people do not learn anything well unless they are both motivated to learn and believe that they will be able to use and function with what they are learning in some way that is in their interest.*
> — The New London Group

> *If I worked for 4 hours on biology I would be absolutely miserable, yet I worked for probably 10 on my Tyger collage alone. This is what college classes should be all about, new approaches to things we thought we knew all about. Thanks for letting me think originally again.* — Alex Shearer

319

CHAPTER FIVE: HOW DO I TRANSLATE MY ACADEMIC WRITING INTO PUBLIC GENRES?

ALEX'S ASSESSMENT OF his experience in a first-year writing class clarifies the work of the New London Group (1996), whose call for multiliteracies reflected in part dissatisfaction with alphabetic literacy but in whole a desire to see students as motivated agents of change. The New London Group used the concept of design to show the interconnectedness of a range of literacies, citing five design grammars (linguistic, visual, audio, gestural, and spatial) and a sixth, synthetic category (multimodal) where literacies converge. But the group offered this refined conception of literacies in the service of a larger project, explaining, "literacy educators and students must see themselves as active participants in social change, as learners and students who can be active designers—makers—of social futures" (1996, p. 65). The group's work offered a helpful corrective to the tendency to link computer literacy to technology-related skills, asking us instead to concentrate on individual engagement and civic opportunities.

But taking the computer out of computer literacies can be equally problematic. Stuart Selber (2004) brought the technological aspects of literacy back into focus by delineating multiliteracies into three categories, one of which is a functional literacy concerned with the operation of computers and software. Selber was careful not to limit functional literacy to "the technical aspects of software applications, hardware components, and operating systems" (pp. 32–33). Instead, we can critique the cultural dimensions of computers even as we learn to use technologies. Selber suggested that educators make use of computers without falling victim to technical determinism, which yields either false hope based on inevitable technical progress or false hopelessness based on the loss of human agency in a world determined by technologies. The trick is to engage technologies while avoiding lenses through which "both utopian and dystopian visions [of technologies] are exaggerated" (Feenberg, 2002, n.p.). We need a model for computer literacy that emphasizes what Bruno Latour has called "the actors in a technical project" (1996, p. 162). Following Latour, we can see technologies as nodes on a network that also includes individuals and ideas, each element having an agency.

The final complication arises when we put the network into motion. Technologies are shaped by humans and ideas and in turn reshape human concerns and individuals. According to Latour,

[technology] is not a human thing, nor is it an inhuman thing. It offers, rather, a continuous passage, a commerce, an *interchange* between what humans inscribe in it and what it prescribes to humans. It translates the one into the other. This thing is the nonhuman version of people, it is the human version of things, twice displaced. What should it be called? Neither object nor subject. An instituted object, quasi object, quasi subject, a thing that possesses body and soul indissolubly. (1996, p. 213)

Latour offered this interchange metaphor when referring to the microprocessor, and the point was that the microprocessor quickly becomes a hybrid that brings things (both physical things and conceptual matters) and humans together. So, too, computer literacy acts as entity and non-entity, a mediator that continually links converging technologies, concerns, and people. For educators, such a conception allows us to turn computer literacy from a thing into an activity, sloughing off definitions that would fix computer literacy as a set of skills in favor of processes through which multiple literacies can flow, processes like borrowing, mixing, layering, and sharing. Further, seeing that literacies emerge through interchanges of things and people, we can affirm a human agency to counter technical determinism. Concrete technologies and functional skills are put into motion to implement human goals and desires. At the same time, the interchange model gives us permission to concentrate on things, to emphasize skills and emerging technologies. Our understanding of literacies, then, moves continually from concrete tools and skills to conceptual realizations and human goals like a finger tracing both sides of a mobius strip.

But is there more to be gotten from the interplay of people and machines? Why bother to bring composition into the twenty-first century if we can't carry over the ineffable payoff that comes from creation? Why else would Latour (1996) suggest that "there really is love in technologies" or explain that "metaphor means transportation" (p. 282)? Why would Gregory Ulmer (2003) build his electronic literacy, electracy, around the punctuum that stings or assert, "the basic device of aesthetic composition (metaphor to put it in one word), marginalized in literate education, becomes central to electrate learning" (p. 69)? The ultimate value of transforming literacies is to help students discover the ineffable possibilities of the creative process. Ulmer was right to point out how such a process is frequently marginalized in education. My experience is that much of education delivers cold information and boredom. If converging humans and machines not only yield multiple literacies but also hold the potential for delivering body and soul realizations, engagement, educational magic, shouldn't that be our focus when integrating technologies into the composition classroom? The question is rhetorical. The rest of this essay will try to explain why.

321

CHAPTER FIVE: HOW DO I TRANSLATE MY ACADEMIC WRITING INTO PUBLIC GENRES?

1. Construction Sites, Pedagogies, and Personal Motivation

In *Reassembling the Social*, Latour offered the metaphor of the construction site to call attention to the "making" that goes into any concept or concern, suggesting that construction sites "offer an ideal vantage point to witness the connections between humans and non-humans" (2005, p. 88). Wandering around such sites, we're likely to experience discoveries unavailable by simply examining a finished product. Latour reported on the experiences of science studies practitioners exploring constructions of facts: "we went back stage; we learned about the skills of practitioners; we saw innovations come into being; we felt how risky it was; and we witnessed the puzzling merger of human activities and non-human entities" (2005, p. 90). The construction site is intimately concerned with innovations, looking toward technologies as agents that bring people and concerns together. It is also a site of risk and experimentation, a place where "silent implements stop being taken for granted when they are approached by users rendered ignorant and clumsy by *distance*—distance in time as in archaeology, distance in space as in ethnology, distance in skills as in learning" (2005, p. 80). At such a site, technologies influence activities and people, "objects become mediators," and accidents reveal connections between humans, ideas, and things. Latour's construction site offers a useful model for thinking about integrating new media into the composition classroom. By relying on free, consumer-level (what I call low-bridge) technologies, we can easily create a construction site that emphasizes things used by people (technologies) and people making things (projects). This approach offers practical benefits for instructors and personal benefits for students.

Creating a construction site based on emerging technologies serves as a catalyst for instructors wishing to reconceptualize pedagogies—technical things shed new light on existing paradigms and open possibilities for new methodologies. Reflecting on her experiences teaching with word processors, Patricia Sullivan showed how learning about new technologies can lever conceptual change and create "the possibility, even the probability, that present and future technology may well 'threaten' some aspects of writing theory and pedagogy" (1991, p. 46). Sullivan's work and early explorations of word processors illuminate one way the discipline of composition comes to know technologies. The process begins with access to new (often soon-to-be-ubiquitous) technologies, enters an experimental phase in which teachers and writers employ the technologies, and then matures into a reflective phase in which theories and pedagogies are layered over activities. Obviously such a model oversimplifies.[1] But, for the purposes of finding practical means of transforming education, the model of technology first, experimentation next, and reflection later offers a direct route to classroom practices through which new literacies can emerge and converge.

I recognize that the claim above raises red flags about technical determinism and the dangers of operating without complete knowledge. I'm loath to delete the section, though, because it will be disingenuous to argue below that students benefit from technical challenges and unfamiliarity without allowing that instructors, too, require skill challenges and will benefit from an ability to experiment with new technologies. Putting technology first promotes opportunities for play and experimentation that can lead to new learning. Albert Rouzie (2005) complained that institutional forces "[blind] most educators to the significance of play already occurring in their classrooms" (p. 27). Margaret Mackey (2002) pointed out that experimentation is "a form of rehearsal [... and] an important part of mastering new media" (p. 187). James Paul Gee (2003) made a similar connection with video games, extending the link to critical thinking:

> The game encourages [the gamer] to think of himself as an active problem solver, one who persists in trying to solve problems even after making mistakes; one who, in fact, does not see mistakes as errors but as opportunities for reflection and learning. It encourages him to be the sort of problem solver who, rather than ritualizing the solutions to problems, leaves himself open to undoing former mastery and finding new ways to solve new problems in new situations. (p. 44)

Unknown technical things create ideal situations in which literacy-enriching problem solving activities might play out. Further, entry-level technologies with

---

1   Clearly, these layerings can work the other way, as recognized in the oft-repeated call to "put pedagogy first" when integrating technologies into the classroom. Nancy Kaplan (1991) pointed out that instructors wishing to promote "a social-constructionist pedagogy" found an easy means of doing so in "[o]ff-the-shelf word processing programs, networks, and hypertext tools [that] seem[ed] ready-made to address writing as a social process" (p. 32). There is also a long history of compositionists building specific computer tools upon a foundation of theoretical and pedagogical knowledge. Early technologies such as the Daedalus Integrated Writing Environment developed at the University of Texas or later technologies such as the Writing Studio at Colorado State are just two examples that illustrate a counter-movement to the experiment first, theorize later approach advocated here. Ultimately, classroom implementations of technology often play out with a continual transitioning between technological thing and pedagogical/theoretical idea, a process that twists practice and theory together as continual strands in a technology integration twine.

323

CHAPTER FIVE: HOW DO I TRANSLATE MY ACADEMIC WRITING INTO PUBLIC GENRES?

simplified interfaces, limited feature sets, and broad availability can ease the way towards innovation.[2] Not surprisingly, instructors who jump-start innovation with entry-level software soon find the experience yields pedagogical insights and theorizing that can be layered over practice through reflection, a process often characterized by borrowings and recuperations.

But engaging technical things comes with a bigger payoff. Experimenting with unfamiliar technologies can facilitate a sense of creativity that can lead to motivation. In one of his many studies on creativity and motivation, Mihaly Csikszentmihalyi (2000) pointed out that "one needs to grow, to develop new skills, to take on new challenges to maintain a self-concept as a fully functioning human being" (p. 199). Csikszentmihalyi channeled his discussion of skills and motivation through the concept of flow, or autotelic experience, a state of consciousness associated with creativity and characterized by a sense of intrinsic motivation and pleasure. The results of flow resemble the higher aspirations of critical and media literacies, providing individuals with opportunities for action, a sense of competence and control, heightened awareness of personal identity, avenues for creative self-expression, and a sense of agency. Sadly, Csikszentmihalyi revealed, "our compulsory and uniform educational system is a sure guarantee that many, perhaps a majority in each generation, will spend their youth in meaningless unrewarding tasks" (p. 100). For tasks to have meaning, there must be an optimal correspondence between their degree of difficulty and the skill levels one brings to them. Overly-challenging tasks can limit flow. In most educational situations, though, the opposite holds true. Familiar tasks fail to present a level of challenge that would lead to flow.

Could it be that low-bridge new media technologies provide the right mix of challenge and ease of use for instructors and students to develop a sense of

---

2   For discussion of the flip-side difficulties that arise when the notion of ease is applied to computers, see Bradley Dilger's "The Ideology of Ease," in which Dilger explains "ease is never free: its gain is matched by a loss in choice, security, privacy, health, or a combination thereof" (2000, n.p.). Dilger showed how students must remain critical even as they reap the benefits of easy-to-use software, ultimately developing a demystified understanding of computing environments and activities. See also Selber's discussion of functional literacies. There is a real danger of failing to recognize the social and political dimensions of technologies, especially off-the-shelf technologies that are frequently seen as neutral tools. Selber pointed out, however, that we are not condemned to such lack of insight. Following Feenberg and Sherry Turkle, Selber affirms the role of human agency in conceptions of literacy featuring tool metaphors: "As a human extension, the computer is not self-determining in design or operation. The computer, as a tool, depends upon a user, who if skilled enough can use and manipulate its (non-neutral) affordances to help reshape the world in potentially positive ways" (2004, p. 40). By combining a critical perspective on technologies with an emphasis on human agency, instructors and writers can take off-the-shelf tools and use them in a process through which they further develop computer and critical literacies.

control, creativity, and flow? The entry-level nature of low-bridge technologies ameliorates difficulties that can shut down flow, but the challenge of composing with unfamiliar forms opens pathways to creativity and motivation. Fulfilling Csikszentmihalyi's criteria, low-bridge media technologies "offer a range of 'flow channels' at various levels of skill and commitment" (p. 80). Of course, there is no guarantee that all students will develop this sense of control when faced with skill challenges based on learning new technologies. Still, for those who do respond well to the tasks, the payoffs extend beyond any service- or content-oriented conception of education, since "at the height of their involvement with the activity [people] lose a sense of themselves as separate entities, and feel harmony and even a merging of identity with the environment" (p. 194). The practical benefits of bringing low-bridge technologies into the classroom yield to personal benefits of identity growth and motivation. Why bother with technical skills and things in the composition classroom? Because the making that occurs through the interplay of things and humans yields creative and personal transformations.

2. The Practical and Personal Become Public

[***]

The links between motivation, new media, multiliteracies, agency, and civic participation can be readily traced. Less clear, however, are the connections between these items and changes in education. The most compelling advocate for considering personal motivation in terms of transformation in composition is probably Geoffrey Sirc. Sirc doesn't argue for either alphabetic or multimedia literacies but rather advocates that compositionists aim for the expressive *process* of production. Again, we must put things into motion. Sirc (2002) explained, "defining composition, exclusively around the parameters of page or canvas, results in that conventional, academic surface" and instead suggested we think of composition "as a record of tracings, or gestures, a result of a body moving through life" (p. 111). Sirc was looking for a composition that might be "anti-conventional, expressive, discursively hybrid, and technologically innovative" but instead finds in most scholarship a composition that "is all about conventions; which sees its retreat from expressionism in academicism as some sort of progress; which prefers a purified, taxonomized, monophony to hybridity; and consigns discourse on technology to a sub-realm of the discipline" (p. 173). Sirc is clear that this over-disciplining of composition bleeds the motivation from students, leading only to "alienation" and "exhaustion" (p. 209).

New composing processes feature literacies like juxtaposition, parody, or pastiche and build upon student interests. These remix modes can overcome the boredom and "exhaustion in most writing assignments" (p. 212), making students "architects of their own aesthetics" (p. 132).

Kathleen Tyner (1998) also connected motivation with educational reforms, explaining, "unfortunately, the ideal of citizen democracy is in conflict with the repressive and undemocratic education that students receive daily in the school environment" (p. 229). Tyner saw the liberal arts and media literacies as providing a possible model of reform, hoping that "as communication forms merge in digitized multimedia formats, new relationships between visuals, texts, and graphics [will] call for creative expression ... ushering in a rich renaissance of artistic expression ... " (p. 229). Similarly, Csikszentmihalyi suggested, "to test the limits of the mind, the first education should be an artistic one—not in the sense of learning about art or even learning to do art, but in the deeper sense of acquiring an artistic vision" (2000, p. 205). The recommendations, then, have come full circle—from the practical things and skills of technology to the personal energy of motivation to the public promise of civic change, and now back to the personal power of creative vision, back to the conceptual promise of moving things. If multimedia is linked to motivation, which is linked to literacy, which in turn is linked to critical participation in civil society, then it should come as no surprise that Sirc asked us to integrate new media in our classrooms by beginning with "a theory of textuality that trie[s] to get in touch with the energies in things, to renew people's engagement with the world" (p. 289). The case studies below trace some of those engagements.

3. Building Bridges from Alphabetic Literacies Using Playlists

Kathleen Tyner suggested that even activities calling for multiliteracies can benefit from a healthy grounding in alphabetic literacy, especially for instructors who likely "are secure in their ability to explicate texts with students ... [and who] can apply familiar principles of alphabetic literacy to [a] further understanding of new genre[s] and media while their tool skills are getting 'up to speed'" (p. 92). Playlist assignments borrow from alphabetic literacies while using the raw materials of music to press toward additional, emerging literacy skills. Students create either a profile or a short narrative by identifying a set of songs that represents the identity of a person or tells a story. The images in Figure 1 represent excerpts from two playlists and demonstrate some of the possibilities.

Fig. 1. Playlists composed by Lindsay Smith and Helen Kearns.

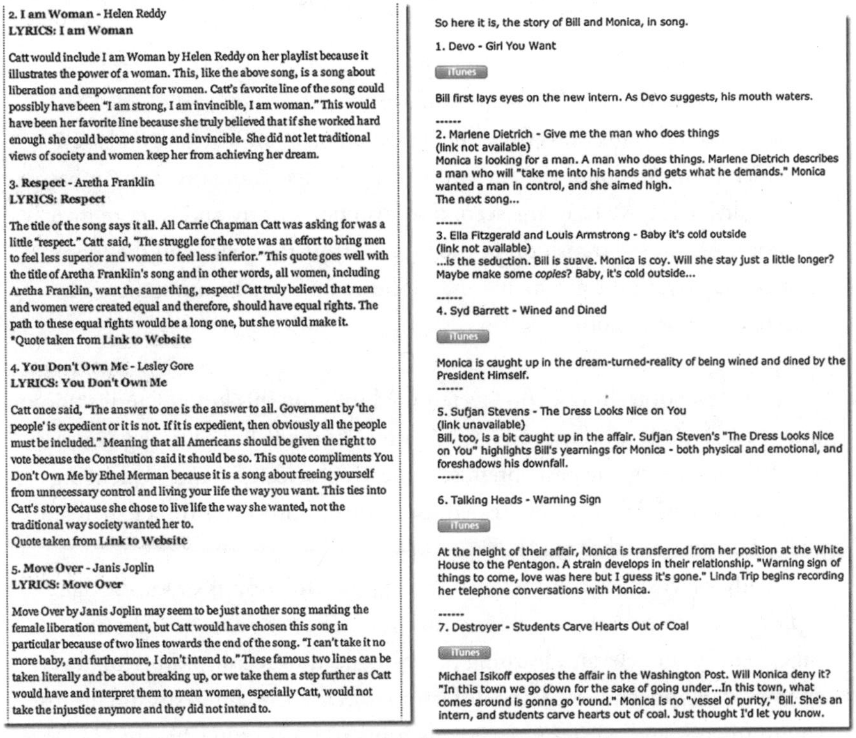

2. I am Woman - Helen Reddy
LYRICS: I am Woman

Catt would include I am Woman by Helen Reddy on her playlist because it illustrates the power of a woman. This, like the above song, is a song about liberation and empowerment for women. Catt's favorite line of the song could possibly have been "I am strong, I am invincible, I am woman." This would have been her favorite line because she truly believed that if she worked hard enough she could become strong and invincible. She did not let traditional views of society and women keep her from achieving her dream.

3. Respect - Aretha Franklin
LYRICS: Respect

The title of the song says it all. All Carrie Chapman Catt was asking for was a little "respect." Catt said, "The struggle for the vote was an effort to bring men to feel less superior and women to feel less inferior." This quote goes well with the title of Aretha Franklin's song and in other words, all women, including Aretha Franklin, want the same thing, respect! Catt truly believed that men and women were created equal and therefore, should have equal rights. The path to these equal rights would be a long one, but she would make it.
Quote taken from Link to Website

4. You Don't Own Me - Lesley Gore
LYRICS: You Don't Own Me

Catt once said, "The answer to one is the answer to all. Government by 'the people' is expedient or it is not. If it is expedient, then obviously all the people must be included." Meaning that all Americans should be given the right to vote because the Constitution said it should be so. This quote compliments You Don't Own Me by Ethel Merman because it is a song about freeing yourself from unnecessary control and living your life the way you want. This ties into Catt's story because she chose to live life the way she wanted, not the traditional way society wanted her to.
Quote taken from **Link to Website**

5. Move Over - Janis Joplin
LYRICS: Move Over

Move Over by Janis Joplin may seem to be just another song marking the female liberation movement, but Catt would have chosen this song in particular because of two lines towards the end of the song. "I can't take it no more baby, and furthermore, I don't intend to." These famous two lines can be taken literally and be about breaking up, or we take them a step further as Catt would have and interpret them to mean women, especially Catt, would not take the injustice anymore and they did not intend to.

So here it is, the story of Bill and Monica, in song.

1. Devo - Girl You Want
[iTunes]

Bill first lays eyes on the new intern. As Devo suggests, his mouth waters.
----
2. Marlene Dietrich - Give me the man who does things
(link not available)
Monica is looking for a man. A man who does things. Marlene Dietrich describes a man who will "take me into his hands and gets what he demands." Monica wanted a man in control, and she aimed high.
The next song...
----
3. Ella Fitzgerald and Louis Armstrong - Baby it's cold outside
(link not available)
...is the seduction. Bill is suave. Monica is coy. Will she stay just a little longer? Maybe make some *copies*? Baby, it's cold outside...
----
4. Syd Barrett - Wined and Dined
[iTunes]

Monica is caught up in the dream-turned-reality of being wined and dined by the President Himself.
----
5. Sufjan Stevens - The Dress Looks Nice on You
(link unavailable)
Bill, too, is a bit caught up in the affair. Sufjan Steven's "The Dress Looks Nice on You" highlights Bill's yearnings for Monica - both physical and emotional, and foreshadows his downfall.
----
6. Talking Heads - Warning Sign
[iTunes]

At the height of their affair, Monica is transferred from her position at the White House to the Pentagon. A strain develops in their relationship. "Warning sign of things to come, love was here but I guess it's gone." Linda Trip begins recording her telephone conversations with Monica.
----
7. Destroyer - Students Carve Hearts Out of Coal
[iTunes]

Michael Isikoff exposes the affair in the Washington Post. Will Monica deny it? "In this town we go down for the sake of going under...In this town, what comes around is gonna go 'round." Monica is no "vessel of purity," Bill. She's an intern, and students carve hearts out of coal. Just thought I'd let you know.

Lindsay Smith's *Carrie Chapman Catt* playlist [left column, Fig. 1] resembles the familiar research essay in its informational focus. Helen Kearns's *Bill and Monica* playlist represents the affair between Bill Clinton and Monica Lewinski through song. These projects reside very close to traditional conceptions of alphabetic literacy—each writer has excerpted and discussed lyrics from songs much as one might do in an essay. However, new literacies converge with these familiar composing skills. First, a variation of information literacy developed through the playlist projects. Using basic HTML linking, the projects operated on a logic of selecting and borrowing from existing sources. Students determined what amount of a song could responsibly be excerpted, what relevance the excerpted piece had to the profile or story, and what kinds of links could be provided to either lyrics or song samples. The project provided an easy route to thinking about information and remix literacies that were layered over the alphabetic literacies built into the project.

Additionally, the playlist offered a bridge between alphabetic and audio literacies. Students practiced listening literacies as they selected and sequenced the songs

327

CHAPTER FIVE: HOW DO I TRANSLATE MY ACADEMIC WRITING INTO PUBLIC GENRES?

that would go into the playlist. Alex Shearer, for instance, created a narrative playlist about a relationship. Discussing the second song in his playlist, he explained,

> all of a sudden the man's attitude changes, and he starts to feel attachment to the woman. This change of attitude comes when the song "Sir Psycho Sexy" transitions from the lyrical phase to an instrumental section which continues until the end of the song. Whereas the first section has a funky, seductive beat, the second section flows freely and is more melodious. Again, the transition in the song mirrors the change in the man's attitude toward the girl he has met. (Shearer, personal communication, November 10, 2006)

A low level of technical effort is required to bring this kind of audio thinking into the composition classroom. While students made links to song samples and Web resources, the basic premise of hearing, selecting, and sequencing songs could have been accomplished using a word processor (or a pencil and a cocktail napkin for that matter).

Finally, playlists expose one of the most powerful aspects of low-bridge multimedia projects: their ability to motivate. The New London Group suggested, "to be relevant, learning processes need to recruit, rather than attempt to ignore and erase, the different *subjectivities*—interests, intentions, commitments, and purposes—students bring to learning" (1996, p. 71). This engagement is no small matter. Reflecting on his playlist, Alex reported, "I liked the idea of the playlist assignment right from the start. There are certain songs that have always been associated with moods that I have. The trick was blending those moods into a story and then attaching songs whose lyrics made sense in a sequence." Danielle Veal offered a similar reaction:

> I was very excited when I learned that I had to create my own playlist. Music is a huge part of my life. I own over 100 CDs and I have played the violin since the 5th grade. Creating a playlist allowed me to play the role of an executive producer at a record label. I chose the songs that went on the CD and the order in which they were listed. Instead of being random songs, like most CDs, my CD told a story. This playlist tells the story of a young girl named Monica who struggles with obstacles in life. This topic was inspired by close friends of mine and even a little from my own life. (Veal, personal communication, December 7, 2006)

Without exception, students found the ability to bridge their personal and academic interests afforded by the assignment to be highly motivating.

4. Bridging Functional and Visual Literacies in Collages

As instructors and students move further away from alphabetic literacies, technical things and skills become more central to the composing process. Composing digital collages, in particular, ratchets up technical difficulties. But there is justification for teaching students to use a digital image editor in the writing classroom.[3] If students are to become visually literate, it helps to spend some time making things with the digital technologies of visual composition. A comparison of two collages can illustrate.

Fig. 2. Moriah Halper's "The Tyger" collage.

3   Shipka (2005), Wysocki (2004), and Sirc (2002) have demonstrated the value of non-digital multimedia assignments. Shipka's students have created gift boxes and other non-digital projects, allowing them to work with multiple genres and media. Shipka suggested that "a much wider, richer repertoire of semiotic resources, coupled with [student] efforts to purposefully structure the delivery and reception of their work, afford new ways of thinking, acting, and working within and beyond the space of the first-year composition classroom" (p. 279). Wysocki's students have created mixed media maps. Sirc's box logic projects revealed a similar ability to go multimedia without becoming fixated on the digital high-end. The point is not to question these approaches but to sketch out additional literacies that become available through similar digital projects.

Moriah Halper's collage in Figure 2 represents an explication of the poem "The Tyger" by William Blake. The collage integrates images of fire, a tiger, a soldier, an angel, a lamb, and a set of manacles. The elements have corollaries with the imagery of the poem. Additionally, this collage makes use of a snippet of text, a couplet from the poem. The couplet reveals how alphabetic and visual literacies can inform each another. Consider how a reading of the collage might progress if it did not contain the text. Would the imagery alone be enough to make the connection with the poem? In terms of visual literacy, it might be tempting, then, to argue that if the poem can be read through the image without the text, it has succeeded in creating a parallel visual message. Moriah explained:

> I interpreted the poem as if there was a young child questioning God and wondering about all of the evil things in the world ... I also placed the little girl so that she was looking down upon all of the "evil, as if she was inspecting it and curious about it ... The red colors in the bottom half of the collage correspond to the fiery imagery in the poem, seen with words like "burning," "fire," and "furnace." (Halper, personal communication, September 23, 2006)

Fig. 3. Kandis Rich's "The Tyger" collage.

FOCUS ON WRITING: WHAT COLLEGE STUDENTS WANT TO KNOW

Simple analysis can bring out elements of visual rhetoric like arrangement, balance, contrast, emphasis, shading, color, shape, and line. But, through production of the collage, Moriah applied these visual concepts to the representation of content-area knowledge, here literary interpretation, "plac[ing] the little girl so that she [is] looking down upon all of the evil."

To consider how far such visual arguments can be pushed, examine Figure 3 depicting a collage created by Kandis Rich explicating the same poem.

Of Moriah's collage, we asked what would happen if we removed the alphabetic couplet. Let's perform the visual equivalent on Kandis's collage by asking what would happen if we removed the hand of creation from the top-left corner of the image. Would the questions about God inherent in the poem be lost with the removal of the hand? If so, this visual element acts as an explanatory reference, linking the concept of creation to the mixed elements of fire, forest, and tiger in the collage (and poem). To fully read the collage, though, we need to bring technical skills back into our discussion, and we'll need another screenshot (Figure 4).

Fig. 4. The Twirl Effect and Layer Manager palette.

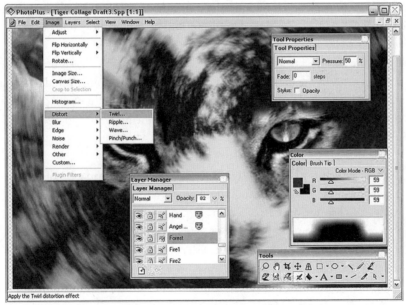

The distortion effect that Kandis has applied to the forest creates a visual twirl that gives the trees a swirled appearance and introduces a sense of motion into the fixed frame of the collage. The Layer Manager palette shows the

CHAPTER FIVE: HOW DO I TRANSLATE MY ACADEMIC WRITING INTO PUBLIC GENRES?

elements in the image. Note the opacity setting of the forest layer; twirling the forest and then lowering its opacity blends the layer with the image of the tiger underneath. Now, recall that there are no alphabetic cues in this explication, necessitating a new grammar of literary interpretation. Here the twirling combined with the lowered opacity creates a smearing of the kind we might find in the tenor and vehicle of a metaphor; forest and tiger are joined and set into motion, expressing the symmetry and creative energy of the poem through software effects. Image editors call for new skills, grammars, and vocabularies (layering, twirling, cropping, masking, arranging, and so on) through which students can explain elements of the poem. Making things with the software, then, enables students to express the literary through the visual. And, once again, the making leads to motivation.

Kandis reported "this [collage project] was a very interesting and exciting assignment to do. When we learned how to use the program for blending the images, I literally spent hours just trying to figure out how the program worked. I used all kinds of images and manipulated them in so many different ways ... This assignment gave me a better understanding of the term collage and gave me a whole new way to create a story or describe something in the form of pictures" (Rich, personal communication, December 7, 2006). Not only did the functional literacies developed by "learn[ing] to use the program" translate into visual literacies, this process deepened Kandis's understanding of the collage genre and the poem. The response also reveals flow-like levels of interest and engagement in the project that extend beyond what one might find if Kandis had been asked to turn in a one-to-two page explication of the poem.

Moriah reported similar "addiction" to learning the program and a convergence of literacies:

The collage was my favorite assignment so far this year. I had a lot of fun playing with the images and tools in Photoplus. I finished my collages really early because once I started on each collage I would get addicted to working on them and would not be able to move from my computer for hours ... For some reason, I never feel completely satisfied with my collages. The more I look at them, the more I want to change something around to make them even more perfect ... In addition to enjoying creating the collages, I also liked conveying the themes and the character analysis through images. It is a lot harder to use images to express how you analyze a work than to simply write a paper. It was interesting and refreshing to take a different approach to analyzing literature.

FOCUS ON WRITING: WHAT COLLEGE STUDENTS WANT TO KNOW

Moriah's response clearly demonstrates the motivational potential of multimedia projects, as seen in her continual desire to revise and perfect the collages. Other students reported similar fixations on revising these visual compositions. Moriah's response also suggested that a good deal of engagement results from working with unfamiliar modes of expression. That Moriah found the visual mode more challenging than an essay might suggest that the grammars of visual literacy (while difficult because less familiar) may also be difficult because they enable a complexity of expression that rivals that of print. Appropriate technical challenges provide engagement, and the degree of difficulty translates not only into motivation but also into intellectual rigor.

5. Bridging Technical Skills and Rhetorical Literacies through Video Slide Shows

The transformations that unfold as alphabetic literacies are applied to new media (as in playlist assignments) or as functional and content-area literacies are blended with visual literacies (in collages) yield high levels of motivation but also raise fundamental questions about what takes place in the composition classroom. At some point we must ask, *as responsible teachers and scholars of composition, how far can we walk from the written word?* To formulate a response to such a question we can think about borrowings and recuperations. Richard Lanham (1993) and Jay David Bolter (1991) have both explored the rhetorical roots of digital spaces. Walter J. Ong (2002), and others after him, leapfrogged print history to recuperate oral traditions that might be applied to aural composition in contemporary media. Hugh Burns (1984) used Aristotle and Kenneth Burke to create invention heuristics for his *Topoi* program. Gail E. Hawisher and Charles Moran (1993) placed e-mail in a tradition reaching back to the Renaissance and through to the middle ages, outlining a rhetoric of e-mail that includes "genres, audiences, voices, uses, and the extent to which any and all of these are influenced by the properties of the medium" (pp. 629–630). These borrowings and recuperations serve as bridges over which one can walk further from a constrictive vision that equates composition with the production of alphabetic text. Broadly speaking, these bridges are built from rhetorical concepts that transcend particular literacies: concepts like ethos, pathos, and logos, and the well-worn modes of persuasion. Examining student video slide shows reveals how these broad concepts can be taught through technical experimentation and the making of low-bridge media projects.

333

CHAPTER FIVE: HOW DO I TRANSLATE MY ACADEMIC WRITING INTO PUBLIC GENRES?

[***]

Fig. 8. Danielle Veal's The Movement *slide show.*

[***]

Danielle Veal's *The Movement* slide show (Figure 8) charts the history of the civil rights movement. In some ways the slide show resembles an informational video; it sequences historical information to document a period of history. Unlike David's informational video, however, the bits of historical information come in the form of excerpts from speeches by John F. Kennedy and Martin Luther King, Jr. This composing process can be partially understood by looking at the arrangement of the elements in the composing timeline of the MovieMaker software, as seen in Figure 9.

The MovieMaker timeline uses video, audio, and title layers to facilitate composing. The combination of sequential, timeline-based composing and the multiple visual, audio, and textual layers create new possibilities of expression. Danielle frequently employed the title track to layer textual snippets from speeches or credos of equality over images of segregation or racial tension. The process resulted in an ironic juxtaposition that used the image to call into question the conceptual kernel of the alphabetic snippet.

Danielle extended this juxtaposition strategy to the audio track as well, taking excerpts from speeches and sequencing them strategically over the image track. If you look closely at Figure 9, however, you'll see that the MovieMaker software provides only a single audio track. To understand the sonic layering process Danielle invoked we need to look at an additional screenshot, an image representing Danielle's work with the audio for the project, as seen in Figure 10.

The visible portion of the screenshot contains four tracks. (The audio composition Danielle created actually contained twenty tracks.) Danielle recognized the one-audio-track limitation of the MovieMaker program and decided to learn an alternative piece of software that affords audio layering. Danielle created her layered audio track in the Audacity audio editor, exported it as a single audio track, and then imported this track into MovieMaker, a work-around that surveyed the available means of production and then moved fluidly between software applications and methods of composition.

Fig. 9. The MovieMaker composing timeline.

Danielle complemented this fluid multiliteracy with a prolonged process of information gathering and remix literacy, using seventy-eight images and twenty-three audio files for the project. The files represent not merely a collection of materials but artifacts of a new means of production in which notions of originality shift as composers become selectors and remixers of media, a mode of production that recognizes the "folly of insisting on a glut of new materials-when there's already so much existing stuff that just need rearranging" (Sirc, 2002, p. 214). For those who might be quick to dismiss this search-and-combine mode of composition as unoriginal or lacking rigor, I offer Danielle's assessment of the process:

> After listening to the King speech over and over again, I cropped out some
> important lines and quotes from his speech, still unaware of what my main

335

CHAPTER FIVE: HOW DO I TRANSLATE MY ACADEMIC WRITING INTO PUBLIC GENRES?

song was going to be. After searching for more pictures that fit with my theme, I came across John F. Kennedy's civil rights speech that was given in 1963. I also found some good lines in this speech to help my video collage. After doing some brainstorming, and even calling my parents, I found a Marvin Gaye song called "Inner City Blues/Make Me Wanna Holler" that expressed a lot of the same ideas I wanted to get across. So I placed all the cropped quotes and sentences over the song and arranged them in an order that would flow well with the pictures. After finishing the audio track, I began the collage, strategically placing the pictures with the lyrics they matched. I became so addicted to this project that I worked on it day and night, trying to get it to the point of perfection.

Fig. 10. The Audacity audio editing interface.

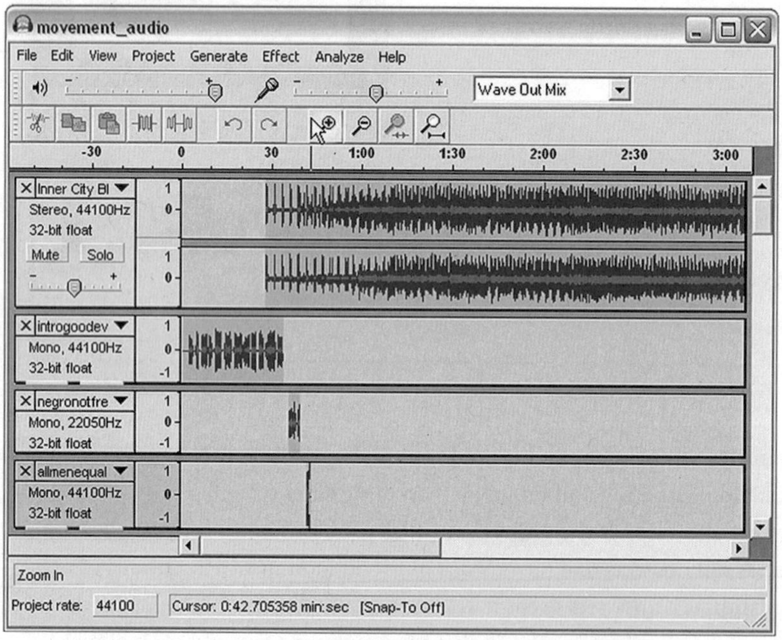

Danielle closely studied her materials, brainstormed possibilities, researched to discover new ideas, focused her thinking, refined her project with the help of others, synthesized, drafted, revised, polished, and so on. And she did all of this with the same addictive motivation that marks other multiliteracy projects. Of her work on the video slide show, Danielle said:

This video collage was the best project I have ever done in my life. I spent so much time on this, and it actually turned out to be an audio collage along with a video collage. I had a vision in my head before I even started the project and I worked at it until it was as perfect as I had seen it in my head. I felt so moved by my own work that I had to extend it.

Clearly, video slide shows like Danielle's serve not only as vehicles for familiar rhetorical concerns but also as transformative projects enabling new modes of composition and literacy including audio, visual, sequential, informational, and remix literacies. But the promise of such projects, as with others discussed here, resides primarily in their ability to create literacy experiences that engage students with learning and allow them into the flow of creativity.

6. The Low-Bridge Studio Model of Composition

After looking at the case studies above, we might wonder if we have lost track of the initial impetus behind this article—to spell out a philosophy for low-bridge integration of media projects into the writing classroom. The projects display uses of HTML and extensive uses of image, audio, and video editors. But let me reiterate the nature of these projects and the approach discussed here. The playlist projects require little unpacking to see how they might be easily integrated into the classroom. They sit closely aligned with alphabetic literacy and, while the lists above use HTML coding, they require no technology beyond a word processor to compose. The projects do, however, provide an entrée into informational and remix literacies and can also open avenues that bridge audio literacies with composition.

The collages call for a greater investment in technical skill development. The projects, however, have a number of qualities that make them low-bridge paths toward high literacy payoffs. The collages shown here were composed using free image editing software, in this case Photoplus software available for Windows. In contrast to expensive and sophisticated image editors, a free, minimally featured editor offers an easy-to-transverse path to a composition space that features masking, effects, and layers—key components of digital visual composition. The payoff that comes from such projects is the long-called-for goal of student production of visual compositions, an outcome that promotes convergences of functional, content-area, and visual literacies.[4]

The video slide shows operate with a similar easy-access logic. The key feature of these projects is their basis in remix literacies. Rather than using recorded video, which brings the attendant challenges of locating cameras, learning to film and work with field sound, and locating computers that can download and edit video, these projects collect ready-made materials in the form of images and audio files. They also rely on consumer-level software bundled with the major operating systems. These projects again have a high payoff for the level of investment they require. The learning curve is low for the software, the logistical difficulties are minimized, and the literacies fostered by the projects range from computer literacy to functional software literacy to visual and audio literacy to information literacy to content-area literacy to rhetorical literacy.

It would be misleading, however, to suggest that these projects do not require transformations in the composition classroom. The simplest way to explain these reconfigurations is through a comparison to the studio arts. For years, composition has called for visual and new media projects to be brought into the classroom. The net effect of many of these calls, however, is to foreground analysis of media works, to limit production activities that do take place to the visual, and to offload media production activities to lab environments or dorm rooms.[5] New media is too often an additive, something layered over existing pedagogies and analytical modes. An alternative model, which begins with the notion of production as the central activity of the classroom, is the studio arts. This production, however, is complemented by layers of analysis and theorizing that bubble up from student-created work. The classroom becomes construction site—a site where technical things, created things, and human concerns, flow together. Composition has, to some extent, established this model for alphabetic text, featuring workshopping of student papers. Even these models, though, give short

---

4   For the last decade, scholars have frequently pointed out the failure of much of the technology integration efforts in education to move beyond print-centric notions of composition and literacy (Anderson, 2003; George, 2002; Johnson-Eilola & Wysocki, 1999; Kress, 1998). Anne Wysocki and Johndan Johnson-Eilola go so far as to question the very term literacy for its alphabetic bias. Simultaneously, scholars have begun implementing and theorizing multimodal composition in the classroom, as evidenced by Kathleen Yancey's (2004) call for the development of a new curriculum based "not only in words" in her 2004 Chair's address to the annual Conference on College Communication and Composition.

5   For more on the status of multimodal composition in writing classes, see Anderson et al.'s "Integrating Multimodality into composition curricula: Survey methodology and results from a CCCC research grant" (2006).

attention to studio-based production—students likely compose their papers on their own, in their dorms or apartments, and then bring them into the classroom for the obligatory review session.

Low-bridge multimedia, in contrast, calls for hands-on time in class for students to work together as they develop technical skills and multiple literacies. The studio classroom acts as Selfe and Hawisher's "technology gateway" because it provides a supportive yet critical environment, a community of peers in which students can "acquire and develop robust sets of digital literacy skills" (2004, pp. 104–105). To create such a context for learning multiliteracies, "teachers [must] become real colearners" (Selber, 2004, p. 202). This often-lauded decentering is required for "writing as experience-exchange, text as process-action" (Sirc, 2002, p. 157). Such a space embraces student creativity and pushes for movement from the practical to the personal to the public, knowing that as multimodal projects are moved from the studio to the networked world they will carry forward "the active mobilization of every individual's latent creativity, and then, following on from that, the molding of the society of the future based on the total energy of this individual creativity" (Tisdall, quoted in Sirc, 2004, p. 157). The studio doesn't shirk from the functional deployment of "skill-based media tools" (Tyner, p. 156). But always the focus is on "a creative, artistic/aesthetic skill set" because "[w]hile the purpose of technology education may be job readiness, the purpose for arts teachers who use media tools with students is to foster self-expression, creativity, and to find their own 'voice'" (Tyner, p. 157). Note the pronoun ambiguity in Tyner's recommendation. When it comes to integrating multiliteracies into composition classrooms, those who create environments where writers can experience the personal engagement that will translate into motivation and rich convergences of literacies are few and far between. When it comes to really transforming education with new media, even many compositionists must still find their voice.

References

Anderson, Daniel, Atkins, Anthony, Ball, Cheryl, Millar, Krista H., Selfe, Cynthia, & Selfe, Richard. (2006). Integrating multimodality into composition curricula. *Composition Studies, 34*(2), 59–84.

Anderson, Daniel. (2003). Prosumer approaches to new media composition: Production and consumption in continuum. *Kairos: A Journal of Rhetoric, Technology, and Pedagogy, 8*(1). Retrieved April 30, 2007, from <http://kairos.technorhetoric.net/8.1/index.html>.

339

CHAPTER FIVE: HOW DO I TRANSLATE MY ACADEMIC WRITING INTO PUBLIC GENRES?

Bolter, Jay David. (1991). *Writing space: The computer, hypertext, and the history of writing.* Hillsdale, NJ: L. Erlbaum Associates.

Burns, Hugh. (1984). Recollections of first generation computer-assisted prewriting. In William Wresch (Ed.), *The computer in composition instruction: A writer's tool.* Urbana, IL: NCTE.

Csikszentmihalyi, Mihaly. (2000). *Beyond boredom and anxiety: Experiencing flow in work and play.* San Francisco: Jossey-Bass.

Dilger, Bradley. (2000). The ideology of ease. *The Journal of Electronic Publishing,* 6(1). Retrieved April 30, 2007, from <http://www.press.umich.edu/jep/06-01/dilger.html>.

Feenberg, Andrew. (2002). Looking backward, looking forward: Reflections on the 20th century. *Dogma.* Retrieved April 30, 2007, from <http://dogma.free.fr/txt/AFLooking-Backward.htm>.

Gee, James Paul. (2003). *What video games have to teach us about learning and literacy.* Gordonsville, VA: Palgrave Macmillan.

George, Diana. (2002). From analysis to design: Visual communication in the teaching of writing. *CCC,* 54(1), 11–39.

Hawisher, Gail E., & Moran, Charles. (1993). Electronic mail and the writing instructor. *College English,* 55(6), 627–643.

Johnson-Eilola, Johndan, & Wysocki, Anne. (1999). Blinded by the letter: Why are we using literacy as a metaphor for everything else? In Gail Hawisher and Cynthia Selfe (Eds.), *Passions, pedagogies, and 21st century technologies.* Logan: Utah State University Press.

Kaplan, Nancy. (1991). Ideology, technology, and the future of writing instruction. In Gail E. Hawisher and Cynthia Selfe (Eds.), *Evolving perspectives on computers and composition studies: Questions for the 1990s.* Urbana: NCTE.

Kress, Gunther. (1998). Visual and verbal modes of representation in electronically mediated communication: The potentials of new forms of text. In Ilana Snyder (Ed.), *Page to screen: Taking literacy into the electronic age.* London: Routledge.

Lanham, Richard A. (1993). *The electronic word: Democracy, technology, and the arts.* Chicago: University of Chicago Press.

Latour, Bruno. (1996). *Aramis, or the love of technology* (Catherine Porter, Trans.). Cambridge: Harvard University Press.

Latour, Bruno. (2005). *Reassembling the social: An introduction to actor-network theory.* Oxford: Oxford University Press.

Mackey, Margaret. (2002). *Literacies across media: Playing the text.* London: Routledge.

Morrow, Leslie M., & Tracey, Diane H. (2004). Instructional environments for language and learning: Considerations for young children. In James Flood (Ed.), *Handbook of research on teaching literacy through the communicative and visual arts*. Mahwah, NJ: Erlbaum.

New London Group. (1996). A pedagogy of multiliteracies: Designing social futures. *Harvard Educational Review, 66*(1), 60–92.

Ong, Walter J. (2002). *Orality and literacy: The technologizing of the word* (2nd ed.). New York: Routledge.

Rouzie, Albert. (2005). *At play in the fields of writing: A serio-ludic rhetoric*. Creskill, NJ: Hampton Press.

Selber, Stuart. (2004). *Multiliteracies for a digital age*. Carbondale: Southern Illinois University Press.

Selfe, Cynthia, & Hawisher, Gail E. (2004). *Literate lives in the information age: Narratives on literacy from the United States*. Mahwah, NJ: Erlbaum.

Shipka, Jody. (2005). A multimodal task-based framework for composing. *CCC, 57*(2), 277–306.

Sirc, Geoffrey. (2002). *English composition as a happening*. Logan: Utah State University Press.

Sullivan, Patricia. (1991). Taking control of the page: Electronic writing and word publishing. In Gail Hawisher & Cynthia Selfe (Eds.), *Evolving perspectives on computers and composition studies: Questions for the 1990s*. Urbana: NCTE.

Tyner, Kathleen R. (1998). *Literacy in a digital world: Teaching and learning in the age of information*. Mahwah, NJ: L. Erlbaum Associates.

Ulmer, Greg. (2003). *Internet invention: From literacy to electracy*. New York: Longman.

Wysocki, Anne. (2004). Opening new media to writing: Openings & justifications. In Johndan Johnson-Eilola, Cynthia Selfe, & Geoffrey Sire (Eds.), *Writing new media: Theory and applications for expanding the teaching of composition*. Logan: Utah State University Press.

Yancey, Kathleen. (2004). Made not only in words: Composition in a new key. *CCC, 56*(2), 297–328.

341

CHAPTER FIVE: HOW DO I TRANSLATE MY ACADEMIC WRITING INTO PUBLIC GENRES?

STEPHANIE ANNE SCHMIER, ELISABETH JOHNSON, AND SARAH LOHNES WATALUK'S "GOING PUBLIC: EXPLORING THE POSSIBILITIES FOR PUBLISHING STUDENT INTEREST-DRIVEN WRITING BEYOND THE CLASSROOM" (2018)

Why I included it

Schmier et al. complicate the idea that student writing for community settings or on digital platforms is always a positive experience. They thus model the way you might respond to a widely held belief about writing by noticing where and when that belief does not work. Close attention to exceptions does not necessarily mean the original belief is discarded; in many cases, the original belief may simply require nuanced thinking. The researchers also provide a helpful model of a case study analysis, which allows them to engage readers with a narrative while also thinking through complex ideas about writing and audience. If you use a case study to make an argument, you might notice how they interpret the case study and rely on secondary research to draw conclusions.

Background

This contemporary essay appeared in the *Australian Journal of Language and Literacy*, but it focuses on American eighth grade students and was written by researchers at American universities. Although the American focus may be surprising at first, it fits with a model of international research that is possible in the digital age because articles are more easily accessed than in the past. High school teachers may be most interested in the findings, and the journal article likely has a wider appeal since the observations and theories about students writing outside the classroom could be applied at any age. The article is particularly timely because students are expected to write for authentic audiences outside the classroom more often since online publication is easier than in the past.

Reading hints and vocabulary

Although at times some of the vocabulary and ideas expressed may be difficult to understand, the crux of the article is the case study. You can rely on the narrative of student publication and the tensions that followed to help you process Schmier et al.'s ideas. The headings and subheadings can also guide your reading and help you trace connections between secondary research and the complexities that arose in the case study.

Please note that the spelling follows Australian conventions, as does the lack of a period when writing "Mr Cardenas." Remember that such writing conventions vary from one discourse community to the next just as word pronunciations or sentence intonation might vary.

ethnographic inquiry: asking and answering questions about people and cultural practices using observation (with the observer sometimes also a participant in the community being studied)

connected classroom: most often used to refer to a classroom that is technological, with students having access to digital tools and those tools being used to support learning. Occasionally the phrase "connected classroom" is used to describe a classroom community that interacts with the larger community in specific ways. In this latter usage, "connected" refers to interpersonal connections

literacy: reading and writing practices

im/material: the use of "/" is a way of saying both "material" and "immaterial" at once. "Material" refers to physical objects such as pens, screens, classroom desks, chairs, and so forth, with the understanding that people interact with such objects and, to a degree, physical objects both allow and constrain behavior. "Immaterial" refers to other elements such as conversation, feelings, sense of identity, and so forth. Putting the two words together implies that they are inseparable elements

embodied identity: rather than a sense of identity relying solely on emotional or cognitive elements, "embodied identity" forefronts the role of the physical body in shaping both perceptions of oneself and perceptions of others, whether in terms of gender, ethnicity, age, weight, mobility, or other elements. This attention to the

CONNECT

As you read, consider responding to the following questions to help you process the material.

1. Even though this article is about students in eighth grade, I find it relevant to students and other writers of any age. Do you agree? Why or why not?

2. The researchers explore issues of power that may arise when students write in various classroom, school, and public settings. What are some examples of topics that may be most likely to spark strong responses and opposition from readers?

3. How do Schmier et al. think instruction and classroom practices might be improved to help students anticipate and negotiate tensions that might arise when writing is published outside the classroom?

4. How do the findings from this case analysis complicate the teaching and digital writing practices supported by Daniel Anderson in the prior essay?

5. Imagine you were one of the people involved in the case study—either Annie, Mr Cardenas, one of the physical education teachers, or the school principal. Do you appreciate the way you are represented in this article by Schmier et al.? How might the article affect your response if such a situation were to arise again?

body implies that interactions—even online interactions—involve physical bodies that affect those interactions

critical digital literacy: "critical literacy" involves reading and producing texts that interrogate power relations, especially those associated with race; "critical digital literacy" extends such reading and production activities to online spaces where power relations might be engaged or interrogated in particular ways

Schmier, Stephanie Anne, Elisabeth Johnson, and Sarah Lohnes Wataluk. "Going Public: Exploring the Possibilities for Publishing Student Interest-Driven Writing beyond the Classroom." *Australian Journal of Language and Literacy*, vol. 41, no. 1, 2018, pp. 57–66.

Abstract

THIS ARTICLE PRESENTS a case drawn from a year-long ethnographic inquiry with secondary school youth who engaged in publishing student interest-driven writing for audiences beyond the classroom. Informed by connected learning researchers' illustrations of the potential impact of connecting student self-interest with publishing in the academic sphere (Ito et al., 2013), we look deeply at the work of youth and teachers as they negotiated institutional spaces in a connected learning classroom. Specifically we share a case study of a student who went public with a text critical of her school's approach to Physical Education classes and advocating for change, highlighting the tensions that arose as her text circulated among audiences beyond the classroom. In doing so, we discover instructional implications and possibilities that can help teachers anticipate and create moments of learning that occur when texts are published for audiences beyond the classroom.

In this article, we engage in a critical exploration of the literacy events surrounding a writing assignment enacted in an eighth grade journalism and digital media studies elective class at a public secondary school in the United States. In our current political era, where journalistic writing is constantly politicised and scrutinised, we find it both crucial and timely to investigate the possibilities and challenges of teaching students about writing for public audiences. Here we draw on data from a year-long ethnographic inquiry with youth who engaged in the study of journalism and digital media, which included publishing for public audiences beyond the classroom (Duke, Purcell-Gates,

Hall & Tower, 2006). Informed by connected learning researchers' illustrations of the potential impact of connecting student self-interest with publishing in the academic sphere (Ito et al., 2013), we recognise the learning potential for student-led authorship. Through connected learning, teachers work with students to enact both digital media and analog projects driven by youths' individual and collective interests, with the products disseminated to public audiences within and beyond the school walls. In doing so, teachers advocate for students by making space for their individual voices, within an often disempowering system of standardised instruction and assessment (Garcia, 2014).

While such work is often couched in an optimistic discourse touting the positive, transformative nature of digital technology for learning (Selwyn, 2010), this discourse often fails to account for the on-the-ground messiness of enacting student interest-driven writing and publication. Further, we recognise the way in which student interest in schools is often shaped by what Gee (1996) described as the secondary Discourse of school as opposed to the primary Discourses of passionate affinity spaces in line with a connected learning framework. Following Soep (2006) and other self-titled Critical Youth Studies scholars (e.g., Dimitriadis, 2001; Sarigianides, Lewis & Petrone, 2015) who posited classrooms to be places where power relations are always present and productive, we ask: What happens when audiences beyond the classroom including school authority figures intra-act with (Barad, 2007) students' interest-driven writing? How do or might teachers and youth navigate these negotiations that have both immediate and long-term implications for student voice and choice in the connected writing classroom? In this article, we look deeply at the work of youth and teachers as they negotiated institutional spaces within and beyond the classroom, in particular through the story of Annie and the tensions that arose as her article—critical of her school's approach to Physical Education (PE) classes and advocating for change—circulated among audiences both known and unknown. To illustrate the tensions and opportunities that arise when student interest-driven writing leaves the classroom and goes public, we draw on scholarship that conceptualises literacy as an im/material practice (Burnett, Merchant, Pahl & Roswell, 2014) and an embodied identity performance (Enriquez, Johnson, Kontokorvi & Mallozzi, 2016). With these lenses come an emphasis on the ways 'literacy is materialised and materialises in different ways through texts, bodies, and screens and the spaces they generate' (Burnett et al, 2014, p. 7).

As students and teachers engage in writing for publication beyond the classroom, the literacies they practice will be im/material. In other words, students' literate identities and subjectivities (i.e., ways they perceive themselves as and

345

CHAPTER FIVE: HOW DO I TRANSLATE MY ACADEMIC WRITING INTO PUBLIC GENRES?

are recognised by others as literate), are interwoven with the texts they write, their feelings, the screens upon which they appear, and the variety of spaces (e.g., school websites and blogs, online social media) these texts, feelings, and screens *make*. How does the im/materiality of literacies shape and shift teacher-student power relations? How might school adults use the im/materiality framework to recognise and advocate on behalf of students' multiple identities as writers, activists, youth, women, students, and critics?

To address the questions we pose above, we additionally bring a needed critical lens (Avila & Zacher Pandya, 2013) to the im/materiality framework. In particular, here we weave together concepts of criticality and im/materiality to foreground aspects of literate subjectivity that existing frameworks addressing digital writing and publication for public audiences (e.g., Boyd, 2014; Ito et al., 2009) might overlook. Thus, in what follows we look critically at connected learning in action through the lens of im/materiality in order to discover possibilities for teaching and learning that materialise when students publish interest-driven texts to public audiences within and beyond school walls. In doing so, we discover instructional implications and possibilities that can help teachers anticipate and create moments of learning that occur when texts are published for audiences beyond the classroom.

From critical digital to critical im/material literacies

Critical digital literacies are 'those skills and practices that lead to the creation of digital texts that interrogate the world; they also allow and foster the interrogation of digital, multimedia texts' (Avila & Zacher Pandya, 2013, p. 3). While literacy practices are not always explicitly labeled critical (Johnson, 2011) and issues of power are not universally foregrounded, we side with scholars who affirm that when youth and adults make media and practice digital literacies in context, power relations and issues of authority are ever present and productive (Fleetwood, 2005; Soep, 2006). Conflicts over meanings, tastes, identities, and values abound and intersect (see work by Lewis & Crampton, 2015; Lewis & Dockter Tierney, 2011). Indeed, power relations that arise in practice weave digital tools and texts (i.e., the im/material bits and bytes) into the analog, material, physical world they are often defined against (Hayles, 1993).

In their framework for the im/materiality of literacy, Burnett et al. (2014) articulated a lens for exploring the interwoven, ever-shifting relationships between material and im/material worlds, and the implications said flows might have for literate subjectivity. Through a classroom vignette of students making meaning between a projected Google map of their neighborhood and their personal experiences living in that neighborhood, Burnett et al. illustrated how students' literate subjectivities hinged on the spaces generated by the intermingling of material and immaterial things, experiences, and screen-based texts. As student authored texts leave the classroom audience of peers and a teacher, audiences shift and the contours of power change. Such shifts warrant critical lenses if teachers are to advocate for and ally themselves with youth.

The critical im/materiality lens nuances praxis for adults invested in alliance with and advocacy on behalf of youth as it draws attention to:

1. The power of invisible, ephemeral *stuff* like feelings and oral speech in shaping (and constraining) multimodal composition as well as the constraints of digitally enabled tools and devices (Lewis & Dockter Tierney, 2011)
2. The ways different *embodied experiences* get recognised, circulated, represented, and censored differently based on normative constructions of age, race, class, gender, sexuality, and academic achievement (Johnson, 2011)
3. The beliefs and practices that undermine or sustain a *virtual* reality of youth publishing *screen-based texts* to appreciative audiences and networked publics for school purposes as well as ways in which imagined audiences are constantly re-configured in praxis (Petrone & Lewis, 2012)
4. Digital *spaces* are fluid and full of potential, but intimately interconnected to off-line face to face spaces that run the risk of reproducing dominant discourses given the importance people perceive said spaces and interactions to have. That importance may shift as invisible audiences are made visible, audiences are diversified, or invisible material investments are made visible.

In this paper, we draw upon this framework to consider the ways power shifts and produces a variety of positions for a secondary school aged youth as her im/material *personal experience* text is materialised and travels via material *things* (school hallway posters) and *screen-based texts* (school website) to generate social *spaces* (populated by fellow students, teachers, her principal, and the invisible audience of the open web community) with differential results for the enduring visibility of her personal experience text and ultimately, the *transformative* potential of the online school newspaper project.

Methodology

Project context
This qualitative study was conducted at a large public secondary school in the United States with a population of 3000 students including 40% English

347

CHAPTER FIVE: HOW DO I TRANSLATE MY ACADEMIC WRITING INTO PUBLIC GENRES?

Language Learners and 90% receiving free or reduced lunch. The eighth grade journalism and digital media studies elective class was designed and taught by Mr Cardenas, an experienced teacher at the school, and included the study of both traditional print journalism and digital media such as audio and video podcasting. Stephanie (Author #1) was a participant observer two days a week over the course of the academic school year.

Data collection

The primary method of data collection was participant observation of the teacher and focal students, including Annie, across various spaces including the journalism and digital media studies class and academic English classes. The constellation of events in this article centre the public writing of one student named Annie. These observations were documented in field notes, with special attention paid to texts, actors, actions, and interactions. Further, two formal in-depth interviews were conducted with participants as well as informal conversations throughout the year, with a focus on the students' experiences writing in the classroom. Finally, digital and print texts were collected including lesson plans, class assignments, students' draft and published writing, photographs, and video.

Data analysis

Data analysis was a multi-stage process that began with indexing of field notes and interview transcripts and identification of literacy events (Heath, 1983) as the initial unit of analysis. This meant looking within and across 'any occasion in which a piece of writing is integral to the nature of participants' interactions and their interpretive processes' (p. 93). Literacy events traversed the multiple social spaces that comprised the site for this study and included live interviews, collaborative writing of a school newspaper, its publication and removal from multiple public locations (bulletin board display in the school's main hallway, school website).

To analyse the literacy events described in this article, we coded data first individually, then collectively, using the im/materiality framework (Burnett et al., 2014) as a guide. We began asking the following questions:

1. What identities, experiences, feelings, and perspectives were materialised and published?
2. How did power shift im/materially?

FOCUS ON WRITING: WHAT COLLEGE STUDENTS WANT TO KNOW

3. How was power negotiated and mitigated? How did power circulate to students?

We then further coded the material and im/material dimensions of three categories that emerged through our initial coding: *texts, identities,* and *space.* Finally, we mapped these codes onto the connected learning framework: *student interest-driven, networked collaboration through public authorship,* and *peer-supported learning.*

In what follows we a) describe the literacy events surrounding the production and publication of Annie's article, b) discuss the material consequences that resulted as different audiences read the text in the different social spaces in which it traveled, and c) offer insights into identifying and creating moments of learning that emerge when texts travel and are read by audiences within and beyond the classroom.

Vignette: The editorial assignment

Mr Cardenas addresses Annie who has set up the first interview of the class. She will interview the PE teacher for a story about his methodology. Mr Cardenas goes over to get her a press pass, and as she waits with her spiral notebook and pencil in hand, the class applauds. She puts the badge on as Mr Cardenas hands it to her and leaves the room (field notes, 9/14).

Annie, a Latina student identified by the school as gifted and talented, was one of 43 students enrolled in the journalism and digital media studies class. In interviews she was described by both teachers and students at the school as a high achieving student who was both well behaved and well liked.

As described above, the journalism and digital media studies class that Mr Cardenas designed and taught engaged students in the study and production of both print-based and digital journalistic texts that were published in different formats (hallway poster, webpage on school website, podcast posted on the website TeacherTube) throughout the year. Students were encouraged to select topics that would be of interest to their readers, which included both *fun* stories like music, movie, and video game reviews, as well as issues in the community that students identified as areas of concern. Mr Cardenas often referred to these topics as *social justice issues,* and encouraged students to write not only about the problem itself, but also offer ideas for solutions. Examples of social justice issues that students published included an article about a community

349

CHAPTER FIVE: HOW DO I TRANSLATE MY ACADEMIC WRITING INTO PUBLIC GENRES?

beautification project and a piece about the disproportionate support for the boy's basketball team at the school despite the girl's having more wins. Though Mr Cardenas did not use the language of critical literacy explicitly, we noted how the curriculum he designed, that centred on taking action about social issues, evidenced his move towards integrating critical literacy into the curriculum (Lewison, Flint & Van Sluys, 2002).

The PE article that Annie wrote for the print and digital issues of the *East Side Tribune*—the name the class chose for the newspaper they would publish throughout the year—was first pitched in a whole class conversation led by Mr Cardenas, designed to help students choose topics for the pieces they would write for their first article. Topics ranged from reporting on school sporting events and dances, to opinion editorial (op-ed) pieces about school violence, cafeteria food, and school uniforms. The PE curriculum at the school was mentioned by more than one student, but it was Annie who chose to take it on. She penned the piece independently, beginning with a critique of practices in the program, which she explained, 'I have witnessed and I can list,' then went on to offer recommended solutions, which could improve 'the flaws' and make the class more successful. The flaws, as described by Annie, included lack of differentiation for students who were less fit, not enforcing the rules while games were played, and spending a significant amount of class time taking attendance while students 'sit down and do nothing'.

After laying out her argument, Annie offered suggestions for improving the PE program, some of which were informed by resources provided to her by Mr Cardenas, including enforcing healthier lifestyles by eliminating the sale of candy and chips to raise funds for sports programs, and focusing on how to exercise properly. She recommended teaching skills like 'how to run' and organising games in ways that made sure that 'everyone is involved'. Finally, she made sure to cite evidence from her research and not make claims she could not back up, as Mr Cardenas had taught the class, including recommendations from the film *Super Size Me* (Spurlock, 2004) as well as from the local newspaper offering ideas for more interactive and supportive curricula using technology.

After receiving feedback from Mr Cardenas, Annie's article was selected by the class as one that would be published in the first edition of the paper. Once approval was obtained from the principal, the first edition of the *East Side Tribune,* including Annie's PE article, was published on a poster displayed in the school hallway directly across from the main office (see Figure 1) and on the school website. Mr Cardenas, Annie, and her classmates all described how proud they were of the first edition that was published and were excited to share it both online and in the main hallway of the school.

Once the article was posted in the school hallway, the potential audience shifted from the classroom to the entire school community. It was in this hallway space that one of the PE teachers read the article and subsequently met with the principal and stated his intention to file a formal grievance with the teachers' union against Mr Cardenas. During the meeting, the PE teacher agreed not to file his case against Mr Cardenas if the article was removed from the hallway. Not only did Mr Cardenas comply with this request, he offered all of the PE teachers the opportunity to respond to Annie's article by writing a rebuttal. Two of the PE teachers took Mr Cardenas up on his offer and wrote pieces responding to the elements of their program described in Annie's critique including large class size (> 50), school district mandates, and tight budgets restricting new equipment purchases which prevented them from enacting the types of recommendations that Annie put forth. The rebuttals were published in the second edition of the *East Side Tribune* posted publicly to the school website.

Findings

In this section we describe what emerged as we drew on theories of critical and im/material literacies to make sense of the experiences of Annie, Mr Cardenas, and the PE teachers. Here we offer insights that can support connected teachers and learners in leveraging the promise of classrooms that encourage and promote student interest-driven authorship published for local school-based and/or more widely read Internet public audiences beyond the classroom. Subsections mirror and map critical im/material lenses onto elements of the connected learning framework: student-interest, networked collaboration, and peer-supported learning (Ito et al., 2013).

Critical im/materiality and connected writing in the student interest-driven classroom

The journalism and digital media studies class that Mr Cardenas designed and taught centred students' interests by inviting them to identify, write about, and

351

CHAPTER FIVE: HOW DO I TRANSLATE MY ACADEMIC WRITING INTO PUBLIC GENRES?

publish on topics of their own choice. Though designed as an elective class, most of the 43 students enrolled in the journalism and digital media studies class were placed in the class because it fitted with their course schedule, not because they had an interest in digital media. In fact, many students expressed frustration that they would have to write in this elective class, which they felt should be easier than their core academic subjects. Consistent with a connected learning perspective, Mr Cardenas recognised that 'when a subject is personally interesting and relevant, learners achieve much higher-order learning outcomes' (Ito et al., 2013, p. 12) and enacted a curriculum that focused on student interests as a means to get students in the class engaged in writing for publication. Annie used this opportunity as described above to write about her lived experience and the experiences of her classmates at school in PE class in an effort to improve these school experiences and potentially the health of the school community.

Recognising ways in which meaning making and being is materialised in texts (Burnett et al., 2014; Davies, 2016), we took note of how Annie materialised her embodied experience at the center of her PE article. For example she wrote, 'Sometimes, the teachers just get mad and yell at the overweight kids who run for 30 seconds then walk the rest.' She further shared her experiences witnessing students being required to synchronise their jumping jacks and sit still for extended periods in a class meant for movement, while her teachers filled out district mandated paperwork. Here Annie inscribes her body into the text for us to read. She blurs her body with peers' overweight, synchronising, restless bodies getting yelled at to move faster and waiting silently for the chance to move. She writes internal and external worlds into intra-action (Barad, 2007) to mobilise change in the PE curriculum. Annie's article also gives insights into the way that she makes meaning of the power and control that she perceived teachers to have to make changes to their curricular programs. For example, she wrote, 'It is combining things that most kids really like doing with things that get kids active, and *voila*!' Annie's choice of language echoes the work of Mills and Dooley (2014) who articulated 'many children who are beginning to write and understand the nuances of quality persuasive texts may similarly use "epistemic modality" (e.g., must stop) and intensifiers (e.g., definitely) in unsophisticated ways, while making little use of hedging (e.g., may, partially, virtually, perhaps) to show humility and politeness in arguments, and to lower feelings of opposition among readers or addressees' (p. 33). Her argument further highlights her understanding that teachers are able to implement new programs and as such she offered a student's perspective

FOCUS ON WRITING: WHAT COLLEGE STUDENTS WANT TO KNOW

on what changes could make the program better. As described above, Annie did intend to interview the PE teachers; however, she ended up interviewing a student instead and including the student's perspective in the article. Perhaps if she had followed through with her teacher interview she would have learned about the challenges that the PE teachers faced before her article materialised an imagined public audience.

We further noted how Annie experienced the space of this student interest-driven classroom, which allowed her to take up the position of author with a voice, giving her the ability to advocate for change in school curriculum—something which traditionally students are not invited to discuss. Mr Cardenas had designed the curriculum and the learning space intentionally as one in which students used publishing to voice their ideas and advocate for change in their school and the broader community. However there was an absence of discussion in the classroom around power (Janks, 2000), specifically how school and community audiences might respond to the published works students were producing in the class. Though Mr Cardenas acted to protect the interest of students in their writing by for example, allowing students to interview outside sources to provide evidence to support their arguments and securing administrative approval before publication, he did not make these actions visible to students. In other words, Mr Cardenas did not make explicit the ways in which the actions he was taking were designed to shift power to students. What was explicitly and regularly communicated to students was the role that journalism could play in raising issues and promoting change. Annie took up a powerful position in this classroom space, realising how she might bring about change that could benefit her and her classmates by contributing to the creation of a program that would promote health and well-being in the school, an issue that she saw as important given the high rates of student obesity in the community.

While the student interest-driven focus of the classroom opened up possibilities for Annie and her classmates to reposition themselves from ways in which students are commonly recognised in school as other and passive, to powerful, active, and confident, some of the spaces in which her article was published reproduced dominant discourses around what is appropriate to write about in school and who is responsible for determining the curriculum that students experience in school. This was further evidenced later in the year by Mr Cardenas's decision not to allow an anti-abortion public service announcement video designed by other students in the class to be shown outside the classroom at the public community film festival (See Schmier, 2013). Additionally, the connections between digital and face-to-face experiences upon publication of the article reproduced dominant discourses and shifted, as material investments were made visible (e.g., union threat, hierarchies of years in the profession, etc.), which we discuss further in the next section.

Critical im/materiality and networked collaboration through public authorship
Research into the skills that students will need to be literate in the 21st century supports classrooms that embrace collaboration. A key component of connected learning is the ability for teachers to facilitate opportunities for students to connect their learning with public audiences in authentic communities of learners that share common interests. Henry Jenkins (2009) identified collaboration as a defining characteristic of 21st-century literacies. According to Jenkins, 'new literacies almost all involve collaboration and networking' (p. 29). The United States Common Core State Standards further support students authoring and publication of text to broad audiences, outlining the expectation that students by the end of eighth grade will be able to 'use technology, including the Internet, to produce and publish writing and present the relationships between information and ideas efficiently as well as to interact and collaborate with others' (National Governors Association Center for Best Practices & Council of Chief State School Officers, 2010, p. 18).

The curriculum of the journalism and digital media studies class embraced this ethos of networked collaboration through writing authentically for public audiences. For example, students shared video productions at an end of the year film festival, which was widely attended by students and their families. The audience for the editorial assignment that led to Annie's PE article was originally designed as other eighth grade students, and printed copies were to be distributed in homeroom classes. Given that the school budget was tight and teachers were being asked to limit paper use, Mr Cardenas decided instead to leverage the digital affordance of the school's Internet resources and post the *East Side Tribune* to the school's website. To publicise the paper further, students printed and displayed their articles in the school hallway across from the main office as described above.

As Annie's article travelled out of the space of the classroom, we noted ways in which the article's posting in the hallway shifted how that space produced different subjectivities for the actors participating in the literacy events surrounding the authoring and reading of the PE article. As described above, Annie's article was selected by the class to be published, which was seen as an honour and a mark of academic success in the journalism and digital media studies class. However, once the posted article was read by the PE teacher in

FOCUS ON WRITING: WHAT COLLEGE STUDENTS WANT TO KNOW

the hallway, Annie's positionality shifted from *successful student* to *agitator*. Simultaneously the posting of the article and reading by teachers and other adults at the school risked positioning the PE teachers as *ineffective*, a term that is increasingly used in United States schools to place blame for students' poor academic progress on teacher effectiveness. Here we see that the opportunity for students to publish their articles beyond the classroom—which Mr Cardenas enacted to create a connected journalistic learning space for students in the journalism and digital media studies—resulted in making 'the material world of the classroom even more omnipresent' (Burnett et al., 2014, p. 95).

By shifting the space of publication from paper handed out to students to a display in the school hallway frequented not only by teachers and families, but community members that included school district officials, the issues that Annie wrote about moved from an immaterial, imagined audience limited to schoolmates, to a material audience of schoolmates *and* school adults. As PE teachers lodged complaints with administration and Mr Cardenas, school adults decided to remove Annie's article from the school hallway and post PE teachers rebuttals above Annie's article online on the school website. This decision effectively silenced Annie's voice in the physical space before a multi-age school community audience and drowned out her voice online. While Annie's article remained visible in this online space, design and functionality of the site turned down the volume of her voice. Online, two PE teachers' rebuttals preceded Annie's text and lived *above the fold*, thus making their texts more accessible to readers. Rather than liberating Annie's voice from the power dynamics of the school and classroom, this positioning reproduced the discourse of the material space. In the flux of power across the three spaces in which the article was available to be read by multiple audiences (classroom, hallway, website) what remained most visible were critiques of Annie's embodied experiences and ideas that materialised in her published text. Put differently, the empowering space of the classroom that allowed for Annie to voice her experiences and ideas through writing for publication shifted once her text went public and was made available to audiences both known (hallway) and unknown (website).

Peer-supported learning in the connected classroom
Connected learning researchers highlight how 'in their everyday exchanges with peers and friends, young people are contributing, sharing, and giving feedback in inclusive social experiences that are fluid and highly engaging' (Ito et al., 2013, p. 12). Based within this recognition of the collaboration that youth are engaging in with their peers on a daily basis, a vision of connected learning in

the classroom would allow for youth to form social networks and communities of interest and expertise, which they could draw upon for support in authoring texts for publication by soliciting feedback and mentorship from their peers.

Some aspects of the journalism and digital media studies classroom embraced this ethos of peer support, which was visible both in the way in which topics were pitched and chosen as a class to be published, as described earlier, and in class discussions that took place once the newspaper was published. For example, Mr. Cardenas engaged the class in a discussion around the reactions that materialised with the publication of the PE article before the rebuttals were written:

> The students are seated at their desks and they are having a conversation about the PE program article. Mr Cardenas asks what the students have heard and Rosy shares that one of the PE teachers told her that the reason he sells Skittles and Hot Cheetos to students is to raise funds for the track team. Otherwise he wouldn't do it. Mr Cardenas then tells the class that he wants to reread the article aloud to the class so that everyone can know what they are discussing.
>
> After reading the article he asks the class if they think the piece is *too bad* or *too harsh* to which many of the students yell out, 'No!' He then looks over to Stephanie who is sitting in the back of the room and asks what she thinks. Stephanie praises Annie for the issues she raises and the thoughtful way she writes about them then asks:

Stephanie:	What are the sizes of the class?
Max:	Like 50.
Mr Cardenas:	They are huge.
Annie:	That's true, they do have a lot of students …
Mr Cardenas:	But my point is …
Stephanie:	(to Annie) But don't feel bad. (field notes 11/6)

Here PE teacher power flows in from beyond the classroom as Annie's classmate Rosy speaks with and through the PE teacher's explanation of the financial (structural) limitations he faces as a track coach. Mr Cardenas responds to Rosy by performing a read aloud of Annie's article and poses an invitation to the whole class to weigh in, informally with a collective, immaterial (but not unanimous), 'No!' This invitation explicitly extends to Stephanie who now, as researcher, must make her entanglement in the event audible and visible (Barad,

2007). Like Rosy, Stephanie raises structural limitations the PE teachers might face in her question about class sizes. A classmate, Mr Cardenas, and Annie all follow affirming the PE classes' large sizes while Stephanie attempts to mediate Annie's embodied feelings, 'But don't feel bad.'

The above discussion highlights Mr Cardenas's attempt to build a classroom community that leveraged peer support. However, in reading these events we noted some absences related to peer mentoring and collaboration. Specifically, though the data illustrated the endorsement of Annie's article by her peers beginning with their applause when she leaves for her interview to their post facto support after her text had been taken down, saying it was not too harsh or bad, their endorsement was ephemeral, and invisible to the publics beyond classroom walls, spoken, not materialised on the article as co-authors or signatures. The collective student voice remained invisible as Annie's name sat solitary at the top of the article. How, we wondered, might Mr Cardenas have shifted the way in which articles were published to give credit to authors while simultaneously making visible the collective of the class as an editorial team?

Similarly, the power and potential of peer support and youth voice in public authorship in online spaces outside of school that connected learning researchers documented (Ito et al., 2009) did not materialise with the digital publication of Annie's article on the school website. We wonder what might have happened had the school website enabled comments. What might have happened if subsequent to the discussion that Mr Cardenas led with students he invited them to comment on the article online? Their collective voice might have been materialised in the digital space.

Implication for reimagining writing in the critical connected classroom
Reading the space of the journalism and digital media studies classroom designed by Mr Cardenas through a critical im/material lens offers insight into ways that teachers can design transformative classroom spaces that open up possibilities for students to author interest-driven texts for public audiences beyond the classroom supported by a community of their peers. Viewing writing instruction and assignments through the lens of critical im/materiality can further support teachers in anticipating moments of learning as well as recognising and creating learning opportunities, as unexpected responses to texts designed in the classroom and published publicly are read by audiences both known and unknown. In the remainder of this article we offer insights to help educators consider ways in which they can re-envision student interest-driven writing and peer support in the critical connected classroom.

357

Student interest in the critical connected writing classroom

What happens when student interests (ephemeral stuff like feelings) follow local (space and bodies) social issues? In the context of this project, we recognise the need for students to look at their social issue from the perspective of multiple stakeholders, particularly if they want to make recommendations for change and effect change. The notion that publication can create social change means we need to put the people we are demanding change from in the web where changes take place. The case we describe in this article points to the need for materialising the experience of the PE teachers in Annie's text by, for example, asking the teachers directly about the constraints and possibilities within their positions as school teachers, or getting their comment on her proposals prior to publication.

Further, as teachers engage students in social issue writing meant to enact change, youth writers need to be taught to deconstruct or evaluate the power, positioning, and perspectives (Janks, 2000; Jones, 2006) on display in the texts they design in order to support them in identifying how their texts might be read by audiences beyond the classroom. Had Annie deconstructed her text in this way before going public, she might have anticipated some of the responses to her article and either made changes to her text or at least have been prepared when those responses materialised. Students also need to be taught to consider the ways that embodied experiences get recognised, circulated, and represented in the popular media. To do so the critical, socio-historical positioning of the actors involved in the social issue that students are writing about needs framing. This may require adult advocacy and material, embodied support gathering evidence from the actors to whom students are making recommendations. It is also important for teachers implementing student interest-driven writing in the classroom to recognise the ever-present power of adults shaping and populating students' developing thoughts and voices. As Schneider (2001) documented, teachers' personal life experiences can impact what they allow as appropriate topics for students to write about, 'or their personal beliefs may [conflict] with the "legality" of topics' (p. 423). We therefore encourage teachers embarking on student interest-driven writing to interrogate the ways in which they may be silencing students through the assignments that they craft and the topics that they sanction as they design instructional experiences for students.

Peer networks in the critical connected writing classroom

When people from structurally and historically non-dominant groups (e.g., youth, people of colour, women etc.) go public with their social issue writing, we must assume a dominant, patriarchal, hegemonic audience will ignore, dismiss, or attempt to silence their embodied experiences and perspectives. Therefore, teachers with more structural power than their students need to work towards materialising the volume of non-dominant voices in anticipation that those in power might dismiss or resist the ideas put forward in their public writing. In this project, that would have translated to Annie materialising peers' voices in her text making their embodied experiences visible, through quotes, anonymised or with pseudonyms, but there in number, so she was not left alone with the authorial *I*. The digital space where her article lived needed to include opportunities for comment, so peer support of her embodied experience might have been materialised beyond the invisible classroom conversation in support of her article and on the web, to balance, or counter the PE faculty rebuttals. As teacher allies of youth writing for a public audience, the peer network is powerful when it is materialised. We must err on the side of materiality when we teach vulnerable bodies. This might also have included collaborative writing and authorship, to ensure Annie stood with multiple writers to advocate for this material change in PE classes.

Finally, we remain hopeful in the possibilities of reimagining the secondary school writing classroom as a place for students to *go public* with the texts they design and share beyond the classroom. As teachers continue to leverage the potential of new media to support students in writing interest-driven texts for public audiences, we are excited by the potential that a critical im/material lens can offer to teachers designing spaces that open up possibilities for student engagement and social action in the secondary school classroom.

References

Avila, J. & Zacher Pandya, J. (2013). *Critical Digital Literacies as Social Praxis: Intersections and Challenges*. New York: Peter Lang.

Barad, K. (2007). *Meeting the universe halfway: Quantum physics and the entanglement of matter and meaning*. Durham, NC: Duke University Press.

Boyd, D. (2014). *It's complicated: The social lives of networked teens*. New Haven, CT: Yale University Press.

Burnett, C., Merchant, G., Pahl, K. & Roswell, J. (2014). The (im)materiality of literacy: the significance of subjectivity to new literacies research. *Discourse: Studies in the Cultural Politics of Education, 35* (1), 90–103.

Davies, B. (2016). Ethics and the new materialism: a brief genealogy of the 'post' philosophies in the social sciences. *Discourse: Studies in the Cultural Politics of Education*, 1–15. doi:10.1080/01596306.2016.1234682

359

CHAPTER FIVE: HOW DO I TRANSLATE MY ACADEMIC WRITING INTO PUBLIC GENRES?

Dimitriadis, G. (2001). *Performing identity/performing culture: Hip hop as text, pedagogy, and lived practice*. New York: Peter Lang.

Duke, N.K., Purcell-Gates, V., Hall, L.A. & Tower, C. (2006). Authentic Literacy Activities for Developing Comprehension and Writing. *The Reading Teacher, 60*, 344–355.

Enriquez, G., Johnson, E., Kontokorvi, S. & Mallozzi, C.A. (Eds.). (2016). *Literacies, Learning, and the Body*. New York, NY: Taylor & Francis.

Garcia, A. (Ed.) (2014). *Teaching in the connected learning classroom*. Irvine, CA: Digital Media and Learning Research Hub.

Gee, J.P. (1996). *Social linguistics and literacies: Ideology in discourse* (2nd ed.). New York: Falmer Press.

Heath, S.B. (1983). *Ways with words: Language, life, and work in communities and classrooms*. Cambridge: Cambridge University Press.

Ito, M., Baumer, S., Bittanti, M., Boyd, D.M., Cody, R., Herr, B. & Horst, H. (2009). *Hanging out, messing around, and geeking out: Kids living and learning with new media*. Cambridge, MA: MIT Press.

Ito, M., Gutierrez, K., Livingstone, S., Penuel, B., Rhodes, J., Salen, K., ...Watkins, S.C. (2013). *Connected Learning*. Irvine, CA: Digital Media and Learning Research Hub.

Janks, H. (2000). Domination, access, diversity, and design: A synthesis for critical literacy education. *Educational Review, 52* (2), 175–186.

Jenkins, H. (2009). *Confronting the Challenges of Participatory Culture: Media Education for the 21st Century*. Cambridge, MA: MIT Press.

Johnson, E . (2011). 'I've got swag': Simone performs and produces space for critical literacy in a high school English classroom. *English Teaching Practice and Critique, 10* (3), 26–44.

Jones, S. (2006). *Girls, social class, and literacy*. Portsmouth, NH: Heinemann.

Lewis, C. & Crampton, A. (2015). Literacy, emotion, and the teaching/learning body. In G. Enriquez, E. Johnson, S. Kontokorvi & C.A. Mallozzi (Eds.), *Literacies, Learning and the Body: Putting Theory and Research into Pedagogical Practice* (pp. 105–121). New York, NY: Routledge.

Lewis, C. & Dockter Tierney, J. (2011). Mobilizing emotion in an urban English classroom. *Curriculum and Instruction, 18* (3), 319–329.

Lewison, M., Flint, A.S. & Van Sluys, K. (2002). Taking on critical literacy: The journey of newcomers and novices. *Language Arts, 79* (5), 382–392.

Mills, K. & Dooley, K. (2014). Teaching persuasive texts: Building a language of evaluation through hedging and moderated intensification. *Literacy Learning: the Middle Years, 22* (3), 33–41.

National Governors Association Center for Best Practices & Council of Chief State School Officers. (2010). *Common Core State Standards for English language arts and literacy in history/social studies, science, and technical subjects.* Washington, D.C.

Petrone, R. & Lewis, M.A. (2012). 'Deficits, therapists, and a desire to distance': Secondary English pre-service teachers' reasoning about their future students. *English Education, 44* (3), 254–287.

Sarigianides, S.T., Lewis, M.A. & Petrone, R. (2015). How re-thinking adolescence helps reimagine the teaching of English. *English Journal, 104* (3), 13–18.

Schmier, S.A. (2013). Designing space for student choice in a digital media studies classroom. In J. Avila & J. Zachar Pandya (Eds.), *Critical Digital Literacies as Social Praxis: Intersections and Challenges* (pp. 15–40). New York, NY: Peter Lang.

Schneider, J.J. (2001). No blood, guns, or gays allowed!: The silencing of the elementary writer. *Language Arts, 78* (5), 415–425.

Selwyn, N. (2010). Looking beyond learning: notes towards the critical study of educational technology. *Journal of Computer Assisted Learning, 26*, 65–73.

Soep, E. (2006). Beyond literacy and voice in youth media production. *McGill Journal of Education, 41* (3), 197–213.

RECOMMENDED ONLINE SOURCES

For direct links to these sources, please visit <sites.broadviewpress.com/focusonwriting>.

1. For interesting and accessible research about the rhetoric of font: Stewart, Nida M., "Typeface and Document Persona in Magazines." *Xchanges*, vol. 6, no. 1, 2010, <http://www.xchanges.org/xchanges_archive/xchanges/6.1/stewart/stewart.html>.

2. For helpful, clear advice on blogging and other forms of web writing: Barton, Matt, James Kalmbach, and Charles Lowe, eds. *Writing Spaces: Web Writing Style Guide Version 1.0.* Parlor P, 2011, <http://writingspaces.org/sites/default/files/web-writing-style-guide-1.0.pdf>.

3. To view and learn the background of a variety of student multimodal projects: Shipka, Jody. *Remediate This*, Blog, <http://remediatethis.com/student/index.html>.

361

CHAPTER FIVE: HOW DO I TRANSLATE MY ACADEMIC WRITING INTO PUBLIC GENRES?

4. To explore famous American speeches (often with transcripts and video in addition to audio): *American Rhetoric*, <http://www.americanrhetoric.com>.

5. To see student-made videos which teach a principle for communication theory in a fun way: Wotanis, Lindsey. *Teach-a-Theory Videos*, YouTube playlist, 7 February 2016, <https://www.youtube.com/watch?v=W2PKKs-lTEU&list=PL6pHoX6AT qfPb8jH6bah77LIJJPxsNcJu>.

6. For a thoughtful and visually engaging video about multimodal composing: Andrews, Kendra L., illustrated by T. Mark Bentley. "Multimodal Composing, Sketchnotes, and Idea Generation." *Kairos*, vol. 22, no. 2, spring 2018, <http://kairos.technorhetoric.net/22.2/disputatio/andrews/index.html>.

7. For a helpful view of current writing technologies in terms of a long history of development and change: Baron, Denis. "From Pencils to Pixels: The Stages of Literacy Technology." Adapted from a chapter in *Passions, Pedagogies, and 21st Century Technologies*, edited by Gail Hawisher and Cynthia Selfe, Utah State UP and NCTE, 2000, pp. 15–33, <http://www.english.illinois.edu/-people-/faculty/debaron/essays/pencils.htm>.

Joining the Conversation

The following formal writing prompts are ways of helping you think through the ideas you've been reading about by *using* the ideas in some way to help you create a text of your own.

MULTIMODAL REMIX

Choose a specific public audience who would benefit from hearing a message from one of your formal writing assignments. Create a composition that uses text as well as other visual and/or aural elements to effectively reach that audience. Consider digital and non-digital project ideas and what would work best for your purpose.

CLASS WEBSITE

Create a collaborative website based on one of your formal writing assignments. Present the class's findings in a way that would interest readers. Share the site on social media to help it reach the appropriate audience.

EDITORIAL

Write persuasively and concisely for the editorial page of a local newspaper to argue for a specific change or to address a local problem or policy based on your study of rhetoric and writing.

INSTRUCTIONAL VIDEO

Using the "Teach-a-Theory" videos (cited in recommended online sources just above) as a model, create a video narrative that exemplifies ideas from writing research in a way that would be accessible to high school seniors or first-year college students.

RATIONALE

Explain how and why you made choices for one of the above assignments to fill a purpose with a specific public audience in mind.

363

CHAPTER FIVE: HOW DO I TRANSLATE MY ACADEMIC WRITING INTO PUBLIC GENRES?

CONCLUSION: NOW WHAT?

One of my favorite parts of the semester is the end.

I know what you're thinking. I admit that I look forward to spending a bit more time on binge-watching television series and pleasure-reading between semesters.

But I'm talking about the end of the semester *before* break. The time when we can look back, assess, and pull together what was learned and what value it may have as we prepare to move forward.

So, let me ask you: **What are you going to take with you when you go?**

You might want to think about your answer to this question by returning to the documents I shared at the start of the book, in the Introduction.

- the WPA *Outcomes for First-Year Composition*
- the "Habits of Mind" from the *Framework for Success in Post-Secondary Writing*

You can revisit the full versions of these documents in the Introduction, and here I include brief references to them in case turning pages feels like a lot of effort so late in the semester.

The WPA *Outcomes*—that is, some goals for students in writing courses—in my own language:

- Consider the rhetorical situation—especially purpose and audience—when you're reading and when you're writing, and make choices accordingly.
- Go beyond the obvious and go beyond your first impressions to read both generously and critically.
- Whether reading or writing, focus on what is surprising, complex, or in gray areas that are worth thinking about.
- Use secondary research and primary research to recap and join ongoing conversations.
- Use the writing process, including workshops and collaborative exchanges, to clarify your thinking, to revise substantively, and to polish your writing.
- Use writing conventions associated with organization, style, and sentence-level choices to respond to specific situations effectively.

That's it for goals. No big deal.

The "Habits of Mind"—that is, some ways of being that help people learn—in my own language:

- Show interest in learning (not just in grades).
- Ask questions, explore possible answers. Rinse, repeat.
- Expect learning curves in new situations.
- Own your learning. Be okay with making mistakes. Feel bad for a limited amount of time, acknowledge your humanity, get back in the fray.
- Do the small projects. Notice how any big project can be broken down into smaller steps. Do the small steps. Do the small steps. At this point, I'm telling myself as well as you. Do the small steps.
- Put yourself in new situations, listen to voices you do not regularly hear, visit places you don't normally go to, do activities you don't normally do. Note: Follow this advice in ways that will not compromise your physical and emotional health.
- Pay attention to how you learn, how you think, how you write. Notice strategies that work and strategies that don't work. Reward yourself for doing the strategies that work.

Some of these habits may have accurately described you and been helpful during the semester, while others may be habits you'd like to gradually develop as you move forward.

You might also revisit the chapter titles and think about how you might have answered each of the questions at the start of the semester versus how you might answer them now.

1. Why write?
2. What is the "rhetorical situation" and why should I care about it?
3. What do effective writers do?
4. What do effective researchers do?
5. How do I translate my academic writing into public genres?

You can also consider what composition scholars call "threshold concepts"—those ideas that reframe a person's understanding, not in a small way, but in terms of an epiphany kind of moment that allows your learning to progress in new ways. To what degree have you had "aha" moments in relation to ideas such as the following (paraphrased from Adler-Kassner and Wardle):

- Writing is always a social rather than isolated activity (even if we are alone when we write; even if we are alone and are writing to ourselves).
- Writing and reading activities always occur within specific situations, never in a vacuum or in a way that is "general" or universal.
- Writing makes things happen.
- Writing is a way we construct our social identities.
- Words and texts are always in relationships with other words and texts.
- Writing helps us learn as we think on the page.
- Returning to our own writing helps us move from understanding our own perspective to using recognizable forms that help us communicate our ideas to others.
- Because writing situations always change, we are always learning how to write.

SHARING YOUR EXPERTISE

At this point, you know a lot. In order to process what matters most, you can formalize the ways of thinking about the semester I outline above by doing one of the following activities:

1. Write to next semester's students in a way that will be helpful to them as they start the semester. What should they expect? What kind of attitude or behavior will help them to have a productive semester? What information do you wish you had known at the start of the semester?

2. Write yourself brief notes that would be useful when you are struggling with writing in future situations. What kinds of reminders would be most helpful? Fold up the notes and put them in an envelope or box for yourself so they are ready to pull out when you need them.

3. Develop a multimedia lesson that your teacher could use in future semesters. Focus on just one part of the semester—something that you consider important and that you feel comfortable teaching other students about. How might you make the lesson entertaining and useful for students? Focus on the message you're delivering and also focus on *how* you might deliver it in an effective way.

4. Write an analogy or extended metaphor for one of the central concepts from the course: the rhetorical situation, the writing process, genre, audience, purpose, motivation, research, and so forth. Simply fill in the course concept in the blank line, answer the questions, and see which answer you'd like to develop with details. Note: This activity is fun to do collaboratively, combining a few metaphors for one concept.

If _____ was a place, what place would it be?
If _____ was a plant, what kind of plant would it be?
If _____ was a household appliance, what appliance would it be?

Keep going! Consider food, a part of the home, a movement, a travel destination, a family member, a sport, a dance move, and so forth.

ONGOING CHALLENGE

I am still learning to write. As each new situation arises, I adjust, pivot, move; I put down some tools and take up others; I make mistakes, I get feedback, I think again. I walk away, I return, I see how I've failed to communicate, I adjust, pivot, move again.

Part of moving forward is recognizing that we don't learn to write in a way that is complete and finished. Instead, we learn to write the way a person learns how to play a sport and make music. We can practice and become good at it, but we are never done practicing; we always hope to improve or hone new abilities.

As you end the semester, you might want to ask your teachers how they still struggle with writing and what they've learned about writing that continues to help them succeed.

Feel good about how far you've come. Know that you can expect to learn much more.

WORKS CITED

Adler-Kassner, Linda, and Elizabeth Wardle, eds. *Naming What We Know: Threshold Concepts of Writing Studies*, Utah State UP, 2015.

Council of Writing Program Administrators. *WPA Outcomes Statement for First-Year Composition (3.0)*, July 2014, <wpacouncil.org/positions/outcomes. html>.

Council of Writing Program Administrators, National Council of Teachers of English, and National Writing Project. *Framework for Success in Postsecondary Writing*. CWPA, NCTE, and NWP, 2011, <ncil.org/files/framework-for-success-postsecondary-writing.pdf>.

PERMISSIONS ACKNOWLEDGMENTS

Anderson, Daniel. Excerpts from "The Low Bridge to High Benefits: Entry-Level Multimedia, Literacies, and Motivation," from *Computers and Composition* 25.1 (2008): 40–60. Copyright © 2007 Elsevier Inc. Reprinted with permission from Elsevier.

Brandt, Deborah. "The Pursuit of Literacy," from "Introduction" to *Literacy in American Lives*. Cambridge University Press, 2001. Copyright © 2001, Deborah Brandt.

Cannizzo, Jessie. "Powerless Persuasion: Ineffective Argumentation Plagues the Clean Eating Community," written for ENG 120 Critical Writing, Pace University, Fall 2016. Reproduced with the permission of Jessie Cannizzo.

Council of Writing Program Administrators. "WPA Outcomes Statement for First-Year Composition (3.0)," July 2014. Reprinted with the permission of CWPA.

Council of Writing Program Administrators, National Council of Teachers of English, and National Writing Project. Executive Summary from "Framework for Success in Postsecondary Writing," 2011; as seen at https://files.eric.ed.gov/fulltext/ED516360. pdf. Reprinted with the permission of NCTE, NWP, and CWPA.

Devitt, Amy J., Anis Bawarshi, and Mary Jo Reiff. "Materiality and Genre in the Study of Discourse Communities," from *College English* 65.5 (2003): 541–58. Copyright © 2003 by the National Council of Teachers of English. Reprinted with permission.

Downs, Douglas, and Elizabeth Wardle. "What Can a Novice Contribute? Undergraduate Researchers in First-Year Composition," from *Undergraduate Research in English Studies*, edited by Laurie Grobman and Joyce Kinkead. Utah State University Press, 2010. Copyright © 2010 by the National Council of Teachers of English. Reprinted with permission.

Gee, James Paul. "Introduction," from *Situated Language and Learning: A Critique of Traditional Schooling*. Routledge, 2004. Copyright © 2004 James Paul Gee. Reproduced by permission of Taylor & Francis Books UK.

Gesler, David. "Research Is Elementary: How 'Blue's Clues' Can Help Teach Communication Research Methods," from *Communication Teacher* 21.4 (2007): 118–22. Copyright © National Communication Association. Reprinted by permission of Taylor & Francis Ltd. (www.tandfonline.com) on behalf of the National Communication Association.

Harris, Joseph. Excerpts from *Introduction to Rewriting: How to Do Things with Texts*. Copyright © 2006 Utah State University Press.

Hayes, John R., and Linda S. Flower. "Writing Research and the Writer," from *American Psychologist* 41.10 (Oct. 1986): 1106–13. Copyright © 1986 by American Psychological Association. Reproduced with permission.

Lamott, Anne. "Short Assignments" and "Shitty First Drafts," from *Bird by Bird: Some Instructions on Writing and Life*. Copyright © 1994 by Anne Lamott. Used by permission of Pantheon Books, an imprint of the Knopf Doubleday Publishing Group, a division of Penguin Random House LLC. All rights reserved. Any third party use of this material, outside of this publication, is prohibited. Interested parties must apply directly to Penguin Random House LLC for permission.

Laskowski, Aleeza. Excerpt from "Domestic Sphere vs. Public Sphere," written for ENG 120 Critical Writing, Pace University, Fall 2016. Reproduced with the permission of Aleeza Laskowski.

Lunsford, Andrea A. "Literature, Literacy, and (New) Media," from *ADE Bulletin* 152 (2012): 49–53. Reprinted with the permission of the copyright owner, the Modern Language Association of America.

Murray, Donald M. "Teaching the Other Self: The Writer's First Reader," from *College Composition and Communication* 33.2 (1982): 140–47. Copyright © 1982 by the National Council of Teachers of English. Reprinted with permission.

Perl, Sondra. "Understanding Composing," from *College Composition and Communication* 31.4 (1980): 363–69. Copyright © 1980 by the National Council of Teachers of English. Reprinted with permission.

Schmier, Stephanie Anne, Elisabeth Johnson, and Sarah Lohnes Wataluk. "Going Public: Exploring the Possibilities for Publishing Student Interest-Driven Writing beyond the Classroom," from the *Australian Journal of Language and Literacy*

41.1 (2018). Reprinted with the permission of the Australian Literacy Educators'
Association, alea.edu.au.

Seible, Marcea K. Excerpts from *The Transition from Student to Professional: A
Pedagogy of Professionalism for First-Year Composition*, a Dissertation Submitted in
Partial Fulfillment of the Requirements for the Degree of Doctor of Philosophy,
Department of English, Illinois State University, 2008. Reprinted with the
permission of Marcea K. Seible.

INDEX

Chicago Manual style, 172

Chicago Tribune, 249

citation, 18, 25, 172, 178, 246, 255, 262, 279

citizen democracy, 326

civic change, 326

civic lives, 20

civic participation, 123, 325

class writing inventory, 233

classroom-to-workplace transition gap, 123, 125

"Classrooms" (Ames), 78

clean eating community, 148–51

client projects, 121–22, 124

code meshing, 46, 113

code switching, 113

cognitive processes, 192, 214–15

collaboration, 27, 90–94, 254, 266, 281, 283–84, 302, 306, 348–49, 354–55, 357

collaborative reading, 94

collaborative writing and authorship, 359

collages, 319, 329–33, 337

collective student voice, 357

College Composition and Communication, 202, 274

college readiness, 26

Common Core standards, 26

Communication Teacher, 288

communities of practice, 85, 108–09, 122

community ethnography, 233

comparative perspective, 60

Compare, Diagnose, and Operate (CDO) model of revision, 225

comparison matrix, 167

composing courses. *See* composition studies

composing digital collages, 319, 329–33, 337

composing processes, 24, 202, 210, 318

composition classroom

integrating new media into, 92–93, 322–26, 337–39

visual and new media projects, 326–38

composition scholars, 123

composition studies, 15, 21, 76, 84, 274–75, 325, 344

ethnography in, 128, 142

computer and video games, 314

computer literacy, 320–21, 338

Computers and Composition, 317

"Concept of Discourse Community" (Swales), 110

concise writing, 180

conclusion, 171, 179, 264

conference papers, 101

connected classroom, 343, 355, 358–59

connected learning, 345, 351–52, 354–55

construction site metaphor, 322, 338

consumerist attitude in relation to education, 82

contemporary literacy, 59

content, 21, 50, 170

content-area literacy, 338

context for reading, 105

contractions, 180

contributive research, 273

contributive research in first-year composition, 274–85

conventions, 25, 105, 109, 114–17, 144, 280

  academic conventions, 117

  spelling, punctuation, and grammar conventions, 179–81

  writing conventions, 179, 366

copyright, 256

correlation *vs.* causation, 259

The Council for Undergraduate Research (CUR), 274

Council of Writing Program Administrators, 27

crafting a message, 116

FOCUS ON WRITING: WHAT COLLEGE STUDENTS WANT TO KNOW

engagement, 27, 29, 121–22, 318–21, 332–33

"Enhancing Student Motivation in Freshman Composition" (Hootstein), 80

entry-level technologies, 323

epistemic modality, 352

Estrem, Heidi, 280

ethical treatment of human study participants, 261–62, 285

ethnographic inquiry, 343

ethnographic method, 143

ethnographic research, 127, 129

ethnography, 128, 144, 146

ethnography in composition studies, 128, 142

ethnomethodology, 128, 130, 142

ethos, 104, 333

evaluative research, 237

event marketing displays, 307

everyday writing, 41, 48, 101, 297

Everything's an Argument (Lunsford), 104

evidence, 49

evidence-based research, 30

evidence-based thinking, 111

exigence, 17, 106–07, 115, 212

expectancy-value theory, 80

experimental designs, 260

experimentation, 323

experimenting with unfamiliar technologies, 324

expert planning process, 220

expert writers, 221–22

  diagnosis of text problems, 226

  revision process, 223–24, 228

expertise, 48, 50–51, 90

extrinsic motivation, 43, 78

extrinsic rewards, 44

Facebook posts, 101

"Fake it 'til you make it," 308

felt sense, 203, 206, 208–11

Feminist Media Studies, 248

Ferrell, Stephen, 94

field observations, 260

Fish, Stanley, 273

flexibility, 27

flow, 76, 78–80, 318–19, 324–25

Flower, Linda, 160, 178, 212–28, 279

focused or exploratory questions, 236

Foer, Jonathan Safran, *Tree of Codes*, 94

format, 177

Forsyth, Donelson R., 78, 80

  "Practical Proposals for Motivating Students," 77

Framework for Success in Postsecondary Writing, 22, 25–27, 34 (table), 365

Franklin, Jennifer, 77

Freedman, Aviva, 142, 146

freewriting, 167, 215

Fulwiler, Toby, 48

Future Time Perspective (FTP), 76, 81, 83

Gaye, Marvin, 336

Gee, James Paul, 323, 345

  Situated Language and Learning, 311–17

Geertz, Clifford, 144

gender-inclusive language, 181

Gendlin, Eugene, 206

Generation NeXt, 76, 82–83

"Generation NeXt Goes to Work" (Taylor), 82

genre analysis, 127–30, 142–43, 145–46, 295

genre conventions, 115–16

genre ethnography, 141

genre theories, 127, 130

genres, 17, 50, 102, 110, 114–16, 121, 280

genres as operational sites of discourse communities, 140

genres as situated actions, 142

FOCUS ON WRITING: WHAT COLLEGE STUDENTS WANT TO KNOW

FOCUS ON WRITING: WHAT COLLEGE STUDENTS WANT TO KNOW

FOCUS ON WRITING: WHAT COLLEGE STUDENTS WANT TO KNOW

FOCUS ON WRITING: WHAT COLLEGE STUDENTS WANT TO KNOW

FOCUS ON WRITING: WHAT COLLEGE STUDENTS WANT TO KNOW